From the moment of its earliest acknowledgement in 17th Century Colonial America, New Hampshire's Old Man of the Mountain was emblematic of the flinty, rugged and individualistic character of the area's inhabitants. It seemed to defy all opposition, existing for its own sake, and answerable to only nature itself. It surveyed the world below as men broke ground on new dwellings and fought against the elements to survive, as their sons and grandsons, daughters and granddaughters gave their lives to be free from British tyranny.

It watched as a new system of governance was created out of the ashes of that mighty conflagration, one dedicated to the insurance of individual liberty and free markets, and fueled by the epochal words of Revolutionary General John Stark:

Live free or die; death is not the worst of evils.

As the rest of America fell prey to a soft and shallow socialism, as the very Constitution written in Philadelphia to insure states' rights and the rights of the individuals therein dissolved under the acidic attacks of self-serving politicians and politically motivated judges, the Old Man stared back, defiant, aggressively contrarian, true to principle, just like the people who lived around him.

For decades, he held firm. But the world was changing. Even in New Hampshire, the individualist nature of its people started to erode. As more refugees from high-tax, large-government states emigrated to the Granite State, they brought with them their leftist ideals. Cracks began to show. Regulations increased. Taxes grew. Judges played games with the Constitution, just like they did elsewhere in the US. 2003 saw what seemed to be the sad, but fitting end. Weathering had done its work. The Old Man collapsed.

Live free or die; death is not the worst of evils.

But the Old Man was merely an icon, an emblem, nearly as transient as the autumn wind. The spirit of liberty never existed in the stone itself. It was the imagination of *people* that gave the façade meaning, and that power, the power of *ideas*, is ageless. The Old Man may be gone, but as long as *real* men and women survive, Stark's words will never die. Here in this volume, two of New Hampshire's best known advocates for liberty carry on Stark's work. Writer and radio host Gardner Goldsmith and his father Paul embark on a decades-long survey of freedom in the United States and the Granite State itself. They trace the lineage of freedom, from Aristotle to Locke, from Bastiat to Mises, from Jefferson to Rand, and they hand this heritage to the reader.

It is up to you to decide what you will do with it, and when you do, remember the words of John Stark to his fellow soldiers in the cause of freedom:

> *Live free or die; death is not the worst of evils.*

Live Free or Die

Essays, Fiction and Comments on Liberty,

by New Hampshire Libertarians

P. Gardner Goldsmith
Paul H. Goldsmith

Copyright © 2007 Gardner Goldsmith
All rights reserved.

ISBN: 1-4196-7533-8
ISBN-13: 978-1419675331

Visit www.booksurge.com to order additional copies.

Preface

This book is a product of the work of many people. Foremost among them is my father, Paul H. Goldsmith, who was born on February 25, 1917, and who passed away on November 21, 2003. He was the most honorable, noble man I have ever known.

In 1942, my father joined the US Navy, and was shipped to the pacific during World War Two. You will read about some of his exploits in this book, but one of the key components of that period was his practice of recognizing wise quotations and writing them in a black book. Between 1942 and 2003, my father wrote two volumes of "Worthwhile Quotations", many of which were his own. He produced observations on life, economics, politics, philosophy, age, childhood, marriage, and love, and my family and I became interested in publishing his books in one form or another.

What you see here is an integrated version of only a small percentage of his work. It is our intention that there will be more to offer in the years to come.

If it were not for my father's guidance in economics and political philosophy, I would not have had an understanding at a very early age about the dynamics of the free market, and the importance of unfettered capitalism in insuring one's freedom. If it were not for my father, I would not have been exposed to the ideas of the Austrian School of economics, to the writing of Henry Hazlitt, or the insights of Leonard E. Read. If it were not for my father, I would not have understood that there is nobility in fighting for one's principles, no matter what the odds against you; and if it were not for my father, I would not have been exposed to the courage to keep smiling and being a good person even in the face of painful adversity. Paul Goldsmith's attributes deserve recognition and praise.

One of his favorite books was "The Merry Adventures of Robin Hood", by Howard Pyle. In its conclusion (beware, those who do not want it spoiled!) Robin is dying, having been betrayed by nuns in the employ of the government. Bled nearly to death, he recognizes the face of his old friend, Little John, who bursts into his tower room in the nunnery. There is no hope. John's face is awash in tears of rage and loss. But Robin asks his friend to lift him to the window, and to help him grasp his long bow. He asks John to steady him as he draws back an arrow for the final shot of his life; wherever the arrow lands will be his burial ground. He lets fly. The arrow pierces the sky, soaring fast and high, and in the end, Robin breathes his last, satisfied that he has done right in his life.

In a way, my dad was both like Robin and like John. He supported me during times of hardship, and ended up relying on me for occasional lifts later in life. That dynamic is at work in this book. If it had not been for my father's direction and encouragement, the ideas set forth in these pages would not have been produced. At the same time, I am proud to be able to unite our work, and do justice to a man whose thinking and integrity surpassed those of many people around him. Together, we've lifted that bow and arrow, and are letting loose a defense of individual liberty.

P. Gardner Goldsmith

Acknowledgements

The book you are about to read is a collection of my articles, short stories, and fiction in other forms that cover a span of approximately ten years, from 1996 to 2007. Many have appeared in, and on: *Investor's Business Daily*, *The Freeman*, *Human Events*, *Mises.com*, *FEE.org*, *The Nashua Telegraph*, *The New Hampshire Union Leader*, *Techentralstation.com*, and *Naked*, of the UK. In organizing them for your perusal, it was important for me to make sure they had long-term value; that they expressed principles that were timeless, and discussed issues that people living many years from now could understand. I also wanted to make sure those who have been integral in helping formulate my work get the recognition they deserve.

There are many people to thank for their guidance, friendship, and influence. Foremost among them is my family. Shirley, my mother, will have her own book dedicated to her. She is the intellectual equal and perfect compliment to my father. Where he concentrated on national issues and economics, my mother has an astounding ability to take local issues and the claims of intellectually corrupt local politicians and tear them apart. She has an uncanny memory, and has often inspired many of the columns included here. My brother, Peter, and sister, Carroll, are much like my parents. Carroll was the scholarly example for me as a kid, and Peter's professional acumen and integrity are examples for anyone to emulate. He has also been very encouraging in the goal of getting our father's ideas in print. My sister Valerie has been a constant source of reading material, and actually lets me "go off" about a subject without shutting off her ears.

I would also like to do more than acknowledge, I would like to *praise*, the good fellowship, advice, and guidance of numerous friends and professional associates, many of whom are one and the same.

First among them are my friends, Bruce Adams, Malcolm Salls, Eric Scheiner, David Tiedemann, Tom Tennisco, and Steve Fox, all of whom embrace the freedom philosophy, and are simply towering people with great integrity. Not only do they understand the principles of individual liberty, they understand the importance of having high standards for music, hobbies, and themselves.

My friends Mark Berry, Ahmed Niazi, and Steve O'Brien, from our old mother country of the UK, have been great supporters, as have been many of the members of the Free State Project who have already moved here.

Some, but not all, of the terrific people in the New Hampshire libertarian movement who deserve recognition include, Don Gorman, John and Rosalee Babiarz, Ian and Mark, of "Free Talk Live", Seth Cohn and his wife Chris Lopez, Denis and Irena Goddard, Jim Perry, Rich Tomasso, Dan and Carol McGuire, Kevin Rohl, Matthew Simon, Dave Ridley, Steve Winter, Wayne Quinn, Domi and Avens O'Brien, writer Jim Davies, and Representative Joel Winters and his wife, Amy. Other great supporters of freedom in New Hampshire upon whom I rely very often include Rep. Dan Itseh and his wife, Lisa, Paul Mirski, Charlie Arlinghaus, Len Dobrowski, Sam Cohen, Keith Melanson, Nancy and Dave Zlotek, Rich Killian, Jenn and Billy Coffey, Ed Mosca, Greg Sorg, Jack Heath, my old producers, Jason (it's okay if you love Billy Joel) Richardson, and Daaaaave Morgan, and Drew Cline, editorial page editor of *The New Hampshire Union Leader*.

Beyond the boundaries of the "Live Free or Die" state, I am thrilled to know that many of the writers and thinkers whom I have seen as some of my intellectual heroes have become business acquaintances and friends. I would like to thank these people not only for their fellowship and kindness, but for the great examples they provided me in many fields of endeavor. They do amazing work, and they include:

Sheldon Richman, writer, and editor of *The Freeman*, published by the Foundation for Economic Education (FEE), in Irvington, NY, Dr. Richard Ebeling, President of FEE, his wife, Dr. Anna Ebeling, Beth Hoffman, of FEE's Publications and *The Freeman*, legendary author Sam Blumenfeld, Marty Zupan, President of the Institute for Humane Studies, and Dr. Nigel Ashford Senior Program Officer of the IHS, Jeffrey Tucker, of the Ludwig von Mises Institute, writer James Bovard, Jim Harper, of the Cato Institute, Jed Babbin, of *Human Events*, and Tom Winter, its Editor-in-Chief, who was a mentor for me when I first began writing about politics and economics, and is a truly outstanding man.

I would like to tip my hat to M. Stanton Evans, Mal Kline, and Chris Warden who gave me training at the National Journalism Center, to Lisa Heyden (debater extraordinaire and cover artist beyond compare), Bill Sly the "Graphics Guy" (again, see that great cover!), my long-time friend Ian McCaleb, who helped me survive one of the worst blind dates in history, to Audrey Mullin of Advocacy Ink, to Bryan Fuller and Michael D. Robins in LA, Sarah Huber of Spence Publishing, and Patricia Jackson of Eagle Publishing, to my friends Sean Naylor and Steve Pizzello, who are both brilliant and engaging writers, Jason and Mike Osborne of Sakal CAI, Charlton Heston (one of the few in Hollywood who has actually *read* Bastiat!), and to my father's closest friend, Jack Leary.

I would also like to thank a few people for their talented inspiration. They include music heroes and writers who have fueled me along the way, even if they might not agree with my politics. If you, the reader, don't know the name Danko Jones, you need to treat yourself to his music, and to do it soon. Thanks Danko. I'm glad we got to introduce you to NH, buddy. To Captain Sensible of the Damned: Captain, I know you're a communist, but we have commonalities, and you are one nice guy. Thanks for the friendly e-mails and great music. You, Dave Vanian and the rest of the band are the best -- the pinnacle of punk rock. Give 'em "BLAH", guys! Thanks also to Richard Butler, Tim Butler and John Ashton of the Psychedelic Furs. Their cutting, intense, ferocious, insightful and original work stands out above the rest. The last essay of this book is named after their form of music, "Beautiful Chaos". I would also like to acknowledge the musical superiority of the Sons of Hercules, Radio Birdman, Wire, the Mummies, New Bomb Turks, Black Flag, Rubber City Rebels, "Demons", Goldfrapp, the Who, and the Stooges, who started it in the US.

When it comes to superiority in the field of fantastic fiction, no one can compare to Richard Matheson. In some of my work, you will hear faint echoes of his voice, as well as that of W. W. Jacobs, TED Kline, F. Paul Wilson, and Edgar Allan Poe. Rod Serling's wife, Carol, has been a mentor to me since I was a teenager, and has been nice enough to keep up a correspondence with me, off and on, since the 1980's. Thank you, Mrs. Serling.

Above all, I would like to thank two people. First, thank you to my niece, Brianna P. Smith. You understand the dangers government poses, and continue in my father's footsteps. You always made his day, and you do the same for me. As Pipa used to say, Bri, "It's nice to have you aboard!"

Finally, thank you, Jill. You make me smile, buddy.

Contents

Introduction: Paul H. Goldsmith
Page 1

Government versus Free Speech
Page 3

Macroeconomics Part One: Money, Immigration, Antitrust and Freedom
Page 41

Macroeconomics Part Two: Federal and State Programs
Page 87

Macroeconomics Part Three: Federal and State Regulation
Page 127

Political Economics, Natural Rights, and Constitutional Government: The Nexus Between Contemporary Issues and Timeless Principles
Page 171

Government and Health Care: Slow Poison
Page 183

Confronting the Political Players
Page 209

Education and the Leftist Attempt To Centralize Decision-Making for It
Page 251

The Bull That Broke Free
Page 305

"Title"
(fiction)
319

"Alone"
(fiction)
323

"Survivor"
(fiction)
325

"Hobson's Choice"
(fiction)
329

"The Jewelbox of God"
(screenplay)
335

Beautiful Chaos
439

Introduction
By
Paul H. Goldsmith

If picked up for slight perusal
One's eye meets thoughts unusual
Some new, some old
Some blue, some bold
Read no more if on supernaturalism you are sold
Or that freedom lies solely in democracy
What about life, and love, and, ah yes, the clergy?

"Oh, what fools these mortals be"
Turn the page, and you will see.

-- 1942, the introduction to "Worthwhile Quotations: First Book", by PHG.

LIVE FREE OR DIE

Government versus Free Speech

When the shark smiles, beware!

**PHG
December, 1985**

"Stifle It!!"
Sept. 1997

During the 1970's there was a very popular television series created by Norman Lear called "All in the Family". It was adored by critics and fans alike. But there was a faction of the American populace that didn't appreciate the program, and for good reason. These were conservative Republicans, who were mercilessly lampooned on the show, often for no just cause. Archie Bunker, the main character of the series, was a perfect example of what Hollywood leftists viewed to be the typical conservative Republican. He was ignorant, lazy, and generally fearful and intolerant of anything that did not fit his worldview. He was constantly being shown the error of his ways by the enlightened left-winger "Meathead", or being taught "subtle" lessons by his seemingly daft, but emotionally brilliant wife, Edith. "Heavy" social issues were explored on the program, and if one didn't appreciate the show, one was either a fascist, or totally bereft of a sense of humor. For years, the media have lauded "All in the Family" as a hilarious, cutting-edges series. But for many, the humor was as simplistic as the political commentary. Even today, when they hear the supposedly classic line "stifle it, Edith!" they cringe.

But there is something very universal in one's reaction to those words. One doesn't have to be a Democrat or Republican to feel it. In fact, about two-hundred years ago, a group of men who probably would have been mocked by Lear had he lived at the time had an intense dislike for the concept of "stifling it." They were just a bunch of ignorant white guys who sat around in oppressive heat in the year 1787, rendered all the wisdom handed down to them from before the times of Greece and Rome, and came up with one of the greatest documents in favor of individual liberty under a limited government ever created. They decided to call it "The Constitution of The United States of America," and to include as the second clause of Amendment One this line, forbidding the Congress from: "…abridging the freedom of speech, or of the press, or of the right of the people to peaceably assemble, and to petition the government for redress of grievances."

In other words, the federal government cannot "stifle" the people.

But the politicians who occupy, both figuratively and literally, the legal edifice the Founders created are of a very different mindset. They fully intend to stifle free speech, and will use every trick in their arsenal to achieve their goal.

The current ploy is called "Campaign Finance Reform", and began as an honest attempt by the Republicans in Congress to discover what the heck the Clinton Administration had done prior to, and during, the 1996 campaign cycle. Thanks to the Democrats -- so eager to cast the light of truth away from their own wrongdoing -- and to the media -- cheerleading for the DNC -- the title has now become a moniker for the suppression of political speech. It doesn't take a genius to realize that when a political commentator on "Washington Week in Review" says the "Campaign Finance Hearings" had better lead, not to the discovery of law-breaking and prosecution of the law-breakers, but to changes in the campaign finance laws, further restrictions on political speech are the goal.

Forget about the meetings between John Huang and Bill Clinton. Forget about the fleecing of supposedly poverty-vowed Buddhist monks in a California monastery, a meeting that Al Gore publicly denied was a fund-raiser, but was proven to have been just that by leaks of his own memos written prior to the event. Forget about the selling of the Lincoln bedroom. Forget about the fact that Al Gore first denied he had made any fundraising calls from the White House -- a felony punishable with up to three years in prison -- then was later proven to have made said calls. Forget the fact that Gore then claimed that he might have made the calls, sure, but with a DNC credit card, so it was a-okay. Clear you mind of the fact that Gore was then proven to have used a White House credit card, thus employing taxpayer money to further the Clinton campaign. Skip the fact the Johnny Chung claims to have paid Hazel O'Leary's favorite charity thousands in order to have gotten access to the White House. Discount any worries you may have had about those innocent "Coffees" between members of the investment community and the Clinton Officials who regulate their businesses, after which many attending coffee drinkers shelled out thousands of Dollars to the DNC (it must have been gourmet coffee). And don't even think about the fact that Bill Clinton unilaterally seized thousands of acres of land in Utah for a "National Monument", a move that just happens to give the Lippo Group a world monopoly on the clean burning coal called anthracite.

What we need to do is fix those darned campaign finance laws, 'cause, gee, the money provided by big business to Republicans "made us do it", say the Democrats.

Without a hint of embarrassment, people such as Al Gore and Bill Clinton tell us that the laws have to be changed because the laws were broken, completely overlooking the fact that *they were the ones who broke them!* It's kind of like a rapist saying that we need to change the laws against the crime he just committed in order to protect women from that crime. It's circular logic, and it's coming from real, dedicated, hard working lawbreakers in order to cover up the truth.

An investigation of the legal mechanism promoted by these lawbreakers as a way to "fix the problem" reveals exactly what their intentions are. That mechanism is known as the McCain-Feingold Campaign Finance Reform Bill, and it is clearly an attempt to curtail the rights of American citizens to support the political ideals and political candidates with which they agree.

Under McCain-Feingold, not only would new caps be placed on the amounts individuals and corporations could donate to political parties, restrictions would be imposed on political advocacy groups that support certain political *principles*. For example, the Christian Coalition publishes annual reports on the voting records of all our Congressmen and Senators. These reports do not advocate the election of one politician or another, they simply compare the voting records of the politicians with the principles the group espouses. It is left up to the reader of the report to decide whether those votes reveal the politician to be someone they would like to support or not. Under McCain-Feingold, any politician who took issue with the publications of a certain advocacy group could call upon the Federal Election Commission to investigate and determine whether the publication was "made for the purpose of advocating the election or defeat of the candidate."

This would have the practical effect of chilling nearly all dissenting opinion by advocacy groups against incumbent politicians and their views, a fact that John McCain himself freely and proudly concedes: "To launch an attack on me (is) participation in a political campaign, and therefore might be subject to some kind of limitation," he recently admitted on NBC's "Meet The Press".

Such fatuous language might be humorous if it were not so dangerous.

To think that an elected official, serving as a Senator in the political system created by the Founding Fathers, could spew forth such utter nonsense, *and have it taken seriously* is almost beyond comprehension.

Almost.

Sadly, this attitude is prevalent inside the Beltway, and it is spreading. The very fact that the current debate about campaign finance reform centers on what new restrictions we can create in order to "level the playing field" is indicative of just how little Americans care about the freedom of speech preserved by Amendment One of the Constitution. Instead, voters are angrier at "Big Business", that Twentieth Century pariah and scapegoat for all that is wrong with our nation. They want to curtail the "influence of corporate greed" on our representatives.

In fact, they should be looking at it the other way around. It is *political greed* that has created the problem, political greed for more power and influence, despite the safeguards written in the very document that allows the politicians to hold office, the U.S. Constitution. The federal government has become so intrusive, is involved in so many things that it is not supposed to be influencing, is doing so much that was not originally granted to it by the Constitution, that businesses have to get involved out of self-interest. That self-interest takes the form of financial support for candidates who will either not impose new restrictions on business, or who will vote in favor of some kind of legislation that will give the business a financial advantage against foreign or domestic competition. "Public Choice" theorists such as James Buchanan expressed the problem very well. Essentially, when a democratic republic such as ours is run according to its strict constitutional safeguards, there is very little risk that cases of "influence peddling" will arise. However, when the politicians begin to stray from the safeguards imposed upon them, creating legislation that showers financial gain on certain favored groups or businesses, it becomes in the best interest of those groups most affected by legislation to try to "buy" influence.

While the interested party will spend large amounts to support a certain bill, knowing that the payoff will bring him much more than he shelled out, the average voter does not have a great enough financial incentive to keep track of all the new bills. In time and money, his opposition to such a bill is more expensive than the taxes he will end up paying after the bill is made law. Thus, we have more and more counter-productive laws written by Congress, laws that favor certain powerful organized interests, whether they be General Motors, A.D.M., the A.A.R.P., or the A.F.L.C.I.O.

So, given the fact that Congress takes carte blanche to write almost any law it wants and to influence any industry it pleases, can one really blame business for either trying to keep Congress off its back or for trying to get

Congress to do it a favor? If you were a dentist who discovered a bill in the works that would impose new regulations costing you up to $1000 a year, would it not be in your best interest to pay up to $999, pool your resources with other dentists, and see to it that the representatives who did not favor the bill got your financial support?

In an America where the federal government has such massive power to help or destroy private businesses, you'd better hope that businesses still have the right to protect themselves. The problem is not business, but the government.

McCain-Feingold, like the 1974 federal campaign finance laws that preceded it, will only serve to expand the influence of the federal government into the field of political speech. This is exactly what the entrenched political class wants. If we, the people, want to see a change in our system of campaign financing, we must force the federal government to abide by the Constitutional safeguards placed upon it. We must not blame businesses for trying to protect themselves or take advantage of a system that has been corrupted from the inside.

We should not be as ignorant as the foolish caricature named Archie Bunker, and shout from our ratty lounge chairs, "stifle it!"

"Bleep"
February, 2004

On February 1, 2004, Janet Jackson and Justin Timberlake gave the world a new perspective on the term "pop music". During the Superbowl half-time show, Timberlake grabbed the right bra cup of Jackson's leather outfit, and exposed her breast to the world. In more ways than one, it was probably the most exposure Jackson had gotten for a performance in years.

Apart from the fact that it was a crude, transparent gimmick by an ageing pop singer -- a ploy to attract attention to herself the day prior to the release of a single -- it was also an attempt to appear relevant to a younger audience. Like Madonna's open-mouthed kiss of Britney Spears on the MTV Music Awards a few months earlier, Ms. Jackson's display of such low, debased behavior did more to make her look desperate for attention than it did to reinforce her image as a rebel.

And it did something else. It got the public, particularly conservative commentators, very upset. Demanding that the Federal Communications Commission finally enforce its standards regarding "decency" on the airwaves, many radio hosts and writers exhorted their listeners and readers to call the FCC and lodge complaints.

There is a clear paradox inherent in the behavior of "small government" conservatives who reinforce the legitimacy of the FCC. It is strange to see "strict-constructionists" calling on people to lobby a federal body the existence of which stretches the meaning of the interstate commerce clause of the Constitution, and contradicts the First Amendment dictum that "Congress shall make no law... abridging the freedom of speech."

The rationale offered by one conservative radio host in support of calling on the FCC was that we already have federal decency laws on the books, and they need to be enforced. Acceptable logic, if one accepts a faulty premise.

Would this same host, I wondered, call for stricter enforcement of the Jim Crow Laws instituted to keep blacks from working productive jobs and leading normal lives during the Twentieth Century?

Which holds sway for a conservative, the laws on the books, or the US Constitution?

Moreover, the FCC codes for broadcast television are called "contemporary community standards". How can conservatives justify the imposition of "community standards" that are created and enforced by a central authority? The irony is so striking it is almost laughable. How can one have a "community standard" dictated to it from outside the community?

It is also difficult to understand how conservatives can support a federal agency that was created during the administration of Franklin Delano Roosevelt as a way to strong-arm enemies and glad-hand friends.[1]

The rationale offered by Roosevelt and his acolytes for the creation of the FCC has been reiterated for decades, and it is entirely unsupportable. According to the boosters of the 1934 Federal Communications Act, the radio spectrum was a limited resource. It also crossed state borders. As such, it was necessary and appropriate that the federal government own the airwaves. As argued by the Roosevelt Administration, the broadcast spectrum was, by its nature, a public good, and it was in the public interest that Washington regulate its use, thus avoiding potential private business conflicts.

Strangely, for other limited resources such as land and water, the federal government wasn't needed as a referee. Somehow, people worked out these claims just fine on local and state levels. Within certain parameters, paper was a limited (though slowly renewable) resource. There were only a finite number of useable trees in the United States in 1934, but, for some reason, this scarcity was not used as a rationale for the regulation of newspaper and book content. Perhaps that was because the American public would have seen it as an abridgement of the First Amendment, just as they should have seen the federal take-over of the broadcast spectrum as the unconstitutional action that it was.

From its inception, the FCC has been a politicized agency that uses taxpayer money to do things which the taxpayers could manage themselves more efficiently and without political favoritism. It has shut down conservative broadcasters and laid pressure on television producers to change the content of their programs. It has dictated to networks what kinds of material they

---

1 In 1938 the FCC revoked the license of the Yankee Radio Network, a conservative broadcaster that often editorialized against FDR's policies. As quoted by Thomas G. West, in "Imprimis", Vol. 33, No. 1, the FCC announced: "Radio can serve as an instrument of democracy only when devoted to the communication of information and exchange of ideas fairly and objectively presented... It cannot be devoted to the support of principles he [the broadcaster] happens to regard most favorably..." So much for freedom of expression.

can broadcast at certain times of the day, and it has fined broadcasters for using language that did not fit its own amorphous definition of "decency".[2]

Its budget has doubled since the early Nineties, and now stands at a breathtaking $292,958,000 for fiscal 2005.[3] But for many conservatives, the FCC does not do enough. It does not punish enough of the foul-mouthed shock jocks on the radio. It does not fine enough radio stations for playing "gangsta rap" that is filled with obscenities. Only now, they say, is the FCC starting to wake up and hear the pleas of average Americans. Only now is it doing its job.

Strangely, the fact that these new public outcries were what made the FCC stand up and act shows how irrelevant and useless the FCC standards truly are. It is only *after* millions of Americans become upset at something they see, that the FCC acts. This signifies that FCC activity is merely a function of public dissatisfaction. If there is public dissatisfaction, what need is there for an agency to tell broadcasters there is public dissatisfaction? If the standards of people have been offended, and they speak out about it, why do we need an agency to somehow put its imprimatur on that public outcry? It is redundant and unnecessary, just like most government programs.

It also siphons away nearly 300 million dollars a year, money that dwarfs the $5.5 million in fines that could be levied against the 200 stations that broadcast Jackson's stunt. What might happen if this tax money were left in the hands of individuals who were free to make their own moral judgments about what they saw on television? What could arise in the media if people were free to exercise their own morals through their own choices, rather than having their choices smothered by the "community standards" of a public official? Would America be a hotbed of licentiousness? Would there be Janet Jackson's running naked on children's networks?

It's highly unlikely. In fact, given their power back, Americans might be more vigilant in policing the airwaves. They already respond to "indecent" material by avoiding it, and avoiding the advertisers who sponsor it. Not everyone will do this, but those who wish to avoid bad content can, and those broadcasters who want to attract people back to their programs will

---

[2] The FCC defines "indecency" as: "…language or material that, in context, depicts or describes, in terms patently offensive as measured by contemporary community standards for the broadcast medium, sexual or excretory activities or organs."

[3] See: http://www.cato.org/dailys/02-08-01.html for these and other statistics on the FCC.

respond in kind. CBS aired the 2004 Superbowl, and it is a sure bet that the network will go to great lengths to assure Americans that next year will be different. They want people to return, so they can offer high viewing figures to their advertisers.

Janet Jackson and Justin Timberlake miscalculated. They didn't understand that not all television is like MTV, not all television caters to the lowest common denominator. People have varied tastes, and those tastes are reflected in the multitude of choices available on television today. They can have their spot for crude behavior, but it won't be on another Superbowl broadcast, and it probably won't be on CBS for quite some time unless they give strong assurances that they will clean up their acts. What the market does is something the FCC can never do. It lets people decide for themselves, with their own money, what is proper and improper, what is decent and indecent. The threat of FCC fines won't be what keeps network executives from hiring Jackson and Timberlake. The threat of lost business will.

One need not be a libertine to criticize the actions of the FCC and the conservative call for more. One need only have faith in his fellow man, and in the ability of the market to respond to what people truly want.

Ironically, just a week prior to Jackson's appearance on CBS, Congress began hearings on two *new* bills that would place even more restrictions on broadcast television. By stirring up such a clamor for federal enforcement, the supposedly rebellious Jackson and Timberlake may just turn out to be the best allies the government moralists could ever have.

"Shout It from the Desktops!"
April, 2002

There are many fronts in the ongoing battle to restore individual liberty and American traditions. From the beachheads of the voting booths, to the guerrilla war of political debate, Americans who believe in the traditional tenets of the Founders are in a never-ending struggle. We take part in elections, we give funds to organizations which represent our beliefs. We try to have an impact.

Yet there is one area of our government in which we have virtually no influence whatsoever: the court system.

Since the time of Chief Justice John Marshall, since the days of the *Dred Scott* decision a few decades later, Americans have seen their Supreme Court acquire more and more power. Today, very few recall that the court is designed to be an *appellate* body, the decisions of which apply only to the case presented before it. A finding of "unconstitutional" by the high court will most likely lead prosecutors in lower courts to not press charges against future defendants, since upon appeal in the highest court of the nation, a defendant would be released by justices who had ruled against the law in the past. Changing the situation would require changing the makeup of the court, and that happens very rarely. Impeachments for dereliction of a judge's Constitutional duty are uncommon. In practice, such changes usually happen when a justice retires, and a new justice must be appointed.

Thus it appears that if supporters of a ban on "virtual" child pornography want to see that ban upheld, they will have to wait for one of the justices of the US Supreme Court to move to greener pastures.

For many fighting in the battle over American culture, that time cannot come soon enough. But the reasons may not seem as obvious as one might first suspect.

In early April, the US Supreme Court handed down a six to three decision in the case of *Ashcroft v. Free Speech Coalition*. The debate revolved around the 1996 Child Pornography Prevention Act (CPPA), which was passed in Congress as part of the overall telecommunications re-structuring of the same period. Under the stipulations of the law, the shipment, distribution, receipt, reproduction, sale, or possession of any visual depiction that "appears to be of a minor engaging in sexually explicit conduct" would be a federal crime. Likewise, any visual depiction that is "advertised, promoted, presented, described, or distributed in such a manner that conveys the impression that the material is or contains a visual depiction of a minor engaged in sexually explicit conduct" would also be federally banned.

The law was inspired by the fear of legislators such as Senator Orrin Hatch (R, Utah) over the growing proliferation throughout the internet of computer generated, nearly life-like depictions of minors engaged in explicit acts. With the level of realism very high, "child porn" without real children involved could become popular among individuals possessed of that particular aberrant desire.

The 1996 law was a departure from the standard established under a 1982 US Supreme Court ruling entitled *New York v. Ferber*. In that case, the Court held that a definition of child pornography required images of real minors engaged in sexual conduct. In the case of the 1996 CPPA, the material in question needed only to "appear to be" or "convey the impression" of a "minor engaging in sexually explicit conduct" for possession or distribution of it to be a federal crime.

In 1999, an organization called the Free Speech Coalition brought a suit to the 9th Circuit Court of Appeals that challenged the CPPA. According to the Coalition, and their lead attorney, H. Louis Sirkin, the CPPA's departure from the "real life" standard set by *Ferber* in 1982 was not a protection against child predation, but an unconstitutional abridgment of free speech that could have detrimental effects on many other kinds of communication.

Numerous members of the Coalition understood the rationale for passage of the CPPA as being an attempt to stop "virtual" child pornography from inspiring child predators to commit more crimes against real children. They keenly grasped the arguments made by Hatch and others that even "virtual" child pornography could possibly spur child molesters and rapists to act on their own, although the Coalition members argued that the data are ambiguous on the subject of cause and effect. It was unclear whether or not exposure to child pornography, virtual or otherwise, increased a predator's propensity to prey upon real children in his surroundings, or it acted as a "release" for those who might otherwise seek out real children to attack.

But the major expressed fear of Coalition members was more nuanced. They argued that an attempt by the federal government to outlaw fictitious images of criminal child pornography, under the rationale that such "virtual" porn could lead to real crimes, could then be expanded to outlaw fictitious depictions of other kinds of behavior, depictions that some argue can lead to increased crimes by those who view the images. If virtual child pornography could be outlawed because of what was called the "Secondary Effects" doctrine, then could crime movies be outlawed because of arguments that such depictions of violence inspire more crime in real life?

Critics of the Free Speech Coalition accused them of using such an argument to gloss over the organization's real mission, to make the United States safe for pornography. Indeed, Sirkin asserted that the Coalition had legal standing to oppose the CPPA on civil grounds rather than merely appealing criminal processions. Since the CPPA's stipulations would force certain adult film producers to forego making films that employ adults depicted as minors in sexual acts, the Coalition pointed out that the law would harm the bottom lines of many film producers.

In his majority opinion, US District Judge Donald Molloy, who sat on the case by designation, said that the *Ferber* standard must still apply.

"To accept the secondary effects argument as the gauge against which the statute must be measured requires a remarkable shift in the First Amendment paradigm… Such a transformation, how speech impacts the listener or viewer, would turn First Amendment jurisprudence on its head." (*Free Speech Coaltion v. Reno*, 1999)

The ruling was not satisfactory to the federal government, and the Bush Administration Justice Department, under the guidance of new Attorney General John Ashcroft, appealed the case to the US Supreme Court.

The arguments brought before the Circuit Court were the same in the Supreme Court, and it may surprise some stalwart conservatives to discover that justices Anthony Kennedy, J. P. Stevens, David Souter, Ruth Bader Ginsburg, and Stephen Breyer made the correct decision, for all the wrong reasons.

The content of the majority decision is a case study of the trap into which many politically minded people stray when they begin debating the relative merits of Supreme Court jurisprudence. They concentrate on the intricate particulars of the issue at hand --the morality of the crime or petition -- rather than looking at the larger, more abstract, but yet just as important, Constitutional issues at stake. It is the issue of federalism that tends to be overlooked as many of us argue about the depravity of an act, or the importance of a law to prevent it, or even the nuances of a Constitutional clause which we believe might or might not apply.

In the case of "virtual" child pornography, it was taken as a given by the justices comprising the majority that the material was a form of "speech" protected by the First Amendment to the Constitution, and it was here that most of their debate concentrated.

Expressing the view of the majority, Justice Kennedy wrote:

"*Ferber* did not hold that child pornography is by definition without value. On the contrary, the court recognized some works in this category might have significant value, but relied on virtual images -- the very images prohibited by the CPPA -- as an alternative and permissible means of expression."

Even if one were to cede the rather unpleasant point that on rare occasions, virtual images of underage sex could somehow have some redeeming value -- and one has trouble trying to imagine such a situation -- the larger scope of the issue is completely missed by such an obvious and sophomoric thought experiment.

Undaunted, Kennedy continued to support the majority decision with still more about the intricacies of the subject, rhetoric that had little to do with the larger Constitutional issues at hand. He attempted to liken child pornography to the genius of William Shakespeare.

"Shakespeare may not have written sexually explicit scenes for the Elizabethan audience," he wrote, "but were modern directors to adopt a less conventional approach, that fact alone would not compel the conclusion the work was obscene."

Such fatuous language would be almost laughable, were it to come from anyone other than a Supreme Court justice. As it stands, it is a truly disturbing reminder of the mental gymnastics these judges are willing to display in their attempts to lower American morals to the basest level. But what is most objectionable is not so much the idea that a judge might try to compare Shakespeare's *Romeo and Juliet* to child pornography, it is the very process of having an unelected federal official decide what is and is not valuable "speech". It is this morality, the question of *who* decides, about which Americans ought to be concerned.

The fact that *Kennedy* is deciding about the levels of depravity, virtual or otherwise, that American's will accept ought to make anyone familiar with the writing of the Founders very concerned. The fact that most legal commentators don't pay such power grabs any heed ought to frighten us even more.

On the issue of speech, federalism is the key.

For a fleeting moment, Kennedy and the majority touched upon slightly more substantive issues, aspects of the case that obliquely deal with matters more important than water-cooler chit chat.

"Pictures of what appears (sic) to be 17-year-olds engaging in sexually explicit activity do not in every case contravene community standards," he wrote, implicating the long-held Supreme Court free speech precedent that as long as something doesn't violate what have been ambiguously called "community standards", it should be protected as "free expression" under the First Amendment.

But the true power of communities to determine their own "standards" has been so diminished by the Supreme Court, the Executive, and Legislative branches of the federal government, that it is virtually non-existent.

The First Amendment specifically states that "*Congress* shall make no law" abridging the freedom of speech, or of the press. It does not address the states on the issue. In stark contrast to the Second Amendment, which utilized the blanket proscription, "the right to keep and bear arms shall not be infringed", the First Amendment clearly allowed for local and state speech and religion laws. Such laws existed for decades after the adoption of the Constitution. State sponsored religious schools existed in Pennsylvania, and town curfews infringed upon the rights of people to congregate in the streets. The Founders understood that unanimity was not to be found on all issues. Therefore, they wisely allowed for the states to create their own laws on subjects like gambling, prostitution, drinking, and myriad other issues.

The "community standards" of what comprises acceptable and unacceptable speech are to be just that, *community standards*. As long as the Fourteenth Amendment provision, that all state laws must apply equally to state citizens, is protected, states are to be free to create their standards, or allow equal power to the citizens of the towns. Justice Kennedy's peculiar views on Shakespeare should have no bearing whatsoever.

This is the essential point. There is a dynamic that is being missed when many contemporary Supreme Court observers give their views on *Ashcroft v. Free Speech Coalition*. It is a thought process that begins with this question.

Does the federal government have jurisdiction?

Well, is "virtual" child pornography a form of speech? That is debatable. If it is, as the majority believe, then it is up to the states to create their own laws, based on their own standards. Thus, the CPPA, a federal infringement on this state right, would be unconstitutional, and the decision of the justices to deem it as such would be correct. Of course, Kennedy and his allies did not strike down the CPPA in deference to the clear state prerogative. They struck it down due to their own group opinion on how this form of "speech" ought to be viewed.

In fact, such a matter was never supposed to be theirs to decide. A federal law would only apply if a state had outlawed such expression and the criminal material was taken over state borders.

But if "virtual" child pornography is *not* speech, and it is a product, then who has jurisdiction over its legality?

According to the "Inter-state Commerce" clause of the US Constitution (found in Article One, Section Eight), the Congress has the power to regulate trade between the States. According to most power-hungry Washington politicians, this is license enough to regulate virtually any item that might pass over state borders, or have even a slight bearing on inter-state trade. To such people, material like "virtual" pictures of child sex, if not defined as "speech", would be products that could be regulated. The primary argument of the regulators would be that outlawing "virtual" child pornography would reduce the incidences of real child molestation and sexual assault by those who view it. The secondary argument would be that a ban would reduce the demand for all kinds of child pornography, thus possibly lowering the number of criminal sexual acts committed in the making of such films.

As practical matters, both arguments can be dismissed. The latter point, that banning "virtual" child pornography could reduce the demand for child porn in general, and thus bring about a reduction in real child porn crimes, is so tenuous as to be fanciful. It is highly unlikely that actual child pornography will be reduced in any way if "fake' child porn is outlawed. There will be no fewer crimes committed by dirty film makers because their competition, "virtual" pornographers, are banned from creating their product.

The primary argument, so feared by the Free Speech coalition as a dangerous precedent that could implicate other kinds of expression, was refuted by Justice Kennedy in one of his more reasoned passages:

Addressing the argument in favor of stifling certain kinds of "speech" out of a desire to reduce the incidence of crimes that *may* be inspired on a secondary level among viewers of that material, Kennedy agreed with Donald Molloy, in *Ferber* and wrote:

"While the government asserts that the images can lead to actual instances of child abuse, the causal link is contingent and indirect. The harm does not necessarily follow from the speech, but depends upon some unquantified potential for subsequent criminal acts."

This is an important point. Are individuals who merely depict criminal acts, when there is no victim and no real crime against a victim, guilty of a crime? Does a writer who describes a horrible killing become an accomplice when a deranged reader carries out such an act in real life? Is a painter who paints a picture of a city fire guilty of conspiracy to commit arson if someone sees his paintings and gets a sexual thrill from the conflagration he sees, thus inspiring him to burn a building in his neighborhood? Is it a matter of intent? What if the creator of the "art", or "expression" in question intended it to inspire or fulfill deviant desires in the recipient or viewer of the product? Can the makers of a violent war film be held on criminal charges because they make a movie in which the main character kills dozens and gives the viewers a vicarious thrill? At what point is there criminal liability?

More to the point, should there be federal laws outlawing the work in order to quell the secondary crimes the "product" may inspire?

As a matter of ethics, such a question ought to be easy to answer. A crime requires a real, actual victim of the act. Entering a world in which crime is defined in an ever expanding circle -- where more and more indirect activity is characterized as having inspired criminal action on a third party, where the responsibility for a crime is not laid solely at the feet of the real perpetrator -- is a dangerous route to explore. It destroys the concept of personal responsibility. A criminal who commits murder is no longer solely responsible for his actions, because he was "driven to it" by something he saw.

Former Vice Presidential candidate Joe Lieberman actually embraced this idea during his campaign of 1999-2000. He expressed his interest in defining films and television programs as "products", which, he said, could then be regulated under the all powerful "Inter-state Commerce" clause. By doing so, of course, "bad" films that (according to him and others who would like to reduce individual responsibility to an ancient human race memory) cause crimes could be regulated and controlled.

The response from conservatives to such insidious and absurd language must be untempered and unambiguous.

It is not Joe Lieberman's place to regulate speech, or even regulate "expression" which has been characterized by him as a "product". The "Interstate Commerce" clause was never intended to give the federal government omnipotent control over any product crossing over state lines. It was written to stop states from imposing tariffs on one another. Under the Articles of Confederation, the original document that functioned as America's founding rule book, states as entities were able to print their own money and impose tariffs on products from other states. This inspired the debt-ridden states to print inflated, worthless money, and place so many tariffs on out-of-state products that the economic well-being of the nation was put at risk, and animosity grew between feuding states. The "Interstate Commerce" clause was written as a remedial measure, to allow the federal government to intervene in inter-state trade disputes and stop state tariffs. It was, as James Madison has been quoted by Lawrence Patten McDonald, not to "be used for... positive purposes," but was "a negative and preventative provision against injustice among the states themselves." (*We Hold These Truths,* Seal Beach, Calif. '76 Press, p. 76). To adopt a stance that the clause allows federal politicians to regulate anything that crosses over state borders is so patently absurd as to be nearly criminal itself.

Lieberman's belief that he and others like him can bring about a utopian world free of crime inspired by offending and dangerous "art" is akin to the belief among prohibitionists in 1917 that passing a federal law against the sale of alcohol would stop crimes committed by people who became intoxicated. For them, the product had enough of a causal link to the behavior that outlawing the product itself was seen as a positive measure. Of course, in 1917 there were still politicians honest enough to propose *amending* the Constitution in order to bring their dream to life. There were also enough justices sitting on the Supreme Court that an attempt to outlaw alcohol on a federal level by passage of a law in Congress would have been recognized as the illicit action it is. Today, with our federal government populated by intellectually corrupt politicians such as Lieberman, and operating under the haze of post-modern thought of judges such as Kennedy, the original tenets of the Founders have been all but forgotten.

It is already being reported that Orrin Hatch is re-writing the CPPA to circumvent the Court's April ruling. The battle for federal supremacy over state issues continues.

As we study the opinions and proposals of people such as these, let us not lose sight of our own dedication to Constitutional principles. If the citizens of the various states want to establish laws concerning the creation and dissemination of "virtual" child pornography, let them do so. Speech laws are their prerogative, not that of Orrin Hatch.

The nuances of the debate regarding what is and is not "acceptable" expression will never be decided, but at least under the federalist system established by the Founders, one could congregate in a state with others of like minds. If one did not like the morality of his neighbors, as expressed in the state law, he was free to move, to join others who felt as he. That is why prostitution is legal in Nevada and illegal in other states, why use of medical marijuana was supported by the people of California, and not on other states.

The insinuation by deceptive politicians and judges of federal influence on clear state issues such as these is a criminal act itself. It should be recognized as such by everyone, even conservatives who would like to see America's culture cleaned up as soon as possible.

"Access Denied"
June 2002

One of the first principles taught in most basic military history classes is the tactical folly of fighting a war on two fronts. Resources are spread thin, geographic challenges are presented that typically hinder movement, and capitulation is usually inevitable.

In the American "culture" war, numerous fronts have arisen to split the defenses of conservatives, forcing them -- or tempting them -- to concentrate on many different threats. None is more apparent than the possibility that children could be exposed to pornographic material on computers. The danger of this has caused many social conservatives to lobby for federal laws to prevent it, or at least decrease it's likelihood.

2000 was a watershed year for such federal legislation. Under the leadership of politicians such as Senator Orrin Hatch (R.Utah), the Neighborhood Children's Internet Protection Act (NCIPA), and the Children's Internet Protection Act (CIPA) were passed as part of the US Omnibus Consolidated Appropriations legislation.[4]

Working in tandem, the laws mandate the use of Internet "blocking technologies" by public libraries that receive "Library Services and Technology" funds to purchase computers for Internet use, or to pay for Internet access. The laws also require the use of screening technology by libraries that receive Universal Service Discounts ("E-rate") for Internet access.[5]

---

[4] Public Law 106-554, 47m U.S.C., sec 254(h)(5)(E)(i)(I).
[5] The Library Services and Technology Act (LSTA) and Universal Service Discounts (E-rates) were federal programs started under the 1996 Telecommunications Act. The LSTA offers federally appropriated tax Dollars to localities in order to facilitate the purchase computers for Internet access, or to acquire Internet access. This money is appropriated through a federal tax applied to all long-distance connections in the US market. It appears on every phone bill in the nation, and is doled out in the form of grants. The E-rate is a subsidy to libraries to allow them to pay for their Internet connections, and is established and funded through a complex application of federal fees on long-distance carriers in order for them to execute their rights to operate in the long distance market. It is essentially a form of federal extortion.

Under the provisions of the laws, libraries must adopt Internet screening policies that address access by minors to "inappropriate" material on the Internet. Although the federal government claims that the meaning of "inappropriate" is to be defined by local school boards and local libraries, the legislation requires that the libraries not only block or filter internet access to visual depictions that are obscene, constitute child pornography, or are harmful to minors, but also that the libraries show *proof* of enforcement. While appearing deferential to local ethics and mores, the federal government clearly has the final say as to what is "inappropriate".

In 2001, the American Library Association brought a suit to the Third Circuit Court of Appeals challenging the provisions of the CIPA and NCIPA, as generally known under the title of CIPA. In closing arguments on April 3, 2002, attorneys for the ALA, Paul Smith and Jennifer Block, offered their reasons for opposing the laws:

"Filters don't work. Blocking technology restricts legal and useful information, while letting though illegal materials.

"Because blocking technology pervasively and necessarily restricts legal information, CIPA is unconstitutional.

"Libraries should not be forced to choose between funding and censorship… CIPA demands these institutions accept a federal mandate in return for vital technology funding."[6]

On May 31, 2002, the Justices of the Third Circuit Court of Appeals agreed. In a 304-page ruling, they stated their decision very clearly.

"In sum, we think that the plaintiffs have good arguments that they may assert an unconstitutional conditions claim by relying either on the public libraries' First Amendment rights or on the rights of their patrons. We also think that the plaintiffs have a good argument that CIPA's requirement that public libraries use filtering software distorts the usual functioning of public libraries in such a way that it constitutes an unconstitutional condition on the receipt of funds."[7]

---

[6] American Library Association, April 3, 2002. "ALA Delivers Closing Arguments in CIPA Trial", p. 1.
[7] ALA, Inc. et al. v. United Sates, et al.: No 01-1303, May 31, 2002.

This ruling has caused an uproar among social conservatives. Seeing their tax money forcibly taken from them for the E-rate and LSTA funds, they find it not only distasteful, but also unethical that this money might be used to provide objectionable material to children over the Internet.

Such protestations are valid and laudable. The ethical dilemmas presented by taxation are infinite, and philosophers from John Locke to Thomas Paine have recognized them. It is not enough to ask if one's tax money is being spent wisely, it is essential to ask if that money should be expropriated at all, to place the morality of taxation in question.

While television pundits argue about the minutiae of what constitutes "objectionable" material, and discuss the value of public libraries having the freedom to "explore" ideas unfettered, this larger question of taxation is missed.

But another important issue is overlooked, even by social conservatives.

The Third Circuit ruling is curious in one striking way. Its justices stated that, "... it constitutes an unconstitutional condition on the receipt of funds."

The idea of an unconstitutional condition on the provision of funds has been visited before, in the 1982 Third Circuit case *Grove City College v. HEW*, and later, on appeal in the Supreme Court as *Grove City College v. Bell et al.* (The name Bell refers to the Secretary of Health Education and Welfare at the time.) What is remarkable about the ruling in the 2002 *ALA* internet case is that it stands in complete opposition to the Supreme Court *Grove City* case, and to the Third Circuit's own ruling on *Grove City*.

The catalyst for *Grove City*, was the attempt by the US Department of Health Education and Welfare to force private colleges to conform to a particular set of federal "anti-sex discrimination" regulations, rules stipulated by Title IX of the Education Amendments of 1972. Under the regulations, HEW notified Grove City College (a small liberal arts school in Pennsylvania) that it would have to sign an "assurance of compliance". Among other things, this paper would stipulate that equal numbers of men and woman had been admitted, that an equal number of sports teams would be offered for men and women to join, and that equal facilities were being provided for males and females. If it did not comply, the one-quarter of Grove City's student population receiving federal grants or loans would have them revoked.

Grove City brought the case to the Federal District Court in Pittsburgh in 1979, and emerged victorious. Loans were deemed to be immune from the federal regulations, and grants were to be viewed as allowable without prior certificates of compliance. Only if allegations of *actual* discrimination were made, and an inquiry conducted, could action be considered regarding federal grant recipients.

But the federal government appealed the ruling, and in 1982, it took the third Circuit only three weeks to unanimously conclude that Grove City College *did* have to comply with Title IX.

Because a portion of Grove City College students received government assistance through Pell Grants, claimed the court, the entire school was subject to government jurisdiction, and specifically to Title IX. HEW could terminate assistance to students solely on the grounds that Grove City refused to sign the "Assurance of Compliance". According to the court, no hearings were necessary prior to terminating the student aid.

Grove City appealed the ruling, but in 1984 the US Supreme Court came to the same conclusion as the Third Circuit. It ruled that federal scholarship grants received by students attending private colleges such as Grove City were *direct* aid, and were sufficient to trigger the provisions of Title IX. They did not accept the argument of Grove City that the federal money was being given to *individuals*, not the school directly, and that these individuals could spend the money without prior federal restraints.

Federal grants are subject to federal regulations, in any form, was the message.

However, it seems as if the message of the US Supreme Court and the Third Circuit in *Grove City* were overlooked in the *ALA* case of 2002.

This is curious, unless one studies the two issues within the context of leftist post-modern legal scholarship.

If a federal education grant is subject to *a-priori* regulations, why is a federal library grant not subject to regulations as well?

One can only assume that it is the goal of the regulation, not the principle of federal regulation itself, that animates a justice's decision. It is a distinction that can only be found by politically active judges who believe that the "ends" of the regulation are more important than the "means".

In leftist ideology, not all the Amendments to the US Constitution are created equal. The First Amendment stands above all others, particularly the Ninth and Tenth Amendments. On one hand, the Third Circuit justices believe that if federal grants are eventually utilized by the students of a private college, federal regulations *can* infringe upon the Ninth and Tenth Amendment rights belonging to the operators of that private school. On the other hand, the justices believe that federal regulations can't possibly infringe upon a federally funded library's -- and a library goers -- right to offer, read or view published material, since this would curtail first amendment rights in numerous ways.

Manifest in such judicial dissonance is a pernicious and pervasive attitude that judges can select which rights they like best, which they wish to protect, and which they wish to neglect. In the eyes of most contemporary legal instructors and judges, the Ninth and Tenth Amendments are "worthless". This is undoubtedly due to the fact that both amendments strictly and adamantly curtail the power of the federal government.

The Ninth Amendment states:

"The enumeration in the Constitution, of certain rights, shall not be construed to deny or disparage others retained by the people."

The Tenth Amendment states:

"The powers not delegated to the United States by the Constitution, nor prohibited by it to the States, are reserved to the States respectively, or to the people."

Apparently, when judges in the Third Circuit look at the Bill of Rights, they not only believe it can be attenuated by the presence of federal money, they believe that people have a greater First Amendment right to free speech than they do Ninth and Tenth Amendment rights to conduct mutually consensual business on their own private property.

The issue of whether or not federal grants are involved becomes moot. It is the *nature* of the right exercised that is important to the post-modernist judge. A federal regulation that effects the decisions of colleges regarding admissions and recreation is irrelevant compared to a regulation that affects the content of a computer at libraries.

Of course, the issue of federal grants is *not* moot. It is central to the entire questionable paradigm of the ALA suit. The question in the ALA suit should not be whether or not it is constitutional for federal grants to be given with rights-restricting strings attached; the question is not whether colleges are being restricted by federal requirements upon student loans of grants.

The question any judge should address is whether or not these grants are *Constitutional* in the first place -- and any reasonable reading of the document which is supposed to be the set of rules under which our government is to operate states the answer quite clearly.

No.

The US Congress was never granted the power to offer federal tax dollars to students, to libraries, to old folks' homes, to scientists, to animal shelters, to artists, to television networks, or anything else not stipulated by the *words of the Constitution*.

In the debate over whether or not a library might have its free speech rights curtailed, or a college ought not to conform to federal regulations regarding sex "equality", the large issue of the constitutionality of the grants themselves is lost.

Until a larger population of Americans becomes curious about such essential issues, the dilemmas presented by federal grants will continue unabated. Unconstitutional farm aid programs will place restrictions on what can be grown, and how. Unconstitutional housing programs will place restrictions on how people can live when accepting the federal lodging. While pragmatic conservatives may feel comfortable with what they see as possible -- and often rare -- "moves towards efficiency" in such programs, they should pause to consider their *principles*. It is upon the principles of the Constitution that our federal government is based, and without them, our nation will forever be caught in a maelstrom of government manipulation.

"Approving the Message"
March 4, 2004

With John Kerry's mathematical lock on the Democrat Party primaries, the head-to-head battle between the likely Democrat nominee and George W. Bush has begun. In fact, major network news organizations are already showing one of the first of the Bush team's political ads, analyzing it like scientists, using Holmesian didactics to pick apart every nuance they can find. In particular, they seem very animated by the fact that Bush has used one and a half seconds to refer to his response to the September 11th attacks. One can understand how the President's political and ideological opponents would like to prevent him from referencing to the war on terror, since it works in Bush's favor. But there is one thing they don't seem to discuss in all their detailed analyses. It is one line. In fact, it is the final or opening line in *every* political candidate's commercials for the 2004 election.

It is the phrase: "I approved this message."

Under the new campaign finance laws promulgated by Washington politicians John McCain, Russ Feingold, Marty Meehan and Chris Shays, and signed into law by the "compassionate conservative" George Bush, political ads cannot be sponsored by any entities or organizations other than the candidates themselves within sixty days of an election. Therefore, when we see lovely pictures of the candidates meeting elderly Americans in retirement homes, and glimpse footage of them sitting with kids in a school, or with blue collar workers in a factory, and we hear their announcers tell us just how terrific they are and how much each one will give us when he becomes the nation's de-facto king, the candidates are required to pop up at the end of the commercial and say:

"I'm So-and-so, and I approved this message."

Now, some candidates have taken notice of how annoying and repetitive this is to see on television about twelve times a day, and they have tried to vary their delivery. Therefore, we get options such as:

"I'm So-and-so, and *I* approved this message."

"I'm So-and-so, and I *approved* this message."

And the ever-popular:

"I'm So-and-so, and I approved *this* message."

Perhaps the most bemusing variation of this phenomenon is the hilarious version of the commercial that sees the candidate *himself* delivering the bulk of the ads self-indulgent copy, and then sees that very same candidate tell us that he "approved this message".

It's a good thing we're given this information, because I'm sure many viewers wondered if he was coerced into delivering such a self-congratulatory ad. Many of us thought he had been forced into it, and wasn't free to truly speak his mind about just how awful a candidate he was.

By telling us this, he seems to be saying, "No, it's okay. I really am that egotistical. I approved this drivel, and I was free to speak my mind."

The ironic thing about it is that he was *not* fully free to speak his mind. As a candidate for public office, trying to express his political principles, no matter how socialistic they might be, the candidate was *forced* to say something he would not normally have said. Right there, in that two second use of his time and money in order to fulfill a government dictate, the candidate has shown anyone interested in noticing it that free speech no longer exists under federal law. This is the first time in American history that a curtailment of the freedom of a US citizen to express his principles can be seen by anyone who is willing to look, and the candidates themselves do not seem to mind!

That speaks volumes about the attitudes of the candidates, about their devotion to expediency over principle, and their willingness to disregard and disrespect the very document that creates the office of President in the first place. In addition, the fact that most of the *viewers* don't object signals the weakness of American respect for the founding document of our nation. It's quite a sad and frustrating thing to see, and it makes one think…

What, I wonder, would it have been like if the Founding Fathers had been forced by law to revise their statements in favor of independence? What if the Declaration of Independence had fallen under the spell of the McCain-Feingold Act? Perhaps the document would not have ended with statements about swearing sacred honor, but would have included this famous and passionate phrase:

"I'm Thomas Jefferson, and I approved this message."

Stirring, isn't it?

What if Thomas Paine had been forced to change the content of his pamphlet "Common Sense", which was one of the major political leaflets behind the push for independence? Speech, be it political or of another kind, is irrevocably tied to economics. The publishers of "Common Sense" and "The Crisis" had to scrape together the time and money to manage their first printings and publications. But in today's political lexicon, the use of one's money to express opinions in a branch of the mass media is *not* considered a form of political expression, it is *not* considered speech. Therefore it is subject to regulation by the very same government officials one might try to criticize!

Under today's rules, the equivalent of Paine's "The Crisis" might open:

"These are the times that try men's souls. But don't get me wrong. It's not all that bad. After all, we have the Crown to protect us, and I'd hate to say anything bad about the Crown sixty days before an election, so just forget that I said anything, and go back to what you were doing. Everything is okay. Oh, and did I mention *souls*? I apologize about that. I didn't mean to get overtly religious here in public or anything. Thank you very much. Sorry for the interruption… Sorry!"

The danger and absurdity of federal speech laws that curtail our ability to express disfavor with the federal government is manifest. The idea that the government is protecting us from "special interests" is a sham. It is preventing us from speaking in favor of our own interests; is it preventing us from doing that which we need to do in order to keep government in check.

The media "experts" who tell us what the ads mean, and the politicians featured in the spots, either do not care, do not mind, or tacitly approve. In every instance, such reactions are frightening, and they are sad commentaries on the politicians themselves, on the voters who would support them, and on the future of our Constitutional republic.

Thanks for reading.

I'm Gardner Goldsmith, and I approved this message.

P. GARDNER GOLDSMITH   PAUL H. GOLDSMITH

A free society has <u>no</u> official, established church supported by taxes.

PHG
May, 1984

"Generation X-Mas"
Dec. 13, 2001

The refusal December 10, 2001, by the US Supreme Court to review a lower court ruling that permits student-led prayer at Jacksonville, Florida graduations harkens back to an era long gone in American history. It was a time when the Court constrained itself from meddling in the affairs of states when no federal intervention was warranted, a period when Justices viewed their oaths to uphold the Constitution as sacred, not meaningless rhetoric used to justify their own politically motivated decisions.

Of course, those days are long gone. Since the beginning of the Twentieth Century, Americans have had to suffer through the vicissitudes of Court wrangling, as various presidents and their Congressional allies and antagonists battle over the composition of the bench, over whether or not the judges placed on that bench will rule on cases according to "strict" or "loose" interpretations of the Constitution. What is worse, we have seen a gradual loss of interest and understanding on the part of the American populace, until only a virtual handful of scholars, special interest groups, and egocentric politicians seem to participate in the Constitutional debate.

To see the almost feral intensity of criticism leveled against the Supreme Court in this Jacksonville case makes one despair for the future of political-philosophical disputation in America. Gray Thomas, counsel for the plaintiffs in the case, said that the decision "further muddies the water" regarding the separation of church and state.

It may come as a surprise to Mr. Thomas, but a "muddying of the waters" concerning the separation of church and state has only come about with the increasing pressure of activist courts during the 1900's; Monday's Supreme Court decision actually helps clean things up.

The Founding Fathers were very clear on the subject. As written and understood at the time, the First Amendment was a proscription against *Congress* establishing a religion, infringing upon the free practice thereof, or infringing on the exercise of free speech. It was not a blanket ban against local speech codes, or state sponsored religions. In fact, state sponsored religious schools were prevalent throughout America; Pennsylvania had many throughout the 1800's.

The reasons such practices were allowed by the Founders were two-fold. First, these wise old birds recalled the experiences of many American settlers, people who had fled their own nations due to religious persecution, and who had congregated with others like themselves in order to practice their religions freely. The inculcation of their children in their preferred belief systems was extremely important, and school, if chosen for these children, was often to have strong religious components.

Perhaps most important for our contemporary understanding of the original concept of Federalism is the fundamental idea of the Founders that there would never be unanimity among Americans regarding all issues. The states were to be left great leeway on important issues; they were to be the "pockets of experimentation", where people of like minds could gather and live, always possessing the ability to "opt out' of a system and move to another, one more akin to their beliefs.

But over the years, the intentional misinterpretation by activist judges, intellectually corrupt attorneys, politicians, and "scholars" of Jefferson's comment on a "separation between Church and State" has turned an Amendment that was originally written to allow religious freedom into a choke collar around the throats of religious children and their parents. At any time, these Americans can have their tax money seized and used to fund a school system that is not only a-moral, but often anti-moral, one over which they have less say than a monolithic teachers' union. If they happen to get a concession from their plunderers to allow their kids a moment to express their own religious beliefs in public, they are not only criticized for supposedly forcing their religion upon others, they are pushed into the legal arena and brought all the way to the highest court in the land.

Perhaps some day, when citizens are no longer coerced into giving up huge portions of the fruits of their labor for government-run schools, we will see a nation in which no one, religious, or non-religious, will feel as if his money is being used for a purpose contrary to his morals and beliefs. People will be able to pray or not pray according to the school system they have voluntarily entered. As a libertarian, I would like to see that day sooner rather than later. But until it arrives, I will be satisfied with the insightful and dynamic system of Federalism that the Founders created, and which the Supreme Court Monday upheld.

**Firearms:
Government Versus the Right to Self Protection**

It has been said that the worst form
of tyranny is a bad law.
It is also true that the worst form of weakness and
stupidity is failure to renounce and rescind it.

PHG
November, 1987

"In Praise of Firearms"
August, 1999

Last month, after suffering through a speech by Arizona Senator John McCain, I ran into an acquaintance who said to me, "That's my man!"

I hated to disagree, but I told him McCain wasn't for me. I disagreed with the Senator on too many big issues, like "Campaign Finance Reform", Federal funding of education, FCC control over telecommunications, and gun control.

At the mention of gun control, Tom's hackles shot up. "I'm completely in favor of it! If it were up to me, no one in America could own a gun."

I told him there were some problems with his position, such as the trifling little fact that total disarmament was, well *impossible*, and that gun control laws are unconstitutional and do nothing to reduce violent crime.

"Let me tell you", he said, leaning towards me as if to adopt some sort of authority. "I've read a lot about this, and the Constitution doesn't..."

I held up my hand. "I know. You'll say it doesn't grant every man the right to keep and bear arms, but only provides that members of the *militia* could be armed, and the militia today is the National Guard."

"That's right!" he exclaimed.

When I told him he didn't know as much about the Constitution and the Founders as he thought, he became very angry.

When I told him that not only do contemporaneous writings from the Founding period make clear the fact that the "militia" was comprised of all free men capable of carrying firearms, but that studies show dramatic *decreases* in violent crime when concealed weapons are allowed in certain areas; when I told him women are 2.5 times more likely to survive a violent attack by using a handgun than "passively complying" to their attackers, he bellowed, "You don't know what you're talking about."

I asked him to refute my claims with his voluminous knowledge, but he refused. So, I challenged him to read some material I could lend him, and then return to me and make his argument.

It was at that point that he appeared ready to make the profound mistake of trying to hit me. Needless to say, he didn't accept my offer. But, being the generous, humble guy that I am, I've decided to jot down a few measly tidbits he may find enlightening.

"The great object is that every man be armed," said Patrick Henry at the Virginia Convention in 1788.

"(Tyrants are) afraid to trust the people with arms," stated James Madison.

Cesare Beccaria, an Italian criminologist greatly admired by Thomas Jefferson put it bluntly:

"False is the idea of utility that sacrifices a thousand real advantages for one imaginary or trifling inconvenience; that would take fire from men because it burns, and water because one may drown in it... The Laws that forbid the carrying of arms are laws of such a nature. They disarm those who are neither inclined nor determined to commit crimes."

Professor Joyce Malcolm, in "To Keep and Bear Arms: the Origins of an Anglo-Saxon Right" (1994), stated:

*"The Second Amendment was meant to accomplish two distinct goals... First, it was meant to guarantee the individual's right to have arms for self-defense... These privately owned arms were meant to serve a larger purpose as well... The customary American militia necessitated an armed public... the militia (being) the body of the people... The argument that today's National Guardsmen, members of a select militia, would constitute the **only** persons entitled to keep and bear arms has no historical foundation."*

The evidence that the Founders believed in the Aristotelian principle of self-defense as the best guarantor of liberty, and that this principle embraced the concept that every man be armed, is so overwhelming that to argue against it is simply foolish, reflecting blind zealotry and a disregard for the facts.

Of course, many in the anti-Second Amendment camp claim that our weapons are so much more deadly today that only the government should have ownership of them. They prattle on that the most powerful weapon of the Revolution was the flint-lock musket. Unfortunately, they forget the weapon called the *cannon*, and the fact that numerous people owned small cannons, and used them to opposed British tyranny.

The intent of the Founders is clear: the citizenry should be *at least* as well armed as the government. Like it or not, this concept of deterring government tyranny with one's own arms also includes tanks, rocket launchers, bombers and, yes, nuclear weapons. If you don't like the idea that private citizens could own nuclear weapons (even though the possibility of such happening is negligible, and the possibility of detonation even more remote than the chance they would be used by governments) then you must advance an agenda of amending the Constitution. You may doubt this reality, but, under a strict reading of the Constitution, the right to keep and bear arms shall not be infringed in any way, and that means *any* arms.

Returning to firearms… Let's say you'd rather overlook the Constitution, you'd rather be dishonest and institute gun control laws that contravene the Second Amendment. Would these laws actually reduce violent crime?

No.

In his monumental analysis "More Guns, Less Crime" (1998, Univ. of Chicago Press), John Lott lays it out for all to see. This unbiased statistical study by a respected economist is necessary reading to anyone who wishes to be conversant on the subject. Among his findings are:

- The probability of serious injury from an attack is 2.5 times greater for a woman offering no resistance than a woman resisting with a gun. (p.4)
- "In Canada and Britain, both with tough gun control laws, almost half of all burglaries are 'hot burglaries' (when people are home). In contrast, the U.S… has a 'hot burglary' rate of only 13%… Convicted American felons reveal in surveys that they are much more worried about armed victims than about running into the police. The fear of potentially armed victims causes American burglars to spend more time… 'casing' a house to ensure that nobody is home." (p. 5)
- There are no crime reduction benefits from state-mandated waiting periods and background checks. (p. 20) (In fact, waiting periods have proved fatal, such as the case of a woman who got a restraining order against her boyfriend, but had to wait to get a firearm for protection, and was killed by him before she could get the weapon.)
- Higher per-capita gun ownership rates do *not* correlate to greater incidences of violent crimes.
- "Violent crimes are 81% higher in states *without* nondiscretionary (gun ownership) laws. for murder, states that ban (concealed guns) have murder rates 127% higher than states with the most (free gun laws)." (p.47)
- Even in violent counties, those that institute the allowance of concealed weapons see dramatic decreases in violent crime, while those that do not allow concealed weapons do not see such changes.

- "(T)he entire number of accidental handgun deaths in the U.S. in 1988 was only 200 (the last year for which data are available for the entire U.S.). Of this total, 22… were in states with concealed handgun laws (allowing them), while 178 occurred in states without these laws (i.e. the guns were illegal to carry). The reduction in murders is as much as eight times greater than the total number of accidental deaths in concealed-handgun states." (p. 54)
- The data indicate that there is a stronger deterrence of violent crime by the allowance of concealed handguns than from higher arrest rates. (p. 119)
- Armed private citizens are much more likely to stop violent crimes than police officers, who usually arrive after the event.

Now, if Tom reads these facts, which represent only a small portion of the evidence in favor of handguns, and he still wishes to bluster without any data to the contrary, so be it. He's merely one of many who act on emotion instead of reason. It may not be possible to stop such a mad dash off the emotional cliff until we are more like Britain, where, as Miguel Faria, M.D., explains, "(O)nly certified members of approved shooting clubs are allowed to own guns (which must be .22 caliber or smaller, and which must be kept locked up at the club…)" (*Human Events*, Jul., 9, 1999, p.10)

Further, he states that in the last several years: "(W)hile robberies rose 81% in England and Wales, they fell 28% in the U.S. Likewise, assaults increased 53% in England and Wales, but declined 27% in the U.S." (Ibid.) By the way, the number of privately owned handguns in the U.S. has shot up dramatically since the feds started to impose threatening limits on our right to keep and bear arms.

As Lott spells out, decreases in crime rates are most dramatically effected by the availability and potential use of guns. Other factors, such as poverty and arrest rates, have much smaller effects.

The "gentile" egalitarianism reflected by gun control zealots is illogical and pernicious. Furthermore, it's only gentile until the zealot is confronted with the facts, at which point he typically becomes angry or enraged.

And that's when the necessity of handguns becomes even more apparent to a person like me….

I'd hate to be assaulted for speaking the truth.

**Macroeconomics:
Part One
Money, Immigration, Antitrust, and Freedom**

Three major foundations of the Free Enterprise System:
1. Personal freedom of choice
2. Private ownership and <u>control</u> of property
3. Peaceful exchange in a competitive market

World leadership requires that we constantly defend the principles of individual liberty and free enterprise.

PHG
December, 1983

"Science Fiction vs. Science Fantasy"
August, 2004

A friend of mine is an award-winning science-fiction novelist. When we first met, I happened to mention to him that I, like him, was working on a science-fantasy novel, and he bristled. He did it nicely, but he bristled nevertheless.

"I write science-*fiction*, not fantasy," he told me. "Those two genres shouldn't even be in the same section at the bookstores."

I took his meaning. It was an early lesson in the difference between those who write books which employ real science to drive the plot, and those who create unrealistic worlds, even if those worlds conform to their own internal logic.

I was not to encounter again the difference between science-fiction and science-fantasy until years later, while in the script department of one of the many "Star Trek" spin-offs.

Sitting in a "story pitch session" with one of the producers, I happened to offer a story outline that involved a "Sting"-like scheme by the main characters to retrieve a sizeable amount of stolen money. But as I told the story, the producer held up a hand and informed me that I needn't go any further.

Seeing my puzzled face, this warm and genuinely friendly person told me something I did not know.

"Gene," the producer said, referring to Gene Rodenberry, the creator of the series, "stipulated before he died that there was to be no money in the Federation."

I was still puzzled.

"No money?"

"Right. He believed that by the Twenty-third Century, mankind would have 'evolved past' the need for money."

I wondered if the meaning of this was that mankind would have come up with some sort of bio-electronic monetary data system, something that would allow the characters to eschew paper money, and walk freely, without bulky wallets and pocketbooks to get in their way on the transporter pads. That was, however, far from the case.

According to this producer, Roddenberry, who was known as the "Great Bird of the Galaxy", simply thought that humanism would strip mankind of the acquisitive tendencies it had shown throughout history, that the use of money was a vice his utopian "Federation" would successfully eliminate.

The producer looked at me and said, "It was one of the biggest mistakes he ever made. You have no idea how much of a headache that rule has been."

Given my background in economics, I actually had a pretty good idea.

Rodenberry's belief was nothing new. In his eyes, money was clearly a vestige of man's base past. It was a symbol of greed, a cause of war and hatred and anger and loss. The drive for it was something mankind needed to overcome, and in Rodenberry's pristine world of the future, man would rise above his dirty urges for riches, and concentrate on more noble goals, like science, and adventure, and green-painted women and mind-melding rocks.

Given this idealistic concept, it can only be assumed that Rodenberry believed man would somehow surpass the need for products and services, that man would move beyond the subtle and noble differences in interest and skills that prompted the ancient differentiation of labor and free trade, and that man would glide towards a socialistic method of living, where there would be no need for money. There would be no need for money, because there would be no need for exchange, and there would be no need for exchange because man would "evolve" beyond the need for private property, differentiation of labor, and the gauche acquisition of goods, services, and funds that come with them.

It was at that moment, sitting there in the Paramount Studios on Melrose Avenue, that I realized "Star Trek" was not "science-fiction", but "science-fantasy".

This is not to deride the series. I like it. But despite the attempt on the part of the producers to back up facets of the stories with well-researched science, the fact that Gene Rodenberry outlawed money means his creation can be nothing other than fantasy.

The reason is simple. Like Rodenberry, many thinkers have tried to envision a world in which there is no need for money, where there is no market exchange, and no property, and every one of those thinkers, be they followers of John Lennon, Michael Moore, or Karl Marx, has overlooked one key insight:

Man's nature does not change.

When men try to fulfill their needs, their varying interests, talents and skills will prompt each of them to concentrate on what he does best. Such differentiation of labor will allow each man to utilize his skills and desires in the most productive way possible. But upon using his skills, each man will soon see the benefits of trading some of the fruits of his labor with those of another person. The way to maximize one's labor in a world of differing abilities and interests is to enter into market exchange with others, offering what one makes or does well, in exchange for what others make or do well. Thus, if you are a skilled lumberjack, you can offer wood in exchange for food from the farmer. In that manner, you don't have to farm, and the farmer doesn't have to cut down trees. Since the two of you are doing what you do best, you are maximizing your work, and there will be more of both products than would exist if you and the farmer had to concentrate on two forms of labor.

But what if the farmer has already traded for all the wood he needs? In that case, you would have to find a product the farmer *did* need, approach the producer of that item, and see if that producer needed wood. If he did, you could exchange your wood for the new product, then approach the farmer to finish your original exchange.

This all becomes very complicated when myriad interests, needs, skills, and products begin to come into play. Therefore, man, in his inventiveness, came up with a very good creation to facilitate universal exchange. He invented money.

When utilized in a market, money allows all participants to employ a universally recognized means of exchange. No longer will you have to find a third or fourth or fifth party to trade your lumber in order to get goods from the farmer. You can use currency. You can hold the currency, you can spend the currency, you can even loan the currency for a higher return some time in the future. The malleability of money, and its ability to let disparate peoples work in harmony is, far from Rodenberry's view, one of the most glorious creations in the history of mankind. Money is the machinery of peace, not of war.

Furthermore, without money, it is not possible to come to any determination of value. Prices reflect the countless valuations of sellers and consumers engaging in non-coercive exchange. They are the end result of each participant's decisions in the marketplace, and reflect how much people value certain products. Prices are essential carriers of information. They not only reflect preferences, but also the relative scarcity of goods in the market. Without the money mechanism, there can be no systematic determination of the value of a good, and no conception of the scarcity of that good. Even in Rodenberry's "Federation", someone had to buy the "dilithium crystals" for Scotty to use in his famous Engine Room.

If one looks closely at "Star Trek" and Gene Rodenberry's ideas, at his United Nations-based concept of the "Federation", and the military life of his space travelers, one is inevitably drawn to the conclusion that he adhered very strongly to the fanciful ideas of utopian socialism. Like the socialists who preceded him, he favored large-scale blocks of control instead of small political bodies or individual control. He rejected private property and market exchange, believing that man would "grow out" of those childish idiosyncrasies. He embraced a paternalistic view of the future that would inevitably lead to scarce resources, impoverishment, and economic stagnation, not a galaxy-hopping culture that found adventure at every turn.

Oddly enough, his stipulation that there be no money used in his high-tech space series has meant that his main characters, when in dire need of some product or service out in the void, have had to revert to the old, inefficient and outdated method of exchange we replaced thousands of years ago. In fact, this is precisely what the producer who sat before me explained when I asked her how in the world they wrote stories that required some kind of market exchange.

Just like the olden days, she said, in the "Final Frontier", they are forced to barter for what they need.

How frustrating, for both the writers, and the characters they created. It's no wonder Captain Kirk always wanted to be beamed away. He just wanted to get to a world where the universal principles of economics applied, not the fanciful dreams of a visionary whose ideas had been tried and failed many times throughout human history.

As Ludwig von Mises has pointed out so well, if someone were <u>really</u> able to forecast the economic future, he wouldn't be wasting his time putting out market letters or economic models. He'd be busy making several trillion Dollars forecasting the stock and commodity markets. Let it be a reminder to anyone tempted to partake of, or give credence to, this modern form of sooth-saying.

PHG
December, 1983

"The Last Horseman"
April, 2004

Many people are unaware of it, but there has always been a Fifth Horseman of the Apocalypse. Overlooked in scripture, he has been there nonetheless, waiting with rancid, baited breath to gallop across the world and leave his destructive hoof-prints in the rubble of Western civilization. He is, according to many government spokesmen and media pundits, the Horseman called "Deflation".

Next to dire warnings of SARS, Mad Cow Disease, and the hegemony of conservative talk radio, the big "scare story" of 2003 was that deflation was upon us, or approaching. Beginning as a trickle in the first quarter of '03, the reports turned into a flood after April. Suddenly, dozens of "experts" and policy analysts lamented with great wailing the forbidding approach of the destructive force known as deflation. Politicians spending other people's money advised us that the Federal Reserve had better do something fast, because the dollar was, as many phrased it, "too strong".

Today, with the passage of a year to allow for dispassionate analysis, the anguish appears to have been misplaced. Not only has the US economy *not* fallen into a deflationary period, it has continued to see a consistent, though low, decrease in the buying power of the Dollar – a continuation of the inflationary behavior of the Fed that has been its salient characteristic for most of its existence.

In May of 2003, members of the Bush Administration began "talking down" the dollar, hinting that they wanted to see it lowered in value relative to the Euro. American Enterprise Institute economist John Makin was quoted in a May 26 Scripps Howard News Service article as believing that a 10 to 20 percent decline in the dollar would increase "economic growth" to 3% by 2004.

Three factors were cited to promote this crusade against deflation.

First, the US economy was supposedly in a recession. Reports abounded that 2.5 million jobs had been lost between August 1, 2001 and June 1, 2003. Despite the fact that new home sales set a record in May of 2003, with a jump of 12.5%, many people believed that the Fed ought to lower interest rates to "jump-start" job creation with less-expensive money.

Second, the dollar was at a premium compared to other currencies. Its value was such that our money bought more foreign goods more easily, and this was seen by US manufacturers and the politicians who pandered to them as dangerous. It had caused a long-term "trade deficit". Americans weren't buying American-made goods, and that was supposedly bad for the US economy.

Third, signs of "inflation" in most sectors of the US economy, especially the all-important sectors which comprise the "M2" money supply data[s], were virtually non-existent. Many people believed that without a little inflation there could be no increase in American wages, thus no increase in demand for US goods, and no increase in demand for US workers. The Fed board members were apparently in agreement with all of these assumptions, and they followed a loose money policy throughout the entire year.

But there was a misunderstanding at the core of nearly all the opinions and prescriptions, one which still persists today. This misunderstanding serves to deceive people about the nature of the problem, and about the remedies needed to cure it.

The trouble stems from the popular mischaracterization of inflation and deflation.

Inflation is often described by reporters as an increase in prices, nothing more. No investigation is conducted as to *why* prices are increasing, or what effect that has on the average person's standard of living. Even the term "standard of living" is left a sort-of mystical phrase, undefined and impenetrable.

In fact, "inflation" is what *causes* prices to increase. It is a general increase in the supply of money in relation to the supply of goods. More dollars chasing the same amount of goods, or a slowly growing amount of goods, means higher prices. Your dollar will buy less. You will have to work harder to get the same products, and your standard of living will be harmed.

Additionally, the loose money that causes inflation also spurs improper investments by businesses, banks, and lending institutions -- what was termed by Austrian economists as a "temporal warping of the supply curve". The presence of inflated capital leads to misallocations of funds for unproductive

---

[s] This is the primary data pool which the economic sorcerers at the Federal Reserve use to measure the amount of money in the market relative to Gross Domestic Product. When they cast their magical monetary runes, the M2 is very important.

ventures. In time, this leads to a collapse when consumers respond negatively to inflated prices, and this leads to excess inventory, loans left in default, unemployment, and a general decrease in the standard of living for nearly everyone.

Many economists used to fear inflation. They watched for it like hawks looking for mice in the fields. But recently the talk has been about *deflation*. Some policy makers have even proposed that we define a slower rate of increase in *inflation* as deflation. Why the concern? Why the manipulation of the language?

First, it should be noted that these terms have become ciphers. Inflation and deflation are often used by government economists to describe the supposed "growth" or "contraction" of the economy. In a world where political appointees try to control the value of the dollar, inflation and deflation are measurements of their own monetary manipulation. They are not really measures of "economic growth", but are estimates of capital expansion, which may, or may not, be connected to *real* economic growth.

According to the "experts", *deflation* is defined as a general decrease in prices, brought on by a decrease in consumer demand. Depending on whether you want to put the cart before or after the horse, this decrease in demand can either be the effect of a recessionary period, or the cause of it. Central bankers rarely seem to have a good handle on the concepts of cause and effect.

Recently, a few commentators at the White House and elsewhere have told us that deflation is caused by a relative decrease in the money supply itself. The scarcity of the dollar makes it more valuable. The dollar buys more goods, and prices fall. The dollar becomes more valuable and exports decrease. The dollar becomes more valuable, and people get laid off.

But in real economics, there is a *reason* for deflation. Deflation is an increase in the buying power of the dollar, it reflects, and is a direct result of, greater productivity. When people are more productive, more goods and services can be produced at less cost, thus making the dollar stronger, allowing it to buy *more*, and allowing prices to *drop*. This is not a bad thing!

The entire purpose of free exchange between individuals is to allow them to be more productive, to allow them to work less for the same amount of goods, or for more goods. Since we have different skills, I can produce one thing well, and you can produce another. Protecting your freedom to do what you do best, for me to do what I do best, and for us to exchange for goods and services on the market, lets society have the best products most efficiently. As you improve your skills and the tools needed to make your product, you will be able to make more for less work, which is what we all want. We want to get more for less work, not less for more work.

Being more productive means less effort is required to make certain products, allowing us to improve our lives, and allowing us the free time and free capital to make new products that will, in turn, improve our lives even more. In a free market, the dreaded horseman "Deflation" is nothing more than the decrease in prices brought about by greater productivity. As prices have dropped for goods such as DVD players and computers, we have had to use less of our money (or less of our effort as represented by our money) to buy them. Our efforts get us more, our toil is less. Our lives are better.

Contrary to the three major arguments of the pundits, one should not fear deflation.

The argument that deflation is the cause of unemployment, that a naturally strong dollar puts people out of work, is manifestly absurd. Unemployment is not caused by a strong dollar. Unemployment is not caused by greater productivity. If that were the case, the proper prescription to solve unemployment would be to destroy all technological advancements that increase productivity, thus making it *harder* to produce things, making *more* effort go into the same products we once built for less, and making it harder to use free capital to begin new job-creating ventures. Reducing the value of the dollar is akin to such a palliative. It harms the patient more than it helps.

It also hides the true reasons for unemployment, which are government spending and taxation, inappropriate monetary policy, regulations, and restrictions on market exchange. The most recent recession was visited upon Americans for precisely the reasons just noted, and due to the powerful financial impact of the terrorist attacks of 2001, not because Americans were somehow "too" productive.

The argument that a strong dollar has harmed American exporters, and thus Americans in general, is only partially right. A strong dollar *does* make foreign products more appealing to American consumers. Many of those consumers are also manufacturers, who can, like retail consumers, buy their products for less. This allows them to be more productive, to sell *their products* for less. That extra consumer capital can then be utilized to buy other products, or invested to start up new, more productive businesses.

Peoples' lives are improved. By trying to protect politically connected US businesses from foreign competition, American politicians do damage to the economy as a whole. For every special US company that is helped by a barrier to trade, consumers are harmed eight times as much.[9]

But what of the "deficit" in our balance of trade?

The balance of trade is just that, *a balance*. Few people are aware of this, perhaps because very few reporters know it or bother to report it, but the numbers that comprise our balance of trade with foreign nations are composed of more than just goods and services. They also include *capital*. For every dollar spent on a foreign good, there is a foreigner with a new dollar. He has to do something with that, and if the US economy is appealing, if the US worker is productive, if the US dollar is *strong*, then all of those valuable dollars that went out to buy foreign goods will return to the US as investments and purchases in the capital market. One need not weaken the dollar in order to help US exporters at the expense of US consumers and manufacturers.

Likewise, one need not weaken the dollar to "help" spur employment.

Those who argue that inflation is needed to keep people employed might as well argue that a fire should be put out with gasoline. Placing more money into an economy does not expand that economy. It does not make the economy more productive. It merely makes more dollars chase the goods being produced, raising prices, and harming everyone. Some have argued that with a little inflation, there is incentive for consumers to buy rather than wait to buy, and that in a deflationary economy, the incentive to wait would stagnate sales.

This is fallacious. As the prices of VCR's and televisions decreased year after year, people did not *wait* to buy them. They bought the products as they needed them. Falling prices were beneficial to everyone, including the producer, who was able to sell more as his price of production *fell*.

In today's world of monetarism, economists often cite a "low inflation" or "zero inflation" policy as the optimum for the United States. But those who truly believe in human ingenuity and productivity as the greatest means by which to improve our lives must recognize the appeal of *falling* prices

---

[9] Bovard, James: "The Fair Trade Fraud"; St. Martin's Press, NY, 1991, p. 5.

and a *rising* dollar. As George Selgin argues in his work "Less Than Zero"[10], such a paradigm would allow long-term improvements in productivity to lower prices in various sectors, and, possibly, in the economy as a whole. Occasional problems such as natural disasters or military conflicts would periodically cause negative supply shocks, raising prices. But these would be natural factors in the equation of supply and demand, natural parts of a dynamic economy that is responding to consumer demand and to real changes in productivity, not artificial government manipulation.

It is a wonder that people who work on monetary policy every day don't recognize the value of what Selgin calls the "productivity norm". Of course, if we had a productivity norm -- allowing real prices to actually *drop* in response to productivity -- many of those policy makers would be out of work. Right now, they can make bundles trying to explain how bonds, CD's, stocks, short-term loans, long-term loans, imports and exports will be affected by their own manipulation of the dollar.

In 1971, President Nixon and other world leaders agreed to drop the flimsy pseudo-barriers against currency inflation their governments had imposed under the Bretton Woods Accords of 1944. From the moment Nixon's team entered the meeting, it must have been understood that all bets were off regarding US monetary policy. Completely removed from any price fixed to a commodity such as gold, the buying power of the dollar was free to be reduced any time politicians saw fit. And they saw fit quite often. From 1972 to 1981 the average inflation rate was 8.48%, compared to the decade prior, which stood at 3.09% [11].

Democrats and Republicans alike were aghast, asking what could be done. But since the years 1982 through 1984, when the US monetarists supposedly took on inflation and got it under control, the problem has not gone away. The ten years following the Reagan Administration's attempt to better husband the dollar saw an average inflation rate of 4.8% (1984-1993, inclusive). The following decade saw inflation at an average of 2.4% (1994-2003, inclusive). This simply means that it has taken twice as long for the government to reduce the buying power of our work by about half.

---

[10] Available from the Institute for Economic Affairs, London. Visit www.IEA.org.uk for more information.

[11] Calculations can be made by referring to the chart provided by the Federal Reserve Bank of Minneapolis. http://minneapolisfed.org/Research/data/us/calc/hist1800.cfm

Put in other terms, in 1972, it took $5 to buy the same amount of goods that $1 could buy in 1850. Ten years later, in 1984, it took $12.44. Twenty years later, in 2004, it is estimated that it costs $22.44 to buy what one could have bought for only a dollar in 1850.

And as government policies continue to whittle down the value of the dollar, there are still economists and media pundits telling us that it is productivity we should fear.

Given their track record, perhaps it is these government boosters who ought to make us nervous. Perhaps we ought to look critically at the monetarists' performance and realize that the value of the dollar ought to be determined instead by the people trying to buy things and make things with it. After all, it represents their sweat, toil, hopes and dreams in the ever-changing market, and as their efforts pay off in the form of greater productivity, the value of the dollar ought to rise, not *fall*.

For Further Information, see these graphs, provided by Oregon State:
Estimated inflation rates from 1865-1916:
http://oregonstate.edu/Dept/pol_sci/fac/sahr/pc166514.htm
Inflation rates from 1915-2002:
http://oregonstate.edu/Dept/pol_sci/fac/sahr/pc1915ff.htm

"Worshipping at the Altar"
August, 1997

Earlier this summer, there was a big celebration in Washington, D.C. The occasion was the unveiling of the new Franklin Delano Roosevelt Memorial in honor of the 32nd president of the United States. There was the attendant pomp and circumstance for a ceremony of such magnitude. There were myriad speeches, and songs, and banners. And there were lots of balloons as well. And while I hate to burst anyone's favorite floater, the pen can be quite sharp, and, out of an appreciation for the truth, I am obligated to use it.

When I was in Milford Area Senior High, I had the sorry misfortune to take a Twentieth Century history class with a teacher who, as I put it at the time, "worshipped at the altar of F.D.R." Little did I know it then, but that colorful phrase would turn out to be a prophetic statement; for there is now -- apart from the massive buildings housing the oppressive regulatory agencies that have been established since F.D.R. set the precedent -- a real, literal totem before which this N.E.A. sap can kneel.

I will dispense with any discussion of whether or not the statue of F.D.R. should have depicted him with a cigarette, or in a wheelchair, or with his hands around someone other than his wife, or with his hands on the warning from military advisors that the Japanese were planning to attack Pearl Harbor, for all those issues are incidental to the discussion of the man's "greatest" legacies: his supposed rescue of the US economy after the Great Crash, and his use of "benevolent government" to help offset the terrors created by rampant free enterprise. To put it another way, it is important that people be exposed to the fact that F.D.R. kept the US in the Great Depression longer than it would have been had he not been President, and the fact that F.D.R. did more than any other man to destroy the U.S. Constitution.

When we were in school, we were often fed the image of the smiling Franklin, sitting beside his hearth, telling Americans via radio that all was well, that he -- through his great wisdom, and antipathy for money grubbing investors and capitalists -- would see the nation safely through the time of troubles known as the Great Depression. Using Biblical imagery, F.D.R. blamed the "money changers" of the investment markets and lending institutions for the stock crash that precipitated the Depression, not mentioning that the loose monetary policy of the newly created Federal Reserve system, a wholly unconstitutional entity, caused rampant risky investment and temporal distortion of the supply curve. Nor did he mention that regulations restricting lending institutions from diversifying their investments and ameliorating their risks caused a systemic breakdown in the ability of these institutions to find alternate funds once the economy started to contract. He didn't mention these things because they were the real reasons for the Great Crash, and they were the causes of government, not the private sector. Franklin needed a scapegoat in order to promulgate and promote his plan to expand the purview of the federal government. And a demoralized populace, not ready to pay the price for years of misallocated investments based on specie government money, was more than eager to take him at his word.

To say that Roosevelt disliked businessmen is an understatement. His antipathy appears to have had no bounds; and this hatred, coupled with tight Fed monetary policy, massive new government regulations and huge new government "make work" programs, had a profound effect on the economy as a whole. Anyone who claims that Roosevelt's alphabet soup of work programs somehow lifted Americans out of the Depression is sorrowfully deluded and has a very dim understanding of economics. Government work programs are inherently less efficient than private projects. When funded through taxation, they commandeer money from the free market -- where individuals, based on their needs, can make the most informed decisions about problems -- and reallocate these funds to politically favored "pet" projects that may have very little real value or cost-effectiveness. When such projects are funded through government borrowing, the value of the dollar decreases, again causing disastrous problems in the private market. Additionally, any government program that is created is a potential competitor for a private initiative, thus pitting government against citizens in a battle for market supremacy. If the fight is between private industry without any government favors and government -- with the power of legislative control and public subsidy -- you can guess which wins.

With as much gusto as he could muster, Roosevelt went about fostering this antagonistic relationship between government and private industry. He not only created his "work" programs, he began instituting, with the help of Congress, as many anti-private property, anti-business laws as he possibly could. Between 1933 and 1940 the federal government passed thirty nine such bills, including: The Agricultural Adjustment Act, The National Industrial Recovery Act, The Emergency Banking Relief Act, the Banking Act of 1933, The Federal Securities Act, The Tennessee Valley Authority Act, The Gold Repeal Joint Resolution, The Home Owners Loan Corporation Act, The Securities Exchange Act, The Communications Act (ever wonder how the heck the FCC was created?), The National Labor Relations Act, The Social Security Act (AKA, "pass the buck"), The Federal Anti-Price Discrimination Act, The National Housing Act, The Civil Aeronautics Act, The Food, Drug, and Cosmetic Act, The Investment Company Act, and the two Revenue Acts of 1940.

In a penetrating article published in the Spring 1997 issue of "The Independent Review" (Vol. 1, No. 4), Robert Higgs writes that all of these acts, coupled with the rhetoric that helped promote them, led to a profound "Regime Uncertainty" on the part of private property owners and investors. By "Regime Uncertainty" he means that businessmen feel "... distressed that investors' private property rights in their capital and in their income will be attenuated further by government action. Such attenuations can arise from many sources, ranging from simple tax-rate increases to the imposition of new kinds of taxes to outright confiscation of private property." (p. 568) As evidence to prove that there was, indeed, extreme "Regime Uncertainty" on the part of investors, Higgs cites contemporaneous polls, such as two from 1939 showing, first, that the majority of business owners believed the government would further curtail their rights to run their own businesses, and, second, that the majority of businessmen felt the government had so affected their confidence that they believed a recovery had been seriously held back (p. 577). He quotes the renowned economist Joseph Schumpeter as having written in 1939: "They *are* not only, but *feel* threatened." (p.571)

How else could a business owner feel when the president of the United States not only verbally abuses him, not only orders the confiscation of privately owned gold, not only pushes Congress to pass legislation curtailing property rights, but begins pressuring, then packing the Supreme Court to interpret the Constitution as allowing such totalitarian measures?

When faced with these facts, many "worshippers at the altar" will shrug their shoulders. First, they are subscribers to the idea that government *should* stand in the way of business in this manner. Second, even if they admit that FDR's policies may have had a teensy, tiny negative effect on the recovery, they will cite his leadership in World War Two, and say "the war got us out of the Depression."

Wrong. As Higgs notes: "During the war years the economy operated essentially as a command system, and as a result the normal measures of macroeconomic performance (e.g. gross domestic product, the price level, and the rate of unemployment) were either conceptually or statistically incomparable with corresponding measures before and after the period subject to the wartime distortions." (p.562) Higgs' statement makes great sense. One can by no means say that a nation which is manufacturing thousands of jeeps and munitions for use in armed conflict overseas, yet instituting food rations and not producing goods that would raise living standards at home, is a "growing economy."

Only when the end of the war seemed near, and FDR's anti-capitalist rhetoric ebbed, did investors begin to take the first halting steps toward reviving the economy. As Higgs shows, while the GDP rose dramatically during the war years, Gross Private Investment did not exceed its 1929 levels until after the war ended. Through 1940, and even with the military buildup of 1941, private investment remained below the 1929 level. (p.565) It is clear that FDR's pre-war policies sent waves of fear through the investment community. As economist Benjamin Anderson wrote in 1949: "The impact of these multitudinous measures -- industrial, agricultural, financial, monetary and other -- upon a bewildered industrial and financial community was extraordinarily heavy." (Quoted in Higgs, ibid., p. 570)

So when we read about the wondrous F.D.R. "saving" the nation, are we hearing the truth, or a fabrication no more real than the statue now dedicated to him in Washington D.C.?

The answer is clear.

But to many of his worshippers this answer is a threat. Why? Because the only thing they have to fear… Is the truth.

History has shown that liberals (leftists) have been spectacularly wrong on all the major worldly issues. I have never been able to figure out why such supposedly intelligent people make such distressingly poor decisions.

PHG
March, 1986

"Immigration: The Latest Front in the War for Freedom"
June 8, 2006

In Washington, DC, protesters rally against "open borders". All over the United States, citizens demand mass deportations. Angry talk show hosts and think tank "experts" tell us something has to be done to "protect us" from immigration. Politicians call for "whatever it takes" to close the southern US border, seemingly oblivious to the fact that the US Constitution doesn't give them such omnipotence.

The political rhetoric about immigration, both legal and illegal, is so heated that defenders of free markets -- and hence, freedom -- are justified in stating that a metaphorical gauntlet has been thrown in the intellectual arena. The fight has begun, and it is time to assess where we stand.

On Friday, May 26, the United States Senate passed a sweeping "immigration reform" package which has, among its provisions, a number of salient factors to be noted by defenders of free markets. First, it would create a "guest worker" program for 1.5 million immigrant farm workers, who could also apply for legal permanent resident status. A separate "guest worker" program would allow 200,000 non-agricultural workers into the US each year.

The bill would also let illegal immigrants who have been in the country five years or more stay here, to continue working and to become legal citizens after learning English, and paying at least $3,250 in fines and back taxes. Illegal immigrants who had been in the US between two and five years would be required to go to a point of entry, and file an application to return. Those who had been in the country less than two years would be forced to leave.

Under the bill, the federal presence at the US borders would increase, bringing the total to 25,300 by 2011, and 370 miles of beautiful new fencing would be raised between the US and Mexico.

As if that wasn't enough, by June 1, 2009, the Senate would force all Americans re-entering the US after ocean cruises, or visits to Canada and Mexico, to show a passport or high-tech identification card, and English would be declared the national language of the glorious USA they re-enter.

Magnanimously, the Senate did set greater allowances for foreign workers to enter the US. The number would increase from 65,000 to 115,000 per year, beginning in 2007, and immigrants with select advanced degrees would not be subject to the caps, which would rise by 20 percent in certain *government approved* sectors. But, within eighteen months, employers would be required to use an electronic system to verify the "legality" of their new employees. Employers guilty of hiring illegal workers would be made to pay a fine of up to $20,000 for each worker and would be liable for jail time upon repeat offenses.

So, in a nutshell, the Senate wants to tell business owners how many and what kinds of foreigners they can hire, force them to report personal data on all their employees, and make sure we all speak English as we cough up our federal ID cards after honeymoon cruises. Just the kind of thing the Founding Fathers would have loved.

Despite the fact that the Senate bill increases the power of the federal government in many ways, anti-immigrant ideologues actually don't think the bill goes far enough. Some of the most vocal critics are self-styled "conservatives" in the US House of Representatives, who believe the Senate has sold out, that the bill creates incentives to bring in more family members of "illegals", and that it does not do enough to seal the border and provide protection against low-wage competition and terrorist threats.

In December of 2005, House members passed their own draconian measure, which would offer no new paths to citizenship, and no new temporary guest worker program. The House bill would also create 700 miles of double-layer fencing along the US-Mexican border, and would make it a felony to encourage or assist a foreigner to enter the US illegally. (So much for promoting the US as the "shining city on a hill"; that might be too much encouragement.) Perhaps most important, like the Senate bill, the House proposal would force employers to report the "legality" of their employees, through the electronic collection of social security data and other information. Maximum fines for "illegal hiring" would range from $10,000 to $40,000, with three year prison sentences awaiting anyone who is a repeat offender. Apparently, "Newspeak" dictionaries and brown shirts are not included with the prison stay.

In studying the House and Senate proposals, one can see just how far the conservative movement has strayed from many of its long-held principles. Among these principles are the idea that the US Constitution should be read in a manner consistent with the intent of the Founding Fathers, the concept that competition in the marketplace is actually good, helps us to be more productive, and betters our lives, and the dictum that all men are created equal under natural law. This is not a whimsical or prosaic observation. It is a sad commentary on a phenomenon that could do severe damage to the United States Constitution and the US economy.

First, there is the Constitutional damage, which is being perpetrated by a gaggle of Senators, Representatives and commentators who haven't the foggiest notion what the Founding Fathers researched, debated, and codified in 1787. Article One, Section Eight of the Constitution gives Congress the power to control *naturalization*, a provision which has often been mistaken for the granting of power over immigration itself, and which has been used to promulgate heaps of pernicious legislation for decades. Despite the fact that there is a profound difference between naturalization (becoming a citizen) and immigration (being on the soil of one of the United States), many so-called "conservatives" have taken it upon themselves to mix the two, as they attempt to justify federal immigration law. For example, Mark Levin, well-known radio host in New York City, and author of "Men in Black", has stated:

"The first effort to control immigration and naturalization came with the Naturalization Act of 1790, when Congress set the residency requirement for U.S. citizenship at two years. In 1795, the requirement was increased to five years."[12]

Unfortunately for many conservatives, and for Mr. Levin's claims, the Naturalization Acts of both 1790 and 1795 pertained strictly to what was constitutionally granted to the Congress: the power to determine *citizenship requirements*. The acts had nothing to do with whether people could *be* in one of the many United States. The power over immigration was a state purview, and the Founders knew it. To try to mix the two is either a mark of an amateur historian, or someone who is attempting to mislead his readers.

The only place where the concept of immigration appears in the US Constitution is in Article One, Section Nine, which reads, in part, "The Migration or Importation of such Persons as any of the States *now existing*

---

[12] Levin, Mark. "Citizenship Up for Grabs", published online by the Center for Immigration Studies. http://www.cis.org/articles/2005/back305.html. March, 2005.

shall think proper to admit, shall not be prohibited by the Congress prior to the Year one thousand eight hundred and eight…" (emphasis added).

This provision of the Constitution tells the careful reader that, prior to 1808, Congress could not write any laws regarding the migration into any of the original thirteen states from outside the US, or from other states in the union. Such wording, and the philosophy of the Founders themselves, would imply that, unless the Constitution was amended, Congress did not have jurisdiction to write laws dealing with immigration in the original states before 1808, and did not have the power to write laws pertaining to immigration in any states that *subsequently* joined the union. This is an important distinction, one lost on most "conservative" politicians, and, sadly, one also lost by Supreme Court justices very early in US history.

It was not until 1875, with the Supreme Court decision in the case of *Chy Lung v Freeman*[13], and the passage of the Page Law in Congress, that federal control was established regarding immigration into more than the original thirteen states. As one would expect, and as we have seen with the push to restrict immigration today, the driving force behind this Nineteenth Century shift in power was political economics. In the west, native US workers were upset by the growing presence of lower-cost Chinese labor in gold mines and on railroads (the Trans-Continental Railroad was built in no small part by low-price Chinese workers). As a result, they lobbied their representatives to restrict their competition. Such activity seems very familiar today.

In 1882, the so-called "Chinese Exclusion Act" was passed. It barred entrance into America by Chinese laborers for ten years, halted Chinese non-labor immigration for sixty years, and prohibited entirely all naturalization by Chinese people. Just like today, as members of the United Auto Workers and Senator Chuck Schumer, of NY, tell us that only certain "kinds" of immigrant labor are acceptable (those that in no way stand to compete against their excessively high wage rates), the politicians and mercantile interests of the 1800's successfully lobbied Congress to protect their vested interests, at the expense of the consumers.

In our contemporary battle over immigration, the unionized mercantile interests find odd allies in the conservative wing of the Republican Party.

---

[13] 92 US, 275. Text of ruling to be found: http://caselaw.lp.findlaw.com/cgi-bin/getcase.pl?court=us&vol=92&invol=275

Today, many of the same people who used to talk about "free trade" during the Reagan Administration are extolling the virtues of quite the opposite. Because they seem to be more and more aware that they cannot stand on the "Naturalization Clause" of the US Constitution, they claim that the influx of immigrants is an "invasion". They tell us that the US Constitution sanctions Congress to protect the United States from "invasion", and it is therefore acceptable to vest Congress with the power to: force employers to collect ID data on all employees, force employers to report that data to the federal government, imprison employers who do not comply, and arrest and deport anyone without proper identification.

But this logic stands on the belief that the United States are being invaded. Whether this is true is clearly debatable. An invasion is an "entrance with malicious intent", and it seems a stretch to think that Honduran and Mexican, Haitian and Salvadoran immigrants attracted to the US standard of living and employment opportunities are coming with malicious intent. Even if one were to believe that the nation is being "invaded", the proper response is spelled out in the Constitution. In order to protect our borders from such a threat, and post soldiers to be our first line of defense, the Congress would have to identify the offending group or nation, and declare War. This would set the proper gears in motion for the President to command the military for our protection against said "invasion". Since, even with the so-called "War on Terror" in full force, Congress has yet to officially declare "War"[14], and since President Bush is sending national Guard troops to the US-Mexican border *without arms*, it is clear that most Congressmen and members of the Bush Administration actually believe we are *not* at war, and therefore not being invaded. As a result, the conservative argument for federal control of the borders is not compelling. It is a shallow attempt to hide what is at its heart a shameless ploy to pander to populist and mercantilist sentiment.

Like Representative James Sensenbrenner, "conservatives" want to stop immigrants for economic reasons. And this point leads us to explore

---

[14] This is an important point. War was understood by the Founders to be a specific term of art. The Bush Administration did not want to see Congress declare War. Alberto Gonzales, one of the architects of the Bush policy, and now Attorney General, stressed that by not declaring War, the US would have more wiggle room when it came to interrogation of terror suspects. The Executive Branch and Congress knew that the "resolution to use force" as it is called, was passed in order to skirt certain aspects of the evidently archaic Geneva Conventions.

the economic damage looming in our future due to politicians like Mr. Sensenbrenner. In national interviews, he has stated he wants to stop foreigners from "taking American jobs"[15], but what he hopes to accomplish will do a great deal to harm the very country he claims to defend.

The economic rationale against immigration, be it legal or "illegal", is very weak. Yet politicians tell people that by restricting the flow of immigrants, they are helping the economy. They claim that "there is no job an American won't take". They say that if immigration were restricted, greedy employers would be forced to cough up all the cash they have been pocketing, and spend it on "good wages" for Americans. But that misses an important point. The employer doesn't have the final say. The consumer does. The argument that Americans would work certain jobs if only the employer was not so evil overlooks the fact that the employer pays *what the market will bear*, and the market will only bear what the *consumer is willing to pay*. The employer is not the one to whom we must look to say "pay the American employee more". It is up to the consumer to decide what is in his best interest. If the cost of the American labor raises the price of a product -- say, an apple -- to a level the consumer is unwilling to pay, no amount of wishful thinking will make him change his mind and buy the apple. Changing the immigration laws to force Americans to do the jobs that lower-priced laborers from other nations were able to do for less simply means forcing American *consumers* to pay more for the same product. This leaves less extra cash in the consumer's pocket, which means other businesses, be they long-standing ones, or start-ups, will never see what they could have seen for their own business. Economic growth is retarded, all because politicians and political pundits wanted to make sure "Americans" did the job.

Perhaps what is most striking about the current debate over immigration is how doctrinaire the proponents of government control have become. From the halls of Congress to the microphones of talk radio, very little intellectual exploration and dissent is being shown. Even talk of reducing the welfare state which immigrants enter is being lost in the endless harangues over "jobs" and security. This is more than troubling, because it means that very few people in the United States understand the fundamentals of the US Constitution, and the free market principles enshrined therein.

---

[15] The Laura Ingraham Show, June 1, 2006.

Proponents of individual liberty and free commerce are likely recognizing we have a long way to go in this march. But it is worth the struggle, for us, our children, and the people who would like to stand on United States soil and live freer lives. The men and women who created this nation came here for those very reasons, and we do a disservice if we do not pick up the gauntlet and defend what they worked so hard to give us.

"The Aliens Are Coming!"
January, 2004

On January 7, 2004, President Bush announced what appeared to be a sweeping plan to grant de-facto amnesty for millions of resident aliens working in the US. In fact, it was little more than a long-term worker-visa program that barely increased the ability of employers to hire whom they wished, and came nowhere near recognizing the right of individuals to move where their abilities could take them. Nonetheless, this has not stopped prophets ranging from conservative radio hosts Laura Ingraham and Michael Savage, to supposedly conservative writers such as Pat Buchanan and Mark Krikorian, from heralding the end of America as we know it.

Much like Kevin McCarthy, in "Invasion of the Body Snatchers", they seem wide-eyed and enervated, exhorting us to beware, because, as he said with such conviction, "They're coming! They're coming!"

Though it might be easy to flippantly dismiss such exclamations, many of their arguments are substantive and important. Due to the paternalistic nature of contemporary government, the proposal to accept the "illegals" as "legal" is fraught with problems.

But apart from these practical, day-to-day considerations, and separate from the debate over whether immigrants are a net gain or loss to the coffers of the federal government, there is a larger, timeless issue that lies at the heart of the conservative assertions.

It is the sweeping claim that immigrants suppress American wages and take American jobs. The argument is used to pander to blue collar workers and high-tech employees alike, and it is bandied about far too frequently by those who should know better.

Perhaps the worst culprit in this regard is Krikorian, who has a deft and stylish way of selectively presenting arguments made by free trade advocates, and using their words to bolster his own anti-free trade position.

In his January 7, 2004, *National Review Online* article about the President's plan, Krikorian (a visiting fellow at the Nixon center, and director of the Center for Immigration Studies) paints a rosy picture of an America which restricts immigration.

According to Krikorian, if the US government were to enforce more stringently the nation's immigration policies, life for American workers would improve.

> [E]mployers would respond to this new, tighter, labor market in two ways. One, they would offer higher wages, increased benefits, and improved working conditions, so as to recruit and retain people from the remaining pool of workers. At the same time, the same employers would look for ways to eliminate some of the jobs they now are having trouble filling.

This hopeful passage brings some nagging questions to mind. Foremost among them is where employers will get the expendable capital to offer higher wages, increased benefits, and improved working conditions. Are they operating on such high profit margins that they can absorb the new costs that Mr. Krikorian would dictate?

He seems unconcerned with this minor problem, and continues to tread along his utopian path. "The result would be a new equilibrium," Krikorian says, "with blue-collar workers making somewhat better money, but each one of those workers being more productive."[16]

It is interesting that he should feel so free to tell employers and workers how their businesses will operate, and that they will achieve a "new equilibrium" which he prefers over the one the employers and workers could establish without his help. Besides the fact that his assumption regarding wages is completely erroneous and reflects little understanding of profit, marginal costs, and the productive use of capital, he assumes employers can simply increase these wages without any consideration of the most important player in the free market economy, *the consumer*.

Krikorian conveniently neglects to consider how consumers would respond to the forced higher costs of products. Perhaps this is because he believes the heady notion that costs just wouldn't go up. As he says:

> [S]ince all unskilled labor — from Americans and foreigners, in all industries — accounts for such a small part of our economy, perhaps four percent of GDP, we can tighten the labor market without any fear of sparking meaningful inflation."

---

[16] One could assume that these workers would not age, either, because Krikorian would get them apartments in Shangri-La as part of their benefits packages.

Such arrogant assurances usually don't sit well with people who understand why we work to decrease costs of production in the first place. This is a basic concept that nearly every consumer going to the market understands.

The entire purpose of a productive economy is to make things *easier*, not *harder*, to buy, to let us use less of our toil to get a product, not more of our energy and time. To embrace Krikorian's naïve notion would be to accept the idea that the farmer should take a wheel off his plow, because, though the machine will move more slowly and he will have to work *harder* to get his produce, it will employ an American to carry the wheel-less side of the plow, or, better yet, force the farmer to hire a team of experts to develop a new, floating plow that may cost him too much to stay in business, but will employ high skilled natives.

This seems to be a very attractive line of thinking to Krikorian, for in his attempts to supercede the preferences of consumers and businessmen as reflected in the market, he cites one of the most legendary free-market thinkers, Julian Simon, and his work on scarcity, as inspiration.

In his breakthrough 1981 publication, "The Ultimate Resource", Simon revealed that most of the leftist fears regarding depletion of natural resources were unfounded. Simon found that the relative scarcity of resources led to greater human innovation, which led to greater productivity, greater market abundance of old and new resources, and improved living conditions.

As Krikorian notes, Simon spelled it out clearly when he said:

> It is important to recognize that discoveries of improved methods and of substitute products are not just luck. They happen in response to "scarcity" — an increase in cost. Even after a discovery is made, there is a good chance that it will not be put into operation until there is need for it due to rising cost. This point is important: Scarcity and technological advance are not two unrelated competitors in a race; rather, each influences the other.[17]

This is absolutely correct. Unrestrained human ingenuity lets us thrive in a world of limited resources. But Krikorian seeks to use this discovery to justify depletion of the US *labor force*! Citing raisin growers in the US and

---

[17] Simon, as quoted by Krikorian, http://www.nationalreview.com/comment/krikorian200401070923.asp. Jan. 7, 2004.

Australia as comparative examples, he explains that in Australia, a nation with a small work force, raisin growers were forced to develop new techniques to harvest their product. This innovation led to greater productivity – more raisins being harvested per worker. In the US, he argues, a surplus of low-wage, immigrant workers suppressed this development, and thus US raisin growers did not adopt the new, productive methods that arose in Australia.

But implicit in his argument is the fact that US employers *did not have to* develop those new forms of harvesting, because their relative costs were lower and labor was not scarce. According to Krikorian, the scarcity of labor in Australia led to technological progress, the kind of thing Simon would have applauded; and the surplus of labor in the US led to technological stagnation, which hurts an economy in the long run.

By embracing the idea that scarcity leads to innovation, Krikorian assumes that a man like Simon would have welcomed greater scarcity. Under Krikorian's paradigm, we ought to eliminate as many resources as we can, be they labor resources or natural recourses, because their scarcity will lead to technological innovation, and greater productivity.

In other words, burn down the forests with eager dispatch! We will come up with new, more productive ways to harvest what is left!

Krikorian makes the dual mistakes of assuming better market knowledge than the US raisin growers themselves, and of confusing all technological innovation – at all times -- with a greater productive use of capital. While the needs of Australian raisin growers led them to come up with new ways of harvesting their crops, and these may have been more productive for *them*, US growers made their own decisions based on their needs. To assume for US growers the responsibility of how best to spend their money and invest in resources is not only arrogant, it stifles the cost analysis that leads to innovation in the first place.

This may all seem academic at first glance. But it is important. As it happens, Krikorian's argument has been widely disseminated, not only in the online and print versions of *National Review*, but also in the broadcast media, where Rush Limbaugh read his polemic on the air to millions of listeners. It is pervasive, and it is dangerous.

Krikorian's messy reinterpretation of Simon's logic is really a tool to support his belief that immigration is not only unnecessary, but that it should be curtailed. At the core of his thinking, and of that of people such as the usually insightful Laura Ingraham, is the honest belief that foreign laborers suppress native wages and harm the economy as a whole.

Perhaps not coincidentally, it was Julian Simon himself who conducted probably the most exhaustive survey of all economic data regarding these claims, and his work refutes Krikorian on every level. In his landmark 1995 paper entitled: "Immigration: The Demographic and Economic Facts", published by the Cato Institute and the National Immigration Forum, Simon looked at the available studies, and concluded:

> The studies uniformly show that immigrants do not increase the rate of native unemployment in the aggregate. The reader need not go further if the conclusion is all that is desired.

However, if one wanted to go further, he could discover that immigration also does not, in the aggregate, suppress *wages* for native workers. Immigration has a slight dampening effect on wages only in certain sectors of the economy, typically those sectors that depend on immigrant labor. These decreases in wages are often very slight, and the wages rise over time as each sector sees economic improvement. As one of the studies reported:

> [T]he evidence we have assembled for the 1980s confirms the conclusions from earlier studies of 1970 and 1980 census data. In particular, we find little indication of an adverse wage effect of immigration, either cross-sectionally or within cities over time. Even for workers at the 10th percentile of the wage distribution, there is no evidence of a significant decline in wages in response to immigrant inflows.[18]

Data like these often go overlooked by commentators, which is a shame, since it would be much more productive to debate when informed by as many facts as possible. With such information on hand, readers would be able to dispel error and seek out the truth, and in the political realm, this practice is not just an academic exercise. When codified, assumptions can cause great damage. Many people assume that an influx of immigrants will harm the bargaining power of the American worker. But they do not see that a decrease in immigrant workers would mean a decrease in the bargaining power of the *consumer*.

---

[18] Kristin F. Butcher and David Card, "Immigration and Wages: Evidence from the 1980s," American Economic Review 81 no. 2 (May 1991), p. 296, as quoted by Simon (1995).

Some claim that the "jobs no one else will do" would pay higher wages if we just got those pesky foreigners out of the labor pool. They never consider that the consumer would be forced to pay more, and the businessman might not be able to attract the consumer to his product if he had to sell it at a higher price.

Most of all, however, they do not see the dynamic effect that a few extra pennies in each consumer's pocket can have on the economy as a whole. The reason immigrants are not dangerous to the US economy is that they allow consumers to buy the best product they can for the lowest price. This, in turn, allows the consumer to have more expendable capital to use on another product, perhaps a *new* American product or business venture, which will employ more people, and, in turn, help strengthen the economy. Despite what the doomsayers claim, immigration helps us all better out lives. It's what economic progress is all about, and it is why people come to this country in the first place.

Addendums re: Immigration
Addendum One: A Letter to a talk radio host in NH
September 17, 1999

Sir,

I listened with interest to your discussion regarding Pat Buchanan's views on international trade, and I see a few flaws in the argument. .

First, as you know, numerous studies have shown that any attempt to protect a particular industry from foreign competition harms consumers to a tune of eight to one over the benefits provided to that industry. James Bovard has written extensively on this, as has Murray Rothbard, and people like Walter Williams, and there have been many studies by Heritage, and Cato and the CBO and GAO that bear this out.

But Pat's protectionist argument usually disregards this point in favor of other issues he sees as more important. Many of your points Friday parallel his.

First, you mentioned that you don't need a college education to work at low wage service jobs such as those provided by Wal-Mart and McDonalds. Of course, one doesn't need a college degree to start a small business, but one *does* need to be able to get low interest loans, and this is based on consumer savings, which is in turn based on the ability of consumers to buy less expensive products made by companies that can be more and more productive.

The dynamic driving start-up small businesses is based on the productivity of the economy, which frees up lower cost money for entrepreneurs who, in turn, can *hire* more people.

The idea that people are stuck in certain positions -- that they just don't have the education or ability to "move up" in the job market -- smacks of a lack of confidence in human nature, and runs counter to historic example. From Irish and Italian immigrants to Cuban refugees and African Americans who were enjoying better lifestyles before the imposition of the Great Society, immigrants and minorities were often uneducated, yet able to learn skills and raise their own living standards and those for their progeny. I'm sure you've read the incredibly detailed studies by Tom Sowell on this. It's a basic historical fact.

"Fair" traders argue two other points:

1. That big business is manipulating government to allow it to bring in cheaper products, then moving plants to other countries to employ cheaper labor, thus destroying "productive" jobs in the US.

Two facets to consider here are the fact that it's in the best interest of the consumer to be able to purchase the least expensive, high quality product, which, again, is the spark for freeing up money for new businesses. Also, to try to block certain specific products is akin to Frederick Bastiat's ironic example of the candle makers lobbying for the extinguishing of their competition, the sun. The paradox presented in "protecting" certain sectors deemed important by those in power in the government is very obvious. Buchanan believes that lobbyists are getting government to play favorites for big businesses that want to use cheaper foreign labor, His answer? To use *government* to protect certain industries (they'll be big too, with lobbyists and unions funneling money for political favors) in this country from foreign competition, from less expensive products that American consumers could buy for less, thus using their money most productively. If people want "protection", they have the power of their wallets, and free choice, to buy or not to buy.

His logic, on economic terms, is circular.

2. He argues on strategic grounds. He believes that if we don't protect certain "essential" sectors of the economy (steel, for example), they will atrophy and we may be in danger should we get into a military conflict. This is his best attempt to rationalize playing favorites with blue collar workers whom certain demagogues say don't have the *capacity* to get training for new jobs. Additionally, the idea of choosing which industries are essential is unfeasible. Steel is often quoted as essential for defense, but if we can buy cheaper steel from Japan and build weapons, tanks, carriers, etc., more productively, that *assists* our military preparedness. Of course, some will say, what if they won't sell it? There are only two scenarios for this:

A. They would sell to us, but cut it off. If this is the case, we would have already been able to build a *stronger* military at less cost, thus heightening our preparedness and decreasing the probability that we'd be attacked.

B. They would just not sell it to us at all, which would mean that we'd be producing it anyway.

And what constitutes "strategic" industries? Is farming an essential strategic industry? Then we shouldn't buy cheaper foreign food for fear that our farming sector will atrophy. Is high technology? Then, in all seriousness, we would want to allow technology based businesses to operate more productively, and compete to produce better products; and we know how that is done. By allowing competition, and by allowing those businesses to buy the best products they need at the lowest prices.

Is steel essential? Is plastic? Are textiles? All are essential during wartime, and all could be fodder for protectionists. Who decides, Pat Buchanan? In his zeal to stop business from getting favors from government regarding tariffs, he wants to play favorites regarding tariffs!

Finally, as mentioned earlier, if we fear the atrophy of sectors, then we have to protect them all, getting worse products at higher costs, harming productivity and suppressing job growth. And it is this very moveable capital that allows for more immediate response to military threat.

The idea that we must protect certain strategic industries reaches an infinite regress both with regard to technology (steel production depends in turn on other products, the makers of which buy from foreign nations because they're cheaper and thus allow those steel companies to be more productive) -- and regarding interest groups and labor interests. Pat's utopian, non-economic view is utterly wrong and unworkable.

It takes more time to reactivate an atrophied agricultural sector than it takes to open up mines in the US and start up steel production.

The best thing we can do to help our strategic preparedness is to open up mineral resources to US companies, allowing us to get those minerals at lower costs.

Morally, the argument against admitting slave-made, or prisoner-made products has some validity. It can be likened to buying stolen goods here in the US. It does have a bearing on Natural Rights, in this case the rights of non-US citizens. The potential problem I see with imposing regulations on such foreign products it really two-fold. First, one again reaches an infinite regress. Clearly reprehensible actions such as slave labor or prisoner labor are easy for us to denounce, and should be. But other groups in the US see child labor in Indonesia as reprehensible (despite the fact that kids line up for the work), and environmental conditions in Mexico as deplorable. Once the mechanism of government moral regulation is established, it only depends on the force of interest groups to define what is "societally acceptable" to buy. And those interest groups invariably will be composed of labor interests, in addition to people honestly motivated by moral ideals.

The imposition of government control over the purchase of products also destroys the concept of individual choice, without which morality cannot exist. If the majority decides you have no choice in the matter, you cannot exercise your own morals. American consumers should be allowed to decide for themselves.

These are some of the issues that should be considered when Pat touts his policies, but he often doesn't allow for such discussion, instead using silly phrases such as: "You know those faces on Mount Rushmore? They all used tariffs." I respect Pat less and less when he comes up with these answers. Yes, he has written books on the subject, but he invariably dances around detailed examination of the debate when in a live discussion. More and more, he likes monologues, not dialogues.

And, as you know, populism is far from conservatism. One could see that Pat was beginning to lean that way in the last election, when he started catering to the GM workers, and donning hardhats at construction sites. Conservatives who have given up on free trade shouldn't call themselves conservatives. Just like Pat, they are now populists, similar to William Jennings Bryon in the last half of the 19th century.

Addendum Two: Neglected Facts about US Immigration Law
June, 2007

In the preceding arguments about immigration, it has been noted that the US Constitution explicitly grants the federal government power to control immigration after 1808 in only the states that existed at the time. I have received some criticism for this observation, and engaged in some rewarding, friendly debates with some who disagree with my analysis. For the record, those who believe the US Constitution grants the federal government the power to control immigration in every state must grapple with a few important facts:

Under any strict reading of the Constitution, the immigration issue is verbally tied to the importation of slaves (Article One, Section Nine). According to the Constitution, Congress was forbidden from regulating the importation of slaves or other people in the states existing at the time, and there was a very powerful political reason for this clause. If it had not been written, the southern states would not have been likely to approve the Constitution.

Here is the layout as it stood at the time of the Founders... By the time the Constitution was written, the Northwest Ordinance had already banned slavery in the Northwest Territory. Southern agricultural interests were reluctant to sign on to the Constitution without some kind of assurance that their way of life would not be immediately threatened by northern states exercising great power in Congress. As a result, the famous "3/5 compromise" was established, making each slave "count" as three-fifths of a man for the purposes of Congressional representation (we can discuss the disaster of slavery at another time, right now, our focus is on how the southern interest in slavery had an effect on Article One, Section Nine, and on the evidence that the federal government was forbidden from messing with immigration in any but the original states).

After the Constitution was written, the Missouri Compromise was achieved. This set a standard for the process of admission of states from the territories of the Louisiana Purchase, whereby the northern free territories and southern slave territories would alternate in admission. If the federal government could set the rules regarding new state *importation* of slaves (or immigrants in general, if we broaden the issue) *outside* the original states, then there would be no need to decide which kinds of territories could gain admission in what sequence, because the territories themselves, upon becoming states, could then have restrictions placed on them regarding slave importation (or general immigration). It is unlikely that the southern states would have accepted such an arrangement when debating the Constitution. What the south wanted was an assurance that Congress would not be able to stop importation of slaves in any of the future states that might be admitted beyond the borders of the Northwest Territory. If one reads Article One, Section Nine, he sees that the use the term "of the states now existing" was intentional, and the exclusion of future states was intentional as well. The 9th and 10th amendments then set the bar higher for any assumption that Congress could adopt this power or assume anything not specifically enumerated.

But stronger than the opinion offered above is the fact that Jefferson took this view on immigration in 1798, when he forcefully commented on the Alien and Sedition Act:

> Resolved, That alien friends are under the jurisdiction and protection of the laws of the state wherein they are; that no power over them has been delegated to the United States, nor prohibited to the individual states, distinct from their power over citizens; and it being true, as a general principle, and one of the amendments to the Constitution having also declared, that "the powers not delegated to the United States by the Constitution, nor prohibited to the states, are reserved, to the states, respectively, or to the people," the act of the Congress of the United States, passed the 22d day of June, 1798, entitled "An Act concerning Aliens," which assumes power over alien friends not delegated by the Constitution, is not law, but is altogether void and of no force.

After he was elected, Jefferson pardoned all people captured under the law, and Congress paid restitution. Later, President Grant, of all people, held the same view: "Responsibility over immigration can only belong with the States since this is where the Constitution kept the power," he once said in a letter to Congress. In Texas, the State Constitution (approved in 1869) had an article in it establishing a "Bureau of Immigration", headed by a "Superintendent of Immigration" for the state. Consider: if the people of Texas believed *Congress* had the power to control immigration in the new states, would they have bothered to include such a provision for their own state government? It is doubtful, in the least.

In numerous Supreme Court cases of the early 19th Century, ("Miln v New York", "Smith v Turner" and "Norris v Boston") participants cited numerous laws enacted by the state legislatures that put restrictions on the kinds of people (such as paupers) that shipmasters could allow in the respective states, and many of the laws were passed after the adoption of the US Constitution. (There was debate as to whether the states could impose taxes on such imports, or if such taxes infringed on Congress' power to impose levies and tariffs, and there were also controversies about whether such state taxes could trump federal treaties with other nations, but there were many non-monetary restrictions on immigrants imposed by state legislatures.

As stated before, it was Supreme Court malfeasance and Congressional politics in the late 1800's that brought about the federalization of immigration policy. It was not the US Constitution. That is something supposed "conservatives" ought to remember when debating.

When you take up with the Devil, don't be surprised if you see horns sprouting from <u>your</u> head.

PHG
Winter, 1983

"Anti-trust"
July, 1999

The antitrust suit brought about by Janet Reno against Microsoft has inspired a great deal of public discussion, and, thankfully, some outrage.

In 1998, Ms. Reno claimed that Microsoft's business practices were "not only un-American, (they were) immoral."

Coming from the woman responsible for the hellish deaths of seventy-six innocent people in Waco, Texas, this statement is more than a bit outrageous.

But her surreal utterance is not the only aspect of this case that deserves skepticism. The very concept of Federal anti-trust law should be in question.

All Federal antitrust laws are unconstitutional. The purported basis for Federal regulation is the "Interstate Commerce Clause."

At the time of its creation, the clause was designed to correct a flaw in the Articles of Confederation that allowed each state to coin its own money, and to establish tariffs on goods entering from other states. But those rules led to problems, for the states began printing their own inflated money in order to pay their debts. Currency of one state became difficult to exchange with that of another, and the protectionist tariffs each state enacted were actually counter-productive, destroying jobs. (Something Pat Buchanan and Ross Perot seem to have forgotten.)

The Founders, wishing to eliminate these problems, placed the power to coin money in the hands of Congress, and also gave it the power to "regulate trade... among the states." They intended to avoid inter-state currency conflicts and eliminate trade barriers, *not* allow Congress the power to intervene in any form of commerce crossing state borders. In fact, the Interstate Commerce Clause applies only to state *governments*, and to the tariff policies of those governments. Its strictures are intended to hamper autocratic state trade laws that would harm individuals in one, or all states.

Unfortunately, with Congressmen and Senators who willfully disregard the intent of the Founders, and a system of "Judicial Review" in which Supreme Court justices can define what the Constitution "means", our nation long ago tossed aside any tenuous link to the laws that established this nation.

In 1893, the barriers against Federal regulation were weakened when, under the Sherman Act, the US government brought suit against the American Sugar Refining Company. And, since that time, wide-open interpretation of Article One, Section Eight, has given the Federal government virtual control over almost all US domestic business.

That control is patently illegitimate. Unfortunately, most Americans accept the practice of Federal regulation, and most who oppose the Reno action do so because they believe it's unwarranted, not because it's unauthorized by the Constitution.

But even if one were to consider the case only on that pragmatic level, one would have to conclude that not just this, but all antitrust cases are founded on faulty logic, and rife with economic fallacies.

The foremost among those fallacies is the misconception of a monopoly itself. When a company acquires majority market share, a strange thing happens to bureaucrats and politicians. They begin to worry about "anti-competitive pricing" that "could eliminate competition and eventually harm consumers." But the cascade of mistakes made in such an assumption is almost overwhelming. First, in order to achieve *any* comfortable position in the marketplace, a company *must* cater to the wants of consumers. The very process of rising to a position of dominance is one driven by satisfaction of consumer demand. No satisfaction, no increase in market share. Thus, big companies are big precisely because they have succeeded in offering something valued by their customers, valued more than a product of their competitors

But once dominant, couldn't large companies utilize their massive assets to offer new products at artificially low prices, thus knocking out smaller competitors? Let's consider the question. If it is publicly held, and potential buyers find the company's plan unwise, the stock will begin to drop in value. By the same token, if the company *can* introduce new products at cheaper prices by utilizing its strength, stock prices will rise. Meanwhile, consumers will be getting a product that is better or less expensive than what was available before, which is exactly the idea of market competition. Why should the consumer be denied the choice to buy a better or less expensive product, thus maximizing his money, simply because that choice might decrease profits of the smaller company? This logic implies that any improvement in efficiency or productivity by anyone interested in entering the marketplace must be proscribed by law. Development must be made illegal.

To most people this line of reasoning makes sense. But they fear that the large company, once it has acquired market dominance, will begin gouging its customers by raising prices. Since the customers will have "no place to go", they will be forced to pay excessively high prices.

This is the most basic of errors, based on a misunderstanding of free exchange and competition. Any business operating in an open market *must* satisfy the customer, for if it does not, it will be vulnerable to new competition catering to dissatisfied customers. Prices *must* be kept at a rate the market will bear, because, if raised, an opportunity for a new entrepreneur will appear.

Some may argue that Microsoft could use its money to suppress other products, so that consumers never even hear about them. But any company trying to develop new products, while at the same time wasting massive amounts of its own money attempting to destroy the innumerable entrepreneurs and products that will compete against it, will be fighting a losing battle. Its only choice would be to beseech the government for some kind of protection…

…Which is exactly what antitrust laws have been used to do. Invariably, antitrust suits are brought about to *stifle* competition, to stop lower priced products and to give consumers less choice.

Computer manufacturers and consumers have selected Microsoft products for a multitude of reasons. No one forced them to buy Microsoft. They saw the choices in the market over the years, and decided what they wanted. Microsoft introduces improvements and additions to its products all the time. Consumers are still free to select other products. If they don't like Microsoft's products, marketing procedures and business practices, they have the freedom to turn to competitors such as Mac, Sun, and Linux. If Microsoft doesn't continue to provide products that consumers believe are of greater or equal value to the money they are willing to spend, its competitors will gain market share.

Janet Reno and her crony Joel Kline want to use antitrust to penalize Gates for his inventiveness. But, in the final analysis, the question comes down to this:

Whom should you really "anti-trust", Bill Gates, or Janet Reno?

It's too bad those seventy-six people from Waco can't answer.

"Testify!"
February, 2002

The dominant news this week has been the rhetorical wrangling over Congressional and Senatorial calls for Enron executive Kenneth Lay to appear before numerous committees. An evidently ubiquitous desire runs through politicians to "get to the bottom" of the Enron financial meltdown. Meanwhile, Lay claims that the elected officials have a "prosecutorial" attitude, which would put him at a disadvantage.

While studying both these claims, one ought to consider, and learn lessons from, another series of high-profile Congressional hearings.

In 1930, Senate Banking Committee Chairman Carter Glass began "investigating" the causes of the banking collapse that had been preceded by the Great Crash. Of course, Glass, his chief counsel, Ferdinand Pecora, and many other politicians had already decided what had caused the bank failures. They blamed the supposedly perfidious and corrupt bankers. Many bankers were called before the microphones to explain themselves, although not many were given a chance to say much, and usually sat listening to the brilliantine, self-righteous preachers tell them how truly venal they had become.

Franklin Roosevelt even used biblical imagery to paint the bankers as evil in the eyes of the populace. Calling them the "unscrupulous money-changers", he claimed that they had, through their own stubbornness and incompetence, "admitted their own failure."

This was, of course, absolute drivel.

The primary reasons for the systemic banking failures, like the reasons for the Great Crash, had virtually nothing to do with private malfeasance or corruption, and everything to do with government regulation and manipulation of the market. Just as loose Fed policy in the 1920's and a tightening of the money supply in 1928 had caused a temporal warping of the supply curve and a subsequent contraction that went deeper than it properly should, the bank crisis that followed the Great Crash had been predicated by federal rules forbidding banks from issuing gold-based currency, and restricting banks from diversifying their investments. "Agricultural" banks could not even do business in urban areas, and vice-versa. If bankers had been able to address the interests of their customers as they desired, the

Great Crash caused by federal manipulation of the money supply would not have had the systemic effects it did.

Of course, Roosevelt didn't want anyone to know that. He was intent on strengthening the vise-grip of government over the market. Thus, his attacks, and those of his political cronies in the House and Senate, helped pave the way for further regulation of the industry.

The Glass-Pecora Hearings of 1930 were, simply put, a sham, a show-trial performed for public consumption in order to facilitate greater centralized control over the financial industry. The culprits were never exposed, because they were the ones asking the questions and accusing the banking industry of being corrupt. Today's politicians are much the same. While they claim to be interested in finding out the wrongdoing of Enron executives -- a job best left to criminal courts -- their actions reveal other motives.

When a man like Dick Gephardt tries to make a connection between Enron's stock dive and the supposed need for "campaign finance reform", and when Democrats infuse every mention of Enron with the fallacious concept that "big business has corrupted government" (actually, overbearing government has set up a protection racket on American business), one gets a strong impression that something else is afoot.

What Democrats want is three-fold. First, they desire further regulations on free speech. Second, they want to evoke a sense that private investment is risky, thus depicting Social Security privatization as ill-advised. Third, they wish to undercut the entire paradigm of free enterprise. Much like the politicians of the 1930's, who blamed bankers for their own misdeeds, today's politicians will make the free market the scapegoat, and will write legislation to curtail our market choices.

The Enron fraud issue is one to be handled by the courts, not Congress. However, other lessons can be learned if one compares the crisis of 1929-1930 to the breakdown of the Enron 401K plan. The key element in both situations was that people did not diversify, thus exposing them to great risk. The most important factor to be remembered is the difference between private choice and government force. No one forced people to work for Enron and to accept the Enron investment plan. They freely elected to place themselves at such risk, with or without the fraud that seems to have occurred. In 1929, government did not give bankers any choice. If politicians are upset that Enron executives did not offer to employees a wide enough choice of diversified investments, they must also recognize the greater risk and *real* coercion that federal rules over investments represent.

Freedom of choice is inherent in the capitalist system. Those who make mistakes suffer the consequences, those who operate fraudulently suffer in many more ways. Under government control, no one has a choice, all must conform, fraud is rarely punished, and those who make mistakes are usually the ones who end up sitting in the House and Senate, answering to no one at all.

**Macroeconomics:
Part Two
Federal and State Programs –
Redirecting the Flow of Useable Capital into
Non-productive Projects**

A socialist (collectivist) society is (actually) one where the vast majority are controlled by a tiny minority that has the power to direct their economic activities. The socialist dream is based on the delusion that men's <u>other</u> freedoms will be enhanced if they are deprived of economic liberty. The socialists hoped to usher in a brave new world by killing economic liberty (free enterprise). Their goose never laid the golden egg because the theory is completely wrong. Its results are the equality of misery – the beginning of a master-slave relationship.

PHG
1983

"What to Do When Business Increases"
September, 2004

According to the US Agriculture Department[19], the number of farmers' markets in the United States has increased 79 percent between 1994 and 2002. There are now more than 3,100 nationwide, and the increase in their number reflects the growing appeal of fresh fruits and vegetables to "Baby-boomers" and "Gen-X-ers" alike. In Ohio alone, nearly 100 farmers' markets are in operation, and in Buffalo, New York, approximately 300,000 people were counted flocking to a 116 year-old market in the two weeks prior to Easter. Evidently, "eating one's greens" is becoming popular enough to allow many local farmers to see "green" of a different sort.

Given this phenomenon, what is the logical course of action to take when the demand dramatically increases for the fruit – no pun intended – of one's labor?

Any sensible person would do what Ohio Congresswoman Marcy Kaptur suggests: turn to the federal government to subsidize it.

On September 14, 2004, Congresswoman Kaptur, a "former urban planner"[20] now serving on the House Appropriations Subcommittee for Agriculture, proposed that the 2006 farm bill spend $50 million to build new farmers' markets and restore old ones in large metropolitan areas.

"The survival of family farmers in our country is going to depend on their ability to market to the consumers, most of which live in the suburbs and cities," Kaptur said as she unveiled her idea to the nation.

Apparently, her sentiment is shared by many people who see the situation of aging hippies, and their growing desire to eat green leafy vegetables instead of smoking them, in a more desperate light.

Ron Paul (not the Texas doctor, turned heroic constitutional Representative), of Portland, Oregon, is trying to garner enough money to build a year-round market to supplant the seasonal one that has been in operation for ten years.

---

[19] http://www.santafenewmexican.com/news/4407.html
[20] http://wwwc.house.gov/kaptur/Article.aspx?NewsID=1293

Of the $15 million cost of his project, Paul was quoted by the Associated Press as saying:

"We are absolutely crying out for an increase in federal assistance for this."

The money to calm Mr. Paul would be provided in direct federal grants, low-interest loans or loan guarantees.

As strange as it seems, there was once a time in the United States when people did not cry out for federal assistance for their growing industry. It was a time of legend and lore, when the recognition that a product was in higher demand led to investment of another kind. During this strange, forgotten epoch, projects designed to accommodate expanding businesses were funded privately, and the loans for those projects were provided by individuals and banks, not the federal government. It may be hard to believe today, but in this by-gone era of the distant, misty past, people pulled swords out of stones, men were chivalrous, and business was conducted by people who used their own money, and took their own risks, to engage in it. Investment and exchange were voluntary, and based on the subjective analyses of those participating in the activity. If an investor saw a benefit in loaning his money to a business owner whose product was in increasing demand, he would risk the temporary loss of his capital in the hope that his investment would bring him great rewards as time went by. Depositors leaving their money in banks could gauge the relative wisdom of their institutions' loan policies, and decide on their own if the projects funded by those banks were too risky, too cautious, or just right.

But today, individual initiative, individual responsibility, and individual thought seem to be quite out of vogue. When it comes to seeing the benefit of investing in a potentially rewarding project, it is not the private sector to which people like Mr. Paul and Congresswoman Kaptur turn, it is the captive taxpayer. Where once, a member of society would have had to approach his neighbor, and personally convince him to voluntarily give up his money to invest in a business venture, politicians and businessmen now extol the supposed virtues of turning to the faceless state, and its powers of coercion, to do the trick..

This is not only unethical, supplanting individual morals and interests with the forces of government glad-handling, egotism, and majority coercion, it is economically non-productive, moving capital from its otherwise chosen course, and redirecting it to uses which, had the market been left alone to operate, would not have been selected at all.

The moral implications are clear. But the economic fall-out from such paternalistic thinking is just as important. At the heart of the matter is a concept which can be called "spheres of control." As many economists have said, and many non-economists understand, the larger the area of control for any human activity, the less efficient its operation is likely to be. Conversely, the smaller the sphere of control, the more likely the decisions over economic affairs will be correct and productive. In fact, the very act of defining "productivity" is a subjective matter, to be made only by the individual whose finances are of concern. The ability of an individual to direct the fruits of his labor towards what he believes will best serve his interests, be that the purchase of a product, the investment of his capital, or the sale of a product or service, is the single factor that drives an economy towards its most productive operation. There can be no true "objective" evaluation of productivity or economic efficiency on an aggregate level, because the aggregate is composed of its constituent parts, and in a free market, these constituent parts are the individual market participants themselves.

As a result, the subjective determination of productivity and the moral primacy of property ownership are inextricably linked. In fact, they are one in the same.

Even a Congresswoman like Marcy Kaptur, despite her high-minded ideals, cannot dispense with the free market and expect to operate in a just and productive society. What one creates is a less prosperous world, where the cute pet projects of well-connected businessmen, and the selfish, ego-driven interests of politicians overrule the personal interests of those who earned the money.

Under Marcy Kaptur's proposal, $50 million will be directed away from choices that would have been made by the people who earned that money. They earned it by serving their fellow participants in the marketplace. It's too bad that in her attempt to build her quaint farmers' market paradise across the USA, Congresswoman Kaptur doesn't realize she is causing harm to the most important market in the world: the *free* market.

"Gouge Away!"
(or "Charley vs. Charlie")
August, 2004

In the wake of hurricane Charley, another powerful Charles, namely Florida Attorney General Charlie Crist, has stepped forward to make it clear that law and order will be upheld in the storm-ravaged areas of the state.

One of the first things on his agenda is to stop what is popularly perceived to be the evil practice of "price gouging".

According to news reports, Crist has moved ahead with legal action against two hotels that have supposedly charged too much for their rooms, and he has stated: "It is important for Floridians to know that they will be protected from any potential price gougers… Anyone who seeks to charge unconscionable prices for vital goods should be warned that they (sic) will face the full force of Florida law. We encourage Floridians to report suspicious price increases to (our) hotline. Price gouging will not be tolerated."[21]

But just what is "price gouging", and what are the "suspicious price increases" that supposedly typify it?

For an easy answer, one could simply rely on popular belief. According to most politicians, many consumers, and the "watchdog groups" that supposedly protect them, "suspicious price increases" are sharp upward spikes in the prices of products (typically "essential" products such as food, water, energy, building supplies and clothing) that rise far above the "market norm" during a time of emergency. When a seller charges such high prices for needed items, he is clearly exploiting the consumer, which, according to Attorney general Crist, is not just unethical, it reflects the worst in society.

But such a notion is far from correct. It may seem counter-intuitive, but supposed "price gougers" are essential for a properly functioning economy, and represent the most important factor in a free market: the need for prices to reflect the relative scarcity of the products to which they are attached.

To begin an exploration into what is typically a scorned and hated practice, one needs to ask a question of those who would characterize price

---

[21] http://www.consumeraffairs.com/news04/hurricane_charley_fl_ag.html

gouging as "prices rising above the market norm." This question has both practical and ethical implications.

The question is: "What is the market norm?"

Simply put, the market norm is determined by those who participate in it. Thus, the market price for a product fluctuates based on the interplay between the wants and needs of the buyers and the wants and needs of the sellers. This interplay can change due to various factors, including, but not exclusive to, location, weather conditions, popular notions of style, technological developments, and time.

As a result, what is perceived by people *outside* the ravaged areas of Florida to be the "market price" for essential products *inside* the ravaged areas of Florida is quite different to those living in the devastated areas. Just as the scarcity of pineapples outside Hawaii makes their prices higher compared to pineapples sold *in* Hawaii, the scarcity of essential goods like food, fuel, clothes and water *inside* storm-torn southwest Florida makes their relative value greater to those who seek to buy them.

Ethically speaking, it seems the height of conceit for a person outside the market to arbitrarily determine for those participating in it what is best for them, be they buyers or sellers. Just as one would not impose his will regarding the exchanges between buyers and sellers of pineapples in mainland America, even though the prices for pineapples might be higher there than on the Hawaiian Islands, one should apply the same standard to the participants in the market for "essential goods" in Florida.

But it is not just good ethics to let one's neighbors determine how much they want to spend or accept for products, it is good economics.

One of the great insights of the thinkers who founded what is known as the "Austrian School" of economics[22] was the importance of the "price mechanism" in the market. According to the Austrian economists, prices reflect the multitudinous valuations of countless sellers and consumers engaging in non-coercive exchange. They are the end result of each participant's decisions in the marketplace, and reflect how much people value certain products. Prices are essential carriers of information. They not only reflect preferences, but also the relative scarcity of goods in the market. Without the price mechanism, there can be no systematic determination of the value of a good, and no conception of the scarcity of that good. And

---

[22] Ludwig von Mises and Frederic Hayek in particular.

without an idea of how scarce something is, a product will not be allocated correctly for those who truly want it.

As a result, sharply increasing prices for popular or essential goods are not only natural, they are indispensable. Higher demand will drive up prices, and these higher prices will eventually curtail purchases, preventing complete depletion of the goods. Without the price mechanism, without "suspicious price increases" for products people want very badly, those products would disappear very quickly. Just as pineapples kept at artificially low prices in the mainland would disappear, leaving a pineapple shortage in the US, prices kept artificially under the market level inside storm-ravaged Florida will cause shortages of essential goods like food, water, clothing, fuel and building supplies. Without "gouging", whatever it means to the politicians, there would be runs on the essential materials, and shortages would occur.[23]

With more Floridians than ever needing plywood and beams for their homes, the increased demand could quickly exhaust the supply. Luckily, there is the price mechanism to reflect this increased demand, which not only prevents depletion, but inspires suppliers to provide more. Eventually, as suppliers move to fill the void, the market prices for "essential" goods will slowly return to a "normal" level inside the ravaged areas, and there will be no more talk of "gouging". In addition, the interplay between consumers and sellers will also ferret out "unacceptable" prices. In most cases, sellers who are perceived by consumers to be "gouging" will either lower their prices, or suffer long-term losses even after the emergency is over. Consumers have long memories, and politicians like Charlie Cris ought to trust consumer opinions as to what is an acceptable price for a badly needed good, not impose their own, arbitrary wills regarding unscrupulous market behavior.

The profit motive decried by Charlie Cris is the one thing Florida cannot do without. Sans the "gougers", and their response to increased demand, there would be no incentive for suppliers to bring in more essential goods to sell to the people of Florida. Given the devastation in many areas of the state, that would simply worsen an already tragic situation.

---

[23] The ironic, but natural, end result of this situation is a high-priced "black market" for essential goods that have been purchased at artificially low "legal" prices. These surplus items will be resold at even higher prices than those of the gougers before gouging was made illegal, because there is the added risk of law-breaking attached to the new sale.

The squeaky wheel may get the grease, but who's attracted to grease?

PHG
1969

"Why Congressman Markey Didn't Give Me a Ride Home"
February 2003

It was sheer coincidence that bought us within proximity of one another.

My airline, trying to get me to my final destination on time, had rerouted me through Reagan International Airport, in Washington, DC. They had gone to a lot of trouble to get me to Boston's Logan Airport, where I could get ground transportation home.

Reagan Airport happens to be a spot where many politicians catch their own flights, and this night was no exception. Strolling aboard the plane behind me, his left hand holding a briefcase no doubt filled with bills to further attenuate my liberty, I noticed Massachusetts Congressman Ed Markey.

Now, Ed Markey seems an amiable fellow. He has a kind smile. His shirts are presentable and his pants appear well-pressed. To me, it seemed that this man who had willingly entered the political arena, and who felt comfortable telling others how to live their lives, wouldn't mind chatting about his work.

But when I told him I thought his bill to increase Federal Communication Commission fines for "broadcast indecency" was a bad idea, he seemed displeased. When I mentioned that the entire rationale of "broadcast spectrum scarcity" employed to support federal control of the airwaves was spurious, and that such logic could be applied to trees and paper, thus justifying federal control over book and newspaper content, he appeared annoyed. When I asked him if he could cite writings of the Founding Fathers that allowed him to stretch the Constitution in favor of his goal, he seemed genuinely bemused, and quickly moved to find his seat and wave goodbye.

Believe me, I wasn't accosting him. It certainly wasn't a one-way conversation. The Congressman laid out his rationale, and I gave him time to make his points before we parted ways. Still, as the plane took off, I couldn't help but think I ought to make amends for our little disagreement. I hate discord. There had to be something I could do...

Soon, our plane was gliding towards the runway in Boston, and I had my idea.

I would give Congressman Markey the chance to do something about which he felt very strongly. I left the plane all smiles, and moved to the concourse to organize my bags. In a moment, he emerged behind me.

"Congressman," I said.

"Hi," he replied.

"Hey, no hard feelings about the FCC thing."

He nodded amiably. "Sure, no problem."

But before he could turn away, I pursed my brow and asked, "By the way, did you vote for federal funding for the 'Big Dig'?"

His smile was like a supernova. "Of *course*!"

"Great! Then... May I have a ride home?"

He looked at me in the sort of hesitant fashion many politicians adopt when they are worried they might be meeting an odd-ball.

"Huh?"

"Well," I explained. "If you feel strongly about building a new Boston tunnel system that will give me an easier ride home, and you feel *so* strongly about it that you are willing to tax some guy in Boise, Idaho who will never come near this city or this airport, I figure you'd agree we could cut out the middle-man, and *you* could give me the easy ride home."

I think he blinked for a moment, until a broad smile crept across his features.

He understood the logic of it... He got it.

I suspected he would ask me where I was from, and that, whatever I answered, he would tell me he wasn't going that way.

"Where are you from?" he asked.

"I'm from Amherst, New Hampshire. It's about an hour and a half away." I replied.

His smile broadened.

"I'm afraid I couldn't go that far."

I smiled too.

"Of course you couldn't." I told him, and we both parted ways, chuckling.

It was obvious that we were never going to agree on anything political. But the lesson to be learned from that brief encounter, and from his silent acknowledgement of my point, was profound: While Ed Markey was unwilling to go that far to give me an easier trip home, he *would*, through the force of the federal government, go so far as to tax people on the other side of the country to pay for it. While he had the freedom of choice to *decline* my request face to face, the taxpayer in Idaho, or Utah, or Hawaii, or any other state, was *denied* that freedom. The Congressman was, in essence, enslaving the taxpayer, forcing him to work in order to provide the capital to pay for a scheme held dear by Markey and a majority of his cohorts in Congress.

At an estimated cost of $14.6 billion, that's a lot of hours to work, and a lot of people to be enslaved.

The "Big Dig", as it has been labeled, is a seemingly never-ending construction project in Boston that was originally proposed in 1985, by Massachusetts Governor Michael Dukakis (please hold your applause until the end of the article). It links three major highways that are often terribly congested, places two of them underground, and expands access to the North Shore by way of a new route that is wider than the original. First slated for completion in 1998, at a cost of $4.4 billion, the project is now not expected to be finished until 2005. Cost overruns, adjusted for inflation, are higher than 300%, and many observers are skeptical that the project will do much to alleviate traffic in the area.

But the real problem with the Big Dig is what it reflects about our political economy, the politicians who populate American government, and the people who vote for them. It is a perfect example of what the 19th Century French economist and political commentator Frederic Bastiat called "what is seen, and what is unseen."

In this case, what is seen is a physical achievement, a construction project so massive and extensive it is said to be the most ambitious in US history, and has been featured in gushing PBS documentaries even before it has been completed. What is seen is an area in Boston that will be easier to access, bringing in more money to the merchants who work there. What is seen is the huge number of engineers and blue-collar union workers who are employed, and who will shower people like Ed Markey with their votes come election day.

But what is unseen is the taxpayer, and all those to whom he could, if given the opportunity, offer his money for products and services he found beneficial to himself, his family and his friends.

What gets discussed are cost overruns. What gets missed are the ethics of taxation, the morality of majority sanctioned plunder, and the opportunity costs forced on people, who, given a choice, would use the money they earned in their own ways. Many small businesses in America are started for less than $20,000. At a cost of $14.6 billion, that means 73,000 new small businesses may not be started in order to pay for my easier ride home along Markey's Big Dig.

This is a dynamic missed by many politicians in America today. But it was a principle that most of the writers of the Constitution understood well.

They knew that people left to fulfill their own interests in the market would make better decisions than politicians working with other people's money. Individuals would be directed, as Adam Smith wrote in 1776, "as if by an invisible hand", to serve the interests of others, thus creating wealth and improvements for all. They believed that each of us had a right to be left alone to pursue our peaceful interests, and that government was instituted to protect us from "messing" with each other as we went about our business. When a government began to do that which we could aggressively do to one another, it became illegitimate, and contrary to its own purposes. It became a mechanism of majority-dictated theft, and should be abolished.

They knew that if a citizen could, through majority rule, force a neighbor to pay for something he valued (be it food for a hungry child, or clothes for a beggar, or even a road project like the Big Dig) that citizen was forcing his neighbor to *work*, enslaving him. They knew that giving it the euphemistic label of "community-minded" did not excuse coercion, even for supposedly noble goals, and that one need only remove the middle-man, as I did in my conversation with Ed Markey, to prove it. If, for example, one believes there is a right to food, and he can force his neighbor to pay for his other neighbor's meals, would he then agree that instead of making his first neighbor work to pay the expenses, they could just take him out of the equation and enslave a farmer and a cook, make them grow and prepare meals for free? We would never do that. But under the artifices of "public works" and "community" we appear more than willing to do what equates to the same thing.

Ed Markey was unwilling to do something which my privately-run airline was more than willing to do. When their delayed flight was going to arrive in Boston quite late, the employee at the desk actually offered to set me up with ground transportation to my house. While I declined, and opted for a transfer to another carrier that could get me in on time, I was grateful for their consideration.

Of course, since their business was at stake, they were willing to go to great lengths to please me, a willing customer, and actually give me a ride home. But Ed Markey would rather take money from someone he will never meet to do essentially the same thing. If that taxpayer complains, and says he has his own plans for the money, Congressman Markey might just criticize him, and call him selfish.

Is it selfish to leave people alone and ask for the same in return? Is it selfish to want to keep that which one earns with his own labor, that which one gains through his own toil and with the use of his own time? Perhaps if I had *forced* Congressman Markey to give me a lift he would have gotten a better perspective on the coercive nature of taxation.

But considering the knowing smile he offered me when we parted company, I suspect he already knows.

And as long as he is reelected, he doesn't mind at all.

LIVE FREE OR DIE

The desire of human beings to be
free took concrete form when:
1. It gave political and religious freedom to all
2. The free market ran its economy
3. Political liberty operated under the rule of law
4. Private property, and the right to it, became the cornerstone of a free people's society

                PHG
              June, 1984

"The Baby Boon"
February, 2005

A popular platitude in the United States is that children "are our future". Armed with that comfortable phrase, politicians have endeavored to shower parents with myriad government favors, secured from the effort and initiative of others. These perks range from government-run school and day-care, to nutrition and "wellness" programs, to special health care and activity programs, all having the wonderful practical effect of making "our" children de-facto wards of the state.

And while Americans tend to pride themselves for being ahead of other nations when it comes to setting social and political trends, evidently, the politicians in Laviano, Italy, have surpassed us in this regard.

A recent *Los Angeles Times* article reported that the bureaucrats of that small southern Italian town have become alarmed by a declining birth rate. As a result, they've come up with an ingenious government solution. The answer? Simply reward people for having babies. Mayor Rocco Falivena and his associates have taken it upon themselves -- through the taxpayers, of course – to literally *pay* parents of newborns for having children. Over the course of five years, the government of Laviano will offer $14,000 to the parents of any newborn child. The *Times* reports that twenty people thus far have taken up the government on its quite generous offer, giving the idea of a nuclear family a whole new meaning.

While it may be easy to derive amusement from this example of redistributive government folly, it might be wise to pause for a moment, and consider that the US government has been doing the very same thing for years.

Those who have taken advantage of it, those who work in tax policy, and those who keep their eyes on the functional disequilibrium of the generic State are familiar with what is being cited. It is the "Earned Income Tax Credit" (EITC), a special dispensation from the Internal Revenue Service of the US government that showers financial rewards on poor people who have kids.

As opposed to a tax *cut* for parents who have children, which has the laudable effect of decreasing the burden of taxation for some citizens, but the pernicious effect of increasing the relative share of the tax burden for others, and reinforcing the fanciful notion that government has a prerogative to favor some behavior over others, the EITC actually *gives money* to people over and above that which they might have paid to the government in the first place. Depending on his income, the EITC for which one could qualify ranges from $1, to nearly $5,000. In most cases, the EITC is collected by poor people who have no income tax liability whatsoever, and it is, in effect, a tax redistribution scheme perpetrated in their favor.

In a recently published report, "Fertility Effects of the Earned Income Tax Credit", University of New Hampshire assistant professor of economics Reagan Baughman asserts that the effect of the EITC, especially since it was expanded in the 1990's to allow for more redistribution of wealth, has had the practical effect of increasing birth-rates among non-white women.

"We do not find evidence that white women responded to the increases in the EITC, but we find evidence that non-white women had small but statistically significant increases in their fertility rates," writes Baughman.

Which just goes to show the behind-the-curve utopians in Italy that they could learn a thing or two from their friends in the United States!

The EITC rewards people for having children. For example, according to the IRS, if you are a single, childless, wage-earner, and the IRS terms your "taxable income" as ranging between $28,950 and $29,000, you get no money in the EITC. If you have one child, you can qualify for a "credit" of $218. If you have two children, the "credit" increases nearly five-fold, to $1,155. If a citizen's tax liability is lower than his EITC, which it often is, then he is making a net *profit* off of another tax payer.

Thus, rather than taking the direct, Italian, route to encourage births in the United States, and possibly inspiring people to sound-off in protest, American politicians have developed a much more stealthy approach. They use the tax code, and call the payments for children "tax credits". The results, however, are the same. As Ms. Baughman's study indicates, the attempt by the government to "help" poor people who are having trouble raising children has had the unanticipated contrary effect. It has incentivized and encouraged births among poor Americans.

It seems counterintuitive to think that a government intent on helping people could do more harm than good, but this is what happens when decision-making is taken out of the hands of free individuals and exercised by others. This is a fact of nature, and the reasons for it are numerous. First, there is the matter of the subjective valuation of money. Only the person who earned the money, who actually employed his skills and energy and time to engage in a free exchange for payment, can properly determine how he will fulfill his desires and needs with the fruits of his labor. This truism is closely tied to the fact that the problems people encounter are best understood by them, not someone who is not in their shoes. Having a child is the decision of the parents, not the state. The consequences of creating a new life, one wholly dependent on his parents and those who freely engage in charitable activity to support their efforts, are properly felt by the individual participants. *They* must make the calculations regarding income, expenses, hopes, and dreams, and it is an economic fact that they will determine the best course of action more often than people not associated with their concerns. The further removed one gets from the individual desires and needs of the money-earner, the less efficient, less informed, any decisions will be. The redistribution of wealth causes a redirection in the flow of usable capital, from those activities that are determined by the wage earner to be most productive, to those that would not have been selected by that wage earner. By definition, this is a loss for the earner. When conducted on a large, national scale, a net loss in the productive wealth of everyone is thus incurred, and unintended consequences arise.

Thus, developing from a tax program that rewards childbirth, that warps the marketplace, and blurs economic reality for parents, we discover a perverse outcome: more children are born into poor families.

It is just the kind of thing the utopians in government wanted to try to alleviate, yet they have made it worse.

The ethics of having an abstract entity, ostensibly formed to protect our lives and our property, become a machine of redistribution based on majority-sanctioned theft are highly questionable. The practical outcome is pernicious. The trouble is that most people working in government will not recognize the fact that their actions are having such disastrous effects on the lives of others. Theirs is a religion. They worship at the altar of the state, and any empirical evidence that challenges their belief is discounted or overlooked.

Don't look for Ms. Baughman's study to be widely quoted by the members of the pop media, and don't look for it to be held up for viewing by the volunteer army in the IRS. Moreover, don't count on many of our Congressmen and Senators acknowledging what her report tells them. They are too busy concocting new means by which to seize the productive labor of Americans to try to relieve crises of their own making.

"Train Wreck"
January 15, 2002
(Op-Ed: *Nashua Telegraph*, Subject: Bass proposal for Nashua – Lowell Train)

On December 22, 2001, Representative Charlie Bass assured voters in New Hampshire that he will continue to do all he can to promote and secure funding for a proposed commuter rail extension from Lowell, MA, to Nashua ("Rail Service Project Makes Sense", *Nashua Telegraph*, p. 12).

According to Mr. Bass, the rail proposal is "a worthwhile project". It would result in 1000 fewer cars on the highways each day. It would help alleviate congestion, and help ensure the growth and success of southern New Hampshire.

Unfortunately, Mr. Bass has confused many things, including what is practical, what is community oriented, and what is sanctioned by the document he swore to uphold when he took office.

It is ironic that just two weeks after Mr. Bass' letter discussing federal assistance for an MBTA/NH project, the Amtrak Reform Council should announce its plan to keep afloat another public rail project, one that has been sucking like a leech off American taxpayers for thirty years.

After 25 billion dollars and numerous promises to do a better job at a lower price, Amtrak has finally been exposed as the boondoggle it is. It has never, ever, operated at a profit. It has always seized money from Americans in one portion of the nation in order to give rail transit to Americans in another part of the country, primarily those in the northeastern US. Ad campaigns have told us "there's something about a train that's magic", while public rail makes our tax dollars disappear. Spokespeople have lauded their new "high speed train" as a breakthrough, yet the people in the Heartland will probably never ride one. Around the world, no fewer than forty countries have been replacing similar government run rail service with more efficient private systems.

The Amtrak Reform Council may yet see the light. On January 11, it proposed that much of Amtrak's routes be offered to private companies to begin competitive service. While the federal government will still own the lines, this introduction of a "sink of swim" for-profit system may begin to expose the areas where rail service is and is not feasible.

The quaint facade of "community values" that public rail service supposedly represents is slowly being recognized as the fraud that it is. Yet politicians such as Charlie Bass still appeal to local voters with enticements of "cheap" rail service that will supposedly cut auto traffic, and benefit the state as a whole.

One thing is certain, public rail service is not "cheap". At a total of $66 million dollars (and probably much more if it is ever attempted and begins running in the red like most other public transit systems in the world), and servicing only one sector of the population, the Lowell-Nashua line's attendant costs far outweigh its small local benefits. The program clearly exemplifies the disturbing ethics of wealth redistribution by offering a small number of rail users benefits at the expense of a large number of taxpayers who will never use the system. Rail users, and those businesses in the immediate vicinity of the rails, will see benefits, while the expenses will be disbursed among people who are never seen. When public attention is given to such wonderful "community projects", only the faces of those who receive immediate benefits are seen on television, only the voices of those who like the system are heard on radio. The man in Boise who had to shell out tax money to help pay for another person's train ride will never be heard.

Additionally, the entire paradigm of "public value" is called into question when a politician proposes spending tax money on a service that could, if it represented a "value" to the consumers in the area, be provided by a private enterprise. If train service from Lowell to Nashua would be as beneficial and as valuable to area consumers as he claims, then one must ask why a private company has not recently tried to provide that service at a profit. The reason is clear. There is not enough demand for such a product on the part of the consumers, and thus such an endeavor would fail. If it was potentially profitable, there would be incentive to try it, like Vermont Transit has done with bus riders. The very fact that no one deems it worth risking his own capital to start a train system ought to make voters question Mr. Bass' proposal to risk other people's money, without their consent. Subsidizing a project that could have been provided by private enterprise, but was *not* because it was unprofitable, indicates one thing: it is an inefficient expenditure.

Peter Gordon, of the University of Southern California, wrote for the Reason Public Policy Institute that a "downward spiral currently affects public transit. It worked best in a world of high concentrations of origins and destinations… and with large numbers of people too poor to own and operate an automobile." ("Does Transit Really Work?" RPPI, 2000.) The population of southern New Hampshire has clearly grown in recent years, but it is nowhere near the density that justifies a train system. Nor are it's citizens inclined to trade their autos for the train in sufficient numbers to make such a proposition financially feasible or ethically justified.

It would be wise if people such as Mr. Bass stopped appealing to our personal interest to get a ride at the expense of others, and instead concentrated on upholding the US Constitution, which never sanctioned such federal spending in the first place. He swore an oath to uphold the Constitution, not to pick the pocket of another American in order to give me a ride to Lowell.

"Trainspotting"
February 11, 2002

The discussion continues regarding a tax-payer funded train system from Lowell to Nashua. On February 2, Mr. Charlie Matthews responded to my criticism of Rep. Charlie Bass' proposal to channel $66 million to such a project. His response is an educational example of how imprecise editing can shade the meaning of a piece, and how people can overlook the larger economic picture when considering subsidies for projects at home.

Mr. Matthews states, "... while Mr. Goldsmith isn't impressed at the prospect of taking 1,000 cars off the highway every day, I sure am!"

What Mr. Matthews fails to understand is that the estimate noted above is not an established fact; it is a *claim*, made by Mr. Bass, the proponent of the expenditure

In my initial letter, I stated:

"According to Mr. Bass, the rail proposal is 'a worthwhile project'. It would result in 1000 fewer cars on the highways each day. It would help alleviate congestion, and help ensure the growth and success of southern New Hampshire."

The published piece, as edited by the Telegraph, broke the statement into two paragraphs, thus making it less clear that the sentences regarding 1,000 fewer cars and less congestion on NH roads were merely claims by Charlie Bass, and not in any way accepted truths.

It would be nice to imagine that there would be 1,000 fewer cars every day, but such an assumption overlooks a great many other considerations, including how people will travel to the train station, where they will park, the general lack of interest in the local bus system in Nashua, public transit's less than stellar history, and the already allocated Route 3 expansion in progress between Burlington and Nashua.

Mr. Matthews attempts to support his facile claims that the tax-funded extension is justified by noting that passenger rail is subsidized throughout the world. This is a tautology, a self-indictment of public systems. In fact, in over forty countries, bankrupt tax-subsidized rail systems are being licensed out to private operators, precisely because they are *not* efficient. While Mr. Matthews looks to a glorious future of tax-funded trains rolling out of Nashua, many people in other nations, many certainly the same nations he noted that subsidize train service because it "makes economic and environmental sense", have turned away from the government run paradigm towards private initiative.

The claim that tax-funded rail systems make economic and environmental sense is patently false, totally insupportable, and makes for very risky political disputation. It is axiomatic that if something makes economic sense, it can sustain itself without the forced seizure of tax money from those who do not use it.

As Edmund Contaski noted in his 1997 book, "Makers and Takers":

"In the same way that profitable enterprise is supported voluntarily, though incidentally, by others because they benefit from it, every enterprise that can't make a profit is providing less benefit to society than its cost. It is doing more to consume wealth than to enrich the lives of others. But it's precisely to such enterprises and individuals that tax money is allocated, to those who offer *less* in return than they receive. Profitable enterprises don't need tax support, and those that aren't profitable don't deserve other people's money. By subsidizing the unprofitable, government acts against the minds and interests of free men. In the case of AMTRAK, for example, the government has forced the taxpayers to buy billions of Dollars worth of passenger rail service which their lack of patronage already indicated they didn't want." (p. 76-77)

Mr. Matthews' citation of differing BTU energy efficiencies between trains and planes, which he employs to support his claims regarding environmental payoffs, overlooks large dynamic economic considerations. If one were not to consider factors such as speed, accessibility, comfort and economic efficiency in a calculation of the relative benefits of various modes of transport, we would be discussing the merits of a tax-funded horse and buggy route from Nashua to Lowell. This kind of Luddite philosophy is, hopefully, only in vogue with certain petuli-wearing hippies and college professors pushing for more federal control of the economy under the pretense of "saving the ecology." From the rest of society, one might hope for more sensible, ethical, and constitutional decision making. Let's leave the military defense of the nation up to the feds, drop the pretense about the environment, and allow private enterprise to risk its *own* capital on ventures such as passenger trains.

The free market is the only system that recognizes the supremacy of the individual as a human being. Moral philosophy and economics cannot be separated. "Social justice" used in the sense of a "value-free" society is a myth. Its champions beget only misery and ignorance for the people.

PHG
March, 1991

"Land Ho!"
March, 2005

New Hampshire is called the "Live Free or Die" state. It has garnered such a reputation as a bastion of freedom that the "Porcupine" members of the Free State Project selected it as the place to which they would like to relocate in order to live more independently and more productively.

Unfortunately, the very principles that have helped keep the New Hampshire government small, and that have helped keep its impact on the economy to a minimum relative to the states around it, have created a market environment that attracts immigrants who do not understand or appreciate the philosophy that fosters such prosperity. Thus, in a place that once reflected General John Stark's Revolution-era motto, "Live Free or Die", the population that has just swelled to over 1.3 million seems more interested in the idea of living off of someone else than in living free.

As the "Porcupines" contemplate relocating to their chosen redoubt, they may want to consider this political reality, and study a case in point.

This spring, towns and cities all across New Hampshire had on their ballots what are called "open space" initiatives. These ballot questions, infused with that peculiar Baby-boomer desire to make everything in society look like a photo from an LL Bean catalogue, asked citizens to support the proposition of floating enormous bonds, which would eventually be paid back with tax money. The bonds, in turn, would be used to buy select properties, "protecting" them from residential development.

As strange as it may seem, the ostensible rationale offered by the well-organized proponents of these initiatives is that they will actually *save* taxpayers money in the long run. How? By buying land and preventing residential development, the sages of "open space" are stopping more families from moving to town. This restricts the growth of the school system, which is the largest portion of any budget in any New Hampshire municipality, sometimes comprising nearly 80% of the overall tax burden. By preventing land from housing more children, the taxpayers are, theoretically, protected in the long run. In other words, we must promise tax money to issue government bonds in order to save citizens from being taxed even more for government services.

Supposedly, the purchase of pristine tracts of New Hampshire woodland and fields will decrease the pressures placed on many residents who cannot afford their property taxes. Older people, who no longer have children in school, are often depicted as the most notable beneficiaries. In twenty-five New Hampshire communities between 2004 and 2005, some $26 million in taxpayer money was promised in order to sell bonds with which to purchase "open space", all under the guise of "helping save" taxpayers' money.

My town of Amherst is no exception.

In a typical gathering organized in the basement of a local church, the members of our "Open Space Advisory Committee" -- which, it was my masochistic pleasure to discover, had been appointed by our own town Selectmen -- presented their arguments for taking from me in order to protect me.

There were posters and fliers, a Powerpoint presentation, and numerous speakers, all selected for their unique ability to espouse the eventual seizure of $5.5 million for the purpose of taking land out of the hands of residential developers, thus keeping our taxes low.

Of course, the ethical principle of seizing money from someone against his will, and the economic complications that arise from deciding *for* someone how best he should use his money, were not discussed. What was stressed was the tax benefit of keeping "open space" free of residential development, with the added sentiment that government ownership of pristine lands allowed our town to retain its "rustic" flavor and visual beauty.

Unfortunately, the proponents did not even have an economic argument with which to convince voters to support their initiative. A person inquisitive about the committee's claim might want to know how much money is, on average, paid into the tax system by a home owner during the time his children are in school and after they are finished. This would give interested parties an idea of whether residential home development is a net gain or a net expense to the town. But when asked if anyone on the committee had an estimate regarding how long home-owners held on to their homes after their children left school, the head of the committee replied, "That would probably be a good thing to know."

Probably.

The proponents also seemed blissfully unaware of another important consideration. Their own Powerpoint presentation indicated that the use of land which is "least burdensome" to the government is commercial use.

Commercial utilization brings in taxes, while demanding few "services" like schools and recreation activities run by the government. Commercial property is -- shocker of all shockers -- actually a *benefit* to the tax base!

This was a point I thought deserved emphasizing, and so I brought it up. "Since," I explained, "your presentation shows that the most beneficial use of land for a town's tax purposes is to allow it to be developed commercially, and we are supposedly here to buy land in order to save taxpayers money, then why aren't we here discussing a $5.5 million bond to buy property and insure that it is developed commercially?"

There were some blank faces, so I went on.

"The very fact that we *aren't* here discussing purchasing land for commercial development, which would have the greatest beneficial impact on tax rates, indicates that this meeting has nothing to do with trying to save taxpayer money. The organizers cannot even support their claims that holding "open space" really *would* decrease taxes, because they do not have enough data regarding how long people pay into the tax system after their children may have left the schools. This meeting is clearly not about saving tax money. It is about taxing our neighbors in order to keep land looking the way you want it to look; it is about taxing your neighbor to pay for something you think is pretty. And before you vote, you need to ask yourselves, would you really take your neighbor's money against his will in order to buy something you think is pretty?"

In an instant, I was greeted with sharp looks, and bold answers in the affirmative.

"Absolutely," said one man.

"Darn right," proclaimed another as he pursed his brow at me.

I left the meeting wondering what had happened to New Hampshire. Two weeks later, by a margin of 3 percent, the supporters of the $5.5 million bond secured their victory, and the supposed protection of all our wallets.

It may seem odd, but I find it difficult to thank the "open space" proponents for their guidance in leading my own life. Perhaps I, and others like me who opposed the initiative, were simply too ignorant to see the wisdom of increasing taxes now to keep taxes low in the future. Perhaps we just spend too much time thinking of other arbitrary government restrictions on property-owners. Things like zoning ordinances and building permits and eminent domain must capture too much of our attention to have allowed us to contemplate this clearly beneficial move towards a brighter community future.

Of course, it could be that they were wrong, and we in the minority were right, but that's irrelevant as far as democracy is concerned, and the leftists do tell me America was founded as a democracy, not a constitutional republic.

New Hampshire used to be a place where individual rights were respected, where economic freedom walked hand in hand with political freedom. Today, it is turning into an egalitarian wonderland, where aging hippies tell their neighbors they know better how to spend their neighbors' money, and where private attempts to preserve "open space" are forgone in favor of tax initiatives enacted for the "public good".

Frederic Bastiat, the French economic-political philosopher who spent much of his life opposing the socialistic bromides promulgated by his 19th Century countrymen, is famous for having garnered many keen insights into the workings of the state. Among his trenchant observations was one that still bothers many leftists, perhaps because it is so appallingly true.

"The state," he noted, "is that great fiction by which everyone seeks to live at the expense of everyone else."

Here is a message to the courageous members of the Free State Project:

Welcome to your new home, where the motto used to be "Live Free or Die".

We are trying to figure out whether that phrase still applies.

The trouble with being a good sport
is that you have to lose to prove it.

PHG
1976

"Second Rate"
Jan. 24, 2002

I hang my head in shame.

The other day I was talking to one of my friends -- well, *former* friends -- and he told me that he just couldn't be associated with me any longer.

Much to my eternal chagrin, he explained why.

"You're second rate, dude. You've got those second rate sports facilities! How can I hang out with a loser like you? They're even laughing at you in a down-trodden city like Berlin!"

Oh, the ignominy. The utter, total dishonor.

"They ought to have non-profit ads featuring all those derelict Amherst kids playing stick ball with broom handles and jagged rocks! What could you possibly be thinking over there? How could you let this happen? For twenty-five cents a day, could I sponsor somebody, maybe get a picture?"

He's right, of course. How could I have missed it. Thankfully, Bill Donovan, speaking for the Amherst Recreation Commission on January 3, pointed it out himself when proposing to the Coop School Board that a $1.5 million domed sports facility be built in Amherst.

Not only did Mr. Donovan claim that we had "second class arrangements", he explained that the community thinks recreation sports is an important part of growing, learning and being healthy and happy.

Perhaps we could pause for a moment to delve into a basic philosophical and historical question.

In the tradition of the American philosophical underpinnings, legitimate governments are formed to protect our lives and property from encroachments and coercion by others. The idea stems from John Locke's articulation of Natural Rights, which stipulates that rights are *negative*. You have a right *from* things, not *to* things. You have a right to be left alone by me, and I have a reciprocal right to be left alone by you. We form the government to uphold that principle, to protect us from each other, and from others who would harm us or our property (in this case that includes the fruits of our labor). When it begins to do that which we could criminally do to each other, government becomes illegitimate.

Many people misunderstand the concept of "rights", which is why we have seen politicians and interest groups clamoring for health care, food, education and other services to be paid for by "government", i.e. individuals being taxed against their will for supposedly altruistic motives. The problem is that the logic chain is never finished when consideration is given to such proposals. If one has a right to health care, or food, or education, if one can forcibly take the productive labor of his neighbor to pay for his other neighbor's medical care, or education, or food, then why not apply this standard of rights to the actual providers of the services themselves? If we can take the fruits of our neighbor's labor equaling many hours of his day, why not just cut out the middle man and enslave all the teachers, or doctors, or farmers for that amount of time? The answer to such an absurd proposition is clear. If one becomes obligated by the government to take *positive* action on behalf of another, he is a vassal, a slave, at the mercy of government whim. Many people argue that certain things are necessary, therefore we have a right to them. Strictly speaking this is incorrect. Need does not equate to right when one forces another to provide something. Education is necessary, but no one would ever propose that we enslave teachers and make them teach. By the same token, one cannot legitimately seize the property or revenue of another for something seen as "necessary". Education was provided for in most states by *private* funding until the mid-1800's. It was necessary to educate children, but people at that time realized it did not equate to a right.

When people embrace the concept of "positive" rights, it is irrelevant whether or not a government takes the form of a dictatorship, an oligarchy, or a democratic majority. It will have license to do whatever it sees fit. The Founders understood this, and repeatedly warned against the tyranny of the majority. When rights are viewed as "positive", then it only depends on majority sentiment in order for a democracy to become tyrannical. James Madison would have been the first to say that altruism is no excuse for the tyranny of the majority.

So, just where in the history of our culture, in the clear tradition of Natural Rights, did it become an axiom that governments are formed to help individuals *recreate*?!

One need not answer such an absurd question. Likewise, one need not try to justify such a proposition by claiming "the town thinks it's important".

I really like punk rock. If I lived in a town with a lot of other punk aficionados, enough to comprise a slight majority, would it then be legitimate to say my views are representative of all, and proclaim that "the town thinks it's important for us to have a mosh pit on the village green, so everyone will now pay for it. And, by the way, if you don't, you'll be seen as 'unneighborly'"?

Of course not.

Propositions such as the "dome" fall into just this kind of majoritarian coercion, and they are illegitimate. One might wonder why, if the individuals behind this public project believe there is such a strong demand for it, they don't attempt to build it privately, without coercing their neighbors to pay under the guise of "community spirit". If they are going to force others to give up tax money, and even attempt to get people to pay from elsewhere by garnering state funds (an idea Fran Harrow reportedly mentioned as prerequisite in the meeting), are they indicating that such a proposal would not fly if tried privately?

If so, how great can the need truly be?

Additionally, how would the management of a place such as Hampshire Hills (which *has* ventured out privately and been successful at providing "recreation" facilities for a fee to only those people who want them) feel knowing that their direct competition for certain customers was a tax-funded dome?

There is nothing neighborly about taking one's neighbor's money against his will, and telling him he lives in a "community" doesn't make it any more justified.

"Taking Credit Where Credit is Not Due"
January, 2005

On January 3, 2005, President George W. Bush held a news conference to discuss the federal government's response to the awesome and terrible destruction caused by the natural disasters in South Asia. When he approached his podium, he was flanked by two stoic and serious men.

"The greatest source of our generosity is not our government," the President explained to the reporters before him, "it's the good heart of the American people.... To draw even greater amounts of private donations, I have asked two of America's most distinguished private citizens to head a nation-wide charitable fundraising effort."

Those two men -- the men beside him -- were familiar.

They were, in fact, his predecessors in the Oval Office: his father, George H. W. Bush, and the forty-second President of the United States, Bill Clinton.

The current President proceeded to tell his audience that the two former Commanders-in-Chief would be heading a special effort to encourage donations to private charities that would assist the "relief efforts" in South Asia.

To a person who appreciates the efforts of private philanthropists, President Bush's choices of two politicians to head an effort to promote American charity might have rung a very sour note.

Why, one was inspired to consider, would the President of the United States elect to place two individuals whose careers have barely touched the private sector to head-up an initiative designed to promote American philanthropy for South Asia?

The reason is that the Bush Administration wants to make the United States look good in the eyes of others around the world. The "Compassionate Conservative" President Bush has not only decided to do this by donating 350 million in US tax dollars to the governments and people of places like Sri Lanka, Thailand, Indonesia, and east Africa, he has decided to co-opt the money donated by *individuals* and use it for a massive public relations scheme to bolster the image of the US government.

There can be no denying the fact that Bush's selection of two of the most recognizable, most well-known American political figures took place at the expense of many other highly qualified people. Ranging from actors, to singers, to entrepreneurs, there is a panoply of high-profile individuals to whom Mr. Bush could have turned. But those individuals are not associated with high American political office, those individuals are only connected to private enterprise. Thus, in what seems an opportunistic attempt to do not only what the politicians believe is "right", but also to look good around the world while doing it, Bush has opted to put a government mask on private charity. The participants of the free market, though their money will be collected, will not be seen by those who are helped.

The government of the United States will take the credit around the world.

Of course, this is nothing new. In an abstract way, the US government has been taking credit for private international aid since the close of World War Two. When the federal Marshall Plan showered $1.7 billion in loans and direct aid on West Europe, it was heralded as a profound success. There was little mention that the money was expropriated from the citizens of America for an entirely unconstitutional program, and that the system actually worked to retard economic growth in the area.[24] It became the template for a continuous line of bureaucratic international aid plans over the decades that followed, and has been instrumental in creating a false impression in the minds of many Americans that if international help is needed, it must be done through the "mighty" power of government.

When studying President Bush's plan to plaster a government façade over the structure of private aid in 2005, one is driven to consider whether it is more unctuous for federal politicians to worm their way into this last refuge of private philanthropy, or to continue to pursue their own so-called "charity" with tax dollars that are not supposed to be theirs to spend.

The record of government-funded foreign aid efforts is abysmal. As noted by James Bovard, the World Bank has funded and helped prop-up the

---

[24] Economist Tyler Cowen, in his work entitled "The Marshall Plan: Myths and Realities", published in *US Aid to the Developing World* (Washington, DC: The Heritage Foundation, 1985, Doug Bandow, Editor) explained that the Marshall Plan stipulated that for every US Dollar offered to a European nation, that nation had to internally secure its own equivalent and spend it on public works. This not only served to redirect the flow of useable capital from the US to politically selected European projects, it pulled capital out of the damaged European markets and moved it to those same politically favored projects. This in no way can be defined as a great leap forward in economic progress.

repressive governments of Tanzania, Vietnam, Indonesia, and Ethiopia, to name but a few. It has seen massive defaults on below-market rate loans, supported backwards economic policies, funded agricultural devastation, and increased the dominance of leftist politicians throughout Africa.[25]

Seemingly few people wonder why this government-funded lending institution's practices lead to such profound failure. In fact, even as George Bush hatched his plan to subvert the image of private charity in the United States, television pundits were pushing for more government money. On January 2, 2005, ABC's George Stephanopoulis asked James Wolfensohn, president of the World Bank, if the victims of the Asian Tsunami would receive "billions" of Dollars. He was told that the response from this wonderful philanthropic institution would be in the "many billions".

A person unaccustomed to challenging the paradigm of government-funded aid packages might wonder why some observers bristle so strongly at this mass push for government involvement. He may wonder why people speak out against former Presidents heading-up private charity initiatives.

The reasons are two-fold. First, there is the ethical dilemma. Government aid, be it direct financial aid, or below-market loans through quasi-governmental entities like the World Bank, can only exist at the expense of private citizens. These citizens either have their tax money taken from them based on the will of the majority in their respective controlling governments, or see tax-payer backed loans handed out to risky and oppressive regimes at rates that would undercut competitors in the free market. Either way, personal liberty is decreased.

The second reason is the practical, economic effect of government disaster relief.

There is no way that government aid can help rebuild a devastated economy as efficiently or as fast as private enterprise. The source of this truism is simple: the profit motive works to channel resources where they will not only be most efficiently spent, but also best improve the lives of those involved.

For example, if a talented landscaper on a devastated island were interested in getting disaster relief funds that would help him buy more heavy

---

[25] James Bovard, "The World Bank and the Impoverishment of Nations", in *Perpetuating Poverty: The World Bank, the IMF, and the Developing World*, Doug Bandow, Editor, (Washington, DC, The Cato Institute, 1994) pp. 59-65.

equipment and hire new employees for rebuilding projects, he might be in competition with a landscaper of less talent. (This second landscaper may or may not be politically connected, that is irrelevant to this exercise. But it deserves noting that often it is the politically connected who receive the bulk of contracts for these types of projects when they are funded through political channels. The favors are later returned during election time.) In a market-driven economy, landscapers A and B would have to approach a bank for a loan. The banker would distinguish between the two, look at their work records, and, looking for the greatest possibility of repayment with interest, decide to whom it was willing to lend its money. This analysis of the prospects of repayment would include a study of the business proposals of the landscapers. Consider that landscaper A could show the bank that he could secure potential clients such as hotels, because he had a reputation as a fast, efficient and trustworthy worker; he only needs more equipment to expand his business. Consider that landscaper B could not lay claim to such a reputation. It is clear that the bank would confidently lend to person A rather than person B, and in this way, it is most likely that the work will be done faster, and more efficiently, providing an improvement in life not only for the landscaper, but for the bankers, the hotel owners, and their customers.

Likewise, the hotel owners themselves would be interested in showing potential lenders that they would efficiently utilize any money lent to them in order to hire a landscaper. Again, the tendency in the private market is for capital to be directed by interested participants towards the most efficient and productive use, and that direction is dependent upon the freedom of the participants to discriminate and use their own judgment.

The profit incentive, the freedom to succeed or fail, is what drives the entire system of progress.

There is no profit incentive in government. Government not only perpetuates sloth, it encourages it by rewarding the most inefficient programs and workers with even more money. To hear media figures push for more government spending in devastated areas is to hear the siren call of bureaucracy, a chorus of the economically ignorant propping up the economically inefficient.[26]

To hear George Bush confidently announce the appointment of two politicians to head-up what would otherwise be a private charity initiative is to hear a member of the political class who thirsts for the US government to be seen in a better light. His actions not only insult the sources of the charitable donations, they can potentially reduce one of the rewards some philanthropists derive from making donations in the first place. While many volunteers and philanthropists donate their time and money due to the sheer satisfaction they derive from helping another person, there are those who also enjoy the satisfaction of being recognized by their neighbors for their work. This is not something that needs to be judged. It merely needs to be considered when looking at two former Presidents who will now be the faces of America's charitable collection effort. George H. W. Bush and Bill Clinton don't need to be recognized any more than they have been in their roles as Commanders-in-Chief.

It is the players in the free market, who risked their own capital, and now freely donate it to causes in which they believe, who ought to be seen around the world.

One does not help bolster the image of the United States by taking credit where credit is not due.

---

[26] To be fair, it must be noted that even private charity is not as efficient at producing a desired outcome as private enterprise. The profit incentive drives private enterprise to work faster and better, to supply more products and more opportunities than even private charity. However, private charity performs better than government "charity" due to numerous factors. First, there is no "public choice" feedback, in which political connections direct money to inefficient recipients in return for later support in elections. Second, the personal connection at the heart of private charity cannot be reproduced by government. Many of America's civic organizations were started because neighbors wanted to help neighbors in emergencies. Those who were assisted had a great incentive to pay back the people who helped them, and the recipients often helped others later. The personal contact of such neighborly charity cannot be matched by any government bureau.

"Doing Good Means Doing Nothing"
January 16, 2002

One of the most satisfying aspects of the manner in which the Bush administration has conducted itself over the past few months has been the "hands-off" approach it has taken towards monetary intervention. Much to the chagrin of liberals cut from the cloth of people such as Bill Clinton and Robert Rubin, the Bush team has seen fit to let the market operate without assuming the conceit that it can better run the economy than individual investors controlling their own money.

Such intervention consistently leads to greater risk and volatility in the future. As many economists know, government-backed money rarely carries the attendant demands for reform and fiscal responsibility that private investment possesses. As with the S&L Crisis of the late Eighties -- when an increase in government insurance of loans up to $100,000 was allowed by Congress -- further government investment in Argentinean debt or insolvent corporations such as Enron would both reward mismanagement, and promote more of it.

But many leftist commentators are unwilling to admit this fundamental fact. Case in point: Washington Post columnist David Ignatius, who, in a syndicated column published in the *Manchester Union Leader* (NH) on January 15, claims that such policies should not become the norm.

While offering tepid praise for the Bush administration's handling of both Argentina and Enron, admitting that "hands-off" was the proper approach, Ignatius claims that such successes are not the norm. Apparently, they are exceptions that ought to be ignored. They are economic curiosities, irrelevant in a lengthy national debate that must, in the minds of the left, conclude with the success of socialist ideology.

To a writer such as Ignatius, it is unacceptable to allow people to fail. But freedom and prosperity require us to have the freedom to do just that. Society cannot progress unless people have the ability to fail, and if that risk is removed, if failures are covered up, or assuaged with other peoples' money, then productivity is harmed, progress is retarded, and eventual failure is made much, much worse.

But Ignatius seems ignorant of these historical facts. Instead, he compares Bush with Bill Clinton, who was involved in "aggressive financial intervention". According to Ignatius, a hands-off policy looks "misguided", especially in the light of a looming financial crisis in Japan, and the assistance we should have been providing to other nations to help stave off international terrorism.

Ignatius actually has the temerity to write: "The Bush administration paradox is that it is wildly interventionist in its foreign military policy but almost passive in international economic policy. That imbalance is a mistake."

It may be difficult for us to fully grasp the degree of perception Mr. Ignatius exhibits when portraying US efforts in Afghanistan as "interventionist". It certainly is comforting to know that military operations conducted to defend and protect the citizens of the United States against acts of war on our own shores can be equated to the limp-wristed, utopian "nation-building" exercises of Bill Clinton that had no bearing on US national security whatsoever. It's reassuring that a perceptive mind such as Mr. Ignatius' can find no distinction between our battle against Al Queda and our wallow in the Balkans, because people such as we are apparently not equipped to handle such feats of mental legerdemain.

We can feel comfort in the fact that Philosopher Kings such as Mr. Ignatius also want to use our money to subsidize international economies. Given his lofty position to perceive Bush's operations in Afghanistan as "interventionism", one must look seriously at his call for more international monetary aid to failing nation-states.

As he says: "One lesson of the war against terrorism is that the United States needs to be involved in the welfare of ordinary people around the world -- sharing the fruits of the global economy..."

Are we to assume that all the financial aid we have already given to nations around the globe, including Afghanistan, all the humanitarian and military aid, all the diplomatic and technical assistance, has not been sufficient to make us look good in the eyes of our "international neighbors"? Are we victims of international terrorism because we haven't "cared" enough?

Despite the time he spent writing his piece, perhaps Mr. Ignatius might want to clarify his statement.

In addition, he might want to consider that there can be no such thing as a "global economy" unless everyone participates in its business. Reckless government handouts do not foster, and have never fostered, such business. To believe otherwise is to mischaracterize as a "global economy" an *American* economy being preyed upon by a world of parasites.

**Macroeconomics
Part Three:
Federal and State Regulation –
Suppressing Economic Growth and Freedom**

> What monstrous mischief can be caused by hoodwinked innocents who think they are improving the lot of mankind, when, instead, they are preparing it for the horror chambers of a madhouse!
>
> **PHG**
> **March, 1984**

"Being Burned by Ethanol"
May 3, 2007

It is nearly axiomatic that anything Cuban "President" Fidel Castro says will be false, incorrect, misleading and downright pernicious. It's not as if the bearded relic from the Cold War – who seems to have replaced his traditional olive military clothing for a more sedate sweat suit look – has a stellar record for veracity or economic punditry. But recently, el Presidente's grumblings have been worth hearing, not because they are precisely right, but because they are at least on the right track.

At the end of March, 2007, Castro spoke out with great fire and resentment about the attempt by the Bush Administration and Congress to increase ethanol usage in the United States.

"More than 3 billion people in the world are being condemned to a premature death from hunger and thirst," he said in a March 29 Op-ed published in *Granma*, the official Cuban Communist Party newspaper.

Coming from a man responsible for the torture, death and exile of millions, these humanitarian claims are more than a bit hypocritical. But despite the source, and the over-blown nature of the rhetoric, there is a barely discernable ring of truth to his words.

Ethanol is, of course, derived from the fermentation of certain carbohydrate-rich plants such as sugar cane, wood pulp, sugar beets, and -- as shocking as it seems – *corn*. And since politicians in Washington, DC, have taken it upon themselves to interfere in not only the energy markets, but pretty much *every* market, for decades, they recently have shown no qualms in forcing consumers to use more ethanol in their automobiles.

As H. Josef Hebert, of the Associated Press, reported on May 1, "There is an ethanol juggernaut moving through Congress that will call for a sevenfold increase in biofuels production -- almost all of it ethanol -- over the next 15 years."

This push includes the passage on May 2, by a vote of 20-3 in the Senate Energy and Natural Resources Committee, of a bill that would require 36 billion gallons of "renewable fuel" use by 2022. It includes a proposal by House Speaker Nancy Pelosi (D, CA) to have an "energy security" bill ready for a vote by the summer, just in time to feed off of anger over high fuel prices, and just in time to promote ethanol even more. The push encompasses loan guarantees, tax breaks, and subsidies for the building of cellulose-based ethanol plants in the US, much like a 2002 law called the Renewable Energy Systems and Energy Efficiency Improvements Program that wasted $73 million through grants and loans to farmers to buy renewable energy systems. And finally, it piles all of this on top of a requirement passed two years ago making oil refiners double the amount of ethanol in their gas products, from 4 to 7.5 billion gallons.

So much for the free market.

Of course, such a comment could come off appearing glib, or merely colorful – a punctuating sentence with little more than rhythmic literary value. But it is of far greater significance, for the interference by politicians in the market for fuel has real world impact, and Fidel Castro, of all people, understands.

The free market in general encompasses every market sector in particular. It represents the dynamic flow of usable capital, time, natural resources, skills, preferences and opportunities each participant utilizes in order to fulfill his needs. Only the individual can make the proper judgments about these factors, and when he participates in any market sector specifically, he helps establish a price system that imparts this information to other participants of not only his sector, but others as well. As a result, the personal needs of market participants drive capital, time, skills, and other resources to their most productive uses, maximizing human effort in all sectors, and minimizing waste.

But by imposing their will on participants in the market for fuel, politicians not only commit the unethical act of coercion, they intercede in, and interfere with, the proper flow of usable capital in all sectors of the market.

As strange as it appears, and as insincere as it is, Castro's statement about starvation and thirst points this out.

US government requirements for increased ethanol use have already caused an increased demand, and thus higher prices, for corn, and the trend will only become worse as more government strictures interfere with the market. These higher prices have devastating effects on people living on the margins. In Mexico, the cost of corn tortillas has more than doubled in the past year. Between August 2006 and December 2006, anticipation of increased demand for corn drove prices from $2.09 per bushel to $3.01

per bushel, making it more difficult for the impoverished to afford the basic foodstuff upon which they rely.

But this unnatural increase in costs is not isolated to corn. Government intervention in one sector has effects on all. For example, the sharp, artificially increased demand for corn, and its relative increase in value to farmers, has prompted, and will continue to prompt, those farmers to shift acreage accordingly. As most economists recognize, but few politicians seem to consider, this rapid, non-market driven shift in acreage has caused reallocation of resources *away* from other produce and towards corn. Such shifts mean rapid changes in the supplies of these other forms of produce, and, as a result, higher prices. According to Keith Collins, Chief Economist at the US Department of Agriculture, "Looking ahead to the 2007 crop of corn, it is quite likely, based on current ethanol plant construction, that corn used in ethanol production will rise by more than 1 billion bushels from the 2.16 billion bushels of the 2006 corn crop used for ethanol. Use of 1 billion (additional) acres, at a trend yield of 152 bushels per acre, would require an additional 6.5 million acres of corn."[27]

This can mean only higher prices for people interested in buying not only corn, but also other forms of produce.

"With ethanol fueling a push for more corn acres, major crop prices are generally expected to be higher over the next couple of years than in the past," Collins told a Senate Committee in January. "Soybeans, while facing competition from ethanol feed co-products… are still likely to face higher prices over time, as lower expected soybean acreage offsets the lower soybean meal demand, and soybean oil is demanded for biodiesel production."

Then, of course, there are all those products which rely on corn for their creation. With a non-market player intervening in the proper flow of capital, prices for everything from cereal, to sodas sweetened with corn syrup, to poultry and pork must increase in cost. Since the passage of the 2005 energy bill requiring an increase of ethanol production to 7.5 billion gallons, the cost of poultry alone has increased forty percent.

As Collins told the Senate, "Livestock and poultry profitability declines under higher corn feeding costs. For example, for hogs, which are heavily

---

[27] Testimony provided to the US Senate Committee on Agriculture, Nutrition and Forestry (without which our nation would self-destruct, of course). January 10, 2007. Available at: http://www.usda.gov/oce/newsroom/congressional_testimony/Collins_011007.pdf

dependent on corn… a $1 per bushel increase in the price of corn would raise the price of producing hogs by about $6 per Cwt ("Hundred Weight")."[28]

These are all costs that will be passed on to the consumer, and will not only make it more difficult for the poor to afford their basic foodstuffs, but will also decrease the capital that would normally be available to purchase other products, thus retarding the pace of economic growth, and harming all our lives. The free market encompasses all sectors, and shifting capital to one means shifting capital away from others.

These economic realities merely compound the problems inherent in the use of ethanol as a fuel itself. As has been noted by Edmund Contoski, in his book "Makers and Takers", corn-based ethanol is still a net energy *loser*.

"The energy needed for growing the corn (for farm machinery, fertilizers and pesticides) and distilling the alcohol is more than you get from burning the ethanol that is produced,"[29] he explains.

This means that not only is the government push for ethanol increasing the costs of raising produce, it is indirectly increasing the price of the fuel required to ship that produce, which harms the economy once more.

And there are other drawbacks. Ethanol is not compatible with colder temperatures. This makes it virtually impossible to run through pipelines, and necessitates shipment by truck or train, which increases costs even more. Upon arrival, the ethanol can only be used above certain temperatures, for if it is cool, the aerosolized particles left over from ethanol combustion stubbornly remain at lower atmospheric levels, causing terrible smog. It was for this reason that politicians from California – particularly Los Angeles -- fought the US government over required ethanol content during the winter months.

Supporters of the Congressional and Presidential pushes to force us to use more ethanol seem oblivious to these scientific and economic realities. They bandy about claims that we need to "help the environment", and "get off of foreign oil".

Meanwhile, they force on us higher costs of living that retard our ability to better our lives, a fuel that creates smog in winter and takes more energy to make than it offers upon utilization, and a series of unconstitutional

---

[28] A Hundred Weight is equal to 100 pounds.
[29] Contoski, Edmund. *Makers and Takers*, (Minneapolis, Minnesota, American Liberty Publishers, 1997) p. 198.

mandates on oil companies that the Founding Fathers would have protested as vociferously as possible. How much better off we would be if they lifted their smothering hands from the backs of these companies, allowed them to participate in the market according to the demands of the consumers, allowed them to explore, drill for, and refine oil without stifling regulations, and set us free to buy what we want based on our preferences and needs…

Of course, that kind of thinking is a pipedream, about as realistic as expecting Fidel Castro to ever be on the right track about economics again.

"Big, Fat Lies"
July, 2004

    It seems perennial. Every season, the mass media find ways to set off the internal alarm bells of Americans about something to do with their health. Usually, the barrage comes in the form of dire warnings about peoples' waistlines. In the fall, we hear pleas from television personalities to watch our caloric intake, because, after all, the seasons are changing, and we may not get out and about as much. In the winter, we are greeted with stern warnings about eating too much during the holidays. In the spring, flash computer pop-ups for diet plans dazzle our eyes, telling us we can lose that extra winter weight, and in the summer, we are told that we can still fit into our favorite beach wear if only we cut back on fattening foods. All the while, we are advised that America is experiencing an "Obesity Epidemic", as if it is some sort of contagious disease.

    In contemporary US culture, the mass media and government bureaucrats have teamed up to create one of the most lucrative symbiotic relationships since Adam Smith first decried mercantilism in 1776. Government "officials" tell us that Americans are becoming obese at an alarming rate; they appear on network news programs warning of the health consequences of being overweight. Politicians talk about taxing fattening foods to stop us from harming ourselves. Meanwhile, morning news programs and pop-culture magazines promulgate the claims, and back them with anecdotes, personal stories, and offers for weight loss products that can change one's life.

    Perhaps nowhere was this more in evidence than on ABC in June. For an entire week, ABC's "World News Tonight", and "Nightline" devoted as much attention as possible to the terrible trend towards morbid obesity in America. Culminating over a year of government warnings that began in January of 2003[30], the floridly titled, "Critical Condition: America's Obesity Crisis" criticized fast food restaurants, advertisers, private insurance companies, employers and, of course, free will. At the same time, the features sang the praises of such ideas as taxing fattening foods, and using government programs to combat this pressing emergency.

---

[30] US Surgeon General Richard Carmona announced in January of 2003 that obesity was a public health risk akin to a weapon of mass destruction .

The high point came on June 2, when correspondent Michelle Martin appeared on "Nightline" to sum up the entire ABC perspective.

Introduced by the urbane and restrained man of journalistic ethics, Ted Koppel, the program began with a derogatory cut on talk radio, where, Mr. Koppel said, he enjoyed "listening to the verbal agility of the host and the absolute certainty with which he plunges into areas about which he clearly knows nothing." This implied that Mr. Koppel knew something the talk host did not, which is clearly what we ought to assume, since Mr. Koppel is, after all, Mr. Koppel.

He went on:

> "Anyway, I gather that my friend, the radio host, was put out by the notion that obesity might be the responsibility of anyone other than the obese person… This was one of those classic rants about freedom and responsibility. We are all free, in other words, to eat whatever we want. And, if we become grossly overweight, it is our own responsibility and nobody else's… Bluntly stated, if you're fat, it's your own damn fault. There is some truth to that. But if, for example, you are poor, live in the inner city, and have no transportation of your own, you are significantly more likely to be obese, than if you are well-off, drive your own car and live in the suburbs. And while education does make a difference, it's not the key factor. Take a look at what 'Nightline' producer Marie Nelson and correspondent Michel Martin found."

The core of the ABC argument was thus stylishly presented, or, to be more precise, it was deftly implied. According to Ted Koppel, Marie Nelson, Michel Martin and "Nightline", true "thinking people" know that obesity is not one's own fault, it's the fault of society. It's almost as if we are being told, "watch the show, and learn!"

Well, let's study the major portions of the presentation…

"The Centers for Disease Control estimates that one out of four adults with incomes below the poverty level is obese," reports Martin in the "Nightline" piece. "The correlation is especially true for women. Those with incomes below the poverty level are more than twice as likely to be obese as women with the highest incomes."

Her opening thesis is stated more generally and more overtly by one of her interview subjects, Dr. Adam Drunowski, of the University of Washington. An outspoken proponent of economic determinism for obesity, Drunowski claims quite defiantly, "Well, some people say that obesity is a result of a low metabolism. I say it is really the result of low wages."

Which means a lot when you think about it... When you think about it the way ABC and Dr. Drunowski would prefer.

In their view, obesity is an indictment of capitalism, the result of an out of control system which caters to the "haves" and neglects the "have-nots". According to Martin, Drunowski, and others who support the belief that higher rates of obesity in the inner cities are not just correlated to, but *caused by* poverty, the free market system which has brought the United States such plenty is rigged against the poor. While it provides unlimited nutritional choices to those who live in the suburbs, drive cars, and can make it to large supermarkets, it offers only junk and fast food to those who need nutritious meals the most, and who can't get outside the city.

To illustrate her point, Martin joins a Detroit resident named George Bogen, a man who weighs over 485 pounds, and who has taken steps to lose weight. One such step is to walk home from work. Unfortunately, according to Martin, his poor environment is bereft of affordable "good" food, and is "a gauntlet of fast-food restaurants and convenience stores." Thus, the noble Bogen is left "on his own" to try to get past the McDonalds and chain stores that call like Sirens to him on his odyssey. This, clearly, is a state of affairs which not only indicts capitalism, the system that put these trashy food places in his way, but also those who would try to keep government small, and not give him help trying to combat the psychic torture of having to walk past such enticing sites. Letting a local doctor speak for her, Martin implies that Bogen is at a disadvantage because government "insurers" will not reimburse for obesity-related counseling.

And so, with a few more flourishes about people "dying from obesity", and attacks on the lack of availability of "healthy food" at corner stores, Martin ends her piece by calling on Dr. Kimberly Dawn-Wisdom, Michigan Surgeon General. According to Dawn-Wisdom, one way to help alleviate the problem would be to:

"Provide affordable fruits and vegetables... And help individuals understand and empower them to know how to cook these vegetables, how to prepare them, how to serve them regularly."

And there you have it. What the ignorant radio host who believed in free will didn't understand was that capitalism has set up so many roadblocks to good nutrition in the inner cities that people simply cannot get good food, and are forced to become obese. Additionally, this daft talk host had better wake up to the fact that we need taxpayer funded fruit and vegetable programs, and obesity counseling to rectify the problem that capitalism has caused! Yes, the "Nightline" crew knows more than the talk host. And now we know as well.

There are, unfortunately, a few holes in this line of reasoning. Besides the fact that the government classification of "obese" could apply to people such as Russell Crowe and George Clooney, the very scientific claims about obesity being tremendously life-threatening are also in dispute. According to *The Guardian*, a 1996 project at Cornell University gathered data from dozens of previous Body Mass Index (BMI) studies "involving a total of more than 600,000 subjects with up to a 30-year follow-up."

According to the macro study: "Among non-smoking white men, the lowest mortality rate was found among those with a BMI between 23 and 29, which means that a large majority of the men who lived longest were 'overweight' according to government guidelines." When looking at non-smoking white women, "The conclusions were even more striking. The BMI range correlating with the lowest mortality rate was extremely broad, from around 18 to 32, meaning a woman of average height could weigh anywhere within an 80-pound range without seeing any statistically significant change in her risk of premature death."[31]

Other statistics would seem to buttress these conclusions. While the "obesity" rate as characterized by government spokesmen has been increasing dramatically, the average life expectancy has done nothing but increase as well. In May of 2004, the Centers for Disease Control reported that life expectancy had risen from 75.2 years in 1990, to 77.4 years in 2002. All of this while people in the inner city were running the gauntlet of fast food and corner stores, and the federal government looked the other way when it came to providing obesity counseling for the poor.

---

[31] The Guardian, April 24, 2004. Reprinted in The Guardian Unlimited online.

And what of the claims made by Martin and her interview subjects that our free market system has hampered poor people in their search to buy good food?

This is a matter of economics. Anyone who runs a retail business or has worked at one, or even thought about how one operates, knows that utilization of shelf space is determined not by the heady notions of marketers and faceless capitalists who control the lives of helpless consumers, but by the store owners, based on what they correctly recognize as consumer demand in their stores. The space provided for apples, oranges, bananas and tomatoes in a corner store is not tiny because the owner is cruelly keeping fruit and vegetables to a minimum in his establishment. It is tiny because he does not sell enough of those products to justify using up more productive shelf space. In other words, people like George Bogen have shown time and again that they prefer junk food and fast food over the "good" food Martin and her coterie of "experts" want them to eat.

One need not get first-hand evidence to confirm this fact. It is simply a matter of supply and demand. But if one did want to back it up, he need only do what I did: walk into a local chain store. In my case, it was the Seven-Eleven located on my way to work, a place where I frequently grab an apple and chocolate milk to go with a sandwich for lunch.

When asked if he would stock more fruit and vegetables if there were more demand for it over, say, Fritos and soda, the manager said, "Of course!"

When told about the argument offered by Michel Martin and the proponents of government intervention in diet, he laughed very loudly, leaning back from the counter.

"That's crazy! They don't know who is in charge here!"

No, they don't, and not many people involved in trying to regulate the choices of consumers really do. But that doesn't stop them from trying. The reason they continue in their Quixotic struggle is that they believe, in large or small degree, in the Marxist myth that the owners of the means of production *make* people buy things. With their Svengali-like powers, these capitalists can mesmerize people, turning them into consuming automatons, exploiting them, and pointing them towards dietary choices like chips and cookies and Big Macs when, under the control of the government, the choices offered would be highly nutritious fruits and fibers. Of course, it *isn't* the business owner who is in charge of the transaction, it is the consumer. Unless the consumer is willing to part with his cash, he will not spend it. Unless the consumer sees what he desires, the business owner will not be able to stay in business. As it turns out, the owner of the means of production is always at the mercy of consumer taste, and the proportion of convenience store shelf space devoted to "good" food is determined by this taste as well.

Based on Michel Martin's report, George Bogen had two sisters. One of them had private insurance and got gastric by-pass surgery when she weighed 350 pounds. The other passed away. His surviving sister told Martin, "If they could see a picture of my sister laying in a casket, and know that on her death certificate it says 'immediate cause of death, obesity,' then maybe that will wake up the government."

It would be preferable to let the government rest. It has been far too busy tinkering with our private lives as it is. The last thing store owners like my neighbor, I, and the other consumers who frequent his establishment need is a government superceding our own preferences regarding what we eat to stay alive.

"Where's the Beef?"
May, 2007

In one of the most stunning examples of federal idiocy and overreaching to have come down the rocky road of regulation in years, the US Department of Agriculture is fighting to stop a small, Kansas-based meat packing company from voluntarily testing *all* of its beef for Bovine Spongiform Encephalopathy, more commonly known as Mad Cow Disease.

You might want to re-read that first paragraph. It really *is* true.

According to the Associated Press, the USDA announced on May 29 that it would appeal a federal court ruling that would have allowed the small company Creekstone Farms Beef to test all of its cattle, and advertise that fact to its potential customers. Evidently, such thorough testing is a threat to the USDA, since the department tests less than 1% of the Unites States beef stock each year.

But this new challenge from the "conservative" Bush Administration's agriculture bureaucrats represents more than just regulatory misanthropy, it is a shocking display of just how pernicious mercantilism and anti-constitutionalism can be.

It should come as no surprise that USDA functionaries are not the only ones who don't want small beef suppliers testing more than 1% of their stock and advertising its safety. Large beef producers are against it as well.

As the AP reports, "Larger meat companies feared that move because, if Creekstone should test its meat and advertised it as safe, they might have to perform the expensive tests on their larger herds as well."

Of course, it does not take Holmesian didactics to figure out who has been pushing the USDA to stop the small guy from checking for safety and advertising that fact. The US Department of Agriculture has been a mechanism of government favoritism and strong arm tactics since its elevation to cabinet position in 1889. By that time, the USDA was not only gathering agricultural statistics, it had also begun handing out loans to politically connected businesses. The practice grew in scope and degree to the point that, by the administration of Franklin Roosevelt, the USDA not only offered or withheld favors to certain businesses and local politicians, it did so based on whether those local politicians had sworn their allegiance to FDR in Democratic Party disputes and elections. As Thomas DiLorenzo points out in his excellent book, "How Capitalism Saved America", the timing of many government handouts through the Commodity Credit Corporation, the Agricultural Adjustment Act of 1933, and the Agriculture Act of 1949 seemed to coincide with the internal politics of the election cycle.

Of course, mercantilism is nothing new. In 1776, Adam Smith devoted much of his seminal treatise "The Wealth of Nations" to the pernicious process of government corrupting businesses with special favors. But today, it seems that Smith could write an entirely new volume.

Between 1996 and 2004, US agricultural subsidies averaged approximately $16 billion per year, not including low-interest loans or even the USDA managed tariffs on foreign produce that could normally sell for less and allow consumers to keep more of their money. Most of this booty went to large agricultural interests with political clout in Washington, DC, and the cash was squandered in very creative ways. For example, the USDA has used its godlike power to shower tax money on plum growers to *not* grow plums, to retain tariffs that allow US dairy farmers to keep US cheese prices 37% higher than world markets, and, according to Daniel Griswold, Stephen Slivinski, and Christopher Preble, of the Cato Institute, to slap restrictive quotas on foreign sugar producers that force Americans to spend nearly $1.9 billion more per year on their food bills.

Daniella Markheim and Brian M. Riedl, of the Heritage Foundation, report that in 2007, the "conservative" Bush administration will allow the agricultural largess to grow to a mind-boggling $25 billion.

We've all heard that Thomas Jefferson preferred an agrarian economy, but this is ridiculous. Perhaps what Jefferson meant was that he preferred the United States to be run by gentleman farmers working with their own property, rather than mercantilist interests using the government to gain favors over their competition and at the expense of the American consumer.

One thing is certain. It's a safe bet that Jefferson would have thought it downright crazy to allow the federal government to stop a man from testing the safety of his own cattle in order to let big farm interests avoid competition. It seems stunning to consider that the owner of a tiny Kansas company would like to make sure its food does not kill people by giving them a variant of the brain wasting disease called Creutzfeldt-Jakob, but the very agency that is supposedly charged with protecting Americans from tainted food is trying to stop him.

It has been noted by Anthony Gregory, of the Independent Institute, that Creekstone Farms loses $200,000 each day due to lost sales to the Japanese market, where safety standards are much higher than in the US. This is revenue that could have stopped 50 Creekstone workers from losing their jobs.

Wouldn't it be better to let those workers hold their jobs? To increase sales? To provide a safer product? To, perhaps, allow the market to work, and let sellers base their safety parameters on what consumers demand, on the carrot and stick of higher or lower sales due to the interests of market participants?

In that case, why should we even rely on the USDA, the FDA, or any other so-called "consumer safety" organization? After all, we don't need politically connected bureaucrats to somehow reflect our preferences, we can display those preferences with our own capital, and our own choices. All the government does is redirect our money, and prevent us from making those choices ourselves.

The story of Creekstone Farms is telling. No thanks to the USDA, a vast outbreak of Bovine Spongiform Encephalopathy/ Creutzfeldt-Jakob has not occurred in the United States, but based on the agency's wasteful, counter-productive and upside-down policies one wonders if we haven't already gone mad.

Thomas Paine observed that civil rights
are nothing more nor less than natural rights – life,
liberty and property – enshrined in civil law. The
primary function of government is to
safeguard those basic rights.

Moreover, he believed that civil rights must be
extended and protected equally:
"Where the rights of man are equal, every man must
finally see the necessity of protecting the rights of
others as the most effectual security of his own."

PHG
On Paine's "Rights of Man"
December, 1984

Abortion for convenience is simply the ash-canning of
a life – one of society's biggest obscenities.

PHG
September, 1990

"Send in the Clones"
Nov. 26, 2001

Three years ago, Bill Clinton called for a world-wide moratorium on human cloning. On July 31, 2001, Congress finally responded to his call by passing the "Human Cloning Prohibition Act". The bill is now before the Senate, the members of which can impress themselves and their constituents by dealing with an issue that is ripe for rhetorical manipulation.

It is a fascinating topic, and one that inspires fear within many. The very idea of human cloning is said to be immoral. We are told that man should not play God. The "world community" should adopt Clinton's suggested moratorium of such experiments.

But these protestations miss the underlying question, which is, "What is the fundamental nature of a human clone?"

Until one comes to grips with this issue, he cannot clearly see the direction any government should take.

A human clone is the extracted DNA of an individual that is subsequently manipulated to create an entirely new life. Until that life is created, an individual is the owner of his DNA. It is his property, and he has the right to do with it as he wishes. According to the principles of Natural Law, a person has the right to do with his property anything he desires, so long as he does not bring harm to the life or liberty of another. No legitimate government has the power to infringe upon this right. Government is there to *protect* it. Therefore, no legitimate government can infringe upon an individual's right to do whatever he wants with his own DNA, so long as he does not bring direct harm to the life or liberty of another.

It is when this DNA is turned into a *new* life that the principles of Natural Law are applied to the clone. One may not interfere with this life without infringing upon its natural rights. One may not experiment on it, use it for parts, or expose it to direct harm. In other words, this living creature is a *human being*, a child, which ought to make people pause to consider the thus far unwritten aspect of this topic. If one cannot *experiment* on a clone as it is developing, since that would be an infringement of its natural rights, can one *abort* it?

Logical consideration leads one back to the fundamental morality of abortion. If, as Clinton suggested, it is immoral to experiment on the developing clone, is it moral to stop its development altogether? If so, why is it not immoral to stop the life of a naturally conceived fetus? These are questions most pro-choice/anti-cloning politicians do not consider, but surely the debate is academic on a federal level. After all, the US Constitution does not give the federal government the power to influence scientific research in any way. It is not a national question. It is a mater to be left to the states.

Unfortunately, the original meaning of the Constitution is rarely given heed in contemporary politics. The idea has long since been forgotten that states could make their own laws regarding issues such as abortion, that states would be the pockets of experimentation, where people of similar morals could congregate and establish laws that accorded with their views within the general framework of rights guaranteed by the US Constitution.

James Madison once said that the "interstate commerce" clause of the Constitution did not give the federal government preemptory power over all aspects of commerce in the US. In fact, it did not allow what Madison called a "positive" power over products and services in any way whatsoever, but instead was to be used as a "negative and preventative provision against injustices among the states themselves." In other words, it was to be a final check against the state governments as entities themselves, something to stop them from imposing tariffs on other state goods.

If only the politicians clamoring to pass prohibitions against human cloning could have a chat with James Madison. They might realize that, no matter how much they fear scientific development, they have no power, and certainly no right, to impose federal laws against it.

Scientific research is not only a humanitarian endeavor, it is also a risky capitalist venture. But the financial foundation of human endeavor should not be used as a pretext for federal usurpation of state authority. Let the states wrestle with the moral implications of cloning, and give our troubled Congressmen time off.

They could use it to brush up on their civics.

P. GARDNER GOLDSMITH   PAUL H. GOLDSMITH

**Deal with the faults of others as you would your own.
PHG
1984**

"Smoke Gets in Their Eyes"
July, 2004

The government of Massachusetts has often given us New Hampshire residents reasons to be cheerful.

During the Seventies and Eighties, the Bay State had such high sales taxes that retailers in southern New Hampshire reaped millions in trade from Massachusetts residents looking for better deals. Income and property taxes in Massachusetts were so high that thousands of refugees flocked to the "Live Free or Die" state each year.

As of July, New Hampshire residents have another reason to celebrate. Once more, the government of Massachusetts has passed another repressive, counter-productive bill, and once more, we in New Hampshire will welcome those who are searching for ways to live free.

The new law, which went into effect with nearly artistic irony a day after *Independence Day*, bans smoking in nearly every workplace and private establishment that is open to the public. This includes restaurants, bars, food courts, supermarkets, offices, hallways, auditoriums, theatres, concert halls, libraries and elevators.

The law replaces an old statute which had forbidden smoking in government buildings, and it overrides the ordinances in one-hundred towns throughout Massachusetts that had outlawed smoking in local private workplaces.

It also contains certain exceptions, which, according to Massachusetts State Senator Richard T. Moore, "strike a reasonable balance between smokers' rights, and employees' rights to clean air."[32] For example, hotels can still possess designated "smoking rooms", and cigar bars can still have smoking on the premises. Smoking is allowed, "under certain circumstances" in private meeting halls for civic groups such as the Odd Fellows and Elks, and nursing homes can apply to get waivers, in order to allow permanent residents to gather in a special room to puff away during their declining years.

---

[32] Public Announcement dated June 10, 2004, from the official website of Senator Richard T. Moore. (http://www.senatormoore.com/news/releases/2004/06/061004_smoking_ban.htm).

Such magnanimity on the part of the government is truly heartwarming. After years of smokers being marginalized by the mass media and government, it's good to see legislators making sure there is a "balance between smokers' rights and employees' rights."

The trouble is, Senator Moore misses the rights that are really in question. Moore and those who promoted the Massachusetts smoking ban give us the impression that this issue is similar to one of those old classroom debates on the "limits of individual rights". Perhaps you've heard of them. They're good ways to explore the dynamics of freedom and what can happen when the actions of free individuals conflict with each other. Often, the questions come in the form of: "Where does the right of your neighbor to play loud music end and your right to sleep without interruption begin?" and "Do I have a right to burn leaves in my yard if my neighbor doesn't like the smoke?" In most of these thought experiments, the instructor leads his pupils to the conclusion that some form of government arbiter or pre-emptive laws restricting the freedoms of those in society are the palliatives which are required. Explorations into the market trade-offs that could be, and historically have been, made between neighbors with conflicting interests are usually forgone in favor of the simplistic government option.

But the issue of smoking in the workplace is not one of those classroom dilemmas. It is a much simpler, basic question. The real issue is that of private property, and who rightly gets to control it, and the origin of the debate can be traced all the way back to Title Two of the 1964 Civil Rights Act.

The Civil Rights Act, an initiative pushed by John Kennedy, and passed with great Republican support during the Johnson Administration, is often touted as the most important civil rights legislation since the Emancipation Proclamation. However, like Abraham Lincoln's famous pronouncement, the act was quite different from what its title implied.[33]

Its primary justification was to insure through federal power the right of minorities to vote and be accepted to government-funded schools. This it did, but the act did a great deal more. Much of it actually trampled on the

---

[33] While the proclamation of the "Great Emancipator" has been depicted as an act that freed US slaves, it applied only to those states in rebellion, those outside of Union jurisdiction. As a result, it had no real impact inside the "United" States, and was recognized by many abolitionists as a transparent political and military ploy designed to disrupt life on southern plantations. See: "The Real Lincoln", by Thomas J. DiLorenzo, available from Three Rivers Press, New York, NY.

civil rights of Americans to use their private property as they see fit, and changed the popular notion of private property itself.

Title Two of the act outlawed discrimination in restaurants, hotels, theaters, and other places that included "public accommodations" as part of their operation. By taking a view of the "Interstate Commerce" clause of the Constitution[34] which James Madison himself had described as contrary to the spirit, design and construction of the document, the lawmakers of the 1960's successfully placed under federal control any establishment that could be construed as effecting interstate commerce. Thus, if a restaurateur bought products from sellers in another state, or admitted patrons from another state, he would be "engaging in interstate commerce", and his property subject to regulation. Essentially, this interpretation turned private property into "public" property, and it has been viewed as such by most Americans ever since.

Today, business owners are required to expend valuable capital in order to comply with a panoply of federal orders. Striptease clubs have had to create accommodations for the virtually non-existent population of wheelchair-bound strippers who might, one day, roll into their dance halls and ask for work. The Pro Golfers' Association has been forced to give a cart to a physically impaired player, despite the fact that its rules say everyone must walk the course, and the Boy Scouts have been threatened for not accepting homosexuals as scout leaders.

These examples may seem familiar, and often they are used to exemplify the absurdity of centrally planning the conduct of non-coercive human interaction. But rarely do observers question the definitional paradigm, the rhetorical means by which that human interaction is regulated. Today, most people believe that any business owner who allows customers and workers onto his property has turned this property into a "public" place, and is therefore open to regulation. To most people, the debate centers on how "fair" the regulation is, not on whether the regulation is legally or philosophically justified in the first place.

Thus, when local Massachusetts governments began passing ordinances banning smoking, there was little opposition. And when these local statutes began causing financial losses to competitors in towns where smoking was

---

[34] Article One, Section Eight.

still allowed, it was widely accepted that people should turn to the state to ban smoking everywhere. To rectify the effects of harmful laws, it was deemed necessary to expand their purview, not revoke them.

How could reasonable people be drawn to such an absurd conclusion? How is it possible that business owners can be vilified to such an extent that even their own property is not theirs to peacefully control?

The answer is simple. Underlying the move to ban smoking on private property is a very old and dangerous assumption. It is the Marxist fallacy that the owners of businesses force employees to work for them, and force customers to buy their products -- the belief that capitalists *exploit* people.

Despite the fact that nearly every assumption of Karl Marx -- from his "labor theory" of value[35] to his idea of a "dictatorship of the proletariat" -- has been proven pernicious, Marx's rhetorical ability to prey upon human envy has had a profound effect on United States culture and politics.

It has borne sour fruit in our progressive income tax, legally-enforced unionism, the minimum wage, and a host of other repressive and malicious statutes on both the federal and state levels. And it has fostered the "us versus them" mentality that assumes employees are at the mercy of those who hire them.

The basic idea is this: the owners of the means of production, much like the feudal lords of old, control the property, and those who labor for them have no clout. The owners can dictate how much the laborers will be paid, and the conditions in which the laborers will work. In Marx's view, both pay and working conditions will never be fair until the laborers take over the workplace and seize the owner's property. To that end, Marx called for a workers' revolution. In America, we employ the less bloody method; we pass laws and regulations to attenuate how a business owner can use his property.

In the eyes of those who enacted the Massachusetts smoking ban, it was essential to protect non-smoking employees and customers from the threat of uncaring business owners who allowed dangerous smoking on their property. In their view, the workers and customers had no choice. If the

---

[35] Marx argued that the commercial value of a product was determined by the amount of labor that went into it. This has been proven false time and again. It does not matter how much labor went into a product, if a consumer is unwilling to purchase it, the product has no commercial value.

workers wanted to make money, they had to work in dangerous conditions. If customers wanted to purchase a product, they had to do business with the uncaring owner of the means of production.

But what the supporters of this legislation do not realize is that in a competitive marketplace, no business owner can exploit employees. He has to compete against other employers for workers. Though Marxists assume that workers are at the mercy of the business owner for their livelihoods, it is possible to look at the equation the other way around. The business owner needs employees in order to operate and stay in business. Just as the Marxists believe the worker is under the thumb of the employer, one could just as easily interpret the relationship as the employer being at the mercy of "money-hungry" employees. Surely no Marxist would support a "capitalists' revolution" based on the belief that the capitalist is at the mercy of the people in the labor pool, and employees will choose to work for someone else if the businessman's compensation and working conditions are not acceptable. Yet, this is exactly what happens in a free market system. Both the employer and the worker are free to choose those with whom they want to work. True, some workers will not be productive enough to demand salaries above a certain level, but employers are also limited in what they can offer highly skilled employees, and often see them move on to businesses that have more to offer.

The result is a negotiated equilibrium in which the needs of the workers and of the employers are balanced, and in which all of their needs are considered within the context of what the consumer is willing to pay.

But these factors are rarely, if ever, mentioned in debates over laws that further attenuate the rights of property owners, employees and consumers to freely engage in peaceful commerce. Instead, we hear paternalistic politicians fuelling class envy, telling people they will balance the rights of the property owner against the rights of the poor, disadvantaged worker.

In a free society, the rights of the employer to hire and fire those he wished, and to create a working and commercial environment that fit his goals and served his customers, would not be infringed. "Improper" choices, would be corrected naturally, through the myriad decisions of the people who comprise the marketplace, not by politicians telling others how to run their lives.

Passing laws that restrict the voluntary choices of participants in the free market does not "strike a balance" of rights. It constrains them. By doing so, high-minded lawmakers constrict the natural flow of capital and labor. When the choice to engage in commerce is made by someone else, the utility of the transaction cannot be measured. When the choice is not that which market participants would have made in the first place, it is, by its nature, less efficient and productive than it would have been. The growth in society's standard of living is therefore retarded.

Anti-smoking crusaders may think that they are saving the world, but employers and employees already had the power to "save" themselves, and efforts to clean the air by outlawing smoking in "public" places harm everyone in the long run.

One is tempted to tell Senator Moore to "put that in his pipe and smoke it", but that might get him fined under his well-intended statute. It's a shame his choices are now so limited, but if he ever needs a change of pace, we will welcome him in New Hampshire.

"Gambling: Where is the Recovery Group for Politicians?"
Letter to the Editor – Manchester Union Leader
May 9, 2001

To The Editor:

Unwilling or incapable of mustering the courage to oppose an unconstitutional State Supreme Court ruling that claims each citizen has a "right" to a state-funded education, the New Hampshire legislature is currently scrambling to find any new tax source it can to fund the budget shortfall the court ruling has inspired.

The latest among the many inventive proposals is to legalize casino gambling at race tracks and "resort hotels". While this has many wondering how they can get their hotel classified as a "resort", it has others worrying that the introduction of gambling will ruin the peaceful, rustic nature of their community.

It's being portrayed as a battle between trade and traditional values, when, in fact, it is a battle between the traditional principles of individual freedom and the arbitrary rule of mob sentiment.

The struggle between those who believe legitimate government is created to stop us from bringing direct harm to the life or property of another, and those who would use government to compel others to make their own non-coercive activities conform to the dictates of "society" has been long standing.

In the early days of the battle, "legislating morality" was quite often boldly proposed, and, just as often eloquently refuted. In his 1689 "Letter Concerning Toleration", John Locke wrote:

"If a Heathen doubt of both Testaments, he is not therefore to be punished as a pernicious Citizen."

But recently the advocates of moral compulsion have adopted a more subtle approach. Unable to argue against the idea that governments are established to stop us from bringing direct harm to the life or property of others, the proponents of moral coercion now try to justify their "anti-sin" laws by claiming "we all pay" for the immorality and mistakes of others.

Hence we have proposals to tax unhealthy foods, alcohol, tobacco, and sundry "dangerous habits" one might enjoy, by claiming they force us all to pay for the higher costs of health care. The fact that only through government-run health care and government-regulated insurance are we "made to pay" for the personal foibles of others seems lost on the advocates of moral compulsion.

Similarly, these moral tyrants oppose legal gambling because, they claim, it hurts others. Gambling, they say, is clearly a waste of good money on a frivolous activity, one that gives no product in return, and one which can inspire misallocations of wealth by parents, husbands, and wives, thus doing grievous harm to innocent children and families. Therefore, it should be illegal; case closed.

Yet we know dozens of activities that provide no physical "product" but are seen as perfectly acceptable. When one attends a movie or play, one leaves with nothing more than memories and a ticket stub. According to the standard applied to gambling, should all entertainment be banned as a useless waste of money?

Similarly, certain products, when purchased, may turn out to be poor investments, causing financial distress in a family. Shall we outlaw furs, boats, recreational vehicles and the like because they might inspire someone to waste money on them, thus making it more difficult to provide for his family?

What about strict financial investments, derivatives, stock options, speculation in currency -- shall these be outlawed because some people are mistakenly drawn in at the expense of those who depend on them?

Arguments are offered that recreational items and the financial markets aren't addictive the way gambling is, that a person doesn't become fixated on these things the way one might with gambling. But surely this is a matter of degree; and the extent to which one views the expenditure of money being a form of recreation, or a "waste" that puts others at risk, is purely subjective.

If a woman has a penchant for shoes that rivals Imelda Marcos and puts herself into debt buying them, shall we outlaw footwear? If an investor makes a bad decision and his stocks go belly-up, shall we outlaw playing the market so that no others will waste money in a similar fashion? In such cases, these financial ne'er-do-wells may have had children who suffered indirectly, but that by no means indicates that we should restrict the parents' freedom to fail.

The "we all pay" argument is also utilized to imply that gambling invites greater crime, which requires greater police protection to combat. Hence, "we all pay" when gambling moves in, either through property-loss via robbery, violent crime, of the costs of stopping them. Yet we could apply that so-called logic to any areas of human aggregation and commerce, thus presenting a case against any association or business whatsoever. When a new shopping mall moves into an area, such as the wildly successful Pheasant Lane Mall, in southern Nashua, it is likely that there will be increased crime in the area. Auto thefts will very likely increase, and violent crime may rise. This will force people to spend more on police protection in the area. Shall we prohibit new malls in New Hampshire as a result?

The fallacies underlying victim-less crime legislation are clear. What makes such legislation, and those who promote it, so dangerous is that there is no longer an honest argument being made on their behalf. Those who wish to run the private affairs of their neighbors now use the excuse that we are all harmed by the supposedly immoral actions of others. But no matter how hard these moral tyrants argue they cannot prove that direct harm is brought about by a person laying money on a pair of dice or a slot machine. A gambler doesn't steal another man's wallet when facing a slot machine or roulette wheel, and the argument that gambling is an inducement to steal or spend money in non-productive ways is vacuous. It leads to a philosophical reduction-ad-absurdum concerning what other activities might cause someone to spend money unwisely and thus make a decision to steal or neglect his loved ones. We form governments to protect us from the coercion of others, not to protect us from ourselves.

"US Supreme Court Orders Affirmative Action for Obama"
January, 2007

P. Gardner Goldsmith –
(Associated Press International Correspondent)

Washington, January 27, 2007

Amidst hollers of protest and support from numerous interest groups gathered outside, the Justices of the United States Supreme Court today ruled by a 23-4 margin that the Democratic Party must institute affirmative action policies at its 2008 Presidential Convention.

"It's a victory for *all* Americans," said Rainbow Shove Coalition president and Poet Laureate Jessie Jackson. "Black, white, cool, uptight. Affirmative action. It continues the fight."

The decision centered on the landmark case *Obama v. Democratic Party of the United States*, in which Presidential hopeful, Senator Barak Obama (D. Ill), brought suit against his own progressive party for what his attorney's called, "a systemic misallocation of delegation votes based on long-standing racial inequities in the political party system."

According to Dennis Moore, Obama's press officer and chief of staff, institutional racism in America, "is still a hurdle that must be overcome, and only through government looking at the skin color of each of us can we ever hope to become a color blind society."

As a remedy, the Court ordered that, regardless of the intent of party members, the votes of delegates attending the Democratic National Convention must be redistributed to those of "disadvantaged groups". This would have the practical effect of shifting votes from some candidates to others, based on race.

For example, if Delaware Senator Joseph Biden were to garner the highest vote total, and former Senator John Edwards were to come in second, a portion of each man's delegate votes would be shifted to Obama, to make up for years of racial inequality in America.

Writing for the majority, Justice Rosie O'Donnell stated that the popular Obama "must receive Convention votes that were to go to other candidates, in a formula to be determined by the party leaders, or, alternatively, by a group of nine kindergarten students using 'rock-paper-scissors'."

But the Justices left room to move. While skin pigmentation must be the deciding factor, others, such as sex, height, weight, familial background and shrillness of voice may also be considered.

"Come on," she said, "You think I could get a fair shot with a voice like mine?"

While most advocacy groups applauded the decision, heralding it as a breakthrough for equal rights in the United States, Joe Gold, a vocal Biden supporter and president of the Center for Peace, Prosperity, and Other Really Neat Things, disagreed.

"Whatever happened to merit?" he asked. "I thought in America that if you worked hard and played by the rules, you had a shot. Now, apparently, the rules have to be constantly rewritten by the racial overlords in the government, not the people!"

When reminded that Senator Biden has spoken out in favor of race-based rules for admission into law schools, and in favor of race-based hiring practices by both the federal government and private businesses, Mr. Gold responded, "That's different! This is *important*!"

But Mr. Biden was of a different mind.

"I like it! Remember, I once said that my father worked in coal mines when I was a kid. We were *dirtier* than dirt poor! Sure, that might not have been *precisely* right, and might even have been lifted from a British Labor Party leader's speech, but it ought to garner me a few votes based on economic grounds!... Right?"

In fact, many legal scholars were of the opinion that the *Obama* ruling, while helpful for the Senator from Illinois, might also be helpful for other candidates.

Hillary Clinton could receive special consideration for being female. John Edwards could receive special consideration for his long association with the downtrodden in civil damage suits brought against Big Business, and Dennis Kucinich could receive votes from more popular candidates because of his long-standing background as, well, Dennis Kucinich.

When posed with such an elaborate schema as a possibility in the real world, Obama's spokesman Dennis Moore paused, contemplating.

"Hmm," he said. "Perhaps this redistribution thing is more complicated than I thought."

The Democratic Convention is planned for the summer of 2008, at a site yet to be determined by lottery, political favoritism, and racial and economic factors.

"The Friendly Skies"
October, 2002

"As I write this, I am sitting on a plane bound from Dallas to Boston. I have had a good trip, despite having been selected for a random search of my bags and shoes at the Dallas airport. The service staff are pleasant, and the pilots appear to be competent, law-abiding citizens. I don't suspect that any one of them is a terrorist plant, and it seems to me that none of them has a criminal background. They retain all the natural rights protected by the US Constitution.

"Why, then, can none of them carry a firearm while in the plane?"

This is a passage I wrote in my notebook as I flew through the orange clouds of a September sunset. On the next page, a question was posited for further exploration:

"What happens when federal regulations begin to impinge upon a constitutionally protected right?"

On September 6, 2002, the US Senate passed by a vote of 87-6 *Amendment S. 2554* to the Homeland Security Act, which would allow a limited number of pilots to arm themselves in the cockpit. The entire bill will be debated when the Senate reconvenes, then reconciled with the House version. Despite previous pronouncements by White House officials that the Bush Administration was opposed to armed pilots, it seems that President Bush will agree to a "test program" for a select number of pilots to carry firearms. Thus, by year's end, the problem may appear to be resolved, and what could serve to be an important debate on the scope of federal power will be avoided.

But the central question remains. *"What happens when federal regulations begin to impinge upon a constitutionally protected right?"*

To my knowledge, none of the debate in Washington over the issue of armed pilots has dealt with this important question. None of the rhetoric on the Sunday morning talk shows has included even a reference to the fact that, under the multitudinous federal regulations imposed on the airline industry, the fundamental right to self-protection through use of a firearm has been infringed by the very government that was created to defend it.

Perhaps this is due to the fact that most politicians don't accept the validity of the Aristotelian principle of self-defense as articulated by the Founding Fathers. Perhaps it is because they have become so conditioned to think that the power of the federal government supersedes the rights of individuals, it never enters their minds that they are working under a faulty paradigm. After all, the airways have been regulated in one form or another since 1925, so most Americans have no experience with free skies.

Perhaps it is both of these factors, and more.

Federal regulation of "the air" began its incubation in 1924, when the US Postal Service established air travel along its lighted Trans-Continental Airway. A year later, the Postmaster General was given the power to contract with private companies to carry air mail. This provided the federal government the opportunity to also influence the structure of air routes. Soon, the Air Commerce Act of 1926 mandated federal safety regulation of the airlines, and created the Aeronautics Branch of the Department of Commerce.

The Roosevelt administration instituted many more regulations on airlines. After subsidizing the construction of new airports in 1936, Roosevelt pushed for and succeeded in getting Congress to pass the Civil Aeronautics Act, which established a more comprehensive regulatory structure over air fares themselves, as well as control over more air routes across the United States. With Roosevelt's successful attempt to maneuver America into World War Two came a complete federal takeover of all air traffic control towers in major airports, and this control was never relinquished.

In 1978, the economic regulations imposed in World War Two were lifted, but control of air routes was given to the Secretary of Transportation. Then, following the terrorist attacks on September 11, 2001, *security* at all major airports was also placed under the aegis of the Secretary of Transportation, then under the Department of Homeland Security, with unionized federal employees conducting the exhaustive work of searching the overnight bags of randomly selected seventy-year-old grandmothers.

If Americans have become acclimated to having their rights curtailed by federal regulations, then is it possible that a debate over the practical effects of this loss could help reinstate those rights?

Certainly. Unfortunately, the current debate over gun rights on planes will not contribute to the process.

It has only been since September 11, 2002 that there has been a public outcry over this lost right, and in the debate, it has not even been mentioned that the freedom to armed self-protection *is* a right. Instead, listeners have been treated to a cacophony of practical points about the relative merits or demerits of the federal government *allowing* pilots to carry firearms. On one side are pilots themselves, who correctly stress the need to have firearms in the cockpit as their last line of defense against hijacking. On the other are bureaucrats like Transportation Secretary Mineta, who announced his opposition to armed pilots on the very day the Bush Administration warned Americans that another attack on a plane was not just likely, it was inevitable.

Perhaps those who debate the merits of arming pilots do not delve deeply into the constitutional issue because it would require them to address a much more difficult political and economic question: the validity of federal airline regulations themselves.

Politicians in favor of such federal rules recklessly point to the "interstate commerce clause" of the Constitution as a way to justify their support for federal regulations. The clause (Art. 1, Sec. 8) states that Congress shall have the power to:

"…regulate Commerce with foreign Nations, and among the several States…"

When the Constitution was written, the Founders included the clause as a way to remedy a flaw in the Articles of Confederation, the original set of rules for the US following the treaty of Paris. Under the Articles, states were allowed to impose tariffs on one another. Thus, when the Revolution ended, many states began imposing tariffs on products from other states as ways to "protect" their own workers. The Founders recognized that this was causing price inflation and was counter-productive for growth. Thus, at the Constitutional Convention in 1787, they proposed that the Congress could act as a check against trade restrictions imposed by the government of any state against the products of others. The measure was instituted to act as a *remedial* measure against state governments themselves.

But since the Roosevelt Administration, the "interstate commerce clause" has been openly interpreted to mean that if *anything* travels over state borders, the federal government can regulate it. The clause is seen as having *preemptory* intent, and has therefore been used to justify everything from "workplace safety" regulations, to food labels, to regulation of airlines and their routes.[36]

---

[36] According to James Madison (as quoted in "Makers and Takers", 1997, by Edmund Contoski, p.408), the "Interstate Commerce Clause" was not intended "to be used… for positive purposes", but as "a negative and preventative provision against injustice among the states themselves."

In order to properly and completely question the federal infringement of the Second Amendment in the air, one *must* look at the faulty paradigm of these regulations themselves. Doing so is difficult for some, because they will be forced to imagine a world in which the Constitution is strictly enforced, and where there are *zero* federal regulations over planes and their travel.

If the fraudulent regulatory structure imposed over airlines were removed, what might happen? Would air travel be left up to the market alone?

Perhaps, if state regulations were not imposed. And by considering such a possibility, one can see how federal regulations are not only unnecessary, they may also be counter-productive.

If there were no regulations over airlines, each airport and air travel company would be free to institute its own security regime. Customers would make their travel decisions based upon the costs of the systems, and the risks those systems presented. It is likely that various levels of security would be offered by various companies, based on the desires of the consumers. Through mutually agreed contracts, some airlines might curtail the rights of passengers to carry arms, others might not. More frugal customers might pick a company with less security. Then again, airlines that provide more security might do such volume that they could reduce prices.

Critics of such a paradigm might deride the concept, because they believe it overlooks those *outside* the plane. If "Cheapo Air" caters to budget travelers, and provides virtually no security, it will not only be those who fly "Cheapo" who will be hurt. Those who are on the ground will suffer if one of its planes explodes due to poor baggage screening, or hits a building under the control of terrorists who passed through lax passenger checks.

Such worries overlook two fundamental principles. First, "Cheapo", as well as every other airline, cannot afford to be so cheap that it risks the lives of its passengers with such lax security measures. The first time it sees passengers die due to a lack of security, it will see a loss of customer interest, and looming financial doom.

Additionally, no company CEO would leave himself open to the liability suits that could be brought against him if people on the ground suffered due to his negligence. Out of his own self-interest, he will not risk lives in the air, or on the ground, and his actions, and those of other business people like him, will spontaneously establish an air travel system that would be open to public scrutiny and consumer response. Under the current government regime, responsiveness is, and has been shown to be, a fallacy. No observer of our contemporary airline system can honestly state that the federal system of passenger and baggage checks is providing us with any real kind of security. In fact, the deadline for having all bags checked in airports has been pushed back twice, because the federally controlled employees cannot handle the task.

It would be healthy for US citizens to explore such ideas when presented with an issue as important as whether pilots can exercise their Second Amendment rights. Unfortunately, such questions are rarely explored on television, in Congress, in schools, or in the neighborhood bar, and this is an historical and intellectual tragedy.

Being at the mercy of political demagoguery over the fundamental right to self-protection is not only frustrating, it is hazardous to our lives, our property, and to our economic liberty. Questioning such rhetoric not only provides a better understanding of our government, it allows us to comprehend the best security system in the world: the free market. Perhaps some day, somewhere, this kind of debate will occur. Until then, we can only watch politicians bluster, and cross our fingers as we step onto a plane.

"AMA Promotes Tax on Sofas"
June, 2006

P. Gardner Goldsmith – (Associated Press International Correspondent)

WASHINGTON, June 18, 2006

Flanked by poster-sized images of Fat Albert and Babe Ruth, the American Mendacity Association (AMA) announced today the launch of a new initiative to institute a federal tax on sofas and lounge chairs.

Emboldened by the recent AMA proposal to lobby Congress for a tax on sodas sweetened with corn syrup (called the "crack cocaine" of sweeteners), the board members of this august group have moved to do more to "protect *our* children" from the ravages of relaxation.

A new study sponsored by the AMA finds that 384% of all children are obese by the age of five, and most experts agree that – just behind plentiful food and the division of labor -- the third most dangerous contributor to this epidemic is comfortable seating. Whereas twenty years ago, there was only *one* lounge chair or sofa per every three households, technology and productivity have brought about a dangerous change, a change our society is ill-equipped to handle. Shockingly, there are now *four* forms of inexpensive, comfortable seating per house. This, says Harriet Hydra, president of the AMA Division of Pleasure Elimination, creates a deadly atmosphere which, "inspires children to sit or lay back, and turn all those extra calories to fat."

"We *all* pay when people relax," said Hydra, citing "negative externalities" incurred on other citizens and on Wellness Providers who see higher instances of obesity, diabetes, nail biting, and insanity in children who sit or lay for longer than three hours a month on comfortable sofas.

"The epidemic of obesity places a strain on our public health care system, and, hence, on all of us. With a 1 Cent per second tax on sofa sitting, we could not only change peoples' behavior, we could generate up to $1.5 billion a year, money which could be used wisely by many of my physician friends who are ready to start up new 'sofa counseling' clinics," Hydra said.

Given the respect afforded the AMA and Wellness Providers in general, such a bill would stand a good chance of passing the US House and Senate. Max Quartlepleen, head of the watchdog group, "American Scientists Who Are Extremely Concerned", added, "We're extremely concerned. We're here to fight Big Sofa."

When asked why the "negative externalities" of socialized medicine should be forced upon free individuals against their wills, thus opening the door to higher costs, price caps on medical services and more government regulation of our private affairs, habits, and living conditions, Mr. Quartlepleen shot back with ferocity.

"I don't know what lobby group sent you here, whether it was Serta, Seely, or Sterns and Foster, but buddy, we don't need loudmouths like you at public forums in America. So why don't you just take your sleep number attitude and get outta here?!"

After the meeting, Ms. Hydra was asked if she saw any impediments to the passage of the AMA proposal.

"Well, common sense is a problem," she said, "But we're working on that in association with the National Education Association. We could also stand to curtail the power of free thinkers and those who follow the US Constitution. A lot has been done in those areas, but we're not out of the woods yet." When asked what the AMA would do if their proposal did not become law, Hydra stated that the organization has a different plan.

"If we can't get a tax to protect our kids and wallets from this deadly scourge, we will work for better *regulation* of sofas, and health initiatives such as time shockers, and spring spikes, to get people off the lounge chairs and on their feet at regular intervals," she said. Many congressmen have openly stated their support for such measures.

As he was led out of the conference by authorities, the reporter who had disrupted the meeting asked Hydra what she was going to do about things like books, music, films and conversation, since all of those tend to inspire periods of sedentary, fat-building behavior.

"What do you want to do, Hydra?!" asked the reporter, whose name is being withheld by authorities, "Regulate and tax freedom into non-existence because 'we all pay'?"

Hydra's response was immediate.

"We're working on that," she said.

It is singly unfortunate that the soul of law has been ensnared by technicalities, so that real justice suffers.

**PHG
January, 1991**

"Nailing Free Enterprise"
May, 2005

On Monday, May 09, 2005, a man named Mike Fisher, from the town of Newmarket, NH, performed an act for which he will pay dearly, under penalty of law.

He engaged in a consentual commercial transaction with another willing individual.

In fact, he performed a manicure.

Mike Fisher, outlaw from justice, enemy of the realm, planted himself outside the state Board of Cosmetology, invited his customer to join him, and committed the unpardonable sin of performing a manicure without a license granted to him from the very agents who worked inside.

The agents didn't remain inside for long.

As Mike lifted his sterile tools to work on his client (certain names have been withheld to protect the innocent), a bureaucrat from the all-powerful Board of Cosmetology emerged to hand him a sheet of paper. On the sheet was information to explain how he was in violation of state law, a fact of which Mike was already aware, since he intended to break the law, and had already been "spoken to" by the state Attorney General, Kelley Ayotte, the week prior.

When Ms. Ayotte asked him not to perform his "stunt", Mike nicely said he fully intended to provide the service to anyone who was interested in hiring him. When he kept his word, he was promptly arrested by the Concord, NH, police.

Mike spent the night in jail, because he was unwilling to pay the state for a license, and unwilling to pay for the mandatory "training" required in order to get the license. Instead, he studied and trained himself, advertised to others that he was going to offer his services at a low price, and willingly accepted a customer, under the watchful eyes of agents of the "Granite State".

Call this crazy, but when was a government established to stop us from entering into a peaceful, non-coercive arrangement with someone else?

Certain people watching what happened to Mike Fisher recalled that we supposedly formed governments to stop aggressive behavior directed at others. Was Mike Fisher on the attack? "Look out! Manicurist gone wild!

Serial manicurist on the loose!" Were those the cries of the people around him?

Not at all. In fact, they supported his effort to work free of state interference, to invite others to accept his services for a fee, and to decline his services if that was their preference. Mike Fisher was engaged in free enterprise; but evidently that type of activity is unacceptable nowadays.

The absurdity of arresting a man for committing the grievous crime of fixing a client's fingernails is obvious. But there are less obvious, though just as important, lessons to be learned about licensing, lessons that can be applied to many other fields of human endeavor.

Licensing is an act of aggressive exclusion. Such policies supposedly are enacted for the protection of the populace. By creating a government-enforced "permission agency", the state protects us, the innocent and uninformed customers, from reckless, money-hungry, fly-by-night charlatans who would bilk us of our hard-earned dough while possibly putting our health or property at risk.

The trouble, or one of the many troubles, with this assumption is that government licensing does not actually do what it is supposed to do. The reasons for this are numerous and manifest. First, government agents cannot be everywhere to watch everyone all the time, and thus the threat of license revocation becomes meaningless when a license-holder rarely sees a state functionary appear to check on his standards and credentials.

Instead, it is the combination of market incentives and punishments that drive entrepreneurs to perform to the absolute best of their abilities. It is the enticement of more profit when one does a good job, and the threat of lower wages when one does not, that keep businesses performing at their highest level. Customers enter shops every day, and reward businessmen for exemplary performance. Agents of the government do not, and cannot. Thus, when it comes to not only keeping a businessman on his best behavior, but offering him incentives to excel, government coercion is no match for market competition.

The second reason government licensing does not actually do what we are told it is designed to do is that what we are *told* it is designed to do, and what it is *actually* designed to do are completely different from one another.

What licensing is actually designed to do is to exclude lower-price competition while it provides more money to the state in licensing fees.

This exclusion of lower-price competition is a destructive force all its own. It not only represents the suppression of individual choice by the will of government (and those using government to gain a competitive advantage), that suppression of choice, in and of itself, means that the free flow of capital is retarded, or redirected away from its most productive use. Thus, even if a handful of malcontents are stopped by licensing laws each year, the vast majority of consumers, in being prevented from shopping among all potential market participants, have lost far more in opportunity costs than they have gained in supposed security.

As the Melvin D. Barger noted in "The Freeman", in April of 1975:

"Under today's licensing requirements, Thomas Edison would not have been certified as an engineer, Abraham Lincoln would have been barred from the practice of law, and Albert Einstein could not have been even a high school science teacher."[37]

Due to licensing, customers lose more than the opportunity to buy services at lower prices, thus allowing them to have money left over to buy other products and services, which expands an already vibrant economy. They lose the opportunity to discover the myriad products and services that would appear if unlicensed businessmen were allowed to enter the market.

When Mike Fisher committed his terrible crime in front of the New Hampshire Board of Cosmetology, he not only represented himself, and his own interests, he represented all the abstract benefits consumers have been unable to acquire in the marketplace due to the absurd notion that the state must give permission for individuals to engage in peaceful commerce. Since there has never been a government anywhere that has produced a product or provided a service without first taking from someone against his will, the notion of bureaucrats increasing our capacity to operate a functional economy is truly laughable.

It was not reported if Mike Fisher laughed as they took him away in handcuffs.

---

[37] Barger, Melvin D., "The Freeman", April, 1975, the Foundation for Economic Education, Irvington-on-Hudson, NY. As quoted by Edmund Contoski, in "Makers and Takers", 1997, American Library Publishers, Minneapolis, MN. p. 108.

**Political Economics, Natural Rights, and
Constitutional Government:
The Nexus Between Contemporary
Issues and Timeless Principles**

"Death Penalty, R.I.P."
January, 2001

"The Illinois capital punishment system is broken. It has taken innocent men to a hair's breadth escape from their unjust execution."

With those words, former Illinois governor George Ryan on January 11 commuted the sentences of 164 death row inmates, and pardoned three others. His actions have been heralded as courageous by opponents of capital punishment, who view Ryan's decision as not only a victory for inmates who have been wrongfully convicted, but also as an idealistic win in the long-fought war against capital punishment itself.

Adopting as their battle hymn the words of Ryan, this group of "pro-lifers" has moved en masse to proclaim their belief that government should not be granted the power to take the life of a human being.

"Public sanctioned killing has cheapened human life and dignity," Ryan said, and so the editorialists, the interviewers, the commentators, and the protesters have repeated it, not so much by rote, but in recognition of a well-phrased distillation of their own beliefs.

But in their vociferous opposition to public sanctioned killing, people such as George Ryan and his supporters might pause to scrutinize the entire range of their own political principles. By so doing, they will slowly discover that beneath the glorious patina of noble idealism, most of them harbor a nearly inscrutable hypocrisy.

They have sanctioned state-sponsored killing every day, and they still do.

The proponents of Ryan's philosophy, although heartfelt in their beliefs, rarely apply their principles across the entire panoply of government resources that their society arrays against crime. They never question certain assumptions which, based on their avowed stance against public sanctioned killing, ought to be placed into serious doubt.

They never question state-sponsored police protection.

One need not be a critic of police officers to admit that police in the United States *often* take the lives of innocent people. A University of Chicago study revealed that in 1993, 330 innocent Americans were killed by police. When one considers accidental shootings, deaths of innocent bystanders in auto chases, and the rare crimes committed by corrupt officers, an honest individual must agree that the potential for state-sanctioned homicide is much greater under the never-questioned paradigm of police protection than under a capital punishment system that allows for hearings, deliberative jury trials, and appeals.

By creating a police force, the citizens of any community are, in effect, sanctioning the possible execution of an innocent life, an execution the likelihood of which is much greater than that seen under capital punishment. Yet opponents of the death penalty never question the utilization of armed men and women to "keep the peace". Occasionally, the system will be studied for possible corruption, usually when a particularly egregious case of police misconduct has occurred. But the actual paradigm is never challenged, not even by those who take the principled stance that government-sanctioned killing is unjustified.

New Yorkers and Comptonites may have protested in the streets over police brutality, but never over the very existence of a police force at all. We may see Barry Scheck, co-author of the book "Actual Innocence" -- which identified innocent people on death row -- call into question the death penalty, but we will never witness him attacking the very institution of police protection that takes many more innocent lives.

And this is odd, for these are people who are typically very vocal about their principles and their moral superiority, they are very "sensitive" to the plight of the down-trodden, they are the first to tell others who *do* support capital punishment that they need to reevaluate their ethics.

If these crusaders are to be consistent, they must apply their stance against state-sanctioned killing to *all* forms of the act, whether accidental or intentional. If they are to remain paladins, they must speak out, they must appear to be as strongly against the existence of police forces as they are against the existence of capital murder laws.

The fact that opponents of the death penalty have not done so forces one to admit that they are not basing their stance on principle. To defend their inconsistent position on state sanctioned killing, these "people of principle" are required to resort to the same argument for which they deride their opponents: that the policy they do not question is, in reality, a deterrent to crime, that the potential loss of one innocent life -- the very reason they oppose the death penalty -- at the hands of police is acceptable when it saves more lives in the community at large.

This is an argument based on utility, and it has nothing to do with principle.

Some may argue that it is unfair to compare a police force, dealing with immediate dangers, to a judicial system that does not need to kill the criminal once he has been apprehended. The criminal in court is going nowhere. He can be imprisoned for life, and society will receive the same protection it would if he were executed. Regardless of the potential for decreased deterrence this policy produces, this facile argument misses the larger point. For the principled opponent of state-sanctioned killing, the end result of giving police the power to use deadly force is the same as that of the death penalty. Any armed officer can take a life, and w*hy* he needs, or believes he needs, to use deadly force, is irrelevant. On this basis, the adoption of life sentences instead of death sentences would equate to taking away the police power to use deadly force while apprehending criminals. Even in England, famous for its Bobbies armed only with batons, the public has sanctioned "S.O. 19" officers who can shoot to kill.

Opponents of the death penalty will not admit it, but what it all comes down to is a consideration of whether capital punishment and armed police are deterrents to violent crime. Principle has nothing to do with it. If they oppose capital punishment and favor police protection, despite the greater number of innocent people who are killed by police, it must be because they believe police provide a greater deterrent against other crimes. They must believe police protection is a prophylactic, while the death penalty is not.

But police rarely *stop* crimes. They investigate the incidents after the fact. Most criminals are not afraid of meeting a police officer while engaged in a crime. There are just not enough officers to cover enough square miles of land. More crimes are prevented annually by privately armed individuals than by police, but the existence of a police force, and, in particular, an investigative police force, is usually seen as having a deterrent effect on the commission of crimes.

Whether it does or not, outspoken opponents of the death penalty ought to admit that they are not as principled as they proclaim. They ought to face up to the fact that they would be forced to utilize the same utilitarian arguments in favor of police protection that their adversaries use in favor of capital punishment. And they ought to consider that the consistent application of their principles would lead to the total dismantling of the state.

LIVE FREE OR DIE

If former Illinois governor George Ryan had been consistent, he would have been chief executive... of nothing.

"Death Penalty Zombies?"
Dec. 13, 2001

With the indictment of French citizen Zacarias Moussaouri on six conspiracy charges related to the terrorist attacks of September 11, the US government has not only taken its first step in delivering justice to those involved, it has inspired a somewhat surprising domestic political debate, and incurred the antipathy of the European Union.

This is because Moussaouri can be put to death.

For most Americans, the prospect of Moussaouri being eliminated seems so sensible as to require no debate at all. If an individual is guilty of murder, mass murder, or conspiracy to commit either, he should be put to death. Those involved in the September 11 attacks should receive swift and certain justice; simple execution is almost too good for them.

But for some, the entire issue of capital punishment is more tricky, a bit more ambiguous. Even the execution of Timothy McVeigh prompted a great deal of debate among Americans over the ethics and practicality of the death penalty. Thus, it seems logical that our international neighbors might express their opinions, even if they alienate many of us.

In most cases, the primary argument against capital punishment is the point made by attorney Barry Scheck and others who believe the state should not be vested with the power to kill. Given that there have been innocent men sentenced to death, and saved from execution by the introduction of new evidence, we must admit that there is a possibility that innocent men have been previously put to death, and others may tragically follow in their footsteps. The ethics of implicating an entire society in the killing of an innocent person are profound, and often work to draw individuals closer towards the position that it is better to keep a criminal in prison for life than to take that final, irrevocable step: execution. Once a criminal is put to death, there is no remedy for a mistake. When one is sentenced to life in prison, he has the chance of being freed if exculpatory evidence is discovered. This appears to be the rationale behind the European Union's opposition to our use of the death penalty.

But there is an inconsistency in the European logic. For them, granting the state the power to kill murderers means granting the state the power to kill those who are potentially innocent, hence their disapproval of capital punishment. But one must ask if the same standard will be applied to the sanctioning of police protection, for police can mistakenly kill, and *have* killed many more innocent people than have been put to death by the courts. If one opposes the death penalty due to fear that the government might take an innocent life, despite the lengthy appeals process instituted to decrease the chance that an innocent person is executed, will he also stand up against hiring local and state police?

This does not imply that police are unethical or sloppy. But mistakes do and have occurred all over the nation, and in other nations, and the death of an innocent by the hand of a police officer who has made a mistake is no different from the death of an innocent by the hands of the court system that has made a mistake. In both cases, it could be argued that the society sanctioning such mistakes is partially to blame. Those who oppose the death penalty on the principle that they do not want to grant a government the power to take an innocent life must also apply that ethical standard to police protection.

Aristotle was one of the first philosophers to express the primacy of self-defense. The public sanctioning of deadly force by a police unit or the jurisprudential application of the death penalty is seen by many contemporary conservatives as an extrapolation of that Aristotelian principle. Most opponents of the death penalty would not go so far. But the least they could do is consistently apply their own moral standards to the debate, and recognize that opposition to the use of deadly force in the form of capital punishment must coincide with opposition to police protection itself.

Guantanamo: A Long Train of Congressional, Executive, and Now, Judicial Abuses
April, 2007

In a stunning contradiction of the principles enshrined in the Unites States Constitution, the US Supreme Court on April 3 denied petitions of certiorari to two plaintiffs who have been held in legal limbo for five years at Guantanamo Bay, Cuba. By doing so, the justices have added another burdensome car to the long train of abuses the federal government has sent barreling down the tracks at US citizens.

The cases were named *al Odah v. United States* and *Boumedienne v. United States*, and in both instances, the court declined to hear the plaintiffs' requests for habeas corpus hearings. The DC Circuit Court of Appeals had already ruled against the plaintiffs, citing the habeas-stripping provisions of the Military Commissions Act passed by Congress and signed into law by the President in 2006[38].

In ruling to deny certiorari, and, hence, habeas corpus hearings for the plaintiffs, the US Supreme Court might appear to some observers to be upholding a long-held power of the Congress to limit the jurisdiction of the federal courts. Congress has done so numerous times in United States history, including a recent law restricting federal courts from hearing liability cases brought against gun manufacturers. But there are other principles at stake here, ones which the majority on the Court, and many reporters, do not seem willing to discuss.

Missed in the *Odah* and *Boumedienne* rulings are the principles of the separation of powers between the three branches of the federal government, and the constitutional stricture against Congress ceding any of its granted powers to any other body. While these points may seem esoteric to some, especially during this time of so-called "war", they are essential, and fundamental to insuring our liberties against government attenuation.

The roots of the April 3 ruling trace back to events just prior to the US invasion of Iraq, when then-White House Counsel Alberto Gonzales approached Congress and asked the representatives to do something not

---

[38] In favor of the Circuit Court ruling were Justices Scalia, Thomas, Alito, and Chief Justice Roberts, while Justices Breyer, Ginsberg and Souter dissented.

allowed under the US Constitution. He asked them to grant the President the power to use the military *without* a formal declaration of War. Such a declaration is the only power granted to Congress to facilitate the President's use of the US military. Instead, the Bush administration wanted Congress to grant him a "resolution for the use of military force", which seems an awfully cumbersome term when one could just, well, *declare War*.

The reason Gonzales and the Bush Administration did not want a formal declaration was obvious: the United States government is a signatory to the Geneva Accords. According to the treaty, which is easily found by utilizing a simple web search, all uniformed and *non-uniformed* enemies captured during wartime in any signatory state (Iraq and Afghanistan are both signatory) would have to be treated according to Common Article Three of the Accords. This insures certain standards of behavior for those holding Prisoners of War, prohibiting torture, and insuring that all signatory nations will afford humane treatment of their POWs.

According to US law prior to 2006, if the individuals captured on the battlefield in this undeclared "war on terror" were not going to be treated as POWs, then they would have to be tried under US criminal code, just like other terrorists in the past. This, of course, would require the courts to provide habeas corpus hearings to the arrested parties, unless Congress utilized its constitutional power to broadly suspend the Writ of Habeas Corpus for all Americans and those being tried under US law[39].

Instead, what US citizens saw between late 2001 and 2004 was a federal government operating outside both the Constitution and the Geneva Accords, with the executive branch apprehending and holding suspected terrorists for long periods of time, without providing treating them as POWs or criminals under US codes.

Enter the Supreme Court case *Hamdan v Rumsfeld*. In 2004, Salim Ahmed Hamdan, the captured and detained former driver for Osama bin Laden, filed suit for a habeas corpus hearing in US court. Held without trial, and as an "enemy combatant" without protection of the Geneva Accords, Hamdan requested what other terrorism suspects had typically received in US history: a hearing bound by US law, in which the evidence against him was presented. The Bush Administration fought the request, on the grounds that

---

[39] Article One, Section Nine: "The Privelege of the Writ of Habeas Corpus shall not be suspended, unless in Cases of Rebellion or Invasion the public Safety may require it."

to reveal certain evidence against Hamdan could put intelligence operatives and soldiers at risk. Such an argument was valid to a point, but it overlooked the necessity to abide by the Constitution and the constitutional treaties agreed to by the US government.

In 2005, the Supreme Court found in favor of Hamdan, setting in motion a number of troubling and revealing actions by the executive branch and Congress that ought to alert even the most disinterested Americans that the "train of abuses" is getting longer and longer.

First, when the Court ruled in the *Hamdan* case that the Administration had to either treat the "detainees" as Prisoners of War or as criminals under US Code, and thus afford them the protection of habeas corpus hearings, the President, Vice President and Secretary of Defense Rumsfeld said that if they had to abide by the Geneva Accords, they would not be able to derive the valuable information from their "detainees" that had helped "save American lives". As powerful as such statements were, they contradicted Bush Administration claims of a year before, in which the same men repeatedly stated that the "detainees" were *being afforded all the protections of the Geneva Accords in Common Article Three.*

The two positions are incompatible. If the Supreme Court ruling that Hamdam should be tried under US criminal code or as a POW under the provisions of the Geneva Accord meant that the Bush Administration could no longer carry out the interrogations it had been conducting at a time when Administration members *claimed* they were affording the protections of the Accords, then, clearly, the Bush Administration was *not* acting in accordance with the Accords prior to the Hamdan ruling. If employees of the executive branch had been conforming, the ruling would have had no effect on their interrogation procedures.

To many Americans this might not sound like such a big deal. After all, the "detainees" or "enemy combatants", as they are called, are all foreigners suspected of terrorist activities against American citizens. But what needs to be remembered is that we have a system under which this country is supposed to operate, and that system is set down in the US Constitution. Avoiding it without trying to amend it is an injustice to the Founding Fathers who wrote the rule book for the operation of the US, and to those of us who were under the mistaken impression that we operated under the rule of law.

Those abuses aside, there is another aspect of the Court's actions that might resonate even more strongly with some Americans. Under the 2006 Military Commissions Act established by Congress in response to the *Hamdan* case, and upheld by the Supreme Court on April 3, 2007, *anyone* can now be labeled an "enemy combatant".

As a result, US citizens can now be designated "detainees" and held indefinitely without trial, or habeas corpus hearing, and if they *are* brought to trial, they can be put on the stand in quasi-federal courts created by the executive branch, not the legislative branch.

Unfortunately, Congress responded to the Hamdan ruling in precisely the wrong manner. It did not pass laws intended to stop the Administration from creating its own "military tribunals", and it did not actually *declare War*, thus setting the US military on the proper track and arranging a POW system for capture, imprisonment and trial under the Geneva Accords. It responded by *codifying* what the Supreme Court had just ruled against. Congress recklessly passed the Military Commissions Act, allowing the Bush administration to set up military courts not sanctioned by the Accords, prohibiting federal courts from hearing any more cases requesting clarification as to the status of "detainees" as either POWs or criminals under US law, and ceding Congress's constitutionally provided power to suspend the Writ of Habeas Corpus.

There once was a time when Congress would not have been so quick to hand its powers over to other bodies. But we now have self-managing agencies such as the EPA, OSHA, and the FDA, and most Americans think they are justified, so why fuss over yet another hand-off to the executive branch, this time involving trials and the suspension of habeas corpus?

There are plenty of reasons to fuss. As it stands under the law, and the recent Court rulings, American citizens can now be arrested by the federal government, held indefinitely without trial, questioned under standards we would not allow for our own soldiers if captured by other nations or subordinates of those nations, and never have a hearing to find out the evidence being presented against them. This is shameful and stunning, and is all derived from a legislative branch that is unwilling to do what the Constitution allows it to do, *declare War*.

When Thomas Jefferson wrote the *Declaration of Independence*, the "train of abuses" by the Crown that he cited filled half a page. Today, Jefferson's quill could fill volumes, and every abuse is being perpetrated by the very politicians and bureaucrats who swore an oath to uphold the government he helped establish. It is a sad commentary on the likelihood that any constitutional republic can long endure without growing to infringe on individual rights, and makes one wonder why anyone ought to put his trust in even the most limited of governments in the first place.

**Government and Health Care:
Slow Poison**

Kiddie Care
August, 2000

Tuesday, August 14, saw the return of Ted Kennedy to the airwaves at a national Democrat convention. Unlike his 1980 DNC speech, his new presentation was a bit less dramatic, a bit more forced, but just as rife with lies, deceptions, and egotistical self-aggrandizement as ever. One of the central themes of his pompous harangue was his boastful claim that he, with the help of people such as Orrin Hatch, and Nancy Kassebaum, had turned the health insurance industry around, had made it more responsive to the public, and had made it more affordable for all Americans. Nothing could be further from the truth.

Kennedy's tactics in the health insurance war have been reminiscent of the Viet Cong forces in the '60's and early '70's. When moving troops or supplies, they would line women and children around the convoys. If the South Vietnamese and American forces wanted to inflict any damage on the convoys, they first had to shoot through the buffer of innocent humanity in their way. They would be killing women and children.

Kennedy and Hatch successfully utilized the disgusting V.C. military tactic in the battle over "KiddieCare", the latest incremental implementation of the Clinton health "care" agenda.

In 1995, many people breathed sighs of relief that the Clintonesque thinking on health care had been defeated. And how could it ever come back? After all, the Republicans held majorities in both houses. Conservatives and Libertarians ought to know by now that this numerical fact means very little. Like a vampire -- like bad Seventies clothing -- the socialist medical paradigm was resurrected, this time in the "historic" '97-'98 budget agreement that spineless Republicans and gleeful Democrats heralded as the salvation of the free world. The political tag-team of Kennedy and Hatch achieved this goal with "KiddieCare", and very few Republicans even raised an eyebrow about it. Why? Because the provision was "for the children", and woe unto anyone with the audacity to inject reason and principle into an argument about helping children.

The primary statistic used to "alert" citizens to the "Child Health Care Crisis" was that there were "10 million American children without health insurance." This statement, offered endlessly by supporters of "Kennedy-

Hatch", and by the President himself, was little more than a conjurers illusion, created to make the observer respond with "oohs" and "ahhs" of amazement and concern. In an excellent analysis published in the June, 1997 issue of *Reason* magazine, John Hood shed the light of truth on these deceptive numbers. They were derived from the March, '97, "Current Health Survey" of the U.S. Census Bureau. According to Hood, "The survey presumes uninsured status when households don't report coverage by a major government insurance program or by employer-provided insurance."[40]

This had the effect of making individuals who were uninsured for a very short period appear as if they were part of a national epidemic of non-insureds, when, in fact, many people drop their insurance when leaving jobs, or drop their insurance for short periods only to pick it back up a month or two later. Hood reported that, adjusted for this fact, the "liberal Urban Institute... estimates the number to be 8.7 million, not 10 million."[41]

And even this number was incorrect. Of those 8.7 million, Hood reported, "... 2.14 million are eligible for Medicaid, and an additional 700,000 will be eligible for Medicaid by the year 2000 because of past Congressional action."[42] In fact, if brought to the emergency room, most eligible children would be "immediately enrolled" in Medicaid, and receive whatever services they needed for no charge.

But even if the purported number of 10 million was not correct, what was to be done with the rest? The fact is, the uninsured already received myriad handouts. Blue Cross and Blue Shield operated a charity program in 28 states for uninsured children whose parents did not qualify for Medicaid. The Federal program "Women and Infant Children" assists many uninsured children through the funds it provides parents. Prenatal care is provided through government or private means for 96% of all U.S. women during the first two trimesters of pregnancy.

Obviously, the posturing that there was a "child health care crisis" was just that, and it was being done on very flimsy footing. Couple the above statistics with the fact that the mortality rate for children between the ages

---

[40] Hood, John. Pediatric Politics. Reason, June 1997: p. 29.
[41] Ibid: p. 29.
[42] Ibid: p. 29-30.

of 5 and 14 has been steadily decreasing for the past fifty years, and you might wonder where the crisis has been.

The crisis arose in the hearts and minds of statist politicians and emotion-based voters who cannot distinguish between private charity and state coercion.

The Kennedy-Hatch proposal was adopted into the budget agreement in the form of a 15 Cents per pack tax increase on the sale of cigarettes. With this plunder, a new bureaucracy was soon created. The new budget allocated 24 billion Dollars to the states over the next five years, tax money that had to be used to establish new health insurance programs for children whose parents would not normally qualify for Medicaid. The Congressional Budget Office forecasted that 40% of the children in such programs would be individuals who were *previously* covered by other insurance plans -- such as their parents' employee benefits plans, or their parents' private plans. These children would be shifted over when parents and employers realized that it was in their best interest to drop their children's coverage in favor of the new government handout.

This proposal should have made any semi-sentient being quite nervous. First, it imposed yet another tax on the current "Great Satan", the tobacco industry. Some might not see this as such a bad thing. After all, smoking is a foul and dangerous habit, and the less of it we have, the better... I could name half a dozen habits that are foul and dangerous, and it would never cross anyone's mind to tax them. Additionally, such a tax does not simply fall on tobacco growers, cigarette manufacturers, cigarette sellers, and cigarette consumers. It is passed on to non-smokers in myriad, unexpected ways

The new bureaucracy has also inspired higher costs in the health care industry. Any time there is a "third party" payer, be it the government, or a tax-favored H.M.O., demand for health services increases. There is a disincentive for the non-paying party to keep costs low. He will seek more services, and costs will rise. The only alternatives under a government plan are to increase taxes, which simply aggravates the problem, or to ration care, which works in contradiction to the purported government goal of providing universal health care to kids. The same dynamic will apply to a government-funded prescription payment plan for "seniors" as well.

Anyone who thinks such government-run health systems can work need only study Canada. While I was in Vancouver in 1996, the government was considering imposing limits on doctors regarding how many patients they could see per day. There was even talk of having certain days reserved for certain maladies. A friend once turned to me and asked, "Does that mean the government will also decide what days we can get sick?"

By claiming they are "helping innocent children", Kennedy and Hatch successfully shielded themselves and their plan from criticism such as that written above. After all, who could find fault with a plan that ostensibly helps needy kids? And who could criticize its kind-hearted framers? Americans learned a great deal from their experiences in, and with, Vietnam during the war. It appears Ted Kennedy and Orrin Hatch have remembered, and put into practice, certain tactics that most of us could never have imagined.

But surely this is academic…After all, the Constitution never enumerated to the federal government the power to regulate "health care", and the Interstate Commerce Clause was originally intended to keep states from imposing tariffs on one another, not to give Congress omnipotent control over inter-state trade. No politician in his right mind would think of getting the federal government involved in health care…Would he?

Then again, no one pays much attention to the Constitution any more, least of all Ted Kennedy and Orrin Hatch.

The dignity of mankind under Communism is that of a raindrop on a sea of slime.

PHG
March, 1984

"The Destruction of the Health Insurance Industry In New Hampshire"
Sept. 2000

A great deal of political hay is being made by the Shaheen campaign over her supposed fight to make health insurance affordable in New Hampshire. In her first campaign for Governor in 1995, we heard the ringside announcement that "she fought the big insurance companies and won." Now, we are being told that she fought the "big HMO's" and is providing affordable health insurance to poor New Hampshire children.

This is far from the truth.

To delve into the reality of the health insurance market in New Hampshire, one must first look back to the administration of President Franklin Roosevelt. It was under his institution of utterly socialistic and unconstitutional wage and price controls that companies began to look for other ways in which to attract productive employees. They did this, in part, by offering health insurance coverage, purchased through "group" insurers, rather than what was typically known as "individual insurers", who covered individual clients.

Thus was established the popular notion that large companies would supply insurance coverage to their employees, and, when the wage and price controls were lifted, the precedent had been set, and had become part of the business landscape for many large employers. It also popularized the erroneous belief that the money being paid for this insurance was coming from the company, rather than the employee. In fact, the paycheck of the employee would have been just that much larger if he had not had to pay for his insurance coverage.

Then, in the early 1970's Congress passed a law providing a tax discount to large employers that purchased "group" or HMO coverage for their employees. Seen as a beneficent stroke by the federal government to encourage group insurance coverage throughout the country, the law had the real-world effect of tilting the tax balance in favor of HMO's rather than individuals purchasing their own individual policies. If an employee had the option to either accept a company HMO plan or take the money in his paycheck and buy his own *non-tax-free* policy, he would obviously recognize the financial advantages of accepting the company plan.

Thus, the power of HMO's began to grow...

Then, in 1993, Bill Clinton went to the airwaves to pronounce that the state of health insurance in the US was abysmal. It was too expensive, he claimed, though, in reality, inflation rates in health insurance were about equal to the inflation rate generally. It was only in the government controlled programs of Medicare and Medicaid that one saw double-digit inflation, over-use by the "recipients", and attempts at price controls. He pronounced that the health insurance industry was callous to those with pre-existing conditions, and told us in his loving way that was too bureaucratic.

So, Mr. Clinton's answer was to nationalize the health insurance industry in one fell swoop. He assigned Hillary Clinton to head up his Health Care Task Force, which held organizational meetings behind closed doors, an act which later cost the White House $300,000 when it was determined to have been illegal. The goal of the Clinton plan was, of course, a *real* bureaucratization of the health insurance industry in the US, to place it under the control of those wonderfully efficient and incredibly responsive dis-functionaries in Washington.

And if Bill and Hillary couldn't nationalize the health insurance industry with one stroke of the pen, they had plans to do so incrementally, via the states, and via stand-alone Congressional legislation.

This began on a national basis with the Kennedy-Kassebaum Insurance Portability Act, which forced businesses with twenty or more employees to have to pay for the insurance plans of their employees even after they had left their jobs, for a period of up to eleven months (just long enough for these people to qualify for federal insurance). Later, in 1997, the Kennedy-Hatch "CHIPS", or "Kiddie-care" plan was passed, which taxed cigarettes an extra 15 Cents per pack and funneled this plunder to the states in order to create their own bureaucracies which would administer health insurance to supposedly "poor" children. At the time, it was predicted by the Congressional Budget Office that 40% of those children who would be placed on this plan in their home states would be children who already *had* insurance coverage, thanks to their parents, or their parents' employers, but would be shifted over to the new tax-funded plan after those who paid for the original insurance plans recognized the fact that they could get health insurance for the kids on someone else's buck.

And, in New Hampshire, Senator Jeanne Shaheen proposed SB711, which has gone on to decimate the individual health insurance market in the state, just as she had been warned it would.

But before we get into the insurance miasma created by Shaheen, let's participate in a quick overview of the dynamics of health insurance.

Obviously, health insurance is a business, not a charity. No one has the right to force a person in this business to *give* him insurance, just as no one has a right to force a supermarket owner to give him food. Such impositions are infringements upon one's right to his own property, and create a social system in which order, justice, and mutual respect are replaced by chaos, injustice, and perpetual coercion. It is no more just for a government, through the mechanism of majority rule, to seize private property than it is a robber or a gang of thugs. Even if it is to serve a supposedly altruistic motive.

An easy way to imagine how the insurance business works is to consider Ben Franklin's famous adage: "A stitch in time saves nine." From the perspective of the client, his regular premium payments are his "stitches". He knows that life always presents risks, and that insurance is a hedge against future loss. He pays his "stitches" to a business owner willing to accept him as a client. In return for this financial obligation, the insurer agrees to pay out "nine stitches" should some injury or calamity occur. The insurer stays in business, and turns a profit, as long as he has more clients paying "stitches" than he expends for claims. This is true for all types of insurance, home, health, fire, auto, life, on down the line to the policy taken out for Mary Hart's legs. If the client is worried that something really, truly, horribly rotten could happen to him (and what sensible person isn't?) he will try to buy some insurance. The insurer will decide to accept the client based on the risk he presents -- the risk that the company will have to expend a lot of "stitches" for claims.

It only makes sense, then, that insurance companies accept or deny coverage, decrease or increase premiums, based on the health and lifestyle of the individual interested in buying its insurance. If the insurance company feels that the potential client -- say a junkie, skydiving, secret agent who enjoys weekends playing Russian Roulette with Andrew Kunanin -- represents too much of a risk to accept, the insurance company has the right to say "sorry!" Likewise if the potential client has diabetes, or any disease that, statistically, means the insurer will be more likely to have to pay claims in the future, the insurer has the right to not accept him as a client, or ask for a higher premium, so that the amount the company takes in premiums will offset the amount the company expects to pay out for claims. The more old, ill, risky clients an insurance company insures, the more claims will have to be paid. As a result, in order to keep afloat, the company will have to raise premiums for everyone. It sounds harsh, but so is life, and insurance is based on the clear and important risks presented by life.

But some people, usually those in the Federal and State governments (and usually those with big "D"s next to their names, but increasingly they have "R"s as well), believe that recognizing those risks is unfair. They think that through the machine of government, all can be made "fair and equal". Of course, it can be empirically observed that they are wrong. And in their efforts to equalize the existences of all they have infringed upon private property, damaged our principles of charity, damaged the charitable institutions that rely on us, warped the true meaning of natural rights, and destroyed the very definition of insurance.

Now, let's look at the state. New Hampshire… Home of the brave… The Granite State… Rock solid… Jeanne Shaheen, its Governor…

Let me tell you about Jeanne Shaheen. In 1994, then State Senator Jeanne Shaheen co-sponsored a bill called SB711 (RSA 420-G), which passed both houses and was later allowed to become law by the supposedly "conservative" Steve Merrill. SB711 essentially forced private insurance companies issuing individual, or "non-group", policies in the state to accept people with pre-existing conditions. It also forced them to place their clients into "Community Rating Pools", in which age categories would be set up, and in which the younger policy holders in these categories would pay artificially high premiums in order to help lower the premiums of the older members. The fact that older people *should* pay higher premiums because they represent higher risks never seemed to register with her.

Of course, the effects of this kind of nonsense could be predicted. With "guaranteed issue" of insurance (the elimination of pre-existing condition clauses in policies) there is no incentive for someone to purchase health insurance while he is healthy. He will wait until he gets sick, then get his insurance. (Kind of like one's family getting a life insurance policy *after* one dies.) This not only corrupts the very definition of insurance, it has the secondary effect of leaving only the sick with policies, which then forces the insurance company to increase premiums to stay in business. The added feature of forcing younger insureds to subsidize the older members of their "pools" increases the incentive for young people to drop their insurance, again raising the price of premiums for those still holding policies. In 1994, the results could not only be predicted, they could be *seen*, in states such as New York, which lost a huge percentage of younger, healthy individuals who formerly had policies, forcing up the prices of premiums for those still being insured. One could see at the time that New York would be lucky if any of the companies doing business there continued to issue policies. Why bother, when all they would end up doing is subsidizing people who were already sick? That's not insurance, that's state coerced redistribution.

I gave the State House a call to contact Senator Shaheen about the issue back in 1994. But the committee office was empty of members, and I was told I should try her at her home. I was assured this would be okay… It was far from "okay". When I asked Mrs. Shaheen if she was aware of the statistics that had been put together in states such as New York, when I asked if she had considered what people would do if they could get their insurance after they got sick, she became very angry. When I asked her if she thought it wise to impose her ideals on individuals and businesses making contracts with one another for insurance here in the state, she hung up the phone.

Well, I've been keeping my eye on the effects of SB711, and Mrs. Shaheen should have stayed on the line. In 1994, there were ten companies issuing "non-group" health insurance policies. As of January 1, 1995, the date SB711 went into effect, four of those companies stopped issuing policies in the state. They knew what would happen to their bottom lines under such a system of state coercion. What follows? What happens when there is less competition in any field? Prices rise. What happens when those companies still issuing policies are faced with potential clients who are already sick, or high risks? Prices rise. What happens when those companies that have stopped issuing policies, but retain their previous clients, see their clients getting older, making more claims, while younger, healthier clients are no longer entering their pool of insureds? PRICES RISE! What happens when prices rise? Healthy people drop their insurance policies because they are too expensive. What happens when healthy people drop their insurance policies? PRICES RISE for those still holding their policies! HELLO! It's a never-ending cycle: government manipulation leads to changes in the behavior of clients and potential clients, or to pre-emptory changes in the policies of companies, which leads to less competition, which leads to higher prices, which leads to more clients and potential clients changing their behavior which leads to... And so on.

If you are the charitable kind, you might believe that Jeanne Shaheen was simply daft or naive. I am not that charitable. She was presented with mountains of information, researched by very highly regarded firms, that warned her of just this kind of effect. For example, in 1994, the Council for Affordable Health Insurance stated:

"Community rating, as mandated in this bill, will result in significant premium increases for young families and small employers."

A letter dated April 1, 1994, from GoldenRule Insurance stated:

"When New York passed similar legislation (in 1993), rates increased 170% for 30-year-old insureds."

Jeanne Shaheen was about as open to this information as she was to mine.

We've seen that those money-grubbing, nasty, evil insurance companies left the state after Shaheen tried to dictate to them the operation of their businesses, despite the fact that the New Hampshire constitution only allows regulation of monopolies and consortiums that are attempting to collusively control prices... But what happened economically? Did her attempt to make insurance more readily available to people achieve success? Did rates go down? Did more people have individual policies?

The answers to these questions can be found in a report issued by the state called: "The Effects of RSA 420-G" (Which was the House version of SB711 that was eventually passed into law.)

The report clearly states that, not only did four of the ten businesses issuing individual policies in NH leave the state on the day Shaheen's brainchild became law, by December of 1997, we had 42% *FEWER* people holding individual insurance policies than we did prior to the passage of her bill. (See p. 36.) This decline occurred despite higher employment in the state.

Additionally, insurance rates for those in the younger "Rating Pools" have increased nearly 100%, just as it was predicted, just as Jeanne Shaheen was told.

But the detrimental results of her absurd creation could be seen in other areas as well. There was a domino effect, extending into the "group" market, and, specifically, Blue Cross -- Blue Shield.

In 1977, BCBS's charter was recodified, as a 501-C-4, Non-profit Service Corporation. Under this status, BCBS was given a special 2% Premium Tax deduction for accepting people with pre-existing conditions. Other companies that did not accept people with pre-existing conditions did not enjoy such favors. As a result, BCBS of NH existed as the "insurer of last resort", or the company to which people with pre-existing conditions would turn if they could not buy coverage from other companies, or found the premiums of other companies too expensive.

But once the other companies were forced by Jeanne Shaheen, through SB711, to accept people with pre-existing conditions, they cried foul that they did not receive the same 2% Premium Tax discount that BCBS received. So what did the state do in 1995? It revoked BCBS's 2% Premium Tax discount. What did BCBS have to do in return? It decided to drop all its clients holding "non-group" (or individual) health insurance policies, and not accept any more! Why? The amount of money it lost in the year between losing its tax discount and dropping its high risk clients was almost exactly the same as the amount of its prior tax discount... Gee, go figure.

And, as a result of SB 711, we have seen the power of the HMO's increase. After all, their competition from individual issuers has been nearly cut in half.

What has the state done to curtail the "faceless, heartless" monolithic HMO industry here in NH? Has Jeanne Shaheen proposed a revocation of SB711 and invited those individual issuers she drove out of the state back into her embrace?

Not at all. She's merely pandered to the public, painting the HMO's as evil giants who are disinclined to give their clients a fair shake, who continually deny coverage for simple procedures, who deny coverage for those in need. Yet, she never states that the <u>real</u> client of the HMO is usually the business that purchased the plan for its employee, not the employee himself. She's paraded herself as a champion of the little guy, the important woman who helped pass the HMO Accountability Act in 1999, which is merely another level of state control over the insurance market, even though it has been state intervention in the insurance market that has caused this continuing stream of problems in the first place.

And today, we see commercials with Jeanne Shaheen sitting behind her desk, popping on her glasses while a dulcet-voiced announcer tells us she's got a quiet style, but she gets results.

Well, if the results of her actions are typified by the insurance debacle she's commanded in the past few years, perhaps it would be better is she stayed out of politics entirely.

Editor's note: With the beginning of the Craig Benson Administration in NH, changes were proposed to the NH health insurance laws. Under Senate Bill 110, companies could once more check for pre-existing conditions, and rate according to risk factors like age, smoking, etc. Unfortunately, part of SB 110 prohibited policy holders from dropping their policies and going to new companies until a year had passed. This being the case, the companies already doing business in NH, and who had clients who could not move to new competition entering the state, increased their prices. This caused a clamor among voters, and was used a lever to revoke the positive provisions of SB110. Senator Ted Gatsis then proposed, in early 2005, a new health insurance bill that would eliminate once more the ability of companies to actually look at the risks posed by potential clients, and to charge accordingly. Instead, Gatsis' bill forced these companies to accept people with pre-existing conditions, without being able in any way to look at their health history – an interesting prospect for what are supposed to be HEALTH insurance companies. Only AFTER the companies accepted the clients could they look at the risk factors, and then, if their actuaries thought a client posed too high a risk, Gatsis' bill gave the insurances businesses the ability to move these clients into "high risk" pools – which, of course, are paid for with money taken by the state from the very health insurance companies being forced to accept the clients in the first place. We have not only returned to the pernicious situation of Shaheen's SB 711, we have made things worse, more coercive, and, eventually, more expensive for insurance companies, and the people who would like to buy policies. Socialism never works, no matter how altruistic the motive, and no matter if the policy is proposed by a Democrat or Republican. Keep it in mind next time you visit a doctor.

"Calling All Comrades!"
November, 1998

WANTED: A post-Soviet Marxist to join energized group of socialists and redistributionists for experiment in utopian government expansion. Requirements: Must be blind to the ethical dilemmas of taxation and redistribution, must believe there is no such thing as private property, especially when the demands of a particular group can be played upon in emotionally charged news stories, must be able to overlook things like the US and New Hampshire Constitutions. Most important, the ideal candidate must be conceited enough to believe he or she can decide what is best for the lives of others. Interested applicants, contact Jeanne Shaheen, Governor, New Hampshire.

Many Americans celebrated upon the dissolution of the USSR. The tired old shibboleths of Karl Marx, Lenin, Stalin, and all the other scheming redistributionists had finally been exposed as unworkable. The primary facets of free economics -- individual initiative, private property, and subjective valuation of one's wealth -- had been proven preeminent, the core principles that drive prosperity. Who would have thought the old redistributionist hallucinations would once again take hold?

Especially here in New Hampshire?

Well, it's happening. Just one look at the report called "Creating a Healthier New Hampshire", recently released by the NH Department of Health and Human Services, tells much of the story.

The report is an introduction to an even larger, more offensive publication called "The New Hampshire Health Care System", which is a glossy, 87 page collection of specific policy proposals that would completely alter the way in which NH citizens select their health insurance.

In this piece, I will discuss the general concepts covered in "Creating a Healthier New Hampshire". I will delve into the nasty details of the larger, 87 page document in a future article.

The report begins grandiosely, with a "definition" of *health* from the World Health Organization: "A state of complete well-being, physical, social and mental, and not merely the absence of disease or infirmity." The fact that the WHO is a teeming hive of redistributionists that receives funding from the US government in opposition to all Constitutional strictures is not the primary problem with the opening of the report. The primary problem is with its definition of *health*, a definition that goes beyond physical and mental maladies that can be empirically noted and addressed, to include "social well-being".

Just what does "social well-being" mean? It means different things to different people. Depending on one's nature, one's interests, and one's abilities, "social well-being" could mean living like a hermit in the woods, living in a commune with others of like interests, being in a rock band, immersing oneself in books, playing cards with one's friends, etc. There are as many different definitions of "social well-being" as there are people, and what those definitions have to do with a health care system being designed and enforced by the government, one cannot fathom. In fact, it is frightening to consider the possibility.

But, that aside, there are more forbidding things in this proposal. Let's begin with the introduction:

"In 1995, in response to changes in the health care system, the NH Dept. of Health and Human Services drafted legislation which was approved and signed into law by the NH legislature that directed the Department to prepare 'a comprehensive and coordinated system of health and human services as needed to promote the health, safety and well-being of the citizens of NH.' The Department responded by creating a statewide Health Care Planning Process - the goal of which was to develop a State Health Plan."

Essentially, what the above says is that the Dept. of Health and Human Services lobbied the legislature to pass a bill that the Dept. itself drafted. It is a bill that would give the Dept. license to move forward with its intent to create a State Health Plan. Additionally, and more important, the introduction doesn't tell you about the "changes in the health care system" that came about in 1995. Well, I can tell you. The changes mentioned were the passage of a law that spurred the departure of 40% of the insurance companies issuing individual health policies to NH residents, the loss of customers for the companies that remained, and the inevitable rise in costs for the customers who didn't drop their policies. All of these problems came in direct response to a regulatory bill proposed and sponsored by then Senator Jeanne Shaheen. (The initial bill was titled SB711, and it was the matter over which Ms. Shaheen hung up the phone when I called to discuss it with her in 1994. Such a nice demeanor!) When the bill became law, many companies left the state, as many people had told Ms. Shaheen they would, the insurance choices for NH citizens dropped dramatically, prices rose, and today, we have about 40% fewer individuals holding individual health policies than in 1994, despite the fact that we have much higher employment!

So, what does the Shaheen administration plan to do to rectify the problem? Impose not just more government intervention, but nearly total government control in the old Soviet style. It's all spelled out in the HHS Department report.

First, it is important to note that the very premise of the department's goal is flawed. Just as in the USSR, the politicians believe they can make better decisions than the individuals looking to address their own specific needs. A successful "comprehensive and coordinated system of health and human services," as proposed by the department, cannot possibly be created by government law. It can only arise through market response to the varied, spontaneous, and ever-changing needs of customers. Only in that way can "needs" be defined, recognized, and quickly addressed.

However, this fact of life is rarely recognized by politicians. In order to carry out this ill-inspired idea, the department, as it puts it, "joined forces with health care and social service professionals, with elected officials, and, most importantly (sic), with New Hampshire citizens.

"Through District Councils set up by the Executive Councilors, and through town meetings and focus groups, hundreds of New Hampshire residents participated in planning the kind of health care system New Hampshire wants and needs and the best way to achieve it."

So, let's get this straight. "Hundreds" of citizens helped plan the kind of health care system that nearly 1 million, including you, will have to accept? The conceit of stating "hundreds of NH residents participated in planning the kind of health care system NH wants..." is mind boggling. How about allowing people to make their own choices, based on their own specific needs, to have their wants satisfied by utilizing their own dollars, in the manner, and with whom, they choose?

And even if one were to buy into the fallacy that such focus groups could choose for everyone else, just how were those District Councils and focus groups composed? They were, as noted in "The New Hampshire Health Care System": "...(N)ot randomly selected. They were either members of groups; recommended by individuals within the Dept. of Health and Human Services or the Executive Councilors; or selected by the Executive Councilors." They were biased from the start.

The politicians then tell us that "…(F)rom the very beginning, the planning group stressed the importance of balancing the roles of government, business and communities to serve New Hampshire residents."

Let's get something straight. There is no such thing as a "balance" when government becomes involved. Immediately, the market becomes skewed by government regulation, regulation brought about to play favorites and garner votes. The "role" of communities in this case will be to act as bureaucratic cells, handling the commands that come down from the state. If you doubt this is the reality that inevitably comes about, you haven't had your eyes open to how government works.

Page one of the report states:

"Our vision is to ensure that New Hampshire (i.e. the government) will promote access (i.e. will pass laws redistributing money and regulating insurance companies) for everyone to *necessary* and *appropriate* health and human services…" (emphasis added.)

But who defines what is necessary and appropriate? If it is anyone other than the doctor and the individual paying, the system is unbalanced and corrupted.

The report then goes on to state its "Health Status Goals". Among these are:

"New Hampshire residents will live with independence and satisfaction as contributing members of their communities."

But how can one be independent, and, at the same time, a "contributing member of one's community" if one's livelihood is seized by the majority and one's freedom of contract is abridged?

Additionally, goal 6 states: "New Hampshire residents will choose behaviors which contribute to health and well-being."

Thanks, but I'll decide what behaviors contribute to my own health and well-being. The conceit of bureaucrats to somehow "define" goals for all the residents in the state is dumbfounding. How about this for a goal?

"It is the role of the state to protect the citizens from threats against their life and/or property made by others."

According to the political principles that formed this nation, that is the only reason governments are founded. The rest is up to us, through our own individual volition.

The report continues along these lines until finally determining what should be done to the health care market in NH:

"(Establish) a standardized set of benefit packages for the health insurance market."

My first question, among many, is, how is it a "market" when the choices have already been determined by the government, and not the customers? The politicians claim that this will allow buyers to do comparison shopping. But they will be able to choose from what? From what the state allows them. And how will comparison shopping be best encouraged, by limiting the number of choices by state dictate, or by allowing buyers and sellers to make their own choices without meddling from politicians at the HHS?

"(The state will) establish a risk adjustment system for the insurance market."

Like the risk sharing system Shaheen forced on HMO's? The one that helped increase HMO costs over the past year? Increases that are being used as an excuse for *further* government expansion? The proposal stresses that "without the incentive to select less costly patients, health plans would compete only on the basis of efficiency and quality."

But efficiency and quality cannot be disconnected from costs. Customers purchase insurance plans based on all of these factors. Insurance companies issue policies, base their business on *costs!* Without the ability to make discriminating decisions regarding who they will accept as customers, and how much those customers will be charged, based on the risk those customers pose to the company regarding benefits payments, no insurance company can operate correctly. What the Shaheen people want is health insurance businesses without the business.

"(The state will develop) health information systems to provide the information all of us need to make informed choices."

How about letting each of us be responsible for creating his own "health information system" by shopping for insurance the same way we shop for food, or clothes, or cars? And just what will be the criteria for this "health information system?" The state decides, not the consumer.

"(The state will establish) partnerships between the state and communities in creating and delivering efficient health care and social service programs."

This does not only imply more welfare, Medicaid, KiddieCare-type programs, more bureaucracy and more immoral redistribution. Taken in conjunction with the next proposal, it has even more terrifying implications.

"(The state would support) community based *planning* targeted at improving our health (emphasis added)."

And this planning gets us to the point that started this article. The mechanism for such planning, the device by which the state politicians would institute their plans, their "partnerships between the state and communities" is called the "District Council". As the proposal explains, the biased, pre-selected "District Councils" that helped formulate this noxious set of ideas, "...should be retained as a permanent part of health planning and policy development..."

For anyone who is familiar with world history, this is almost exactly what the Marxists created in the USSR after the revolution. They were called "Soviets", hence the name Union of Soviet Socialist Republics. These Soviets were cells of bureaucracy that executed the dictates of the central government, that dictated to the localities how their lives would be run, in every way, from business production, to travel, to health care. Jeanne Shaheen has stumbled onto a New Hampshire version of the Soviet. Or, perhaps she has been interested in creating a system like this all along. Whichever her motives, the end result will be the same. You will have less control over your life. Politicians will make your choices for you, and they will call it moral. Prices will rise, options will disappear, quality will suffer, and bureaucrats will claim they're doing something good and worthwhile.

You know, I have a piece of the Berlin Wall on my desk. I never thought it was made of granite.

"The Cost of Abasement"
December, 1998

What is the cost of abasement? What is the amount one must surrender in our current American climate of paternalism, in the atmosphere of state authority, the system of property seizure and redistribution? What must one give up in order to be "taken care of" by the majority?

At one point in history, and it seems so very long ago, one would have had to relinquish a great deal: things such as personal integrity, personal responsibility, the moral and ethical treatment of one's neighbors, an old fashioned, indefinable thing called pride...

But not any more.

Now, it's not only acceptable to kneel in supplication to the majority, to be servile to the state, it's expected. One must never question the morality of majority decisions, whatever the issue.

This is the mindset behind many of the most deplorable injustices ever perpetrated against man. And it is the twisted philosophy that promotes people like William J. Clinton and Jeanne Shaheen to advocate for ever greater state interference in people's lives. It's good to surrender control of your own life to the state, because the state will care for you better than you for yourself. It's good to relinquish your livelihood and property to the dictates of the majority, because the majority obviously knows better how to spend it, how to be more caring with it, than you. In return, the state will include you in its great schemes; you can have the satisfaction of receiving majority sanctioned affection and care. And isn't that grand? You'll no longer have to worry.

And Heaven help you if you should disagree, because then you'll be painted as callous, heartless and cruel. Why, a *different* way? A way that works better? One that doesn't involve highly publicized political plans and "caring" bureaucrats making careers out of what was once done voluntarily?

It's no longer conceivable! *Of course* the state has to manage our lives, or at least the lives of our daft neighbors, who obviously can't handle their own affairs.

The health care issue is a perfect example of this twisted philosophy of state control. As discussed last month ("Calling All Comrades", November, 1998), the New Hampshire Department of Health and Human Services has recently released a blueprint for the complete takeover of the health insurance industry in the granite state. Predicated upon the fallacious idea that HMOs are a "free market" system (they arose after federal wage controls in WWII forced businesses to compensate employees by offering health policies, then were further strengthened by federal tax incentives), the HHS makes the daring claim that there is a market "crisis" in the industry.

Rather than calling for the removal of the artificial government manipulation that has inspired the whole mess, including Jeanne Shaheen's absurd law codifying the idea that people can buy their health insurance *after* they get sick (kind of like buying a life insurance policy for a deceased relative), the liberals in Concord have proposed getting the government *more* involved!

Setting out to win people over, the HHS has produced an 87 page document called, "The New Hampshire Health Care System". Early on, they attempt to define health, saying "Health care should not be understood merely as treatment for illness; it should include necessary and appropriate services, medical, social or other, that is (sic) intended to promote the highest possible level of function and independence for an individual...." "Health care should include physical, emotional and spiritual growth..." (p.5)

How quaint. At one time, terms had very clear definitions. Now, people can manipulate them to fit any amorphous, new-agey goal they have in mind. Just what do they mean by "spiritual growth"? Does that mean the state health plan will include a low deductible for Yanni concerts? Am I covered for used copies of "The Celestine Prophesy?" I thought health care had something to do with services provided by medically trained individuals intended to relieve or eliminate empirically observable maladies. But obviously, I'm deranged; I must be in need of some "emotional services".

The writers then list their "New Hampshire Health System Values":

"1. Every New Hampshire resident will have access to necessary health care services regardless of individual circumstances." (p. iv)

In other words, "universal access", which is based on redistribution of income, suppression of the free market and individual choice, and fuels inflation unless price controls are instituted, which in turn would inspire shortages and losses of quality.

"2. The health care system will be based on desired health outcomes as determined by well-defined indicators for measuring health." (p. iv)

In my previous article, I discussed the frightening prospects of having the state determine the "desired outcomes" of a health care system. There are so many different demands, brought about by the hundreds of thousands of consumers in the state, that such a brazenly audacious and conceited statement as the above seems almost laughable. But don't count on the statists in Concord to recognize the absurdity of their lofty goal.

And, by the way, why aren't these "well-defined" indicators defined in the publication? The answer is obvious: because they are only definable by the individuals seeking the care. Only the consumer can determine whether or not he is satisfied with his care.

"3. The health care system will emphasize quality of care and focus on managing costs."

Before reading on, please refer to number One above. If the state is going to institute a plan of "universal access", then demand will increase. If demand increases, costs will rise. If costs rise, demand will decrease, but this would imply that some people couldn't afford the care, which would mean that the state's goal of "universal access" is not being achieved. The answer the state proposes, and its the same idea Nixon tried with oil, is to institute price controls. As with oil, price caps inspire producers to produce less, and quality often goes down. So the goal listed as number Three is internally contradictory. The state cannot emphasize quality of care while at the same time managing costs through legislation.

"4. Health care consumers will be empowered and assume primary responsibility for their health and for the care they receive."

The only thing that need be asked here is: who pays? If the consumer pays with his own money, then yes, indeed, he will be inclined to try to get the best care for the money. The market will have to respond by providing that quality care at the most reasonable price. The market is competitive, and each participant must answer to the demands he receives if he wants to succeed. But if the consumer is using *someone else's* money? Then he will not assume primary responsibility for his care. He will not watch costs. *Because it's not his money!!!!* Again, the state proposal is internally contradictory. By "empowered" the writers mean the state will give the citizen the purchasing power (i.e. money). But if the state "empowers" the consumer, the consumer will have no incentive to manage his own affairs. By definition, he will be utilizing someone else's money, so he won't even be managing his own affairs; they'll be those of someone else.

"5. Communities will play a role in the organization and integration of health systems and in the delivery of health care services."

As mentioned last month, this is one of the most pernicious proposals in the entire plan, and there are a great many bad ideas with which to compete. Basically, what this outlines is the creation of small bureaucracies to not only execute the state dictates, but to actually *become* part of the health care delivery process!

Now, each of these proposals has a slew of tiny details to be worked out by the state, details that will further control your lives. Indeed, part of the plan to "protect and empower consumers" (that used to be the responsibility of the consumer himself, but I guess we're all too stupid to take care of our own business) is the creation of a "state information infrastructure" (p. vii). This system would review your health status… In other words, the state will control and monitor all your health information. Nice, huh?

But perhaps that invasion of privacy through force of law isn't as frightening as it sounds. After all, who better to take care of the details of our pesky private lives than the government, the same entity that gave us an electric monopoly on the state level, and social security, welfare and farm subsidies on the national front? Health care is in *crisis* after all, so we'd better turn to some folks with a *proven* track record of success…

When considering all the fallacies presented by politicians to promulgate their malicious plans, I'm reminded of an insightful quote from "President Gas", by the Psychedelic Furs, about the manipulation of the electorate:

"It's sick…
The price of medicine.
Stand up…
We'll put you on your feet again.
Open up your eyes just to check that you're asleep again.
President Gas is President Gas again."

How appropriate. In order to appear "compassionate", the politicians will lie, twist the meaning of words, and present false "crises" that they then offer to solve. They do this to achieve and retain power. And people accept the falsehoods, they buy into the lies; they willingly accept the increases in state control of their lives, all the while believing they are doing something good for themselves and their neighbors.

Meanwhile, the government grows, unchecked.

Are you ready to kneel before the state? Apparently, it's okay. I'm told it's very comfortable to live on your knees.

**Confronting the Political Players:
Preserving Freedom Is Not a Game**

P. GARDNER GOLDSMITH   PAUL H. GOLDSMITH

**If you are two-faced, you won't know
whether you're coming or going.**

**PHG
August, 1991**

"Missile Defense vs. Terrorism?"
Sept. 13, 2001

Two hours after the destruction of the World Trade Center, Boston's largest AM radio station featured a live interview with Massachusetts Congressman Marty Meehan. At approximately 11:50 AM, WBZ 1030 asked the Democrat just how he and his staff had handled the terrorist threat. He responded by giving a few details about how hectic the scene in Congress was, how he ordered his staff members to leave the building, and he explained that he had not been in touch with many of them since. But Mr. Meehan didn't stop there. He then wandered into a screed about how these events show that President Bush's missile defense plans are truly misguided. To paraphrase:

"We're planning on spending $100 billion on missile defense, when I think these attacks prove that missiles aren't the greatest threat, terrorism is the greatest threat."

There are only two possible reasons Mr. Meehan would have brought this up.

If one were charitable towards him, one might think that Mr. Meehan is truly animated about the threat of terrorism, has been worried about it for some time, and is expressing thoughts about which he feels so strongly that he doesn't even realize it's just an inappropriate time to be discussing them.

If one were not so charitable, which is probably more justified, given the continual opposition to even the abstract principle of missile defense that he and many other liberal Democrats have displayed over the past fifteen years, one can only conclude that he was trying to use the tragedy for political reasons.

In the first instance, Mr. Meehan is simply displaying his ignorance. From whence comes the idea that missile defense and anti-terrorist planning are mutually exclusive? How does one adopt such convoluted thinking that he sees the two policies as being in complete opposition to one another? Particularly notable in this regard is the fact that Mr. Meehan frequently votes for bills that have nothing whatsoever to do with the primary reason the federal government was created, which was to defend the United States. Does he think that spending on social programs is more important than missile defense? Why aren't midnight basketball and the National Endowment for the Arts two programs that stand in opposition to protecting us against terrorism?

The belief that missile defense is unworkable, or too expensive, is pervasive among Congressional Democrats. Yet we now know that an operational Navy Theater Wide program could be instituted in stages beginning eighteen months from today.

As quoted by "The Shield" (July/August, 2001), Rear Admiral Rodney Rempt, the Assistant Chief of Naval Operations for missile defense, has stated that our most advanced missile defense system could be operational in nine years. This is a sea-based system that could destroy long-range ballistic missiles from all points of the globe, and could be implemented for a cost of just $8 billion to $12 billion.

A less sophisticated system that could destroy missiles from Iran and more advanced threats from North Korea could be up and running in six years, for $3.5 billion to $4.5 billion. A more basic system of sea-based defense, one which could shoot down missiles from Libya and North Korea, could be prepared in four to five years, at an aggregate cost of $1.4 billion to $1.8 billion. Finally, for just $150 million to $200 million, an "emergency" defense against missiles from North Korea and China could be up and running in twelve to eighteen months. Does Mr. Meehan possibly think this is too much to spend, that this somehow stops us from dedicating resources to the terrorist threat America faces as well?

It is almost impossible to fathom what reasonable justification liberals could provide against moving forward with such systems. Of course, reason is something typically lacking in most liberal arguments against missile defense. Theirs is a knee-jerk hatred of the idea, based on the twisted concept that if we actually try to defend ourselves against missile threats, we will "destabilize" the world.

With this in mind, one has to give serious consideration to the possibility that Marty Meehan was not simply expressing his belief that we are misallocating funds that could be better spent on anti-terrorist programs. Meehan's rhetoric is part of an ongoing strategy to block missile defense at every opportunity. The primary argument employed by liberals in the 1980's when Ronald Reagan would not bow to Soviet calls for him to drop plans for SDI was that we would ruin the "balance of power". When the Soviet Union dissolved, the argument was that missile defense would abrogate the ABM treaty. But that particular treaty is a document which was signed by the US and the USSR, a nation that no longer exists. Thus, the liberal rhetoric has fallen on deaf ears throughout most of America, except in the hallowed halls of the media giants.

Now the line of attack is the "mutually exclusive" argument. Meehan's sloppy appearance September 11, on Boston radio, fits right in with the transparent and misguided arguments liberals have made for years. For them, it seems, any method employed to undercut the concept of defense against missile attack is justified.

Even if it means utilizing the greatest tragedy in American history to achieve their ends, people like Marty Meehan will feel no shame.

"The Rise of 'Moderation'"
May 28, 2001

Although Shakespeare's adage "...a rose by any other name would smell as sweet" is well suited to the struggle of Romeo and Juliet, it has its limitations when viewed in the context of contemporary public relations. In a world of P-R spin, the expressive qualities of words and phrases have tremendous significance, and they are used to great advantage every day.

In no field is this more obvious than politics, for politicians continually attempt to hide their intentions and gain political advantage through the use of euphemisms and catch-phrases. Case in point, the legislative organization called the "Mainstreet Republican Caucus", which has attempted to push the NH House republicans to the left during this legislative session.

In an interview published April 20, 2001, "Mainstreet" member Rep. Peter Bergin claimed the group was founded to "get back to the basic principles of the party -- fiscal responsibility, social tolerance and common sense problem-solving."

His claim is interesting, especially when one compares his amorphous "principles" to the *actual* principles of the party, which were voted upon last year and written down in the Republican Party Platform. These are clear statements, to which he could have referred, but -- either intentionally or due to ignorance of them -- he did not.

For example, the Republican Platform unequivocally states:

"We reject the Supreme Court's erroneous Claremont rulings...We hold that the Claremont I and II rulings by the state Supreme Court are (judicial activism)... and that, therefore, the Justices who wrote them should be removed from office..."

Yet, by their earliest public pronouncements, the "Mainstreeters" find as their unifying theme the *adherence* to Claremont I and II and the attempt to impose a long-term, broad-based tax on the state in order to comply with the intellectually corrupt rulings. How is their stance at all consonant with Republican principles? Additionally, how do their policy prescriptions, which include broad-based income taxes, sales taxes, or combinations of the two, correspond to the most widely publicized principle of the Republican Platform, the opposition to any broad-based income, sales or capital-gains tax?

The obvious answer is that the political positions of the members do not adhere to the major planks of the Republican Platform. The truth is that the "Mainstreet Republican Caucus" is an assemblage of liberals who obviously got tired of the appellation "RINO" (Republican In Name Only) and decided to seize the P-R advantage and create a new title for themselves.

It doesn't take an expert in semiotics to deduce that the title "Mainstreet" was specifically selected because of its visual and aural similarity to "mainstream", and because it connotes the "middle of the road", which is where most leftist politicians wish to convince people they stand. This allows them to claim the rhetorical high ground, and assign to their opposition the image of being "out of step". Hence we see Mr. Bergin's implication that the "Mainstreeters" are attempting to restore certain fundamental tenets to a party that has supposedly lost its way.

But the opposite is clearly the case. It is the "Mainstreet Republicans" who wish to hide their rejection of the basic party principles through the use of euphemisms and spin, even while they try to replace those party principles with their own, politically correct double-talk.

One need only compare the votes and policy positions of the "Mainstreet" members to the stated positions of the party itself to see this borne out.

For example, in addition to the differences on Claremont, on taxation and on Judicial activism noted earlier, one might ask if the majority of the "Mainstreet" members support the party plank that declares Republicans will "… work to limit growth of spending to not more than 2.5% annually."

This is doubtful. Mr. Bergin's stated "principle" was "fiscal responsibility", which, speaking generously, gives a politician a great deal more latitude to define what is "fiscally responsible".

Additionally, there are other major aspects of the Republican Platform that might cause problems for the "Mainstreeters". For example, the Platform clearly states:

"… the unborn child has a fundamental right to life which cannot be infringed."

It is a safe bet that the majority of the "Mainstreet" members would never go so far as to embrace such an explicit statement of principle.

Then there is the party position supporting "right to work legislation", which might cause some problems for the "Mainstreeters".

The party Platform also vows support for death penalty laws, support for the Second Amendment to the US Constitution, and opposition to firearms restrictions, as well as the promotion of school choice and charter schools, and the increase of market forces in health care.

One has to wonder just how many of these major planks of the Platform have caused, or will cause problems for the members of the "Mainstreet Republican Caucus" when manifested in proposed legislation.

But perhaps most important is the philosophical statement written into the Platform, and from which all other considerations regarding the justifiability of laws is derived:

"The rights of our people always preempt the actions of government."

There is no such clear expression in Mr. Bergin's statement of "principle", and this is not only extremely troubling, but even more revealing. It tells us which side the "Mainstreet Republicans" believe takes precedence. It tells us which they consider first, the rights of the people, or the prescriptions and proscriptions of the government. It informs us where the "Mainstreeters" first look when considering how to address problems, and it is not to the people themselves.

The introduction of the "Mainstreet Republican Caucus" was conducted with great fanfare. Its members have boldly asserted certain claims to the heritage of the Republican Party, and attempted to use whatever political clout they can derive from these claims to force the party to the left.

But there are reasons people join parties, and these reasons stem not from the fact that people like the letter "R" better than the letter "D". These reasons must be based on *principles*, and the party platform is written to express those principles. Certainly, there will be some aspects of the platform with which one might disagree. But when one reaches a point where he cannot adhere to the most fundamental, most explicit principles of his party, it is time for him to reconsider his affiliation with that party. It is *not* time for him to try and portray his differing agenda as "moderate" or the "mainstream". Yet this is precisely what the "Mainstreet Republican Caucus" has done.

The obviousness of the "Mainstreet" members wouldn't be quite as vexing if one could assign to them the originality of creating the title on their own. At least then one could compliment them for their political instincts. But the fact that there is also a Federal "Mainstreet Republican Caucus" -- a liberal group of Reps on Capital Hill that caused a major plank of George Bush's education reform bill to be killed -- means that one can safely assume the choice was not original here in NH. It also means that one can assume the groups are associated with each other, which is something to ponder when thinking about the inner workings of party politics in New Hampshire and in Washington, DC., and when considering the supposed earnestness of "Mainstreeters" who would like to redefine for us the principles of the Republican party.

"Judd Gregg's Conversion"
January, 2005

Upon taking the helm at the powerful Senate Budget Committee, US Senator Judd Gregg (R. NH) announced that constituents in his home state should expect the federal government to tighten controls over spending.

"I intend on being very aggressive. My goal is to put in place a budget that will reduce the deficit in half over the next four years," he told the Associated Press.

Such rhetoric fits well with Gregg's image as a conservative from the supposedly flinty state of New Hampshire. But, just like the government of New Hampshire, Gregg has been much less conservative with other people's money than his statements imply.

When one evaluates the thrifty language of our senior Senator in light of his actions only a few months previous, some nagging questions arise. For example, how is one to believe Judd Gregg espouses true fiscal responsibility, and actually *believes* his words, when a matter of weeks before, he had seen his name attached to a weather center at Plymouth State University in honor of his showering of $1.3 million in tax money on the school? Long ago, in a bygone era, names were attached to educational edifices when benefactors donated their *own* money. Judd Gregg's government philanthropy comes at the expense of other people, not himself. The names of the taxpayers who involuntarily "donated" will never appear at Plymouth State University, but the name of the man who helped shift their cash to New Hampshire will always be remembered.

In a similar fashion, is one to feel pride upon hearing Judd Gregg announce that Washington will tighten its belt, when mere months before he was steering $250,000 to rebuild the site of the original State House in Portsmouth? Judd Gregg has endeavored to shower federally garnered tax money on these and other patently unconstitutional projects, including an underwater cable television connection from the coast of the US to public schools, so children can watch the wonderment of sea creatures from the comfort of their own classrooms. For Senator Gregg, who portrays himself as an environmentalist, the spending fits. But for anyone familiar with the US Constitution, which does not contain provisions for underwater environmental education, or education at all, the spending does not sit well.

It indicates a lack of candor and honesty when there is a sudden conversion to fiscal responsibility by that very senator who dealt the pork. One is led to wonder why, prior to an election, this same "conservative" was so interested in sending out boastful press releases announcing one federal grant after another.

A man's nature does not change when his position on a committee changes. It smacks of hypocrisy for Judd Gregg to proclaim his devotion to fiscal responsibility, when only a few months before, his office was busy telling people about how much pork he had brought back to New Hampshire. When a man suddenly talks about keeping the federal government in check, though he long ago broke an oath to uphold the very constitution that gave him an office, it indicates that he is not trustworthy. Judd Gregg's sudden conversion to fiscal conservatism may bring about some lofty rhetoric, it may even bring about tighter federal spending, but it cannot bring back those of us in New Hampshire who lost faith in a senator who once promised to be a conservative, but long ago broke that promise.

"The Boot"
Oct. 1998

Have you had enough?

Of course, you know exactly to what I refer, the Impeachment of Bill Clinton.

And, again, I ask, have you had enough?

Bill Clinton and his slack-jawed, Democrat acolytes are betting that, if you haven't yet, you soon will. You will grow so tired of the whole sordid affair that you will wish it away, out of your mind, out of public discourse, and out of the Congress.

They are depending on the quite observable trend that people would much rather be contented with a lie than expend mental energy in order to uphold truth, virtue and the rule of law.

Since the revelation early this year that Clinton spent some valuable "downtime" in the White House with an intern less than half his age, and that he denied having a sexual relationship in both a civil deposition and before the cameras of the world media, we have been tortured by a parade of liberal buffoons telling us:

A. That he didn't have the affair.

B. That he didn't have the affair, and that the entire thing is a fabrication by the "Vast Right Wing Conspiracy" (Hillary's keen insight).

C. That he didn't have the affair, and the entire thing is a concoction of Independent Counsel Ken Starr (according to the blathering Cajun, James Carville).

D. That there was no *evidence* Clinton had engaged in sexual relations with Monica Lewinsky.

E. That, well, okay, there may be evidence that they fooled around, but Clinton (since he has no other way out of this mess) is now going to come clean with the American people (he didn't, but whether he did or didn't is irrelevant. As far as the law is concerned, he committed perjury at least three times in his civil deposition, and once before the Grand Jury. Both of these types of crimes are felonies).

F. So, all right, he had the affair, but it wasn't really an *affair per se*, and it wasn't *sexual* according to Bill Clinton's definition of the term *sex* during his

LIVE FREE OR DIE

Paula Jones deposition, and it was a private matter, and shouldn't have been looked into by Ken Starr in the first place.

G. Okay, so he had the affair, lied about it in his civil deposition in the Paula Jones suit, lied about it to America, tried to use every legal maneuver he could to delay the investigation for seven months, came clean only when he knew that the Independent Counsel had undeniable proof that he had engaged in the affair, lied in his grand jury testimony and claimed he couldn't remember the answers to questions that any reasonable person would have been able to answer, performed a supposed mea culpa for four minutes on August 17 -- a speech that was really a childish attempt to deflect blame onto others and create the public image of Bill as a victim, traveled the world proclaiming himself to have already said he was at fault and to have asked forgiveness, then returned to the U.S. to begin visiting with a motley assortment of lackluster "religious leaders" such as Jesse Jackson in order to create the image of himself as "repentant" while at the same time setting his legal spinmeisters to the task of attacking the Republicans and trying to portray them as power-hungry maniacs, and sure, he then got his flacks to begin blurring the lines about such clear standards as impeachable offenses...

BUT HE DID IT FOR HIS FAMILY!!! HE'S REALLY A NOBLE GUY!!!

Whew!

I certainly hope you have not bought into this line of foul excuses. But if this kind of sophistry has gotten you to the point where you just want nothing more to do with the impeachment issue, or if you are so poorly educated that you don't know where the provision for impeachment of the President is located in the U.S. Constitution, or if you are one of those poor ignorant slobs who has had the disadvantage of sitting through twelve years of a public education, plus four more of a watered-down, federally subsidized and federally manipulated college system, and you don't know the origin of the term "High Crimes and Misdemeanors"... Or, if you just plain don't know the meaning of the word sophistry... Let me mention something interesting.

It's a line from George Orwell's "1984". When Winston Smith, the protagonist, is captured by the forces of the government and tortured by a man named O'Brien, O'Brien gives him an idea of what the world will be like under the rule of Big Brother: "If you want a picture of the future, imagine a boot stamping on a human face -- forever." (p.220)

If you have had enough of the Clinton impeachment issue, then you have willingly laid down on the dirty pavement, turned your head to the side, and accepted the boot.

I feel sorry for you. Like Smith at the close of the novel, you believe "2 plus 2 is 5," you believe "Freedom Is Slavery", you believe Clinton has done nothing that approximates impeachable offenses; you are comfortable with those who have convinced you. And you are comfortable with a lie being accepted as truth.

The constant drumbeat by the liberals in office and in the media that Clinton made a mistake that should not jeopardize his presidency, that this whole affair should be dismissed with a "censure" by Congress, is akin to someone telling you the sky is green.

Let's take a critical look at some of the major points of the whole affair.

The liberals tell us that the Monica Lewinsky affair was said to have been ruled immaterial in the Paula Jones sexual harassment suit. This is incorrect. The matter had to do with whether or not questions about an affair between Bill Clinton and Ms. Lewinsky should be reserved solely to the Independent Counsel, who was conducting a criminal investigation. The Jones suit was civil, and Starr's office did not want sensitive material to come out about Lewinsky prior to his office having the opportunity to investigate it.

The liberals tell us that the Jones suit was a political plot from the start. This is also incorrect. Paula Jones was "outed' by the magazine "American Spectator", in a report that portrayed her as having willingly joined Clinton for a sexual tryst after being solicited by Arkansas state troopers. She subsequently came forward to say that the story was erroneous, that she had been sexually harassed by the then governor, and that she had witnesses to prove her upset state of mind after he propositioned her to "kiss it" in the hotel room.

If the Vietnam Draft scandal didn't convince people that Bill Clinton is a doughy, perfidious, over-grown teenager who will play with the facts to get his way, who will lie, then try to cover-up those lies, the subsequent sex scandals should have.

For example, in 1992, while in New Hampshire campaigning for the Presidency, Clinton was asked if he had had an affair with Gennifer Flowers. This, because it would have ruined his chances of being elected, he denied.

But in 1998, when he was questioned about the Flowers affair during the Paula Jones Suit deposition, he knew that if he denied it the evidence would prove him guilty of perjury. He knew he couldn't get out of it, so he answered "yes". At the same time, he was unaware that Ken Starr had tapes of Lewinsky speaking with Linda Tripp about the affair, and so he thought he could get away with lying about it.

The liberals claim that he lied about the affair with Lewinsky in order to protect his family. But, if that's the case, why would he have admitted to an affair with Gennifer Flowers in the same deposition? The answer is obvious. He thought he could get away with a lie about one, while he knew he couldn't get away with a lie about the other.

Similarly, his response to the charges in the Paula Jones sexual harassment suit reveal his propensity for obfuscation and lies. When first accused of exposing himself to Ms. Jones in an Arkansas hotel where she worked, Clinton said that he hadn't even been at the hotel that day. Later, when it was proved that he *had* been at the hotel, Clinton said essentially, "Well, yeah, I might have been at the *hotel*, but I wasn't in that room." A few days later, when it was proved that he had, in fact, been in the room, Clinton retorted with something along the lines of, "Well, sure… I might have been in the room, but I wasn't ever alone with her." Later, a state trooper testified that Clinton *had* been alone in the room with her. And it was at that point that Clinton tried to use every legal ploy ever invented, and some here-to-fore uninvented ones, to delay Ms. Jones's suit.

Liberals are eager to claim that Ken Starr has been on a witch hunt. That his "Four Year, Forty Million Dollar" investigation (as the mindless mantra goes) dug up nothing except a private sex affair.

First of all, Ken Starr's Whitewater investigation has led to the conviction of eleven of Bill Clinton's closest friends and business partners. Included among these are: Webb Hubble, Jim Guy Tucker, Jim MacDougal, and his wife, Susan. Second, the cost of the investigation has been inflated as a direct result of Clinton's absurd claims of privilege, his appeals of rulings about simple, straight-forward matters of legal procedure, his refusal to produce evidence when requested (or even six months after it was requested) and his staff's attempts to intimidate witnesses. And, third, in addition to revealing the twisted character of the President, who, according to founders such as George Washington, is supposed to be virtuous, the Lewinsky affair and subsequent cover-up are purely public issues. They pertain to a civil suit, a suit for which Clinton was deposed, and a deposition in which he lied. If you don't like Paula Jones, at least you can ask yourself this: If you were suing your boss for sexual harassment, would it be okay for him to perjure himself in order to get out of the suit?

It is sheer buffoonery to claim that Bill Clinton's lawlessness does not rise to the level of an impeachable offense. And in this regard, the liberals are counting on the fact that the vast majority of the American public hasn't a clue what impeachment is all about.

Contrary to the drivel you hear from the left-wing pundits, impeachment does not have to be brought about only for wrongdoing such as treason or bribery. It is a long-standing tradition that can be traced back to our common law heritage in Medieval England, and has, since its inception, been a mechanism to protect an office from a holder who is venal, who acts with perfidy, who brings disgrace upon the office, whose character proves him unfit to hold the position. During the Constitutional Convention of 1787, James Madison noted that he "thought it indispensable that some provision be made for defending the Community against the incapacity, negligence or perfidy of the Chief Magistrate."

The fact that Clinton's actions *are* criminal offenses only makes the argument for impeachment more valid. But even if he hadn't broken any laws (which he has four times over) his actions in the White House are so far above the "level of an impeachable offense" they are like a flood.

And anyone who tells you that, perhaps, a deal can be struck, that Congress can simply "Censure" Clinton, is telling you that two plus two is five. There is nothing, not a line, NOTHING in the Constitution that allows Congress to do something called "Censure" of the President. The liberals who tell people this might as well use a term like "Doughnut". Dick Gephardt might as well say, "We are considering *doughnutting* the President." It *means nothing!* Under the Constitution, it is the sworn duty of the houses to proceed with impeachment hearings. Public polls have nothing to do with it…

Or, I should say, public polls *should have* nothing to do with it. Unfortunately, in a nation where "War Is Peace", "Freedom Is Slavery", and "Censure Is Constitutional", few of our elected representatives are willing to stand up for the truth.

After all, each of their constituents has willingly laid down, and is smiling as the boot smashes on his face.

Note:

I have avoided discussing matters such as the rifling of over 900 FBI files by the Clinton administration (an offense for which a Nixon official was imprisoned -- for pulling just *one*), as well as the loosening of defense guidelines over sensitive missile technology that was eventually provided to the Chinese, possibly in exchange for Chinese money given to the DNC through agents of the Chinese government. I have also postponed mentioning the revocation of an Interior Department approval for an Indian tribe casino, a revocation that appears to have been prompted by department head Bruce Babbitt after he solicited a donation of $300,000 to the DNC from their neighboring Indian rivals. I have avoided mentioning the firing of Billy Dale and the White House Travel Office, and I have not mentioned the lawlessness of Al Gore when he solicited campaign contributions from the White House. I figured that if some people had trouble with "2 plus 2 is *4*" then they might have a harder time with algebra.

"The *People's* Business"
February, 1999

I was pulled over by a police officer the other day. Given the fact that I was traveling at Racer X speeds, blaring Iggy and the Stooges from the stereo, and sporting a bumper sticker reading, "Hey, fuzz-man, I Dare Ya!", I suppose I was a good target. The sonic booms I left in my wake only served to further justify his decision.

But when he strolled up next to me, his uniform pressed, his buttons shining, I made my case quite clear: it was *he* who was in the wrong.

"Hey! Can't you see I'm doing The Peoples' Business here?!" I vociferously demanded (I let Iggy and the Stooges blare on the stereo, just for his pleasure).

His stunned hesitation merely allowed me to press on.

"I mean, geez, here I've got Social Security to think about, and old people on Medicare, and children eating Sweet Tarts for lunch, and all those worries about education! Can't you see you're distracting me here?"

I think he mumbled something about doing one-twenty in a school zone, but I was ready for him.

"I mean, heck, can't you see society is functioning perfectly well despite what I've done? What gives?! I'M A BUSY GUY!"

He tried to say something about the law, and obvious breeches of it, but I just thumbed over my shoulder at Tom Harkin and Pat Leahy playing Scrabble in the back seat.

"You'll have to talk to the 'Triers' about it, they're very familiar with the facts of the case. Right guys?"

Harken's exclamation wafted forward.

"*Constitution!* That's a Triple Word Score!"

To which Leahy solemnly replied, "Constitution's not a word. I'm a Senator, I oughta know!"

And thus it was over. Silly cop, thinking he could try to uphold the law, when I had so many more important things to do.

Isn't it nice that the impeachment trial of Bill Clinton has given all of us this defense, and it's been so heartily affirmed by Senators like Harkin and Leahy? In fact, hasn't the entire spectacle of the trial been a wondrous sight, almost like watching puppies play in their dirty cages at a Doctor Pet?

Such intellect. Such integrity. Such adherence to principle.

Thus far, we've been treated to a Senate arguing over the "rules" under which the trial will be conducted; to Senator Harkin -- who'd only days earlier sworn an oath of silence on punishment of imprisonment -- interrupting the presentation of the House case for impeachment; to a "State of the Union" speech by Bill Clinton before the very people who shall decide the fate of his presidency; to two weeks of TV appearances and press briefings by these same senators, who, though sworn to impartiality, have been beating the drums for dismissal even before they heard the case; and to a Supreme Court Chief Justice who would rather sit through a performance of "Showboat" than perform his proper Constitutional role as presiding judge at the trial.

The Constitution orders that, upon impeachment in the House, a president shall stand trial in the Senate, where the Chief Justice shall *preside*. It's very simple. The Senate is to hear the articles of impeachment, and the facts of the case, and determine the president's guilt or innocence. The Constitution gives no further instructions than that. And the reason the Founders didn't spell it out any further was because they didn't feel it was *necessary*. The system of jurisprudence had been firmly established in Anglo-Saxon Common Law long before the US Constitution was conceived. It was understood that the Senate would act as a jury, not control the procedure of the trial. Such a responsibility was understood to be the purview of the presiding judge. Thus it is *not* the role of the senators to determine the "form" of the trial, or whether witnesses are called, or rule on any of the nuances about which we so often hear. Just like any other trial, the presiding judge is supposed to do all that. He's the one in control. He *runs* the trial. There aren't supposed to be goofy "votes" on whether witnesses will be called, or "bi-partisan agreements" as to who will eventually be on the witness list. The presiding judge makes those determinations, based on the requests of the House prosecutors and the White House defenders. Senators, like any other jurors can *request* to see witnesses, or hear testimony again, but those requests must be presented to the presiding judge for his approval.

There aren't supposed to be eight senators on "Meet The Press" talking about their opinions on a trial that's not even half-over. The *presiding judge* should tell them to BE QUIET and, if necessary, sequester them.

Compared to William Renquist, and his useless Captain Kirk stripes, Judge Ito was an Iron Man. It seems as if Renquist is just filling up space, dreaming about Tyne Daily and the latest Tony Award nominations until the supposed "trial" is over.

And believe me, I'm not just moaning over a lost cause, not just upset that "my side is losing". My side isn't that gaggle of spineless wretches known as the Republican Senators. My side is the Constitution. I have yet to meet a single person who can articulate a cogent defense of Bill Clinton's obvious perjury without resorting to ad-homonym attacks or excuses such as "it was a sexual witch-hunt." Such mindless, emotional arguments are the last refuge of ill-informed partisans who would like us to believe the removal of the President can't be justified -- even if the law is very clear. They try to make the rule of law sound petty.

Just like Bill Clinton. He can't be bothered to pay attention to is own impeachment -- the first of an elected president in US history. He's just too busy! After all, he's doing "The Peoples' Business."

And thus it goes. He uses the excuse and belittles his accusers. *I* use the excuse and send the well-intentioned, perfectly justified policeman back to his cruiser in defeat.

If I recall, the name on his uniform was something like "H. Hyde".

Well, at least he made the attempt.

He just didn't realize I had Senators playing games in the back seat.

"A Tale of Two Forums"
Dec. 19, 1999

A funny thing happened on the way to the forum Friday, December 17.

The forum was the "Nightline Candidates' Forum", at Daniel Webster College. What was funny, or more precisely, strange and sad, was that the gathering was about as far from a "forum" as could possibly be imagined. It was a managed, staged event created by the producers of a major network program, intended to foster the image of authentic spontaneity, when, in fact, it was planned to the last detail.

When I use the word planned I don't mean the typical preparations for a live-on-tape program that anyone in television or radio knows are required, the logistical and monetary considerations. I mean an intentional pre-selection of the topics and questions to be discussed by intellectual titans Al Gore and Bill Bradley in a "no holds barred" fight-fest supposedly dictated by the varied and unanticipated questions of audience members.

The producers of "Nightline" could easily anticipate the questions, because they selected them.

The first piece of information to absorb about this breathtakingly mind-numbing event was that only a certain number of people were contacted to be potential audience members. I happened to be given the heads-up, and was told to call John Eppinger, a producer with the show.

Upon calling Mr. Eppinger, I was asked "What question do you want to ask?" I responded that I wanted to investigate the constitutional parameters under which the candidates believed they functioned. When I was told that such a question was "too deep", I resorted to my second idea, which was to quiz Gore on his infamous "No Controlling Legal Authority" quote when it was discovered that he had made fundraising calls from the White House, a felony punishable with up to three years in prison (that is, as long as the Attorney General is willing to prosecute).

With incomprehension in his voice, Eppinger asked me why I wanted to ask that question. "Because none of the major media correspondents have asked it," I replied. He told me that he would let me know details about getting to the event in a few days.

I was given the okay to attend, and arrived figuring that there would be so many people interested in asking questions that I'd probably have to fight to try mine. I wasn't going to be disappointed if my efforts went unrewarded because of the competition.

But when I entered the auditorium and discovered that around each microphone, certain seats had been labeled "Reserved", I began to suspect that the chat I'd had with Mr. Eppinger had been for reasons other than conversation.

They had already decided who was going to ask questions, and met with them earlier in the week.

As people milled about, they, like me, began asking the floor managers if they were going to get a chance to ask their questions. The managers handed out index cards, which, they said, could be filled out. If a subject came up that had a bearing on the question, they might be allowed to ask it.

Of course, those subjects had already been decided upon by the producers.

Koppel offered the explanation that if they let all the people with questions line up at the microphones, there would be a long line, and they would get in camera shot. That's if you accept the premise that people should line up at the *microphones*. Anyone involved with a live performance could figure out that numbers can be handed out to audience members, who can remain seated until their number is called. Alternatively, questioners can be held outside the doors in a line, whereupon they can be called in one at a time. Koppel's justification was as weak as his questions.

As the program went on and the candidates droned monotonously about their Great Achievements and Experiences With The People, the floor managers would speak into headsets telling the producers what questions had been handed to them. The producers, in their great beneficence, would then grant permission to certain Special People to be added to those already selected to speak at the mic.

So, we were treated to such monumentally important queries as "Do you support a manned mission to Mars?" and "Would your wife make a good First Lady?" and "Is this election a battle for the soul of America?" and "How can you stand running for office when your private lives are turned upside down?" They were suited to "Oprah", not a debate.

And these were the questions the producers of "Nightline" determined would carry the night in this "slug-fest" of ideologies.

To the candidates' credit, they did, on rare occasions, stumble like drunken sailors into real issues. They fell into a discussion on gun control and school vouchers when asked a typically innocuous question on "Columbine". They later charged forward heroically to tell us that SDI would endanger the ABM Treaty (which was agreed upon 27 years ago, was done so with a nation that no longer exists, and was broken by that nation many, many times)

In contrast, I attended a forum with Bill Bradley two weeks ago at the studios of TV 50, WNDS. Thanks to Jack Heath and his staff, this was a real forum, where the audience had the opportunity to ask any question that fit into the hour, and Mr. Bradley was surprisingly candid, for a candidate.

My question was: "Mr. Bradley, many people try to justify federal involvement in education, health care, and gun control by claiming the Constitution is what they call a "living document", or invoking an open-ended interpretation of the Inter-state Commerce Clause. Since this leaves the states, businesses, and individuals at the mercy of Congressional and Judicial whim, do you think it's justified? If so, how can you reconcile this with the literal wording of the Founders, and, if you can't, why should we have a written set of Constitutional rules at all?"

Mr. Bradley's response was very polished, and very telling for anyone interested. He said, "I consider myself a child of the Declaration of Independence rather than the Constitution."

What he was saying was that he paid no attention to the Constitution, the rules of the government, the document he swore an oath to uphold when he became a Senator. But by invoking the Declaration, he evoked visions of July 4th, the flag, and patriotism. He said that the government had a responsibility to provide for "life, liberty and the pursuit of happiness". Of course, for him, those terms meant that government was to provide all the essentials of life by taking the productive achievements of some and dolling them out to others. He overlooked the real meaning of the terms. The "right to life" means that you are sole owner of your person, and have the right to defend it, as in, *using a firearm*. "Liberty" means the ability to do as you please as long as you do not infringe on another's right to do the same. And "the pursuit of happiness" means the right to utilize your talents and property as you see fit, without regulation by the federal government, or seizure of your productive labor.

I had anticipated he wouldn't care a bit about the original intent of the Founders, I just didn't expect him to be so smooth in doing so.

But at least he admitted it. The producers of "Nightline" don't even have that level of honesty. They promote a broadcast as a forum for real questions from real voters, but those questions are selected by the producers of a media monolith in order to cover the issues they want to cover. Those important issues like a *mission to Mars*.

If only the staff of TV 50 could have the reins at ABC for a week.

"Bill Bradley's Hook Shot"
August 15, 2000

It was a lot more enjoyable watching Bill Bradley pull back for a fifteen-foot jumper during his days in the NBA than it was seeing him let loose his political views on national television Tuesday, August 14.

Perhaps this is due to his shameless and stomach-churning re-interpretation of the Founding Fathers, a re-interpretation I got to see in person about a year ago.

During the recitation of his laundry list of liberal causes, Mr. Bradley had the audacity to say:

"When the Founding Fathers wrote that we have the unalienable right to life, liberty and the pursuit of happiness, they didn't think we'd have to take turns."

And this quote reminded me of an answer he tossed my way while I attended a forum last year at WNDS, TV-50.

My question to him had been fairly simple and direct. Easy enough for a former Senator to answer. I said this:

"Mr. Bradley, many people try to justify Federal involvement in education, health care, and gun control by invoking an open-ended interpretation of the Inter-state Commerce Clause (of the Constitution, Art. One, Sec. Eight), or claiming the Constitution is what they call a 'living document'. Since this leaves states, businesses and individuals at the mercy of Congressional and Judicial whim, do you think it's justified? If you *do* how can you reconcile this with the literal wording of the Founders? And if you can't reconcile it, why should we bother having a written Constitution at all?"

To which he replied something in the order of:

"Well, I consider myself to be a child of the Declaration, rather than the Constitution. I believe that we have certain unalienable rights, to life, liberty and the pursuit of happiness." Fine, as far as it went, but he went further to say that he believed government existed to supply us with these things. Regarding "life," he said that in these times of plenty, government has the ability to help us all receive medical care. Of course, he neglected to mention that government provision of medical care and insurance requires that the productive labor of certain Americans must be seized and redistributed, whether it be through taxation, regulation, or legislation.

Regarding "liberty", Mr. Bradley believed that the Federal government should help all people raise their standards of living. For him, this is to be done through Federal programs, rather than through freeing entrepreneurs to start new business and employ more people who might otherwise be on welfare -- a liberation that occurs only through removing the iron fists of Federal taxes and regulations. And, when Mr. Bradley spoke of "the pursuit of happiness", he seemed to be implying some sort of New-Age, feel-good measure of "fulfillment" that could be measured by government and fostered through Federal education programs and government subsidies.

Bradley's misuse of the Declaration of Independence bordered on rape. His Machievellian attempt to invoke the Declaration when I had specifically asked him about the Constitution was completely deceptive, and it illustrated how little he cares for two things.

First, it showed how little he regards the audience. By invoking the Declaration, he was trying to deflect my question away from specific Constitutional restraints and direct it towards a more "patriotic" and more popularly known document. After all, the Declaration is something we celebrate each year on July 4th, with flags flying high, and fireworks blasting in the air. The assertion that he is a "child of the Declaration" imbues Bradley with a patriotic color, despite the fact that his answer really says he pays no attention to the *Constitution*, which is the set of written rules under which this nation is supposed to function, and which Bradley took an oath to uphold when he became a Senator.

Second, it shows how little he cares for the real meaning of the Declaration. By "life", Thomas Jefferson didn't mean that one had a right to have his life taken care of by the government (i.e., by his neighbors, through involuntary taxation and redistribution of funds). Jefferson, in the tradition of Natural Rights, meant the primacy of one's *own* person. Life was a God-granted thing, and belonged to each person upon creation, which implies upon conception, which stands in direct opposition to Bradley's belief in the supposed "woman's right to choose" regarding abortion. One's life was the purview of each individual person, and, as such, could be defended by him when placed in direct harm. This implied the free use of weapons for self-defense, as first espoused by Aristotle and recognized by the Founders, and this principle obviously included the utilization of firearms. This view of the Founders, as expressed in the Declaration, stands in direct opposition to Bradley's misguided support of restricting gun ownership.

When the Founders spoke of "liberty", they clearly meant the ability of each man to apply his God-given skills to his work, without the interference of others -- whether through their direct action, or through government coercion -- and to the fruits of his labor, i.e. his *money*. Mr. Bradley's whole-hearted embrace of socialist redistribution of wealth on the pretext that it somehow insures the "liberty" of all Americans is completely absurd, and would be revolting to anyone with an understanding of the Founding Fathers and their principles. One does not "insure" the rights of Americans by having the government curtail the rights of some, by having the government determine what is a "fair" amount of freedom and what is "unfair", and trying to equalize the lives of everyone.

And, finally, by "pursuit of happiness", the Founders meant the ability to do with one's own property and life what one wants, as long as it does not place the life or property of another in direct harm. It's a simple principle, first articulated by John Locke in "Two Treatises of Government". But Mr. Bradley doesn't seem to get it. To him, the government should be the mechanism of controlling everyone's ability to pursue happiness. It should be the regulator, the judge of what is too much "happiness", of what is "fair". You can't pursue your goals unless the government says it's okay, even if you're not placing another individual in direct harm.

Bradley's answer to my question at TV 50 seemed so blatantly absurd to me that I almost laughed right there. But I looked around me and saw the faces of the others in the audience, their wrapped gazes, their slow-motion nods. And I knew that he had done it. He had successfully appealed to their senses of patriotism with a statement so completely unpatriotic that it might have prompted the Founders to string him up then and there. He had appealed to their senses of "wealth fairness" so effectively, Karl Marx would have been proud, and he had catered so well to their belief in the benevolent state that Fidel Castro would have lit a cigar.

It was amusing to hear him use the same rhetoric during his DNC speech. But it was disturbing as well. Why?

He received a standing ovation.

"The Race for Last"
December, 1999

A political battle is underway in New Hampshire, one that threatens to fracture the long-standing Republican monolith of the "Granite State", and tip the balance in the US Senate.

Two-term conservative Senator and Independent 2000 presidential candidate, Bob Smith, is facing a challenge from the equally conservative two-term Congressman, John E. Sununu. But while these men are often seen as champions of low taxes and constitutionally limited government, the forces behind them betray a strong division in the NH Republican Party, a division that also exists nation-wide.

For years, New Hampshire conservatives have fought a losing battle against hordes of invading "RINOS". These "Republicans In Name Only" have crossed into the state to escape taxation in wonderlands such as Massachusetts and Connecticut. But packed with their belongings have been the very intellectual qualities that caused economic devastation in their former homes, specifically, a pernicious belief in the communitarian benefits of wealth redistribution and a general ignorance of constitutional history.

The result of their invasion has been a diminution of the Granite State's conservative character, as exemplified by recent gubernatorial elections and by the current conflict between two seemingly conservative Republican Senatorial candidates.

In 1996, Democrat Jeanne Shaheen was elected to the office of governor, and her tenure has seen increases in state spending averaging 10.6% per biennium. Such massive expenditures have arisen despite the fact that state unemployment decreased through the entire period, making one pause to wonder why, during a time of plenty, *more* state handouts were needed. It would seem self-evident that when prosperity is on the rise, there should be less demand for state spending, but to Jeanne Shaheen and the "RINOS", greater employment simply means there is more tax money to add to bureaucratic coffers.

Perhaps the most troublesome aspect of this shameful display of government mismanagement is the fact that the population of New Hampshire, once so flinty and proud of the motto "Live Free or Die", has seen fit to re-elect her twice, and actually considers her a serious candidate for the US Senate.

Now two Republican Senatorial candidates battle to see who can challenge this liberal profligate spender. On one side is Sununu, who appeared content to stay in his Congressional seat until party operatives began to whisper that he would be a better candidate to field against Shaheen. To the party apparachiks, Sununu has a more "moderate" image, something appealing to "RINOS" who have about as much understanding of fiscal responsibility and constitutional history as Hillary Clinton has of cattle futures.

Set against the Republican elite is Smith, a man who left the party in 2000. After delivering a justified attack on the rudderless drifting of the Republicans, Smith eventually returned to the fold, securing a powerful committee chairmanship.

Now, this conservative senator promotes himself in different garb. Smith caters to retirees with his "prescription drug program", a federal spending plan that the once strict constitutionalist would have correctly voted against. News reports detail Smith's involvement in securing federal funding to "save the Florida manatee", something that is clearly not sanctioned by the Constitution.

But who is to blame? Is it Smith, who has had a sterling record on most Constitutional issues? Is it Sununu, who has one of the highest American Conservative Union ratings around? Or is it a Republican Party mindset that promotes victory over all else, that repeatedly capitulates on principle in the feckless hope that it will appear more likable in the eyes of people who don't care about them anyway? The ego-centrism of politicians *can* lead them to damage their own integrity. But when smothered by a party establishment that consistently overlooks the importance of educating people about the fallacies of liberalism, a party blind to the reality that it must expose new voters to the principles of constitutional government, men such as Smith and Sununu will always be placed in these awkward positions.

An employee of Sununu once asked me, "Whom would you rather see debate Shaheen?"

Unfortunately, that question can't really be answered, because any Republican debater will be hampered by the advice of party players ringing in his head:

"Look moderate! If we talk about free markets or the constitution, we're dead!"

Which is precisely why we're in this situation.

"Let's Make a Deal!"
July 19, 2000

It's peculiar, how little things will set one off.

A person can be calm and relaxed one minute, then be confronted with the most mundane inconvenience or annoyance and simply lose all sense of reality.

I must admit this was my situation Wednesday, July 5, as the House Judiciary Committee completed nearly two weeks of hearings on the possible impeachment of Justices Brock, Broderick, and Horton.

After discovering that these justices had knowingly allowed disqualified members of the court to be involved in cases; after realizing that Judge Brock had testified in a contradictory manner to the committee regarding his receptiveness to improper influence by Judge Thayer; after realizing that the Justices knew they were committing class B felonies by not reporting this improper influence to the Attorney General as Howie Zibel did, and after sitting through the infinite arrogance of the contemptuous John Broderick preaching to the committee that if the public shines light on the Supreme Court, it "will destroy this body", I suppose I had justification to be annoyed.

But I guess I must have been looking for something to set me off when the subject of recusal came up as a possible impeachable offense for David Brock, and my own representative, Rob Rowe, stated at 10:50 PM:

"Yes, it was wrong, but everyone did it."

For a moment I just sat there, wondering if I had really heard what I thought I'd heard. It was a rationalization that is so weak that no one takes it seriously. But there it was, and it seemed that, instead of latching onto the statement and exposing it for the twisted inanity that it was, the majority of the committee were quite ready to embrace it. After all, to say that the recusal policies of the Justices had been unethical from the days of David Souter would actually call into question the workings of him and all the others who had engaged in such activity on the bench. And we couldn't have that, now, could we?

But even if the committee had restricted itself to the actions of Brock and Thayer regarding recusal, it was unwilling to recognize the malfeasance of even these men in its impeachment proceedings. Rep. Rowe's sentiment won out quite handily:

"Yes, it was wrong, but everyone did it."

Let me get this straight, if we hadn't prosecuted people for some crime, say, arson, for a number of years, but then, we caught an arsonist thanks to someone reporting him, would Rob then say the same thing? We'll just let him go, because everyone was doing it! Unbelievable.

I'm sure the people of Detroit would really appreciate that sentiment on Devil's Night each year. (For the uninformed, Devil's Night is the fun evening each October 30th when the gangs of Detroit come out and set the city ablaze.)

But that little bit of irritation over Rob's statement, that *tiny* annoyance wasn't enough to really get me steamed.

It took Rep. Andy Peterson to do that.

Just seconds after the committee had voted in favor of three items of impeachment to move before the House, Rep. Andrew Peterson emotively proposed a bill to actually give David Brock his pension.

I know, I'm quick to anger, a termagant. I really ought to get some help. But, in my addled brain, I thought I had just heard the committee vote to impeach the man. They then said, "let's have the state pay his pension if he resigns"?!!

The emotion-laden twaddle that came forth as they discussed the bill reminded me of the attorney for the Menendez Brothers asking the court for leniency because they had "suffered the psychic trauma of losing their parents" -- when *they* were the ones who had killed them, and just been convicted for it.

The problem that Brock may be removed from office one year before he could have received his pension is no one else's fault but *his own*. Not the judiciary committee's fault, and certainly not the fault of the taxpayers, the people who will have to be paying for this intellectually and ethically corrupt malcontent for the rest of his life. He knew what being a judge meant at every stage of his rise up the ladder, and he made decisions and took actions that put his pension at risk. That's it, end of story. If he's removed, he's removed due to *his own malfeasance*, not somebody else's.

The attempt to offer Brock his pension is nauseating. Thanks to pure political gamesmanship, we have gone through the process of impeachment hearings only to end up offering the man we are ready to impeach a wad of cash to step down.

Representative Rowe said that other states have been watching us closely to see what we do about the Court. Thank goodness the entire house killed the proposition that was introduced in the Judiciary Committee by Andy Peterson. Otherwise, other states would have learned that impeachment hearings can skirt around the major issues, let arrogance have its way, allow wrongdoers to get away with their actions without any real consequences, and award unethical behavior.

I'm not sure if Mr. Peterson knows this, but those are lessons no one needs to learn.

What is more dangerous than an eloquent
man with good intentions captured by
evil ideas and desperate motives?

Only the ignorance that spawned the
ideas in the first place.

PHG
Summer 1984

"The Seven Principles of Foolishness"
December 14, 2004

Would you like to take something special with you from the holiday season?

How about a thought, an idea, a concept to help warm one's heart?

How about a Christmas story?

Well then! Here goes...

The other day -- Sunday, December 12, to be exact -- my sister and I decided to walk from our brother's house near the Amherst Village Green, to the center of town itself. It was nearing five in the evening, and we had been looking forward to joining other Amherst residents in the traditional "Christmas Tree Lighting Celebration". Having both grown up in the town, we recalled the many times we had visited as kids, holding small candles, drinking hot chocolate, singing Christmas songs, awaiting the arrival of Santa Claus, and gazing at the tree as it was set alight with color.

We embarked on the short walk, the cold air reminding us of those old times, and warning us of the winter yet to come. But as we approached the crowd surrounding the tree and the riser at the tree's base, I observed that no one was holding candles. It was then that my sister mentioned something that struck me as odd.

"Didn't you see the notice in the paper? They asked that people *not* bring candles, because they're a *hazard*."

The sarcasm in her voice was notable, and appreciated. Immediately, I felt uneasy. The announcement in the paper was the kind of weak, neurotic and politically correct nonsense I had seen invade so many other formerly simple ceremonies. How many kids, and how much property, were hurt or injured because of the tiny candles used for this brief event?

My bemusement and speculation were short-lived, for in a moment, a fellow resident, "moderate" Republican in the state legislature, and a fixture at the Christmas Tree Lighting Celebration took to the microphone. My sister and I watched as he welcomed everyone to what he then called the "Tree Lighting Celebration".

Again, something about it put me off. It seemed strange. I noticed immediately that he had excluded the mention of "Christmas" in the title of the event. Peter knew better than to make a mistake. He had to have known he was avoiding the word; at least, that was my strong suspicion.

My sister and I looked at each other. She had noticed as well.

Not holding candles, standing in the cold among the multitude, we then heard the carolers on the riser begin singing "Come All Ye Faithful", and we joined in. But when the song was over, Peter once more took to the microphone.

"And now, will you please welcome Mrs. Findlay, the music teacher at Clark School, for her ninth year at the Tree Lighting Celebration, and her students from the first grade, as they sing, 'The Seven Principles of Kwanzaa'."

There seemed to be a pause in my thought process as I assimilated what he'd just said. The second song at what used to be called the "Christmas Tree Lighting Celebration", the song being sung by first graders, taught to them by their music teacher, was... A *Kwanzaa song?!*

"Okay!" said my sister. "I'm all set. I'm outta here."

We turned away in disgust and frustration. It wasn't that we were upset that the town officials and volunteers who had helped put together the "Tree Lighting" celebration had wanted to be inclusive, to cover a few more bases for the holidays, it was that the entire atmosphere had been one of simplistic political correctness, of egalitarian, narrow-minded pandering by people who didn't even know what they were doing.

How many people there, I wondered, were aware of the heritage of Kwanzaa when they taught it to the kids? How many knew its background, and the background of its creator? How many were aware that it was not even a religious holiday, was not even a *real holiday* at all, but rather a totally fabricated event created by a former felon in 1966?

The "holiday" of Kwanzaa was invented by one Dr. Mualuna Karenga, AKA Ron Everett, a former "social activist" who helped form the radical organization United Slaves (US) in the 1960's. Engaged in a power struggle with the Black Panthers, Everett kidnapped and tortured two women to garner information from them. He was subsequently arrested, and found guilty on two counts of felonious assault and one count of false imprisonment for the beating and torture of Deborah Jones and Gail Davis. Everett was sentenced to serve one to ten years in prison, beginning in 1971.

Upon his release, he suddenly, and thus far inexplicably, was welcomed by the University of California, Long Beach. He became a professor of Black

Studies, and ran the department. The school has yet to cite his qualifications for the job.

Perhaps all of these facts are unimportant to the people of the "Tree Lighting Celebration" and the staff at the Clark School. Perhaps they see the "overall good" the man has done by creating the holiday overshadowing, or redeeming his past.

Unfortunately, the so-called holiday is nothing of the sort. It is a socio-political construct with blatant racial overtones created by a criminal for the express purpose of racial separation and economic war.

Karenga's "Kwanzaa" is supposedly a celebration of the east-African fruit harvest, the "holiday" derived from elements of African tradition. As such, it is often lauded by innocent and high-minded teachers as a way to introduce kids to cultural diversity and racial inclusiveness. The only trouble is that Kwanzaa is a lot more than a celebration of a traditional African harvest. What Karenga sought to do with his fiction was establish a pseudo-religious holiday based on race, and infused with political ideology. His is a modern political manifesto to be taught to the kids, not a link to ancient times and ancient traditions.

At the core of Kwanzaa are the "Seven Principles" about which the first graders sang. Those principles are:

umoja - unity

kujichagulia - self-determination

ujima - collective work and responsibility

ujamaa - cooperative economics

nia - purpose

kuumba - creativity

imani - faith

Karenga himself has said that the philosophy underlying Kwanzaa is distinguishable from Marxism only in its added embrace of racial hatred and certain aspects of Chinese and Cuban socialism. Certainly the "Seven Principles" reflect this claim. Ought one to be justifiably concerned that six year-old children are being taught the laudable attributes of the supposed "African tradition" of collective economics and collective work and responsibility? Ought one also be concerned when he knows that these "Principles" were cobbled together by a felon who has been intent on spreading his philosophy, not spreading good will among his fellow men?

Evidently, the need for teachers in tax-payer funded schools to acclimatize children to "social awareness" precludes them from actually teaching students right and wrong. It also seems to prevent them from even investigating the fact that one cannot have a "collective" anything without the presence of the individual first. There is no "collective" action or responsibility, no "collective" economics, because every "group" action can be reduced to that of an individual within the group, a man making his own decision for his own reasons.

Collectivism is not necessarily a traditional tenet of east Africans, the people around whom Karenga based his fictitious socio-economic political "holiday" of Kwanzaa. It is an enslaving philosophy that has brought nothing but poverty, death and pestilence to those who have had it imposed on them.

It is not something to teach to first graders, and it is certainly not something to espouse during a post-modern "Tree Lighting Celebration" conducted by people who ought to know better.

That's my story. Happy holidays. Enjoy that warm feeling of the season.

It think that feeling is called frustration.

P. GARDNER GOLDSMITH   PAUL H. GOLDSMITH

Love may be "blind", but ignorance, parading as eruditon, is blindest of all.

PHG
September 6, 1985

"The New Impropriety"
March 31, 2003

For the first time in my life, I have been chastened by my niece.

I should have known this day would come, for in growing older, each of us becomes accustomed to using language that might seem inappropriate to the more tender ear of a seven year old girl. We grow tempered, inured, and occasionally reckless in our speech.

Now, I find myself guilty of what I thought I would never do.

I uttered the "S" word in front of my niece.

I can excuse it as an act of frustration, an expletive derived from my own emotional response to something my niece had said, but I know that is merely rationalization. I should have held my tongue. Now, I will never appear the same in this sweet girl's eyes.

You see, my niece recently returned from Disney World, where she had the most wonderful vacation of her life. The weather was warm, the sun shone brightly in the sky, and she not only got to meet all the fantastic icons of the Disney realm, but she got to enjoy rides and play games and try foods she might never have been able to experience had she stayed in her cold home of Mt. Desert, Maine. Pretty as that island town can be, it doesn't quite compare to Disney in the winter.

And this is where I made my mistake, for I mentioned to my niece, Brianna, that she could now tell each of her friends all about her wonderful trip, about the rides and music, and fireworks and animals. She could tell them about flying in the plane to Florida, and riding the Monorail at the park.

But her reaction told me I was sorrowfully mistaken.

"We can't do *that*," she informed me, "Miss (xxx) says it's not right to tell people about things they might not have been able to do or see. It will make them feel bad."

When the pregnant pause her reaction inspired finally gave birth to words on my part, I pursed my brow and asked her if she was kidding.

"Oh, no!" she said.

"But that's crazy!" I exclaimed. "You can't tell your friends about things you enjoyed because it will hurt their feelings?! What do you do for show and tell?"

"We don't *have* show and tell."

At that moment, I was stunned. I was almost dumbfounded, and I guess, I went too far.

"That's the stupidest thing I've ever heard!" I said.

She pointed at me with a shocked and slightly superior expression, as if she had caught me with my hand in the cookie jar.

"You said a Baaad Word!!!"

Now, I'm familiar with most of the Bad Words in the English language, and some in Spanish, and I very, very rarely use them. I don't like foul language when other language is just as useful. I couldn't really understand what I had said. I tried to recall the words I had used.

Thing?

Heard?

"You said the "S" word!" she announced with shock.

"What?"

"You said the "S" word! You know! 'S-T-U..' "

"Stupid?!"

"You did it again! Gardie said the "S" word!…TWICE!"

"But Bri," I implored, "Stupid isn't a bad word, who told you it's a bad word?"

"Miss (xxxx) told me so. You shouldn't use bad words like that. They make people feel bad."

"But Bri," I explained, "sometimes people do stupid things. Saying something is stupid, or someone is being stupid, isn't always bad. Sometimes it's true! And you know what? What your teacher thinks about not telling other kids about places you've gone or things you have seen? That's stupid! Isn't it interesting to listen to someone tell you a story about a trip? What if a friend went to Paris and saw the Eiffel tower, and told you all about the flowers growing nearby, or talked about a funny thing that happened on his trip? Wouldn't you want to know? What about when I went to England and visited Big Ben? You've never been there, but you can learn about how old it is, and how big it is, and how much I liked it. You can learn all sorts of things from the experiences of others and it can help you imagine what it was like, maybe even make you want to go and learn yourself!"

"Bri," I said, "I'd like you to ask your teacher what teaching is, except telling people about things they might not have experienced themselves, or had never thought of. See if she understands that she ought to let you guys talk all about things that are fun and exciting and new to you. And you know what? You can tell her for me that I think what she is doing is just plain dumb."

I patted her on the head, having completed my own little lesson. But in an instant, she was looking for her mom.

"MOM!!!! Gardie just said the "D" word!" she yelled.

I was left to contemplate the fact that, even as our newspapers are filled with debates over the reasons for war in Iraq, with arguments over the use of our soldiers and the efficiency of the war plan, with disagreements over the position of the press in the entire event, one has to realize that the other struggles of American society continue unabated. The bizarre attempt to sensitize children against things that are natural to all human beings is ongoing. Inquisitiveness, competition, and excitement are becoming verboten. The fervor to re-structure minds so that the nuances of the English language have no meaning is today so pervasive it has even found its way into a first grade class in remote Maine. Someday, when most contemporary issues have become history, this problem will return to the spotlight.

Meanwhile, there are children who don't know the importance of nuance in speech, who believe "stupid" and "dumb" are swear words, and who can't tell each other about their interesting personal lives because that might make another child feel inadequate.

My niece has since stepped away from her teacher's doctrine. She's a smart girl. Let us hope there will be time left to correct the teachers' silly, dunder-headed mistakes. Otherwise we may see a day when *learning* itself becomes a forbidden word.

**From the Federal Level to the State:
Education and the Leftist Attempt
To Centralize Decision-Making for It**

The upper echelon of the educational community is an esoteric wasteland, almost totally captured by a minority of well-meaning intellectual dilettantes whose major goals have "legitimized" the rather simple, basic, productive and noble activity of education and teaching into a pseudo-science research profession.

Their "innovative" ideas, "progressive" programs, fiats and prattling are followed, lemming-like, by innocent liegemen, careening down the road to Never-never Land, scattering in their wake the bodies of millions of children and young adults upon the dump-heap of humanity.

Why?
Because the poor souls are functionally illiterate – the tragic reaping of the "Look-say" method of reading, and the disembowelment of a past traditional, classical, basic-curriculum into spoon-fed mush.

PHG
Washington, DC, April, 1983

"Reforming Robin Hood"
January, 2003

Many Americans are justifiably worried about the malignant, and growing, role of the federal government in the daily operation of their local schools. Informed about federalism, and cognizant of the fact that local information is best handled on a local level, they have fought hard in what seems a losing battle to stop Washington from usurping more of their sovereignty over their own schools. But while that fight has been long engaged, and very much in the spotlight with the institution of President Bush's "No Child left Behind" initiative, another, less noticeable guerrilla campaign soon may be lost to the advocates of larger government. This battle has been raging for years, but has gone virtually unnoticed by defenders of individual freedom nation-wide. It has slipped under their radar screens because it has been fought in isolated states, with little information passing from state to state. The central focus of the battle is whether localities will control their own school funding, or state bureaucracies will rule them like feudal lords. It is an issue of paramount importance, and it is often prompted by something called the "Robin Hood Law".

During a recent conversation with an acquaintance from Texas about public school funding, I became aware that the citizens of the "lone star state" were dealing with a legal problem that was eerily similar to one that had plagued my home of New Hampshire.

She was happy to inform me that, although taxation for local education had once been "unfair" in Texas, it was now more equitable, thanks to the passage of new "Robin Hood Laws". These statutes allow the state government to "take money from the rich towns, and give it to the poor towns", in what is widely construed as a large-scale application of the principles of Locksley's most famous son.

This was both amusing and discouraging, of course, for the impression that it is appropriate to take money from one "rich" town and give it to another, "poor" town, and the idea that Robin Hood did this on an individual level, are not only incorrect, they do a disservice to a great fictional (and possibly historical) hero. Robin Hood was, after all, a tax protestor.

After mistakenly shooting a prize deer on the King's lands, and killing a man in self-defense, Robin, AKA Robert Fitz-Ooth, chose a life of exile in

Sherwood forest, where he gathered about him a band of stout and merry men who had come to be alienated from Henry the Second's society of royal plunder and privilege.

With friends such as Will Stutely, Allan a Dale, and Little John, Robin Hood vowed that:

> "…even as they themselves had been despoiled they would despoil their oppressors, whether baron, abbot, knight, or squire, and that from each they would take that which had been wrung from the poor by unjust taxes, or land rents, or in wrongful fines; but to the poor folk they would give a helping hand in need and trouble, and would return to them that which had been unjustly taken from them." [43] [44]

Today the image of Robin Hood is being "reformed" by Texan politicians who would act in a manner completely contrary to the principles held by the hero, and who would like to convince society that their surreptitious corruption of the figure and his ideals establishes a better paradigm for their state.

Texas is not alone. Over the past twenty years, state courts and legislatures all across the US have methodically attacked the traditional system of local control over public school funding in order to establish a "fairer" system, a system based on socialism writ large. At every opportunity, politicians have sneered at the idea that localities, not to mention the individuals who comprise them, have the ability to handle their own affairs. They have established law after law redistributing wealth from "rich" towns to "poor" towns, or from "rich" people to "poor" people, all conducted under the guise of "fairness", and given appellations such as "Robin Hood Laws".

---

[43] The most famous literary version of the Robin Hood legend is the 1883 novel "The Merry Adventures of Robin Hood", by Howard Pyle. This quote is taken from page 4 of the 1968 annotated version published by Classic Press, Inc., of Santa Rosa, California. It is highly recommended to anyone interested in both Robin Hood, and in Howard Pyle, a writer of considerable strength and skill.

[44] It is important to note that in Thirteenth Century England, property was controlled by a network of feudal lords and dukes. Land rents, therefore, were payments made to the government under penalty of injury or imprisonment.

Since the first suit over "education funding fairness" went before the US Supreme Court, in the form of "*San Antonio School District v. Rodriguez*"[45], there have been thirty states in which similar cases have been brought to trial. Across the US, there has been an organized effort on the part of teacher unions and school administrators to bring suits that will shift wealth, eliminate local control over education funding, and centralize it in each state capital.

In many cases, such as those in Connecticut, New Jersey, Texas and Vermont, state supreme courts have ruled that local taxes imposed to fund local education were violations of state "equal protection" clauses, because they led to disproportionate levels of funding from town to town. In New Hampshire, the rationale was more convoluted, but the end result was the same. One after another, states fell to these lawsuits brought in the name of "fairness".[46]

In each state, politicians have been led to impose state-wide property taxes. The statutes, or "Robin Hood Laws", increase the property taxes paid by fiscally prudent towns, and redistribute the wealth to "poor", often less prudent towns.[47] One of the crowning ironies of these "Robin Hood Laws" is that many of the citizens in the "rich" towns justifiably oppose their aggregate status as property tax "donors", but support the redistribution of wealth on an *individual* level, be it an income tax or a capital gains tax. They believe these are really the "fairest" taxes, since *they tax the richest residents of the state*.

The various practical considerations of this fallacy are academic when analyzed beside the philosophical principles, but these important

---

[45] This was a 1973 Texas-based case in which the US Supreme Court ruled that there was not a constitutionally protected right to "education funding equity".

[46] In Kentucky (*Council for Better Education v. Collins*, 1988), Arizona (*Roosevelt v. Bishop*, 1994), Ohio (*DeRolf v. State of Ohio*, 1997), New Jersey (*Abbot v. Burke*, 1997), Texas, and twenty-five other states, the rallying cry has been "equity and fairness for the poor", and courts have responded in favor of the plaintiffs.

[47] In one case, the majority of citizens in a "poor" town called Claremont would not change their zoning to allow a new business to open in the area. This "poor" town also spent approximately $3 million to build a town opera house. They then brought suit against the state, blaming it for Claremont's "unfair" position of not having enough to spend on school budgets.

philosophical principles are rarely addressed. Politicians never seem to ask themselves why taxing the "rich" is "fair".

Yet this twisted concept is the basis for almost every form of tax redistribution. It can be a capital gains tax, an income tax, or a property tax that takes from "property rich" towns and gives to "property poor" towns because the property rich towns can "afford to pay", but the sentiment is the same: It is only fair to tax those with more, because they will not miss it as much as those who are poor.

The problem with this philosophy is that it flies in the face of the economic principle of "Subjective Marginal Utility". Roughly stated, the principle holds that while it seems possible to assume "rich" people would value X percent of their incomes less than "poor" people would value X, when an attempt is made to actually put this into practice, the assumption must be applied to *individuals*. An attempt to graph the "value" each individual applies to his or her wealth is impossible by anyone save that individual. Thus, as a matter of mathematics, taxation based on "ability to pay" is impossible to justify. "Ability to pay" is unique to every individual, and cannot be determined by outside observers. It is only in the realm of politics that people display the conceit to decide for others how they should value their own sweat and toil.

Of course, the "rich" are supposed to buy into the idea that taking their money, and giving it to whomever the majority deems more worthy, is somehow ethical. Indeed, it is portrayed as the highest virtue in a society. It means we are all part of the same group; we aren't just out for ourselves.

But opposition to wealth redistribution is based on a *principle*, the principle that I do not have the right to force my neighbor to pay for what I believe is noble. I do not have the conceit to decide for my neighbor how he should spend his money. I do not have the moral prerogative to supersede his rights to his own property in order to do what I believe is "better for society".

This is the principle that drove Robin Hood in 1247 to steal back from the lords that which had been taken from his neighbors. It didn't matter if the royal government claimed a noble purpose for that plunder; the property did not belong to the government, and it was unethical to claim that it did.

It is just as unethical for state politicians to employ the name of Robin Hood in the contemporary seizure of majority sanctioned plunder. If he could hear his name being used in such a manner, the great hero of Sherwood

Forest would once more reach for his long bow, and resume his noble fight against the enemies of private property.

The "Old Boy" Network of the Academic Elite:

They are lost in a self-made swamp of intellectual miasma, slowly sinking in its ooze. All that will be given to education and society (i.e. the real world) are some softly rising bubbles, bursting malodorously on the surface with an almost inaudible sigh!

PHG
1983

"The Fix Is In"
January, 1998

A few weeks ago, the New Hampshire Supreme Court issued a ruling that has sent political shockwaves through the Granite State. The issue was the Claremont educational lawsuit, and the ruling -- a perverse oligarchic decree imbued with as much semantic trickery as George Orwell's "Newspeak" -- should make each one of us pause to explore the foundations of his own political principles.

The crux of the lawsuit brought by the plaintiffs was that the state had a Constitutional obligation to fund education equally throughout all towns. According to the plaintiffs, towns with high populations of school-age children relative to the amount of taxable property were at a disadvantage compared to towns with low populations of kids and higher property values. In order to achieve the same level of educational funding, the taxes "property poor" towns had to impose were much higher per $1000 of assessed value than those of "property rich" towns.

It is not my intention to delve into a lengthy discussion of why the charge of "unfairness" is completely groundless, but suffice to say these are different towns, with different industries and backgrounds. They operate under different systems, some more efficient than others. Once tax burdens rise to an intolerable level in one town, there will be sufficient incentive for many dissatisfied citizens to leave, thus reducing the burden on schools and services. It is a utopian argument to claim that every town, or individual living in them, must be made "equal".

Unfortunately, the N.H. Supreme Court disagrees. Reading in Section Two, Article 83 of the N.H. Constitution that the state will "cherish" education, the black-robed demi-gods, in all their "Big Brother" wisdom, found an economic subtext in the word that was heretofore unknown to English-speaking man. Where it once meant "to hold dear", it now means "to equalize through confiscation and redistribution."

The actual text of the Constitution reads as follows:

> "... it shall be the duty of the legislators and magistrates, in all future periods of this government, to cherish the interest of literature and the sciences, and all seminaries and public schools, to encourage private institutions, rewards, and immunities for the promotion of agriculture, arts, sciences, commerce, trades..."

The passage then concludes:
> "Provided, nevertheless, that no money raised by taxation shall ever be granted or applied for the use of schools or institutions of any religious sect or denomination."

Now, it is clear that by employing the word "cherish", the writers of the State Constitution meant "to hold dear." However, they *did* provide for the option that the state legislature could support certain kinds of schools, seminaries, etc., through tax revenue if the majority of voting legislators so desired. But the Supreme Court held this to somehow mean that the state had an obligation to "provide a constitutionally adequate public education." How the justices came up with such an interpretation is a complete mystery. And what "constitutionally adequate" means is even more unfathomable.

The Supreme Court then observed that the State currently mandates many requirements on school districts, including a minimum property tax of $3.50 per $1000 of assessed value that each district must institute and collect itself. This is a key provision of the ruling, since it is the area where political obfuscation and semantic argumentation will be most apparent once the debate over how to respond to the ruling begins. Democrats and liberal Republicans eager to institute a state-wide property tax will now claim that, in order to fulfill the ambiguous court mandate of a "constitutionally adequate" education to New Hampshire children, all they have to do is refine the state-wide property tax that is already on the books. But the mandate of $3.50 is not collected by the state. It is *mandated* by the state onto the towns. It is a debatable point as to whether or not this is actually a state *tax*, or a state *mandate* for local taxes. It is not administered by the state, and does not appear on the state budgets. I mention these points because of the fact that, when running for governor, Shaheen pledged to veto any state-wide, broad-base income, sales or property tax. If the $3.50 mandate was already on the books at the time, why didn't anyone bring it up as a broad-base tax that already existed? Shaheen is currently hedging, playing the semantics game, saying that she will stick to her pledge to veto any *new* broad-base tax. But that is not the pledge she took as a candidate. The word "new" has been added. She is obviously leaving herself room to apply the $3.50 mandate as a broad-base tax, which will then be managed by the state and expanded.

Since her husband is an attorney with the law firm that represented Claremont in the suit, I suspect that she was aware from the start of their argument about the state mandate, and that she planned to use it to institute a broad-base, state managed tax.

Once the justices had stated their claim that the $3.50 per $1000 was a state tax, they then made the incredible jump that any *additional* taxes imposed by local districts for their budgets were somehow part of the state tax. From there, they referred to Section Two, Article Five, which states, in part, that the legislature can:

"…impose and levy proportional and reasonable assessments, rates, and taxes, upon all inhabitants of, and residents within, the said state…"

And since each district has different budgetary requirements, and each town has different property values, the justices lumped them in with the state $3.50 mandate and determined that differences in the property taxes of these districts did not abide by the above constitutional requirement. In other words, the fact that the residents of each district have the ability to determine what they want for their schools, and set their tax rates accordingly, is unconstitutional.

Now comes the debate. If future lawsuits over "funding disparity" are to be avoided under the current Supreme Court interpretation, no town can tax their citizens more than any other. For then, under the "proportional and reasonable assessments" clause quoted above, the taxation mechanism would be unconstitutional.

In other words, there can be no way to produce "proportional and reasonable assessments" of property taxes unless all districts are taxed at the same rate.

And the only way to do that is to apply a state-wide, broad-base tax.

But strangely, people such as Jeanne Shaheen and House Minority Leader Peter Burling have tried to tell the public that they can produce a system that will fulfill the Court's requirements without imposing a new broad-base tax! How can they do it?

By claiming that the $3.50 per thousand already on the books *is* a broad-base tax; by making it a state-funding mechanism, rather than a district funding mechanism, and then raising the tax rates for "property rich" districts. This new plunder will then be redistributed to the "property poor" districts, funding them at a certain legislated "minimum standard," and allowing the districts to lower their tax rates.

At least, that's the most likely proposal.

Unfortunately, that means each district could still increase local taxes in order to fund their own schools beyond whatever the state decided to set as the "minimum funding standard," which could then be challenged as "not proportional." The only way the state bureaucrats can prevent this from occurring is to abolish all forms of local control, or at least set guidelines as to how high individual school funding could rise.

Did you ever think that perhaps people have favored local control for a very important reason? That perhaps, despite their dissatisfaction with the schools in their community, they realize that relinquishing the decision-making process for funding to the state also means relinquishing the decision-making process for content? Did you ever think that those closest to a situation know best how to deal with it? That each time the decision-making authority is moved one step further away from the individuals upon whom the decision will have its effect, the process becomes less efficient, and more bureaucratic?

Did you ever think that Jeanne Shaheen and Peter Burling don't want the citizens of New Hampshire to retain that local control?

I have.

And this is where each of us should think about his own political principles.

One must ask himself if it is any more moral for him to take the money of another through the mechanism of majority rule than it is through employment of a weapon in a dark alley. He must ask himself if the seizure of property is the same, even if the end is supposedly altruistic, say, for example, the funding of someone else's education, or the alleviation of someone else's property taxes. He must ask himself if he could make the decision to take another man's property in order to do with it what he thought was right.

The obvious answer is "no." Unless you're Peter Burling.

And the only reason governments are justly established is to protect us from doing just that -- taking each other's property, or bringing direct harm to the life or property of another. The moment a governmental system begins to do that which it was designed to keep us from doing to each other, that system is coercive and corrupt, and should be abolished. (It should be noted that there are some who believe that even the most basic policing functions of government could be provided on a private basis, through free association, and that even the coercion of having to pay for a government police force could be tossed. For more on this branch of political philosophy, look up "Anarcho-capitalism".)

But, some might argue, isn't tax-funded education the bedrock of democracy? Isn't it just as important to our future as a police force to protect our rights?

There are only a few historical examples of private, free association providing for the "common defense" on a large scale. But there are many examples of private funding producing quality education on a wide scale. In fact, at the time the New Hampshire State Constitution was written, public (tax-funded) education was virtually unknown to its authors. How, then, could the justices of the Supreme Court determine that the word "cherish" meant to fund public education on a massive, collectivist level? Even in the 1800's, observers such as Alexis deToqueville noted that the majority of Americans were literate, well-educated people, people educated by a system mainly composed of private schools. A study of Boston area children conducted in 1812 found that 96% were educated through *private* means.

Is it possible that parents made the best choices for the education of their own children? Is it possible that the competition of private schools in a free-enterprise system created a more efficient system of education? Is it possible that children didn't "fall through the cracks" of funding because private philanthropy, conducted through close personal contacts rather than impersonal, bureaucratic operatives, was their safety net?

Absolutely.

Is it possible to get the government out of the education business altogether?

Yes.

But at least, for now, the citizens of New Hampshire can retain the small amount of local control they already have. And they can do this by compelling their representatives to demand a Constitutional Amendment that explicitly leaves the power to tax with the local communities, one that secures for each district the right to determine the funding and direction of its school curriculum. One that allows for differences in communities, and for the right of citizens dissatisfied with their community to move to another. Under any plan proposed by the statists such as Burling and Shaheen, the entire state will operate under one inefficient, collectivist system, a system in which there will be no place to go should a person be dissatisfied. A system where choice and responsibility are no longer in the hands of the citizens, but in the hands of the state.

The hands of Big Brother.

Wanna shake?

The educational system is the most powerful determinant of who controls whom. George Orwell put it well:

"The Party is not interested in the overt act: the thought is all we care about. We do not merely destroy our enemies; we change them."

This may be the best explanation for the Progressives' centralization of educational authority in pursuit of its goal to Socialize America.

PHG
January, 1985

"Public Enemy Number One: EDUCATION?"
The New Hampshire Education Lawsuits, a Case Study in Judicial Activism
January, 2001

This election season in New Hampshire, one issue was trained under the media spotlights more intensely than a wild-eyed escapee from a State Prison. One subject was so heavy with importance that it could crack the foundations of the Granite State. One problem could change our motto from "live free or die" to "live off someone else or die."

That issue was and still is education funding. Now that the election is over, the debate rages on. But most news coverage casts more heat than light. It lacks the key element necessary for the well-informed citizen to make his choice on election day, it lacks an understanding of how New Hampshire got into an education funding crisis, and how this crisis will effect people for years to come.

As the Gubernatorial candidates worked to attract attention and approval for their various education funding plans, it was essential to learn precisely what was at stake; and what was at stake was nothing less than control over our own local schools. Given the outcome of the race -- the re-election of Democrat Jeanne Shaheen to a third consecutive term -- it appears few Granite Staters have paid the issue much heed. And it appears that New Hampshire's unique position in New England as the only state among its neighbors without an income or sales tax is in great jeopardy.

At first glance, the problem may seem very complex and hard to follow. But it can be rendered down to some very important and easily retained facts and principles. The facts revolve around one word:

Claremont

In December of 1993, the New Hampshire Supreme Court issued a ruling that sent political shockwaves through the Granite State. The issue was the Claremont education lawsuit, a suit brought by the school districts of Claremont, Allenstown, Franklin, Lisbon, and Pittsfield, in which it was claimed that the state was not meeting a Constitutional duty to provide equal education to all students.

The crux of the complaint was twofold. First, the Claremont attorneys claimed that there was a right to a taxpayer funded education codified into the State Constitution. Second, they claimed that since this right existed, it was the State's obligation to insure that all the students received an "adequate" education. According to the plaintiffs, towns with high populations of school-age children relative to taxable property (or property values) were at a disadvantage compared to towns with low populations of children and higher property values. In order to achieve the same level of "adequate" education funding, the taxes "property poor" towns had to impose were much higher per $1000 of assessed value than those of "property rich" towns.

The Supreme Court agreed.

There were two major problems with the decision.

The Constitution

The New Hampshire Constitution is broken into two parts: Section One, the "rights" section, and Section Two, the "form of government" section. Section One delineates all the rights which the State government was being created to protect. Section Two is the "rules of operation" under which the three branches of government will work.

Nowhere in Section One is education delineated as a right. And this makes profound sense, since rights are held to be "negative/preventative" rights, preventing us from coercing our neighbors, not forcing them to do something on our behalf.

According to John Locke, the first man to fully articulate the concept of "Natural Rights", we form governments to protect our lives, liberty and property from direct harm by others. We have a right to be *free from coercion*. We do not have *positive* rights, the rights to demand certain actions and things from others. Once one accepts the view that he has a right *to* something, he opens a Pandora's Box, allowing any individual or group to demand whatever they claim they have a right to take.

The philosophy of Natural Rights embraces the idea that we have a right to *pursue* an education for ourselves or our loved-ones, as long as we don't coerce the provision of that education, or the funding for it, from another. At that point we infringe upon another's rights to his life, liberty, and property.

But the black-robed Philosopher Kings in the NH Supreme Court came to the twisted utilitarian conclusion that because education is *necessary* it is therefore a *right*. Avoiding Section One, since it would not support the conclusion they wanted to reach, they turned to the "function" section, specifically, Section Two, Article Eighty-three, which reads, in part:

> "…(I)t shall be the duty of the legislators and magistrates, in all future periods of this government, to cherish the interest of literature and the sciences, and all seminaries and public schools…"

The justices read that very clear clause and determined that the state had a duty to provide education to the children in each town. They concentrated on the phrase "cherish… literature and the sciences, and all seminaries and public schools", determining that this was a mandatory, rather than hortatory, requirement of the state to fund public education. Unfortunately, they overlooked a great deal in the phrase, and in the nature of the state at the time the Constitution was written.

The phrase does not only say "cherish", it says "cherish the *interest* of literature and the sciences and all seminaries and public schools." How to best serve "the interest" of these constructs is obviously debatable. The justices apparently believe that further inculcating children in the patently misguided, intellectually corrupt, and economically inefficient public schools -- the very schools that have contributed to a massive, obvious and frightening lowering of education standards, and general dumbing down of children for the past thirty years -- would best serve the "interest of literature, and the sciences, etc…"

But others have a quite different idea. We believe that taxpayer funded education is, at best, a system of coercive taxation and redistribution imposing majority morality upon all. We know that our State Constitution was based upon the original concept of Natural Rights as articulated by John Locke. We believe that it is not a fundamental precept of Natural Law that we have the right to force our neighbor to pay for our child's education. We believe that Natural Rights are *negative rights,* not positive rights, that they *stop* us from doing things to one another, such as taking one another's property, or injuring each other. We believe that the responsibility to educate a child rests with the *parents* of that child, that the *parents* can make the most informed decision about the well being of their child. Finally, we know that stealing this power and placing it in the hands of the government immediately removes a certain degree of responsibility, and decreases the chances that those who care most for the child will be making the decisions for that child.

But beyond these differing philosophies regarding education, there was another problem in the court's ruling. Since the court decided that the word "cherish" in the clause meant that the state would support via taxpayer funds, their ruling also implies that the state must support science and literature through taxpayer funds. Perhaps we can look forward to the day when a scientist or writer approaches the state to fund his "Constitutionally" favored avocation.

Worst of all, this weak "pragmatic" view of rights ran contrary to the real "rights" spelled out in Section One.

Being firmly grounded in Lockean Natural Rights theory, Sec. One nowhere delineates education as a right. But it does say something that the Court completely disregarded. Section One, Article Six states:

> "… (T)he several parishes, bodies, corporate, or religious societies shall at all times have the right of electing their own teachers, and of contracting with them for their support or maintenance, or both."

This clause, utilizing the archaic English of "parish" for "town," explicitly states that it is up to the local governments to hire teachers and enter into contracts with them. But by trying to establish a *state* obligation to fund education, the Court created a contradiction. It is not possible for the *state* to have the power over education funds while reserving to the localities the power of deciding whom they want to hire, and for how much. The two simply cannot coexist.

Couple these fundamental problems with the fact that not only did New Hampshire not have public schools at the time the state constitution was written, but its citizens had explicitly *avoided* creating public schools despite British commands to do so, and one might wonder where Chief Justice David Brock and his partners got their bizarre ideas.

We may wonder all we want, but the fact remains that they made their decision.

"Spheres of Control"

The second major problem with the "Claremont One" decision of 1993 was that it contravenes the system of "small spheres of control" built into our State and Federal governments.

The Founders of the New Hampshire and Federal Constitutions knew well that the closer people were to a problem, the better they could handle that problem with accurate knowledge. They understood that by keeping areas of control small, they would better insure people the chance of changing laws they did not like, and better insure, for those who still could not find satisfaction, the option of leaving to find a new, more acceptable area in which to live. It was understood that localities would differ -- in their geographies, in their industries, in their citizenry and their moral and religious beliefs. By creating a system of self-controlled States on the Federal level, and self-controlled towns on the state level, the thinkers of the Founding Period were building a set of systems that would allow us to experiment, to live with those of compatible philosophies, to have the option of leaving a locality that did not resonate with our own views.

Local control of schools is one of the best examples of this concept of "small spheres of control". By allowing us to control our own education budgets, the State Constitution set into motion a process wherein those who were dissatisfied could try to change things simply by working with their neighbors. If they still could not find redress, they could move to a different area, where they might be joined by people of like minds.

The contemporary example of this process could be found a few years ago in the town of Merrimack. When a controversy arose among taxpayers over the degree of sexual content in the school curriculum, the more conservative parents in the town became outraged, claiming that their tax money was being used for purposes they found immoral. When the next school board election came along, these conservative people banded together and won the majority of seats on the board. They then went about changing the sexual content in the curriculum. But they also changed other aspects of the curriculum, such as the English reading list, which made the more liberal taxpayers in town upset. The liberal citizens began claiming that *their* tax money was being used for purposes they found repressive and immoral. But neither of these groups recognized that it was the system of taxpayer-funded education which created this dilemma, and that the real "moral" crisis was the fact that a minority, of either stripe, had to give up its tax money for purposes it found reprehensible.

Small spheres of control allow those disaffected taxpayers the moral choice to leave, provide the closest approximation to market competition. As long as there are other small areas of control, people have a chance of finding an area more compatible to their views. What happens when the area of control is large? Then, mistakes affect many more people, and, worst of all, there is nowhere else to go.

But centralized, state control of local schools is exactly what the New Hampshire Supreme Court justices had in mind when they came to rule on "Claremont One". For them, the ends justified the means. Even if the New Hampshire Constitution did not allow for state control of education, such a fact was irrelevant to the justices.

With "Claremont One", they were able to introduce the spurious idea that education was a "right", the philosophical premises of which do not exist. Such judicial activism is bad enough, but with their decision in "Claremont Two", in December of 1997, they were able to implement their plan to eliminate local control of education.

Claremont Two

"Claremont Two" represented the second phase of the education suit process. Having decreed that the New Hampshire Constitution insured a "right" to a taxpayer funded education, the only task remaining for the court was to invent a way to claim that the state was not fulfilling its constitutional obligation to provide that education to the citizens. The justices did this by employing a series of calculated mischaracterizations of various state laws and applying them to certain sections of the constitution.

First, the Supreme Court observed that the state mandated many requirements on school districts, including a minimum property tax of $3.50 per $1000 of assessed value that each district had to institute and collect itself.

Once the justices had stated their claim that the $3.50 per $1000 was a state tax, they then made the incredible jump that any *additional* taxes imposed by local districts for their budgets were somehow part of the state tax. From there, they referred to Section Two, Article Five, which states, in part, that the legislature can:

> "...impose and levy proportional and reasonable assessments, rates, and taxes, upon all inhabitants of, and residents within, the said state..."

Since each district has different budgetary requirements, and each town has different property values, each town will vary in how far above the $3.50 minimum they set their tax rate. The justices used these differences to their advantage, lumping the variations into the supposed state mandate, calling them all "state taxes" and then claiming that the property taxes of these districts did not abide by the above constitutional requirement of proportionality. In other words, the fact that the residents of each district have the ability to determine what they want for their schools, and set their tax rates accordingly, is unconstitutional.

Now comes the debate. If future lawsuits over "funding disparity" are to be avoided under the current Supreme Court interpretation, no town can tax its citizens more than any other. For then, under the "proportional and reasonable assessments" clause quoted above, the taxation mechanism would be unconstitutional, opening the door for more lawsuits.

In other words, there can be no way to produce "proportional and reasonable assessments" of property taxes unless all districts are taxed at the same rate.

And the only way to do that is to apply a state-wide, broad-based tax.

Thus, we see the justices goal of forcing the state to adopt a broad-based, Concord-controlled tax coming to fruition.

A few state legislators stood against this manipulation. People such as state Reps. David Corbin and Paul Mirski stressed that the legislature did not have to abide by the court's ruling, since the ruling obviously ran against the original intent of the founders of the state constitution, and since the court had no power to *make* law. They suggested that the court was wrongheaded and politically motivated, and that the justices should be removed for breaking their oath to uphold the constitution itself. But these legislators were overwhelmed by a House of Representatives and Senate filled with politicians who cared little for the actual constitution they swore to uphold, and more for the political end-game: state control of education.

In order to facilitate their desire to eliminate local control of education and place the power in their own hands in Concord, certain Representatives, Senators, and Governor Jeanne Shaheen utilized political obfuscation and semantic argumentation once the debate over how to respond to the ruling began. Democrats and liberal Republicans eager to institute a state-wide property tax were able to claim that, in order to fulfill the ambiguous court mandate of a "constitutionally adequate" education to New Hampshire children, all they had to do was refine the state-wide $3.50 per $1000 property tax that was already on the books. This is how Jeanne Shaheen changed her original "no broad-based tax" pledge offered during her campaign of 1996, to a "no *new* broad-based tax" pledge. In fact, the mandate of $3.50 was not collected by the state. It was *mandated* by the state onto the towns. It was a debatable point as to whether or not this was actually a state *tax*, or a state *mandate* for local taxes. It was not administered by the state, and did not appear on the state budgets. Shaheen decided to play the semantics game, saying that she would stick to her pledge to veto any *new* broad-base tax. But that was not the pledge she took as a candidate. The word "new" was added. She was obviously leaving herself room to apply the $3.50 mandate as a broad-base tax, which would then be increased and controlled by the state.

Since her husband was an attorney with the law firm that represented Claremont in the suit, could she have been aware from the start of the argument about the state mandate, and did she plan to use it to institute a broad-base, state managed tax? It's a question worth pondering, and, perhaps, asking Jeanne Shaheen herself.

The Financial Impact

The final outcome of the legislative maneuvering that ensued after the "Claremont Two" ruling was a state-wide, broad based tax of $6.60 per $1000 of assessed value, a tax that collected $24,000,000 to contribute to the overall state education budget of $824,657,000. This money was seized by the state and redistributed from the supposedly "rich" towns to supposedly "poor" towns, thus achieving the purported goal of "tax fairness".

For example, while the town of Amherst, with one of the highest per-capita income levels in the state, received $4,061,916 in state re-allocated education funding via the taxation of other towns and the redistribution of their wealth, the city of Portsmouth was forced to "donate" $557,296 to their wealthy "neighbors" living ninety miles away. It's difficult to understand how politicians can call something a "donation", when the money is being "donated" only upon threat of force by the state. *Coercion* would be a more appropriate term.

The "Fairest Tax"

One of the crowning ironies of the creation of these "donor" towns is that many of the citizens in these towns oppose their status as property tax "donors", but support the application of the redistribution of wealth on an *individual* level, be it an income tax or a capital gains tax (or, in many cases, both).

Many people who were upset over the redistribution of wealth from town to town applauded Governor Shaheen's subsequent 1999 statement in favor of a capital gains tax to fund government education. They explained that they believed this was really the fairest tax, since *it taxed the richest residents of the state*. Both practically and philosophically they are quite wrong.

The practical considerations are academic when analyzed along side the philosophical considerations, but let's take a moment to see just how "fair", or wise, such a policy is. We're supposed to be concerned with "fairness"… Then one must explain to a retired couple living on a fixed income, but with a large nest egg stored away in investments, that taxing them to do what Governor Shaheen believes is "fair" is the ethical thing to do. Tell men and women who work incredibly long hours in order to save and invest that they are part of the "Wealthy Class" and should thus pay more than others. Tell start-up companies that they'll be punished for utilizing their after tax profits in any form of investment, or that their investors will be taxed on their stock returns. Then try to convince them that this will not have a negative effect on investment and their bottom line.

Beyond the practical implications, there are the matters of principle and philosophy. Somehow, many politicians such as Jeanne Shaheen and her ally, Democrat House Minority Leader Peter Burling, believe that taxing the "rich" is "fair".

This twisted concept appears as the basis for almost every form of tax redistribution. It can be a capital gains tax, an income tax, or a property tax that takes from "property rich" towns and gives to "property poor" towns because the property rich towns can "afford to pay" (and because redistributing that wealth is what is "fair"), but the sentiment is the same: It is only fair to tax those with more, because they will not miss it as much as those who are poor.

The problem with this is that it flies in the face of the economic principle of "Subjective Marginal Utility". Roughly stated, the principle holds that while it seems possible to assume that "rich" people would value X percent of their incomes less than "poor" people would value X, when an attempt is made to actually put this into practice, the assumption must be applied to individuals. An attempt to graph the "value" each individual applies to his or her wealth is impossible by anyone save that individual. Thus, as a matter of mathematics, taxation based on "ability to pay" is impossible to justify. "Ability to pay" is unique to every individual, and cannot be determined by outside observers.

For example, we have seen the argument of those in supposedly "property rich" towns that there are many who live in them who aren't wealthy at all, and would have to move if their taxes increased. Yet many politicians in these towns, such as Portsmouth, have no trouble assuming that "rich" *individuals* don't have circumstances unique to their lives that would be just as troubling. If the argument can be made that we just don't understand the economic circumstances of certain *towns*, how can it be justified to overlook the fact that *all* towns are comprised of individuals, and that each individual lives within his own circumstances, be they property-based, income based, or expense-based? And aren't those circumstances even more varied than those of different towns?

If a man who earns $70,000 a year has plans to start a business that will potentially employ thousands of low income employees, is he somehow a better target for taxation than a single mother living on $20,000 a year? What about a retiree living off the triply taxed "income" from stock investments? Do we somehow *judge* one's motivations to be less worthy than those of another, based on our own valuation of what "rich" is? It's *someone else's* money, after all, how are we to know how much he values his efforts? It is only in the realm of politics that we find the conceit of people to decide for others how they should value their own sweat and toil. But that conceit doesn't matter to those who support an income tax, or a capital gains tax, or a redistributive property tax. As long as they can stop the recognition of the individual, and portray people as "rich", they can sucker voters into thinking it's okay to tax. They can paint those who would argue against such immoral taxation as "selfish", when, in fact, it is they who are selfishly assuming they know better what to do with someone else's money.

Some proponents of socialism try to make their ideas more palatable by backing what they call a "flat" income tax. Under such proposals, each worker in the state would pay the same percentage of his income to be used for redistribution. Somehow, this is supposed to make the act of majority-sanctioned theft more acceptable. Former gubernatorial candidate Mark Fernald pushed just such a plan, saying that since we all enjoy the fruits of government education equally, we should all pay the same percentage of our income to support it.

Since the standards and output of the government schools have steadily decreased over the past three decades, and since privately educated children consistently outperform their government-schooled counterparts, the idea that Mr. Fernald's favored education system is benefiting society is highly in doubt. But in addition, even if one were to accept his dream-like notion, one has to apply some logical analysis to his idea that a flat tax is somehow fair. If, Fernald argues, we all share equally in the fruits of government schools (you know those fruits: illiteracy, teen pregnancy, indoctrination, etc.), then we are told we should all pay the same percentage of our income. But why should a person getting the same fruits from the system pay a *penny* more than someone else? Why should a person earning $50,000 per year, and who pays 4% on that to support the government schools, be forced to pay *anything* more than a person earning $20,000 a year and paying 4%?

If we all get the same size ice cream cone from the lovely government, why should the rich man have to pay more than the poor man, regardless of *percentage* of income? The focus is on equality of output, equal enjoyment of the fruits of government. That is the premise upon which the flat tax for education argument is made, in order to try to convince us it is "fair". Clearly, it is not. Taxes are inherently unfair, and making excuses to get the money of the "wealthy" is beneath contempt.

Of course, the "rich" are supposed to buy into the idea that taking their money and giving it to whomever the majority deems is more worthy is somehow ethical. Indeed, it is portrayed as the highest virtue in a society. It means we are all part of the same group, that we aren't greedy, we aren't just out for ourselves.

But being against redistribution of wealth doesn't have to be based on an attitude of self preservation or greed. It is more often based on the principle that I do not have the right to force my neighbor to pay for what I believe is right. I do not have the conceit to believe I can decide better than my neighbor how he should spend his money. I do not have the moral prerogative to supersede his rights to his own property in order to do what I believe is more moral and "good for society".

And this was a concept the Founders understood. When they wrote Section One, Article Six, of the New Hampshire Constitution, they believed that the closest they could come to allowing *individuals* to decide how their money was to be spent was to create a system of *local control*. It was anathema to the writers of our state constitution to place the control over education in the hands of the politicians in Concord.

But those politicians are now *in control*, and they have been wallowing in the mire of political offal over the past year, trying to tell voters that they have created a system by which "tax fairness" will be achieved, and through which we will be able to equitably fund education in every town throughout New Hampshire. They say the problem has been fixed.

Not at all.

While the new system of stealing from some towns to give to others has supposedly achieved "tax fairness", it hasn't achieved any semblance of a long-term fix for education funding.

As of June, 30, 2001, the estimated education funding deficit in the state will be $46.7 Million, and the overall state deficit will be $3.9 Million.

This means that the state-wide property tax will have to be raised from the current $6.60 per $1000 to approximately $10.00 per $1000 next year. And the amount will only increase unless something is done. The only other option is to raid the New Hampshire "Rainy Day Fund", in order to hide the deficit.

Now that the overall decision-making is going to be done in Concord, just how powerful a voice does the citizen of a single town, in a single county, have? And, if one isn't satisfied with what's happening in Concord, and can do nothing about it, where is he going to go? Economists estimate that the rate of growth in state education spending will be at lest 7% per year. Does the average taxpayer think he'll have any influence on that rate? How often would he like to drive to Concord and testify in the House in favor of his position? Does he think he'll enjoy hearing the testimony of all the dozens of others, from various areas of the state, with myriad opinions as to what should be done? And does he think he'll enjoy the sight of dozens of lobbyists who have much more sway than he?

The entire face of local education spending in New Hampshire is changing, due to the "Claremont" decisions, and thanks to the slavish devotion Concord's political class has for centralized authority. It is a change our forefathers would have unquestionably deplored, and there are plenty of reasons for this.

As mentioned earlier, the Founding Fathers of New Hampshire knew well to keep local decisions on the local level. They understood in its most rudimentary form the concept of "Subjective Marginal Utility", and they had a keen grasp of the idea that the most efficient, most ethical political decisions were made by those people living in their own towns, with their own neighbors, knowing the precise problems they and their neighbors faced.

Under the new system of education in New Hampshire, decisions will be made in Concord, and effected not by the wants and needs of individual parents, but by lobbyists representing teachers' unions, representing contractors, representing dozens of such groups who have vested interests in directing the plunder from the increasing state education tax burden towards themselves. It is much easier for a lobbying group to effect legislation in one centralized body than in hundreds of small town meetings.

Budgets will grow without constraint from parents; taxation will increase, and education will become even more bureaucratic than it is now.

How can one know these things? Fundamental principles of economics teach such truths, and the experience of others states that have had similar education court rulings bears it out.

Elsewhere

In 1977, the Connecticut Supreme Court ruled (*Horton v. Meskill I*) that the use of local property taxes to fund education was unconstitutional. In response, the state instituted in 1979 a "guaranteed tax base" system, whereby no district over the 98th percentile of comparable wealth in the state would receive financial aid, while those beneath the 98th percentile *would* receive it. In other words, 98% of all school districts received aid under the new plan. A number of variations in the plan were instituted between 1979 and 1985, variations intended to make the payout scheme more "equitable" and less prone to gouging by poorer towns looking to increase expenditures dramatically, while keeping their local taxes low. The goal was to achieve a level of spending "equality" from town to town, and more and more regulations were required as the system's inherent flaws became utilized by those receiving funds.

But these fixes did nothing to make the tax situation "fair", and merely contributed to the bureaucratic nature of the new state education system. As a result, in 1990, the state enacted a new plan, a "foundation aid plan" that was little more than pure redistribution of wealth on the level we see now occurring here in New Hampshire.

What has been the result of the Connecticut Supreme Court ruling and the subsequent scramble by politicians to make education spending more "equal' throughout the state? Not only are the poor districts spending more, but almost *all* districts are spending more. And it's not just being spent on education. The vast majority of towns in Connecticut have increased spending in other areas (parks, special projects, etc.) upon recognition of the extra money being sent to them via the state tax system. There has been a spending "shift" by citizens in most towns, who know that they can re-allocate tax money from education to other facets of the town budget.

But let us assume this is acceptable, the prerogative of the citizens to carry out. Town spending in non-education areas has increased even while education spending has increased, thanks to the redistribution of wealth via the state. The most important question to ask about this entire situation is this: What has been the actual effect on education performance?

The effect has been disastrous.

For the school year 1989-1990, total overall education spending in Connecticut equaled $3.8 Billion, or $7,463 per pupil. By 1997-1998, total education spending was $5.0 Billion, or $8,580 per pupil. Over that period, aggregate education spending in Connecticut increased 31.5%. And what kind of measurable result did the state see for all its efforts to fund education "equitably"?

For the period 1989-1990, the mean verbal SAT score was 512. The mean math score was 498. By 1998, the SAT scores had declined to 490 verbal, and 479 math. (This measure takes into account the "re-centering" of the SAT scores in 1995, which added roughly twenty points to the verbal score and thirty points to the math score at the median levels on the exam. The "re-centered"/inflated scores would have been 510 for verbal, and 509 for math. The new, inflation-adjusted numbers of 490 and 479 math do not, and cannot, take into account the *qualitative* changes made in the exam, which also contributed to grade inflation. These changes included the addition of an extra half-hour to take each test, and the allowance of calculators on the math section. If one were to take into account these changes, one would have to assume an even sharper decline in verbal and math scores between 1989 and 1998.)

So, while Connecticut's education spending increased 31.5%, student performance *decreased* roughly 4.25 % in verbal SAT scores, and 3.8% in math.

Since the Connecticut Supreme Court ruling was intended to achieve education spending "fairness", or the attainment of an adequate education for all students, how does it sit with the Connecticut politicians that the only result has been the attainment of *less* adequate test scores for the entire state? If, as in New Hampshire, the state has an obligation to educate the children, how can the system of tax redistribution which has led to this drop in scores be characterized as fulfilling that obligation?

The answer, obviously, is that it can't. And we in New Hampshire should be bright enough to recognize that our attempt to travel down the same road as Connecticut will inevitably bring us to the same dead end. A system of state-wide property tax confiscation and redistribution will do nothing to increase the accountability of local schools. On the contrary, it will make them even harder to control. It will do nothing to "raise standards", on the contrary, it will move the decision-making process to Concord, and concentrate it in a pressure-cooker of special interests. It will do nothing to recognize the myriad differences between localities. Instead, it will create a uniform, mandatory system of regulations imposed by the politicians on high, sitting in Concord. The only individuals who will benefit from a state-wide property tax for education are those in the stifling education unions, for they will be able to manipulate and coerce the people of New Hampshire for their own ends.

Playing with semantics, and juggling with various kinds of "fair taxes" will make no difference. A sales tax and income tax will not make the system of centralized government education any better. Not only will these taxes bring about the same problems of addressability that the state property tax has begun to create, economist Thomas R. Dye has estimated that an income tax will increase state spending by a total of $27.2 Billion between the years

2000-2010. It will damage state personal income to the tune of $8.3 Billion per year, and on a per-capita basis, state personal income would be $11,762 lower annually by 2020.

A state sales tax would be just as pernicious. Not only would state spending increase, but the rate of growth for aggregate sales would diminish. Such a tax would remove the comparative advantage New Hampshire businessmen have over our neighbors throughout New England.

The only answer to our current dilemma is to return to the original meaning of our state constitution, to the intent of Section One, Article Six, to the *real* message written by our Founding Fathers: if you are going to accept a government paradigm, local control is best. It is the closest approximation we can have to individual responsibility and market competition. We should leave individual towns and the taxpayers therein to decide how they want their money spent, and, if they do not like that spending, they should have the ability to leave, and try another town. Under our current regime, foist upon us by a reckless and fickle Supreme Court and weak legislators, we are undercutting the ethics of personal responsibility, the responsiveness of government, and, most important, the future of the children living in each town in New Hampshire.

If the issue of education is to be trained under the NH media spotlights in the future, let's hope that attention centers on the substance of the issues. Let's hope it concentrates on the fundamentals of the education lawsuits, the literal wording of the Constitution, and the *real* malfeasance of those in power over the past few years. Only then will the residents of New Hampshire be given the opportunity to clearly study the problem, and produce their answers in a forthright and honest manner.

"Cicero's Legacy"
April 17, 2001

"These are the times that try men's souls. The summer soldier and sunshine patriot will, in this crisis, shrink from the service of their country; but he that stands *now*, deserves the love and thanks of man and woman."

So wrote Thomas Paine in his torchlight treatise *American Crisis*, published in 1776. Mr. Paine was an outspoken revolutionary, dedicated to the principle of individual liberty. He was a man who avoided capture by the British in England by only twenty minutes, and who, due to his adherence to principle, would have been beheaded in France had it not been for the error of a French bureaucrat.

For Paine, there was no higher cause than the struggle for liberty, and his announcement in *American Crisis* was an articulation of his adherence to his principles.

When considering his words, I'm struck by how they compare to the shallow and sophomoric attempt at statesmanship a few weeks ago by a contemporary New Hampshire official, one of my own Representatives, Paul Spiess.

Speaking on the Claremont II Supreme Court ruling, before a gathering of his fellow "Main Street Republicans", Mr. Spiess had the audacity to claim, "Like Caesar, we have crossed the Rubicon, and there is no turning back. New Hampshire must produce a permanent solution to the education funding crisis, and it must be done now."

Listening to his words, one was struck by his weak attempt to infuse authority into his speech, to invoke a sense of importance in his presentation, and, most of all, how his ignorance of history made his statement uncannily apt. For, in his zeal to compare the education funding issue with a monumental event from the past, he completely overlooked one important fact:

The crossing of the Rubicon by Julius Caesar marked the final destruction of the Roman Republic.

For those who understand the implication, I need say no more. These are people who, when they heard Mr. Spiess's rhetoric, might have decided that if he wishes to be associated with Caesar in this conflict, each one of them ought to adopt the moniker Cicero.

Yes, Cicero, the Roman statesman who warned Caesar not to take the drastic measures he did, the man who in 44 B.C. wrote: "The chief purpose in the establishment of states and constitutional orders was that individual property rights might be secured... It is the peculiar function of the state and city to guarantee to every man the free and undisturbed control of his own property."

To Cicero, there was no virtue in living under the guise of something called "civilization" unless its government, if there was to be one, operated under a fixed set of rules. To Cicero, civilization -- a body of civilized men -- was impossible without an immutable order, *written down*, one that protected the primary focus of individual rights, private property. For Cicero, demagogues such as Caesar made sport of the true meaning of laws, and of truth itself.

If Paul Spiess, and others who would step forward with lusty bravado to proclaim they are "moving forward" into the future, wish to associate themselves with Julius Caesar, they do so to their own embarrassment, not just in the eyes of those who are cognizant of the history of Rome, but those who are familiar with New Hampshire Constitutional law and history.

Cicero's admonition that civilization must be protected by constitutional laws instituted to protect private property, that no "other law overrode it... Nor is it one thing in Rome and another in Athens, one thing today and another tomorrow..." stands in stark contrast to the bold boasts of Caesar that he and his soldiers killed 258,000 Helvetii people and 430,000 Germans while controlling the area known as Gaul. It stands in complete opposition to Caesar's attempts to avoid Roman Constitutional safeguards against one man rule, and it is a telling reminder of what is at stake these next few days in Concord, New Hampshire.

The battle here is between those who adhere to the literal wording of the Constitution, who adhere to the Constitutional order, who recognize the separation of powers between the Judicial and Legislative branch, who recognize the ethical superiority of local decision-making and local responsibility, and those who, either through their ignorance or their duplicity, would be willing to accept a completely anti-Constitutional state Supreme Court decision, adhere to this decision in a manner which undercuts and makes a mockery of the separation of our governmental branches, and would force upon others a financial burden which, philosophically and practically, should not be theirs, namely, the funding of education in other towns. The decisions to be made go beyond emotional issues of "fairness" and "equality". They strike at the center of why we elect people to go to Concord in the first place. If we elect them to enter the political realm with an understanding that they are to uphold the Constitution, that they take an oath to do so, and that their primary responsibility is to act in a manner that is in concordance with this oath, then we must hold them accountable when they act in opposition to that oath.

By his statements, Paul Spiess, and by their association with his statements, Cynthia Dokmo, Peter Bergin and many other Representatives, have abrogated their oaths to the Constitution. Mr. Spiess's statement would have been more appropriate if expressed thus:

"Like Caesar, we no longer believe in our oaths to uphold the Constitution of New Hampshire. We have come to the conclusion that the Supreme Court can tell us that black is white and that two plus two is five. We have decided that there are no immutable laws, that all such laws are up to the "interpretation" of the Justices and ourselves. Despite the fact that none of us can deny that the Supreme Court is an *appellate* body and that its opinions are in no way supposed to *make* law, we are going to take it as law. Whatever the Justices say, goes, unless it grates against our emotion-based sense of "fairness" or pierces through the thick wall of ignorance we have erected in all matters of Constitutional principles and political history. *This* is our credo: Like Caesar, we have crossed the Rubicon, we don't know exactly what crossing the Rubicon means, but it sounds good, and makes us feel better as we decide just how we are going to bring about the final blow against New Hampshire's Constitutional order."

"Claremont as Civics Class"
May, 1999

There is a very important point missing from Rob Rowe's defense of many of his fellow Republicans in Concord, and one which followers of the Claremont issue should keep in mind. In his May 8 letter, Mr. Rowe indicates that NH must invest in education because the Constitution requires it. This is not only false as a matter of Constitutional law, which can be confirmed by reading the document and the history of its amendments, but the assumption is unwarranted because Mr. Rowe's statement strives to legitimize the doctrine of judicial review becoming de-facto law.

According to the original principles of both our state and federal Constitutions, the Supreme Court is an *appellate* body. Cases brought before it set precedents for future cases, but do not *change* laws on the books. It is the sole prerogative of the Legislature to pass laws, just as it is only the purview of the Executive branch to execute them.

When a Court ruling is produced that finds in favor of a defendant regarding a state law, that ruling does not automatically negate the law. It only has a bearing on that specific case. Say the issuance of a speeding ticket based on a particular state law is found to be unconstitutional by the Supreme Court. In such a situation, the defendant would be allowed to avoid punishment, and future cases brought before lower courts would most likely fall in favor of future defendants, allowing them to avoid prosecution based on the precedent of the Supreme Court. In practice, prosecutions for such breaches of law would end. But until the Legislature changed the law, it would still stand.

The situation of the Court finding in favor of a plaintiff over the defense of the State (such as in the Claremont rulings) seems much more difficult, but it is not. The only thing that such a ruling does is set a precedent for future cases to be brought before the Court. It does not negate the law, and, based on the principle of Separation of Powers, the Court has no power to order a remedy from the Legislature. Such action would be an encroachment on the Legislative prerogative to pass laws, and thus change the very nature of the composition of state government. The answer to such action is to impeach the justices, which, I must note to Rob Rowe, is actually a written part of the 2000-2001 New Hampshire Republican Party platform.

The founders well understood what we seem to hold sacrosanct: that the Supreme Court is the final protector of the minority against the tyranny of the majority. However, they also knew that if justices were to be able to create de-facto law through their rulings, they would become oligarchs. In this precarious balancing act, they relied on the court to absolve people in <u>individual</u> cases should they find the laws tyrannical, but always gave the balance of power to the legislative body of the people and the executives who were to carry out the laws they produced.

In an 1820 letter to William Charles, Thomas Jefferson said:

"You seem… to consider the judges as the ultimate arbiters of all constitutional questions; a very dangerous doctrine indeed, and one which would place us under the despotism of an oligarchy. Our judges are as honest as other men, and no more so. They have, with others, the same passions for party, for power, and the privilege of their corps… Their power (is) the more dangerous as they are in office for life, and not responsible, as the other functionaries are, to the elective control. The Constitution has erected no such single tribunal, knowing that to whatever hands confided, with the corruptions of time and party, its members would become despots. It has more wisely made all the departments co-equal and co-sovereign within themselves.

"If the (Congress) fails to pass laws for a census, for paying the judges and other officers of government, for establishing a militia… or if they fail to meet in Congress, the judges cannot issue their mandamus to them; if the President fails to supply the place of a judge, to appoint other civil or military officers… the judges cannot force him. They can issue their mandamus or distringas to no executive or legislative officer to enforce the fulfillment of their official duties, any more than the President or (Congress) may issue orders to the judges or their officers…"

In a matter involving a blatantly unconstitutional ruling by the state Supreme Court -- a case such as Claremont that would give cover for townspeople to withhold their taxes, knowing they would either not be prosecuted or would win on appeal -- the paramount action of the legislature <u>must</u> be to impeach the justices. This insures that future tax cases brought before the court will not run according to the Claremont precedent, hence removing the risk of tax evaders holding their local property taxes because they feel they can win in the courts. If the Supreme Court had found that statutes against murder were somehow unconstitutional, setting up the possibility that some NH citizens might feel freer to commit the crime because they would go free when reaching the same Supreme Court on appeal, the legislature wouldn't hesitate to refute the court and remove the justices, thus eliminating the likelihood of greater crime. This illustrates why it is so important to remove justices such as those who invented a "right" to tax-funded education in the NH Constitution: bad precedent can be overturned. And this makes it even more frustrating when elected representatives shun their Constitutional oaths in favor of political gerrymandering, all the while buying into a false premise: that the judicial branch can make law.

Only if all three branches abide by the clear, written text of the state Constitution, will the government function properly. Right now, the Governor, the Supreme Court, and the majority of the Legislature are so far from conforming to their Constitutional duties that they might as well be playing politics with the rules to the game of Risk. No other conclusion can be reached; not one of "they're trying to do the right thing in a difficult situation" or "they're trying to work in a new paradigm that fits our times," or any other shallow excuses. If they were operating according to their oaths, and if Republicans were operating according to the principles of their party, the remaining Justices who were involved in the Claremont rulings would be off the bench. Those Reps who have supported impeachment deserve respect and our indulgence as they try to deal with the funding problem caused by their fellow members' lack of will. Those who have never supported refuting the court and removing the justices deserve nothing but contempt.

"Response to Michael Valuk"
(To the *Manchester Union Leader*)
November, 2001

I was disappointed by Michael Valuk's October 15 editorial on education funding, the most important issue to have been thrust upon New Hampshire in years.

It concerns not only economics, not only taxation, but legislative prerogatives, local control, constitutional authority, and judicial arrogance.

Unfortunately, one would not get the impression that these issues were at stake in the debate presented by Mr. Valuk.

With recursive logic tumbling across the page, Mr. Valuk tells us we must accept fundamental principles. One, according to him, is that the education funding issue is a *property tax problem*, concerning "how your property taxes relate to your income."

Let's get something straight. The problem is *not* one of property taxes. The mismanagement of Claremont's tax base, and its citizens' subsequent attempt to coerce other towns to make up for their own mistakes, illustrate this well. This is a problem of dismissed constitutional authority, of clearly written constitutional clauses being intentionally misread by a politically motivated Supreme Court. It is a problem of gubernatorial and legislative ignorance, weakness, and culpability, wherein people sworn to uphold the NH Constitution don't know it, don't know its history, don't have the faintest clue as to the principles underpinning it, and apparently don't care. It is a problem involving the fundamental separation of powers between the judicial and all other branches, between the state government and the localities; and it is a problem that involves, in its practical consequences, the very nature of how we control our schools.

To see Mr. Valuk dismiss this as simply a matter of whose ox gets gored, i.e. who gets taxed, is extremely disappointing.

But his piece is worse than disappointing, for it advocates action on education funding that is not only illogical based on his own suppositions, it is outright pernicious on constitutional grounds.

While first telling us "Claremont" is a property tax problem, Valuk proceeds to praise a state-wide property tax as a "good way to begin to even out the rough spots." Obviously, a property tax that is imposed state-wide and may be completely removed from local concerns does not trouble him as much as a locally controlled property tax, with people free to leave the system if it is unacceptable. He views "tax disparity" as the essential factor when evaluating an "unfair" system, not whether those being taxed had control over their own budgets, zoning and taxation.

But while he praises what is in essence the aggregate redistribution of local wealth, and the removal of local control over property taxes, he implicitly acknowledges the fundamental flaw in such a system.

It is not, as he assumes, a problem of disparate interests battling in Concord to see who is taxed the least under some form of monetary seizure. It is not even the fact that proponents of income taxes, such as Valuk, don't care that their attempt to establish "constitutionally fixed, low rates dedicated to education" will require them to amend the Constitution, a process which Valuk himself describes as dangerous and difficult.

The problem is that a politically motivated Supreme Court and a Machiavellian Governor have spurned the Constitution, imposing a new, post-modern idea of "education adequacy" on us all. It is a perverse, twisted, unworkable system which can never be correctly understood. The problem is that "adequacy" is as subjective as the valuation of money, and imposing a state-wide level of adequacy will never, ever work. No matter how many Michael Valuk's try to establish "reasonable taxes" to fund it, it will change, always growing, never quite fulfilled.

Mr. Valuk's dissatisfaction with the stop-gap measure of last year's budget will return, because he is trying to grasp a writhing serpent, a poisonous, vicious, socialist reptile that can never be tamed. That is why the state Constitution reserved for localities the right to contract with education professionals, so that these smaller entities could determine for themselves what they thought was adequate.

I was unimpressed with Mr. Valuk's sophistic arguments, and particularly disappointed given the fact that he is the Chairman of the Nashua Chamber of Commerce. Based on the level of discourse among Nashua's political players, including the recently proposed ban on smoking in privately owned restaurants, it makes one wonder whether they are up to the task. The proposals coming from Nashua have been insidious at worst, childish at best. Childish ignorance can be forgiven, but Mr. Valuk and his associates are adults.

When a child plays with a snake and gets bitten, one can feel sorry for him.

Adults who play with bad animals deserve to get bitten.

"Of Oaths and Rules"
April 1999

In December of 1997, I wrote an article called "The Fix Is In", explaining the NH Supreme Court's "Claremont 2" ruling and its implications for education in the state. In that ruling, the Philosopher Kings in Concord ordered the state to produce a funding mechanism for "adequate" education by April 1, 1999.

By the time this hits print, April Fool's Day will have come and gone, with no resolution to the funding issue in the legislature.

But why is that the case? An in-depth look at the problem might help us understand. It also might help us determine what issues are really at stake.

The "Claremont 2" ruling of December, 1997, was based on a prior ruling of the court, "Claremont 1", in which the justices read Section Two, Article 83, of the NH Constitution as if they had been spending a week testing new forms of LSD. The article, which has received a great deal of attention since "Claremont 2", reads, in part:

> "...(I)t shall be the duty of the legislators and magistrates, in all future periods of this government, to cherish the interest of literature and the sciences, and all seminaries and public schools..."

The black robed Philosopher Kings read that very clear clause and determined that the state had a duty to provide education to the children in each town. They concentrated on the phrase "cherish... literature and the sciences, and all seminaries and public schools", determining that this was a mandatory, rather than hortatory, requirement of the state to fund public education. Unfortunately, they overlooked a great deal in the phrase, and in the nature of the state at the time the Constitution was written.

The phrase does not only say "cherish", it says "cherish the *interest* of literature and the sciences and all seminaries and public schools." How to best serve "the interest" of these constructs is obviously debatable. Socialists such as Sen. Mark Fernald and Rep. Peter Burling believe that further inculcating children in the patently misguided, intellectually corrupt, and economically inefficient public schools -- the very schools that have contributed to a massive, obvious and frightening lowering of education standards, and general dumbing down of children for the past thirty years -- would best serve the "interest of literature, and the sciences, etc…" But others, such as I, have a quite different idea. We believe that taxpayer funded education is, at best, a system of coercive taxation and redistribution imposing majority morality upon all. We believe that it is not a fundamental precept of Natural Law that I have a right to force my neighbor to pay for my child's education. We believe that Natural Rights are *negative rights,* not positive rights, that they *stop* us from doing things to one another, such as taking one another's property, or injuring each other. We believe that the philosophical tradition of establishing government only to do those things which we cannot do for ourselves is the basis of our US and New Hampshire Constitutions. We believe that the responsibility to educate a child rests with the *parents* of that child, that the *parents* can make the most informed decision about the well being of their child, and that stealing that power and placing it in the hands of the government immediately removes a certain degree of responsibility, and decreases the chances that those who care most for the child will be making the decisions for that child.

Additionally, beyond these differing philosophies regarding education, there is a manifest problem in the court's ruling. Since the court found that the word "cherish" in the clause meant that the state would support via taxpayer funds, their ruling also means that the state must support science and literature through taxpayer funds. I look forward to the day that a scientist or writer approaches the state to fund his "Constitutionally" favored avocation.

Couple these fundamental facts with the fact that not only did New Hampshire not have public schools at the time the state constitution was written, but its citizens had explicitly *avoided* creating public schools despite British commands to do so, and one might wonder where Justice Brock and his partners in crime got their bizarre ideas.

We may wonder all we want, but the fact remains that they made their decision.

Interestingly enough, the "Claremont 1" ruling came down prior to Jeanne Shaheen's first run for Governor, and, as some may know, her husband worked for the law firm that represented Claremont in the suit. It stretches credulity to believe that Mrs. Shaheen could not have known about the "Claremont 1" ruling when she took the famous "no broad-based taxes" pledge during her campaign. Also, it would have been disingenuous of a person with the knowledge that there was already a ruling on "Claremont

1" (stating that there was a "right" to education in New Hampshire) and with the knowledge that the Claremont plaintiffs were pushing for a state-wide tax, to not notify voters of this knowledge. Based on her excellent position to have this information prior to her first election, I can only say that Mrs. Shaheen was either deliberately deceptive, or devastatingly stupid.

The "Claremont 2" ruling that came down from Court Olympus was based on a continuation of the original suit brought by the people of Claremont and a few other "property poor" towns with large numbers of children and lower property values. A brief explanation of the continuation and the fallacies inherent in the argument are in order. Given the "Claremont 1" ruling that there was a "right" to a state-funded education, the plaintiffs continued to allege that the system of taxpayer funded education in the town of Claremont was fundamentally unjust.

The state requires that a minimum $3.50 per thousand education tax be collected by each town. Because funding comes from local property taxes, and, of course, these taxes are based on property values in the town, and since each town's taxes vary beyond the $3.50, according to what each town decides to budget, differences between the town rates arise. Given the fact that each town is different, has different economic advantages and disadvantages, and differing numbers of kids attending school per capita, one would *expect* there to be differences. It is as impossible to make all towns the same as it is to make all *people* the same. But having established their absurd "Claremont 1" ruling that there was a state responsibility to provide education, and seeing that the state already "imposed" a minimum $3.50 per Thousand tax (a tax that was never on the state budgets, and never collected by the state), the justices then moved to Section Two, Article Five, which says that all taxes imposed by the state must be "proportional and reasonable". The Back Robed Kings then ruled that *any* tax differences that arose between the towns, despite the fact that these are based on their own zoning, budgetary choices and inherent differences, are disproportionate and, therefore unconstitutional.

It was a seamless bit of legal prestidigitation, unless one actually compares the justices rulings to the document upon which they were supposedly based.

In both their Claremont rulings, the justices broke numerous explicit and implicit constitutional provisions. The first, and most glaring, was their disregard of Section Two, Article 78, for both rulings. This article states that no person can sit as a judge who has lived beyond the age of 70 years. Although this article sounds arbitrary, it is still extant, and it is not the place for the Supreme Court to decide which articles it will abide, and which it will not. The proper way to change such a stipulation is to *amend* the Constitution. For both rulings, the justices of the court temporarily seated judges to fill empty spaces. In both instances, those they seated were over the age of 70.

Additionally, in stating that there was a right to education and a concurrent state obligation to provide it, the court completely disregarded the "Rights Section" of the Constitution -- Section One. They contradict Section One, Article Six, which states:

> "... (T)he several parishes, bodies, corporate, or religious societies shall at all times have the right of electing their own teachers, and of contracting with them for their support or maintenance, or both."

This clause, utilizing the archaic English of "parish" for "town," explicitly states that it is up to the local governments to hire teachers and enter into contracts with them. By establishing a *state* obligation to fund education, the justices have created a contradiction. It is not possible for the *state* to have the power over education funds while reserving to the localities the power of deciding who they want to hire, and for how much. The two simply cannot coexist. Many people see that if the state imposes an *upper limit* on how much towns can spend, hoping by doing so to avoid any further lawsuits over "discrepancies" between property tax rates, such a limit would infringe on a town's right to contract with the school employees its citizens want. However, most people miss the fact that any *minimum* standard also sets a limit for the towns. Thus, when the court's "Claremont 2" came down, requiring the state to fund an "adequate" level of education, and leaving the determination of what is "adequate" to the legislature, they completely contradicted Section One, Article Six. *Any* level of adequacy set by the state, forcing the towns to spend a certain amount on education, whether collected by the towns or the state, is blatantly unconstitutional. It's patently obvious.

Such derelictions of constitutional authority easily merit removal from office for each and every justice who supported the actions. And it is the responsibility of the legislature and/or the governor to remove them. However, although Jeanne Shaheen has the power to remove any justice with a simple address of the legislature, she has shirked her responsibility. Why? Because she is in favor of the Court's decision. To her, it is not the breech of the Constitution, nor even the *extent* of that breech, that determines her actions to uphold the founding document of our state, the very document that allows her to hold power. It is the *outcome* of that breech that determines her actions. And Mrs. Shaheen has approved of this piece of sorcery from the start. Her Democratic and liberal Republican allies in the House and Senate feel just the same.

But these manifest breeches of the Constitution are not all of the court's malefactions. By *demanding* that the state legislature produce a new funding mechanism based on some form of "proportional" taxation and redistribution by April 1, 1999, the Supreme Court justices have taken a giant step across the boundaries of "separation of powers". With such a command regarding an issue of tax policy, which is strictly the purview of towns and the legislative branch, the court has imposed its will where it is not constitutionally allowed. This is judicial fiat, judicial tyranny, and it is behavior which easily merits removal from the court. Want to know why the Democrats and liberal Republicans haven't lifted a finger to stop it? Because to them the ends justify the means.

With these people, principle is nothing, lies are commonplace, and quickly forgotten. For example, during a state-wide address on television during the first week of March, Jeanne Shaheen told viewers that if the legislature did not produce a new funding mechanism, there should be a statewide crisis in education. When I reminded her at a news conference the next day that she had derided gubernatorial challenger Jay Lucas for saying exactly the same thing during a fall debate, telling Jay that he "just didn't get it", she looked very displeased. When I then asked her if her television address of the previous night meant she was acknowledging that, indeed, Mr. Lucas did "get it," she outright lied, saying, "Oh, I wasn't talking about the education issue, I was talking about other issues." Every reporter in the room must have known how sadly false her answer was.

There are lessons aplenty in this year-long nightmare, but perhaps one of the best came from a meeting I attended in Amherst, at which our elected representatives tried to show us all the "choices" of tax plans we had, when, in fact the choices were non-starters based on the philosophy of redistribution, ignorance of the law, and appeasement of judicial tyranny. The meeting was like watching a bunch of children; the *sole*, not just primary, concern of 99% of the attendees was "how will this effect Amherst?" No one seemed to give a moment's thought to how it would effect the people of other towns, who would have their livelihoods depleted in order to facilitate *"fairness for the children"*.

Rep. Peter Bergin actually tried to justify the concept of redistribution by playing on jealousy. He pointed out that people in Bedford pay much less on their school taxes than we in Amherst because they send their high school aged kids to Manchester. Of course, the fact that we in Amherst used to be connected with Milford, but decided to build our own high school, which has raised our taxes dramatically, seemed of little importance to him. *It was our own choice!* To try to play on people's senses of envy, to play on their belief that these types of differences, where towns make their own decisions, are inherently "unfair" is very base. But that's where we are. We've got to be jealous of folks in other towns, despite the fact that doing so means we have discarded any adherence to the principle of individual responsibility, and have become blind to the very reasons we have long exercised "local control."

We've reached a point where majority sanctioned plunder is not just acceptable, but laudable, where one's neighbors can reach into one's pocket and take whatever they want, as long as it's for a majority supported goal. The government no longer protects our private property, it offers it up for the jackals of modern redistribution to devour, and the jackals are now our neighbors.

Have we become so docile that when it's all over at the end of the night, we shake hands with the plunderers and walk off as friends?

Testimony to the Legislature
Finance Committee
March 30, 1999

The Claremont rulings of the state Supreme Court have had at least two positive effects. First, they have placed legislators in the position of either upholding their Constitutional oaths, or promoting lawlessness. Second, they have prompted thousands of citizens to pick up and read the document under which our state government was created, under which you, the governor, and the justices hold your positions. And when they read it, they inevitably come to the same conclusions. I will outline some of these now, as a means of supporting the legislation before you.

Legally, in its Claremont rulings, the Supreme Court has brazenly abrogated Article Two, Section 78. Although seemingly arbitrary under today's standards, this section stipulates that no individual shall sit as a judge who has attained the age of seventy years. Many may feel that this section of the Constitution is archaic, out of date, but the key is that it is still *extant*, and it is not the place of the justices to haphazardly decided which sections of the Constitution they wish to abide, and which they wish to ignore. Additionally, when such an obvious breach of the Constitution occurs, it is completely inappropriate for the legislature to approach the very individuals who broke the law for a ruling on their own lawlessness! This is childish and absurd. It is the place of the legislature and the governor to *remove them*. It is the *duty* of the legislators and governor to remove them.

The Supreme Court has also broken the implicit and explicit principles of separation of powers, so finely crafted by the founders of the state and nation, wherein the court acts as an appellate body, and the legislature is reserved the power to make laws. The concept of Judicial review, a concept not explicitly laid out in the constitutions, and, in fact, debated greatly over the past two hundred-plus years does not endorse judicial tyranny. Under the philosophy of judicial review, those judges who sit on the highest appellate body in our state were to keep foremost in their minds the marked delineations between political issues, requiring political, ie. legislative, address, and legal issues. Political disputes, disputes pertaining to matters that are purely subjective and best left to individuals or their elected representatives, were understood to be the purview of the *people*, subject to their individual desires, or their representatives, subject to the give and take inherent to the legislative process. They are not to be placed under the control of unelected individuals wearing the cloak of supposed impartiality.

Additionally, the justices have infused Section Two, Article 83 with a meaning that is clearly nonexistent. As we all know, Article 83 states, in part:

> "...(I)t shall be the duty of the legislators, in all future periods of this government, to cherish the interest of literature, and the sciences, and all seminaries and public schools..."

The justices read that very clear clause and determined that the state had a duty to provide education to the children in each town. They concentrated on the phrase "cherish... literature and the sciences, and all seminaries and public schools", determining that this was a mandatory, rather than hortatory, requirement of the state to fund public education. Unfortunately, they overlooked a great deal in the phrase, and in the nature of the state at the time the Constitution was written.

The phrase does not only say "cherish", it says "cherish the *interest* of literature and the sciences and all seminaries and public schools." How to best serve "the interest" of these constructs is obviously debatable. Many members of the legislature believe that further inculcating children in the patently misguided, intellectually corrupt, and economically inefficient public schools -- the very schools that have contributed to a massive, obvious and frightening lowering of education standards, and general dumbing down of children for the past thirty years -- would best serve the "interest of literature, and the sciences, etc..." But others, such as I, have a quite different idea. We believe that taxpayer funded education is, at best, a system of coercive taxation and redistribution imposing majority morality upon all. We believe that it is not a fundamental precept of Natural Law that I have a right to force my neighbor to pay for my child's education. We believe that Natural Rights are *negative rights,* not positive rights, that they *stop* us from doing things to one another, such as taking one another's property, or injuring each other. We believe that the philosophical tradition of establishing government only to do those things which we cannot do for ourselves is the basis of our US and New Hampshire Constitutions. We believe that the responsibility to educate a child rests with the *parents* of that child, that the *parents* can make the most informed decision about the well being of their child, and that stealing that power and placing it in the hands of the government immediately removes a certain degree of responsibility, and decreases the chances that those who care most for the child will be making the decisions for that child.

Additionally, beyond these differing philosophies regarding education, there is a manifest problem in the court's ruling. Since the court found that the word "cherish" in the clause meant that the state would support via taxpayer funds, their ruling also means that the state must support science and literature through taxpayer funds. I look forward to the day that a scientist or writer approaches the state to fund his "Constitutionally" favored avocation.

Most glaring of all the legal problems with the court is their brazen willingness to contradict an article that *was* intended to denote a right, Section One, Article 6, which states:

> "… (T)he several parishes, bodies, corporate, or religious societies
> shall at all times have the right of electing their own teachers,
> and of contracting with them for their support or maintenance,
> or both."

This clause, utilizing the archaic English of "parish" for "town," explicitly states that it is up to the local governments to hire teachers and enter into contracts with them. By establishing a *state* obligation to fund education, the justices have created a contradiction. It is not possible for the *state* to have the power over education funds while reserving to the localities the power of deciding who they want to hire, and for how much. The two simply cannot coexist. Many people see that if the state imposes an *upper limit* on how much towns can spend, hoping by doing so to avoid any further lawsuits over "discrepancies" between property tax rates, such a limit would infringe on a town's right to contract with the school employees its citizens want. However, most people miss the fact that any *minimum* standard also sets a limit for the towns. Thus, when the court's "Claremont 2" came down, requiring the state to fund an "adequate" level of education, and leaving the determination of what is "adequate" to the legislature, they completely contradicted Section One, Article Six. *Any* level of adequacy set by the state, forcing the towns to spend a certain amount on education, whether collected by the towns or the state, is blatantly unconstitutional. You should be certain that if any state law is passed that infringes upon Section One, Article Six, lawsuits will follow, lawsuits that *will* be based upon clear Constitutional mandates, lawsuits that will make the Claremont arguments look like feverish delusions.

I have nothing but contempt for those legislators who have willfully and with great partisanship decided to ignore their Constitutional oaths. And I ask them, why *have* a written constitution if those who hold power under its rules refuse to recognize its strictures? Why not run the state with the rules to Monopoly, or the Manchester bus schedule? Why bother paying lip service to some amorphous totem called the Constitution is we only do so for political expediency?

Philosophically the rulings, and the plans produced by such people as the governor, Liz Hager, Cliff Below, Donna Sytek and others, are all deserving of opposition. The governor has stated that we *all* have a responsibility to provide an adequate education for *our* children. I wonder what she implies when she says "our". I am not her child, nor are her children mine, or yours, or anyone else's other than hers and her husband's. To say that each of us has a *responsibility* to educate another person's child, one must accept the supposition that each of us also has the concurrent *control* that goes with that responsibility. And I think you will agree that, upon placing this education question in the state house, where decisions are made on the basis of majority rule of representatives, it is impossible to accommodate even the slightest bit of individual control. If I have a *responsibility* to educate another's child, I must also have a say in how that child will be educated. I'm sure many people who would like others to pay for their child's education would like to promote the idea that I have a responsibility to pay for that education. However, I doubt they would agree that I should have just as much say in how that child is educated as the parents have.

The problem of control is one which can be traced back to the Founding Fathers and beyond. It is inherent in the concept of Natural Rights. If, as some say, there is a "right" to education, then that supposition is based in the philosophy of Natural Rights as laid out by the Scottish political philosopher, John Locke. But Locke stressed that we establish governments to secure our rights to life, liberty and property, to protect them from encroachments by others, this facilitates control of our own lives. Our rights are explicitly "negative" rights, where we are *prevented* from doing certain things to each other, not obligated to do certain things for one another. There is no such thing as a "right" to education, because the very nature of "rights" spelled out by our political heritage is one of negative rights, not positive ones. When governments begin to infringe on our rights by establishing these positive obligations on us, they are illegitimate, and must be abolished.

Finally, let me discuss some matters of efficacy. The diving force behind the acceptance of the Court's rulings is the feel-good application of the term "fairness". We must be fair to the children of NH and provide every child with an "adequate" education. Let me present you with the reality that it is as impossible to make every child's education circumstances the same, as it is to make every adult's living circumstances the same. To believe otherwise is utopian and dangerous. Additionally, if it truly is the goal of those who would change the way in which we control our education in NH to create the best system of education they can, for the largest number of students, then they are talking about aggregates, and an analysis of the aggregate test scores of NH students, whether they be standardized test for fourth and eight grades or the SATs, shows that NH consistently ranks in the top ten of all states for student performance. We get the best, most efficient education when we leave the funding decisions up to the parents and local control. Therefore, those who want to "create the best system of education for the greatest number of children" must recognize the system we already have.

Local control is not only the most efficient, it is the most ethical next to complete parental control. When you have small spheres of control, there is a greater possibility that the needs of those in the sphere will have their needs addressed. The larger the sphere of control, the less likely this is to happen. For example, in the town of Merrimack, there was a debate a few years ago about the distribution of condoms in the schools. The conservative people in town viewed such a policy as contrary to their morals. They didn't want their tax money used for something they found repugnant. A year later, they organized and took over the school board, changing the policy, and going one step further. They decided to change the reading curricula for the schools, eliminating certain authors they thought represented lifestyles they disliked, such as homosexuality, or promiscuity. At this point, the more liberal citizens spoke out. How dare the school board use their tax money to promote their moral views?! Well, obviously, whomever was in control had the final say, a problem inherent in public education, and one which deserves more explication. However, the overall lesson shown here should be obvious. And that is at least these people could leave! They had, as the philosophical principle is called, the "right to exit". With small spheres of control this can still happen. But once the state takes over, where are you going to go? Nowhere, because the sphere of control will be the entire state. And don't try to kid yourself that you're likely to find a better system by moving to another state.

In closing, I would like to point out that a lot of the rhetoric recently centered on how to produce the "most fair" tax plan possible. This is based on the acceptance of an illegitimate court ruling, and on a facile understanding of economics. To claim that any tax other than a user fee is fair is absurd. To claim that a tax which is based upon someone's "ability to pay", as the euphemism goes, is the fairest is just as absurd.

"The Fallacy of 'Fair' Taxation"
October 26, 1999

Recent debate over how to fund the $825 Million education budget foisted upon us by a politically motivated Supreme Court in the "Claremont" rulings has brought to the fore many fallacies that require attention.

First, let's look at Governor Shaheen's statement last week in favor of a capital gains tax. She explained to us over and over that this was really the fairest tax, since *it taxed the richest residents of the state*. Both practically and philosophically she is quite wrong.

The practical considerations are academic when analyzed along side the philosophical considerations, but let's take a moment to see just how "fair", or wise, such a policy is. We're supposed to be concerned with "fairness", right? Explain to a retired couple living on a fixed income, but with a large nest egg stored away in investments, that nailing them to do what Governor Shaheen believes is "fair" is the ethical thing to do. Tell men and women who work incredibly long hours in order to save and invest that they are part of the "Wealthy Class" and should thus pay more than others. Tell start-up companies that they'll be punished for utilizing their after tax profits in any form of investment, or that their investors will be taxed on their stock returns. And then try to convince them that this will not have a negative effect on investment and their bottom line.

But beyond the practical implications, there are the matters of principle and philosophy. Somehow, people like Jeanne Shaheen and Peter Burling, and many others in politics believe that taxing the "rich" is "fair".

This twisted concept appears as the basis for almost every form of tax redistribution. It can be a capital gains tax, an income tax, or a property tax that takes from "property rich" towns and gives to "property poor" towns because the property rich towns can "afford to pay" (and because redistributing that wealth is what is "fair"), but the sentiment is the same: It is only fair to tax those with more, because they will not miss it as much as those who are poor.

The problem with this is that it flies in the face of the economic principle of "Subjective Marginal Utility". Roughly stated, the principle holds that while it seems possible to assume that "rich" people would value X percent of their incomes less than "poor" people would value X, when an attempt is made to actually put this into practice, the assumption must be applied to individuals. An attempt to graph the "value" each individual applies to his or her wealth is impossible by anyone save that individual. Thus, as a matter of mathematics, taxation based on "ability to pay" is impossible to justify. "Ability To Pay" is unique to every individual, and cannot be determined by outside observers.

For example, we have seen the argument of those in supposedly "property rich" towns that there are many who live in them who aren't wealthy at all, and would have to move if their taxes increased. Yet many politicians in these towns, such as Portsmouth, have no trouble assuming that other types of "rich" individuals don't have circumstances unique to their lives that would be just as troubling. If the argument can be made that we just don't understand the economic circumstances of certain towns, how can it be justified to overlook the fact that *all* towns are comprised of individuals, and that each individual lives within his own circumstances, be they property-based, income based, or expense-based? And aren't those circumstances even more varied than those of different towns?

If a man who earns $70,000 a year has cancer and a mother in a nursing home, is he somehow a better target for taxation than a single mother living on $20,000 a year? Of course he isn't. But that doesn't matter to those who support an income tax, or a capital gains tax, or a redistributive property tax. As long as they can obfuscate the recognition of the individual and portray people as "rich", they can sucker people into thinking it's okay to tax them. They can paint those who would argue against such immoral taxation as "selfish", when, in fact, it is they who are selfishly assuming they know better what to do with someone else's money.

Of course, the "rich" are supposed to buy into the idea that taking their money and giving it to whomever the majority deems is more worthy is somehow ethical. Indeed, it is portrayed as the highest virtue in a society. It means we are all part of the same group, that we aren't greedy, we aren't just out for ourselves.

But being against redistribution of wealth doesn't have to be based on an attitude of self preservation or greed. It is more often based on the principle that I do not have the right to force my neighbor to pay for what I believe is right. I do not have the conceit to believe I can decide better than my neighbor how he should spend his money. I do not have the moral prerogative to supersede his rights to his own property in order to do what I believe is more moral and "good for society".

Don't count on any of these considerations to be discussed in the public debate over what is the "fairest" tax. Taxation is inherently unfair, and taxing some more than others for services we are all supposed to be receiving on an equal basis is completely unethical, no matter how much people try to couch it in terms of "caring" for the less fortunate. The "fairest" tax is not one based on "ability to pay", but one based on use of services. A fee-for-service tax system is the closest a society can come to taxing each according to the demands he places on government. Such a system would inevitably shrink to primarily those services for which governments are supposed to be formed: protecting ourselves and our property from damage and from incursion by others.

Education, no matter what anyone says, is not a right. Rights are *negative*. They *stop* us from taking things from one another, and from forcing others to do certain things we deem important. I do not have a right to approach a teacher and demand that he teach my child for free on the pretext that my child has a "right" to education. Similarly, I do not have a right to tell my neighbor he must pay for my child's education. Education is not a service that can be justifiably provided by taxation. No matter what arguments people make that tax-funded education is required to make our society function, that therefore we are *all* recipients of the benefits of public education, such an argument does not support taking another's money, just like it doesn't justify forcing a teacher to teach for nothing. Additionally, it has been historically proven that tax-funded education is actually less efficient at teaching children, which further negates the "societal need-societal benefit" argument for taxation.

I don't care for the less fortunate by taking my supposedly "rich" neighbor's money and giving it to someone else. And neither does Jeanne Shaheen.

LIVE FREE OR DIE

The Bull That Broke Free:

Men are enslaved with shackles made by
others and by themselves.
Animals do not have the capacity
to forge their own chains.

There is nothing nobler than the bull
that resists, and breaks free.

P. GARDNER GOLDSMITH   PAUL H. GOLDSMITH

With the "New Age", common courtesy
is no longer common.

PHG
December 11, 1992

"Boomer Culture, RIP"
Dec. 2, 2001

In a perverse way, the media coverage of former Beatle George Harrison's death may have been the greatest disservice to the man and his work that could have been committed.

This ought not be an unorthodox view of the round-the-clock, in-depth reports about the musician. After all, by dwelling on the supposed world-changing importance and glory of Harrison and his cohorts, the Baby Boomer-dominated media have served not to celebrate the life of a creative man, but to irrefutably verify their own myopia and childish narcissism.

Large segments of the aging, former-hippie Boomer population have shown time and again that they are so self-involved, so egotistical, that they actually believe the naive notion that their "Age of Aquarius" changed the world for the better. Adhering to the belief that their devotion to free love, eastern mysticism, post-modernist art, socialism and rebellion against parental authority has had a positive bearing on the generations that have come before and since, the Boomers continue to look at the Sixties as monumental, as the social watershed of the twentieth century.

Ironically, it is this generation, the population of Americans who embraced the fallacy of moral relativism, that finds it beyond its capacity to recognize the relativistic nature of generational interests.

To the Boomers working in almost every facet of the mass media, whatever strikes their fancy must immediately become part of the cultural lexicon, no matter how silly or ignorant they may appear by promoting it.

For some unfathomable reason, retirement investment seems not to have existed before the former anti-capitalist Boomers realized they were getting older and ought to invest. The stock market was anathema until they recognized its value. Social Security and Medicare were unimportant until the Boomers saw old age creeping up on them.

Perhaps most telling of all has been the sudden adoration of the "Greatest Generation", the World War Two vets whom it instantly became fashionable to admire once the Boomers recognized their own mortality and started seeing the deaths of their parents. Only when the "Greatest Generation" started to pass away, when it became nearly too late to thank many of them, did the members of the "Me Generation" contemplate the possibility that perhaps their parents weren't as ignorant and awful as they believed they were while smoking pot and sitting in the lotus position in the muddy fields of Woodstock.

The Boomers in charge of the pop-media seem to have an uncanny ability to turn truly valuable aspects of our culture into apparently frivolous, mindless fads, imbued with as much significance as a frock coat or love beads. Conversely, they over-estimate the importance of fads until they are viewed as historically significant. The Boomers infecting the media are effusive. They haven't changed a whit from the days when they cried at the sight of George Harrison and his mates taking the stage. They are not only led by their emotions, they reflexively celebrate that fact and promote it as a high virtue in society.

It's sad. The Baby Boomers always claimed they would remain young forever.

Based on the self-indulgent nature of the coverage of George Harrison's death, it appears they still haven't grown up.

LIVE FREE OR DIE

When a state's underclass learns that it can live off its producers, that state will slowly sink into socialism, and strangle…

PHG
November 29, 1990

"Welcome to New Hampshire... Now GO HOME!"
October, 2003

On October 1, the 5000 members of the libertarian "Free State Project" gathered in New York City to decide where they will soon move in order to live more freely.

Their choice was New Hampshire, a place which has as its motto revolutionary general John Stark's famous dictum, "live free or die". The selection of the "granite state" has been mentioned in papers from Great Britain to Japan, studied by political analysts all over the globe; and though the plan to migrate to a new, freer area, and the selection of New Hampshire as that land, say a great deal about the sorry state of liberty in America, the reaction of political pundits in New Hampshire says even more about the obstacles these free-thinkers have to surmount in their chosen home.

In response to the vote, New Hampshire Democrat Party Chair Kathy Sullivan issued comments that show she is quite unhappy with the decision, and that the members of the Free State Project are not welcome here.

They are, in her words, "a sort of fringe group that can best be described as anarchists." According to Sullivan, Craig Benson, the Republican governor who has welcomed the immigrants to NH, needs to "explain to voters why he is supporting such a radical, antifamily agenda."

So much for the vaunted left-wing inclusiveness.

Apparently, inclusiveness is only reserved for those who share the same orthodox socialist view as Kathy Sullivan. It means that one is welcome and included only if he agrees with Ms. Sullivan. He must agree that it is a good thing to take the productive labor of his neighbor and give it to his other neighbor, and that non-violent activities among consenting adults are to be controlled by the ever-changing whim of the politically-connected majority. Then, and only then, is he to be welcomed as a fellow New Hampshire citizen. Then, and only then, does he apparently embrace "family values".

Thomas Jefferson would have been stopped at the border. Sam Adams would have been asked to leave. Thomas Paine, for those in the Democrat Party of NH who know who he was, would probably have been apprehended, held for questioning, and escorted out as soon as Ms. Sullivan could arrange it.

If one desires to leave his neighbor alone, to be left alone, to make government adhere to what John Locke called its legitimate function of stopping us from coercing one another, he is not welcome by Kathy Sullivan and the Democrat Party in New Hampshire. Likewise, he is feared by less-prominent Democrats.

"I'm ballistic. We have enough trouble passing school budgets as it is. These people will come in and try to eliminate services," said Ken Perry, 58, a Realtor in Wolfeboro and retired public school principal who made his living off money legally expropriated from his neighbors.

"I was hoping they'd go to Wyoming," Perry said in an Associated Press interview.

Such comments are interesting in light of the fact that Mr. Perry assumes his "services" are properly provided by government, through the seizure of other people's money, and not properly provided by the private sector, without forcing anyone else to pay.

"I like to be left alone by the government. But I need my trash picked up," Dennis Pizzimenti, a lawyer from Concord was quoted by AP.
Such faith in the ability of people to provide for themselves is truly heartwarming. No wonder Democrats believe in social welfare programs; they don't even think people can handle getting their own trash removed. One hates to contemplate how they manage to potty-train their own kids.

In stark contrast to this fear driven, paternalistic rhetoric, stands the philosophy of classical liberalism that the Free State Project embraces. As FSP founder Jason Sorens, a lecturer in Political Science at Yale told the *Guardian* (UK), "The classical liberal (libertarian) philosophy has a long and respectable pedigree. We see ourselves as a kind of chamber of commerce, promoting the state as somewhere where people will come and live freely and do business."

Whether the FSP members will be able to effect the change they seek remains to be seen. Given the population of New Hampshire, which is 1.3 million, the 20,000 people the FSP plans to relocate to the Granite State will have to pick their spots very carefully, studying demographic maps and political districts as much as possible. They may even be hampered by their own success, for if they make New Hampshire an even freer place to live, with lower taxes and regulations, it will become an even more attractive haven for refugees from Massachusetts, Connecticut, New York and New Jersey. For years that has been New Hampshire's dilemma; in being freer than its neighboring states, it has attracted refugees from those states. Those refugees have typically been unfamiliar with the principles of individual liberty and small governments, and have moved due to simple economic necessity. If the Free Staters are successful, they may end up creating political change, only to see it undone by the very refugees they attract.

One thing is certain: the left-wing political establishment in New Hampshire is frightened. Despite the relatively small FSP population, it is composed of articulate, motivated and politically driven individuals who will no doubt begin playing a very prominent role in state politics. They will work hard to remove the yolk of government oppression that has been weighing more heavily on the backs of people in the Granite State for years. They will appear in town meetings, post candidates for public office, and raise funds to combat the adherents to Kathy Sullivan's amorphous and ever-permuting "values". They will, in short, work to live free.

And as crazy as it sounds, they might, just *might*, get their own trash removed.

Goodbye, Dad
A Eulogy for Paul Goldsmith, November 25, 2003

The other day, I was telling my niece, Brianna, a little bit about the word *Panglossian*, which entered our vocabulary thanks to the great writer Voltaire, and his novella, "Candide."

In the story, Candide is a care-free society member who subscribes to the philosophy of one Dr. Pangloss, a cipher for the 19th Century philosopher Leibnitz.

Voltaire and Leibnitz were at odds over their views on many things, foremost among them, a statement by Leibnitz that all was "for the best, in this the best of all possible worlds." In Leibnitz's view, God created this world, and therefore anything that happens in it is for the best.

Voltaire scoffed at this attitude, believing that any sane man who observed the tragedy, sadness and suffering people endure around the world would conclude that sometimes all is *not* for the best. Those who believed as Leibnitz, or as Dr. Pangloss, did, were either naive, insane, or afraid to face the truth. Voltaire's book, which he supposedly wrote in a day, was such a phenomenally controversial publication, the term Panglossian became part of the vernacular, and came to stand for the habit of looking through the proverbial "rose-colored glasses".

My father admired Voltaire, as I did after I acted on his suggestion to read "Candide". To me, it seemed that Voltaire's view easily trumped Pangloss's conception of the world. But I always wondered about how my father felt. I could snicker at those who said that all was for the best, that it would all turn out okay in the end, and I could say, "what about crime, disaster… what about death?" But my father didn't snicker. He went about life with a growing sense that all *was* going to be for the best.

Before I came here, I wasn't so sure.

I think everyone wonders how he will deal with the loss of a loved one. My father was a true hero in many ways. He was the kindest, gentlest and wisest man I have ever met. He conducted himself with integrity and sincerity, and always showed me how much he cared for me, how much just my being around made him happy. He was always asking me how I was doing, and even when I might have been down, he would say, "Hang in there, pal. That's the way." He would always treat the rest of the family with great kindness and show us the warmest form of love. He was just one of the best men around.

And now, he is gone. And I look for him, and he is not there. He is not there to talk to, to see laugh, to see smile and sigh at the sight of his lovely granddaughter, nor to impart wisdom to us, mixed with his adventurous, humorous spirit. And I look around me, and I cannot believe it.

That sorrow, that deep, unfathomable confusion and heartache, makes me wonder if things are *not* all for the best. They can't be if this is the way the world operates... If the man who was such a good and caring man, such an innocent, yet wise and hopeful man, could be... gone.

But looking back on what he has achieved, and the way in which he conducted himself, looking at the wonderful people I see here today, I wonder...

My father's life was amazing. Born in Massachusetts, February, 1917, he entered an America caught in the grip of the First World War. His formative years were spent attending school in Marblehead, honing his skills as a hockey player on local ponds, and flourishing as a pitcher during the summer months. This was a period when most households used iceboxes to keep food cold, and teenagers could walk down the street with 22 gauge rifles over their shoulders on their way to take target shots at tin cans. It was an America closer to the social environment of Abraham Lincoln than to that of Bill Clinton and George Bush, a nation where school children could still sit with Civil War veterans to discuss their experiences on the bloody fields of terrible battle.

On one occasion, my father even recalled seeing a pi-plane land with little trouble on the avenue in front of his house in downtown Marblehead.

Lawrence Academy, in Groton, Mass., welcomed him prior to college, and he acquired an interest in law and science. Despite the hardships of the Great Depression – travails that he later realized were prolonged by government policies – his athletic skills were formidable enough to secure him a baseball scholarship at the University of Michigan. The summer prior to embarking on his college tour, he was recruited by the Boston Red Sox to join their "Hooligan Squad" of young prospects, pitching on the mound in Fenway Park. As you might have read in the obituary of him, he actually played against Satchel Paige, and during the inaugural year of Nashua's Holman stadium.

But an injury to his shoulder brought an end to that career, and he shifted over to hockey, becoming captain of the University of Michigan team, and an All-American.

It appeared that he was destined for a career as a star national player, but once more the vicissitudes of life and an international conflict would change everything.

On December 7, 1941, my father emerged from a movie house in Ann Arbor, and heard the news of the Japanese attack on Pearl Harbor. He was in the South Pacific within a year. His brother was soon marching with Patton.

Baking beneath the equatorial sun of islands such as Guam, New Guinea, and New Caledonia, he helped push back Hirohito's forces as an aviation navigator. He has recalled running naked from his barracks to try to save an Australian fighter pilot who was being burned alive in his downed plane, swimming with sharks, and playing volleyball against New Caledonian headhunters during his off time.

Upon returning home, my father found he could earn more money to support his ailing parents by turning away from a pro hockey contract and going into non-athletic endeavors. His principles were sound, his priorities straight. He worked, married, had children, and even coached youth hockey during his spare time.

Through it all, he fostered and inculcated a ravenous desire to learn. As a teenager, he found the dictionary to be one of the most interesting books in the world, and he read it all the way through. At the age of twenty-five, he began noting intelligent or wise aphorisms in a tiny black book, a book that, by the time he turned 80, spanned two volumes. In it, he quoted, among many, Ovid, Thomas Paine, Aristotle, Jefferson, John Locke, Milton Friedman, Bastiat, Madison, and even his own children.

This predilection for intellectual pursuits eventually drove him to inquire as to how to determine a set of irreducible principles for human interaction, a group of ideals derived from observation of human nature, that, when closely followed, would foster the greatest freedom among people. As was his disposition, he had faith in others, and his studies led him to the works of economist and political philosopher Ludwig von Mises. An Austrian dissident from World War Two, von Mises was one of the first economists since Adam Smith to articulate the idea that markets are driven by mutual self-interest, and that the valuation one places upon his own work and earnings is purely subjective. Government intervention was found by von Mises, and by many of the other economists to follow, to not only be immoral, but also counter-productive, driven more by the ego-centric views of politicians than by the subjective desires of people acting of their own accord, with their own free-wills.

My father eventually synthesized the economic argument in favor of laissez-faire economics, with the moral case for individual freedom. He often said that the person who earned the money ought to make the decisions about that money; it was both the most ethical way to treat one's neighbor, and the most effective, since the individual could best determine his own needs and how to fulfill them. He was in the vanguard of school choice here in New Hampshire, seeing vouchers as a step towards removing altogether the smothering blanket of government bureaucracy and union control.

His efforts led him to be recognized by the Reagan Administration, where he was selected to work at the National Institute of Education – one of a hand-picked few who actually wanted to eliminate his own department, seeing it as not only inefficient, but unconstitutional. He has recalled periods when Carter Administration holdovers would break into his filing cabinets to discover that he was about, when he had to meet in restaurants to hold private conversations.

When he was 67 years old, and still working in Washington, my father returned to his Alexandria apartment to discover a robber unplugging his television. The young man pulled a knife, and my father wrapped his winter coat around his arm and went on the attack. And ambulance took the twenty-six year old out of the apartment on a stretcher, bearing with him a concussion and a shattered jaw.

He retired to New Hampshire shortly thereafter, where he headed up the non-profit organization Freedom Through Strength. Under its auspices, he diligently pushed for a national missile defense long before it was a fashionable subject. Until his last few days, he kept up with his favorite publication – *Human Events*, *National Review*, *American Spectator*, *Chronicles* and *Reason* – often engaging in conversations on the material he read. He had seen his parents, his brother, and many of his friends pass away. He had seen world conflict and horror many cannot even imagine. Yet his good nature and kind disposition still held firm. He shared those traits with his children and grandchildren whenever they were around.

Those who know me, know I am driven by my political principles, that I study and read economics and political philosophy as if I were in school. The reason I bring up these things here, now, is that my father was just as driven. It was important to him that people educated themselves, they they, as Socrates said, sought out truth, and dispelled error, that they studied the foundations of western civilization, and tried to keep those foundations firm by stoking within themselves an appreciation for the good, the just, and the ethical. My father was a lighthearted man, but he was serious about this. And he worked very hard to turn his knowledge into action.

When I was in my twenties, I ordered my first set of highly difficult, but important texts on economics and individual liberty. When they arrived, I was shocked to discover first editions of books such as Ludwig von Mises's "Human Action" in his library. I said to him, "Dad, you already HAD all these books?!"

As you can see, he not only HAD them, he had annotated them and written in them comments for his kids. His modest response when I told him how amazing his efforts were was, "Well Gard, the ideas just made sense."

And this is what he wrote to us (in "Human Action"):

June 1970

To My Gang – Pete, Carr & Gard

Someday, somewhere, sometime it is my hope that all of you will read all or part of this work.

May it act as an infinite beacon to guide you through the rocks and shoals of shallow philosophies and thinking whose tapestry is held by cobwebs.

With everlasting love and appreciation –

Dad

My father was my hero. He was a humble, kind and delightful man. The memories I have of him helping us collect fireflies, or fishing together, listening to our reel-to-reel tape recorder in the darkness as it played "Night on Bald Mountain" and "The 1812 Overture", are all very clear. The thoughts of how he adored our dog, Snowball... of a night when he carefully removed porcupine quills from Snowy's mouth after she had bitten into one in the middle of the night, of his accompanying me to the Smithsonian to let us see the wonder of the Dutch Realist painters, of hot summer nights barbequing, and loving it all, of three legged races and hops in the surf... All those memories are so vivid and warm, and they are combined with the knowledge that he was preparing us for our adult lives, and for the roles we needed to play in society.

I look for him now, and he is missing, and missed, but when I think of such a wonderful life, of a young man who was thrust into terrors and yet kept his hope, of a man who always smiled as he turned towards the future, and a man who led his life, a life like any other, that cannot be predicted or totally planned, and yet he did it right, a man who was good, and honest, and just, and got happiness out of it that was well-deserved and never asked for... I realize that perhaps he might never have said it outright, but he always suspected Dr. Pangloss was right, that all will be for the best. And I think that one of the greatest lessons he has taught me, one of his final lessons, is that I can agree.

I just wanted to make one last observation. I've thought about it, and... you only have a certain amount of time with your family, and with the people you love. Everybody knows it goes by quickly... So when you look at those pictures, think about the people near you, and think about the fact that you want to cherish those times with the people who are important.

Thank you. I'm just going to pin something on my father's lapel that I thought he might have liked.

(The American flag.)

"Title"
2004
(Fiction)

What can I express about this strange phenomenon that will not inspire within you merely a subtle sense of disquiet, rather than utter, uncontrollable dread?

To you, the tale I intend to recount will seem a trifle, the most ordinary of occurrences, dismissible as a simple twist of fate or the combination of average circumstances as seen through one man's *paranoid dementia*. But to me, the witness of these preternatural events, it is a story so horrific as to implicate the Devil himself.

In my lonely and solitary existence here in New England, I have endeavored to trouble no one. The pale and silent snows of winter blanket my surroundings, delivering peace and tranquility to my once tormented soul. They bring to mind the deep arboreal stillness of my homeland, where a man might walk for miles and encounter no one. His companions, mute and unmoving, would consist of the majestic firs and brooding oaks, and the crisp air would fill his lungs and caress his skin. Invigorated and enlivened, he would march with a bounce to his step, planting his boots in the snow and delighting in the crunch of the one against the other.

I can recall with vivid clarity the varied colors of the wood: the deep green of the pines and pearly white of the snow, the somber browns of the shadow-filled valleys, and the ghostly grey of my own breath, billowing into the air. The frosted canopy had its own wonderful presence, and I encountered it like a subject does his king, with heartfelt and profound reverence.

Many years have passed since then, the days and trying times accruing like layers of tarnish on silver. But the brilliance of those memories remains, of a time when I was young and vital, standing alongside my friends in a great and noble struggle.

Tragically, almost all of them are now gone, buried beneath those knee-deep snows, their pale bones turning to dust in unremarkable graves. It is all too clear that I cannot return to see them, but I *do* have my memories. And although my loneliness is sometimes profound, I can relive those halcyon days be exercising my mind, and thumbing through my care-worn diary.

My recollections from that time are set down on some one-hundred-and-eighty pages in an almost unintelligible script, written with an uncooperative fountain pen over the course of three years. The sheets themselves are yellowing and delicate, like centuries-old vellum, and bound in a brown leather cover embossed with the glorious seal of my people.

It may seem to you that all of these images are rather sedate and bucolic: a cottage in the woods, the drifting snow, a cherished diary. Had I not experienced what I have, I might be inclined to agree. But such a judgment could be no further from the truth. Think me mad if you must, but it is these very underpinnings of my ordinary world that have conspired to drive me to paroxysms of fear, the sort of terror that is chill and unvanquishable, and worst of all, never-ending.

Winter evenings here can be very cold; the air can numb one's skin, and great harm can be dealt the delicate constitution of an old man. I, therefore, wisely retire early, retreating to my familiar rocker by the fire, where I wrap myself in homespun Yankee blankets and contemplate the leaping flames. How lively they are sometimes, rising up as if to engulf my entire world. Their lambent orange glow is more than sufficient to illuminate the cottage, the pop and crackle of the flames the only sounds in the haunting night.

On my lap rests my diary, a tiny looking glass to days gone by. As I scan the pages and remember, a curious sensation of warmth o'erspreads my aged form, bringing with it contentedness and lethargy. The scribbled words speak clearly to me from so long ago, telling those familiar stories I hold so dear, and I cannot help but feel a pang of emotion upon reading them. Occasionally, I am even driven to weep.

Perhaps it was the saltwater coalescing in my eyes, or a manifestation of my failing sight, but three nights ago, as I felt slumber coming on, something most… *peculiar* occurred.

The fire was slowly dying, its light retreating to the interior of the wood, and I sat content in my warm and comfortable chair. I had been fighting off drowsiness with an ever weakening resolve, hoping to finish a particular chapter written in 1942. Had I been a younger man, perhaps, I would have stayed awake, listening to the howl of the frigid wind. But as it happened, my head began to nod, my chin to rest on my shrunken chest, and my eyes to close.

It was then, when I was most susceptible, that it happened.

As I tried to remain awake a moment longer, the letters on the page seemed to *move*, shifting ever so slightly.

I dazedly blinked and came back to myself. But the odd moment had passed and, there being nothing remarkable to see, my eyes quickly lost their focus. I proceeded to fall into a deep, uninterrupted sleep.

This sequence of events occurred on the night following as well, in precisely the same manner, under entirely similar circumstances. The fire had expired, the room had grown dim, and the grieving furies wailed like tormented souls outside my little cabin. But what my eyes beheld this time, as I retained that final bit of self-awareness, made me jerk awkwardly to life.

The ink had blurred and moved! As surely as I breathed! And, most unholy of all, a *word* had appeared.

I stared at the faded script on the page, but, like quicksilver, the message was gone! I was left with only an *impression* of what had been – a fleeting impartation of something horrid and unspeakable. The diary invited further investigation, but I could not bring myself to read it, to read what I *knew* to be the simple recollections of a young soldier! I shivered convulsively, and, suddenly aware of my age and solitude, I sought the refuge of my bed.

When I awoke this morning, all memory of that uncanny experience had vanished from my mind. The day was bright and sparkling with possibilities, and although I at first drifted about absent-mindedly, as if there were something important that required my attention, I quickly shed my listlissness in favor of a stroll through the woods and some late afternoon hours spent collecting fuel for the fire.

I returned to the cottage tired, but contented, and recalled with a smile those days I had exhausted myself in the service of my country, marching back and forth along the stark, frozen perimeter of our camp.

A hot meal of beef stew and a touch of sherry to rekindle my heart and I was ready to recline by the hearth; my belly was full and my spirits were high.

But, as I settled into the old rocker with my diary in hand, a strange sense of unease seized upon me. It was slow to comprehend, building ever so gradually, but it palpably existed nonetheless. The twilight and the glow of the fire reminded me of something, something from the night previous that I should have recalled, but could not. Like a half-forgotten dream...

It was a word. A *word*.

I must have slipped into an uneasy sleep then, for when I opened my eyes some time later, the fire had died completely. Outside, the pale face of the moon shone just over the blackened tips of the trees, and it cast strange shadows on the floor.

Perhaps I was still in a dreamlike daze, but, looking at those otherworldly designs, I felt a peculiar chill grip me, as if something most unholy had found deliverance from the grave and touched me with its cold and lifeless hand. I rose, gripping my diary to my chest, and hastened toward my bed, where I thought I might find peace. I moved stiffly, without much grace, my thin legs weak and unsteady.

Coming to rest upon the mattress, I laid my diary down on the night-table and slipped beneath the covers. I shut my eyes and for some time sought the intoxicating nectar of sleep.

It remained elusive.

The moon rose higher, and my unease grew. I felt that the letters in my diary had tried to tell me something. I knew it was a warning, a premonition of the future, of *that* I was certain.

But the meaning remained unclear.

I sat up, propped against the pillows, a weak, frightened old man staring into the gloom. My body stretched out before me, spent and emaciated, covered by the blankets as if by a death shroud, repulsing me, reminding me of *them*…Confused, I turned away, I tried to avert my gaze.

Very slowly, my eyes fixed on the blanched flooring of the room as I listened more closely to the howls beyond the walls.

The howls… Like tormented souls.

Suddenly, I understood.

The moonlight, shining garishly through the twisted limbs of the denuded forest, slid slowly across the old planking of the floor. And in the swirling grain of the faded pine, I saw their faces, twisted and tortured, screaming out at me like inhuman things, their mouths tearing apart, eyes bursting with fear.

They were the faces of the past. The faces of the camp.

Before I fell asleep, I ventured one last look at my diary, at the cursed black insignia emblazoned on its cover, and I knew the word that I had read.

I closed my eyes.

The word was Hell.

"Alone"
2003
(Fiction)

He was alone.

The soft, ratty recliner embraced him like a diseased paramour, its tattered and decomposing arms wrapping around him as if in a love embrace. The beer moved automatically to his lips, flat and bitter. The last of the lot. The last beer he'd been able to find. It had been sitting in his clutch for an hour, warm as soup, foul as brine, but he held it nonetheless, as if tenaciously gripping a vestige of himself.

His fingers and palms ached, not from the intensity of his rictus hold on the drink, but from the hammering, the staccato blows against the spikes, driving them deep into the two-by-fours, slamming the beams against the frames of the doors and windows. The drywall wouldn't do. He had needed wood. They would be coming for him eventually, and he knew that plasterboard wouldn't hold.

His wife and daughter were decaying in the other room, what was left of their human bodies swelling and turning to rot. Soon, the flesh would be falling off their bones, their skeletal frames exposed -- the essence of their lives, lost for all time.

But it was better than the alternative.

He wanted to take them out before they began to stink, before the acrid perfume of their bodies seeped throughout the house to permeate everything, and before that foul, noxious stench could drown his memories of what had been. It would get into the carpets, into the chairs; it would invade the curtains that were going yellow and dusty behind the lattices of pine he had nailed to the frames. But he couldn't take them outside. He had to live with the smell, with the reality…

That he was the last man alive.

It was strange how one's mind dealt with horror. True horror. The fear he had felt had moved in on him with stealth. First, it had manifested itself as a nagging, irritating sense of disquiet, an indefinable *something* that bugged him a tiny bit each day. Things outside were different, the people were different. It wasn't a pleasant place to be any more. It had changed.

They had changed.

And as the burden of the days accumulated, the realization became more defined.

Something was happening. They were becoming something *else*.

Sitting here now, at the end of everything, it seemed almost humorous how innocent he had been. How he had missed everything for so long, overlooked the changes until it was too late. Upon finally opening his eyes to reality, he saw that it was all around him. Within weeks, the world was inside-out. It was over.

He never imagined people could turn into such unspeakable creatures.

There had been so many -- friends and coworkers, neighbors and passers-by. He'd seen it happen to each of them. He could think about it all again, but now their names seemed irrelevant, their faces a blur, and the inhuman sounds of their voices merely part of a horrific fugue. Perhaps that was how the mind defended itself during fights for one's life, by pulling away from the details, creating protective abstractions, overlooking the closest, deepest terrors in favor of a larger picture, a picture of survival.

Even the images of his wife and child had become part of it.

Was this how it was to end? Humanity's last haggard breaths taken in a state of near oblivion?

Perhaps. But even now, he held on, out of sheer strength of will and adherence to principle. He was the last human, the only one who could remember how it had been. As the world closed in, he would fight it. He had seen what had happened to them, and was not going to let it happen to him. He would resist. He would be himself to the last, and in the end, he would die a *man*.

He heard the thick buzzing of a large, heavy fly.

They were coming. He knew.

And he was waiting. Waiting…

Outside, the traffic flowed freely along a hot and shimmering road.

"Survivor"
August, 2002
(Story Pitch to the "New Twilight Zone")

It's World War One. Joe Emerson (20's) is a soldier on the Western Front. He is also a coward. Caught in a terrible battle, Joe watches as his companion, Derek Jacobs, falls from a shot to the leg. Enemy fire zips everywhere. Derek calls to Joe for help, but Joe hesitates, then flees! He runs through the woods, finally stumbling onto a German sniper, who holds his gun on Joe.

"I saw what you did down there," the sniper says, "you left him to die..."

He lowers the gun.

"I approve."

Joe is stunned. The German continues. "You do not care about the others, only your own survival. What if I were to tell you that *I* can allow you to survive anything?"

Joe shakes his head in disbelief, but the German tells him, "Inside this *shell*, I exist. A thing you have never encountered, a thing from beyond the night's stars... And if you accept me as my host, I can make you invincible! You can return to your men and outlive them all!"

Joe thinks the man is crazy, but to prove his words, the German spreads his jaws and we see a strange, snake-like thing whip around inside his mouth.

"As long as I am in you, no harm can come to you," the sniper says.

Disconcerted, but driven by his pathological fear of dying, Joe accepts, watching with disbelief as the creature leaves the mouth of the German to enter his own. Suddenly, the thing is beneath Joe's skin, and he blacks out.

He awakens on a medical cot in his base. When asked what happened, Joe says he can't recall. But slowly, he begins to remember, and when he steps on a broken glass and sees his cuts immediately heal, he realizes he wasn't imagining things. He goes back to the front lines, volunteering for the worst duty, getting caught in gunfire and hit many times in the arms and chest, but the wounds heal. His ego grows. Soon, he's a hero, braving mine fields to take new territory, reveling in the killing of the enemy, surviving mustard gas attacks to rescue three of his American company, and capturing two Germans in the process.

The commander of his company congratulates Joe. He asks if anyone speaks fluent German, and Joe surprises everyone by answering the call. He is asked to interrogate the Germans, but he enjoys the torture too much, doing terrible things to them. Finally, his sadistic side overwhelms him, and he brutally kills both men. His commander is outraged! He demands Joe hand over his pistol, and it appears Joe will, but he suddenly lashes out, killing the commander slowly with a knife, taunting the other man cruelly as he dies. Then, he's on the run, AWOL once more.

He races through the horrors of war, unstoppable, indiscriminately killing people (Germans and Allies) until finally coming into a small Belgian village. There, he pauses, wrestling with himself, experiencing waves of horror and delight from this new strength and desire.

Suddenly, there is a sound, and a beautiful woman holding a small boy appears. Joe pulls his gun, ready to kill her. We see the struggle of his evil and good natures, and he finally puts down the gun. He's attracted to her, but we're not sure whether he can overcome his innate wickedness. He speaks to her in French, asking if she needs help. Her son needs food, they need shelter. Joe finds a small, secure apartment in a bombed-out area. He braves bullets to get them food. In a quiet moment, she tells him what happened to her husband years before, how they were left alone, then shelled out of their home.

Joe's features reveal attraction, and, perhaps, some guilt for what he has done. He comforts her, and she returns his affection. They embrace… And Joe snaps! He attacks her in a libidinous rage, pushing her about, trying to get at her clothes. The child enters from another room, screaming. Joe grabs his gun, fires, and the boy falls. The woman is shocked, and Joe, crazed with elation and a distant remorse, almost insane, bolts!

He doesn't get far. Barely out of the building, he is captured by the Germans, and brought to a POW camp in Landsburg. There, he is thrown in an iron isolation cell, and as the iron door closes on the man, we see the alien thing writhing about in his screaming mouth.

With a slam, all turns to darkness.

A graphic is displayed: "Five Years Later"

We dissolve to a bright, sunny morning in the prison work yard. Crazed and malnourished, Joe walks by himself near the fence. He has been left here, his crimes deemed so heinous that he, like many other prisoners in WWI, would not be extradited. His path in the yard brings him beside a young man at a bench. The man is a German soldier, doing six months for a political offense. He's writing in a small notebook. Joe glances at it, then he speaks in German.

"You are like me," he says, "what if I were to tell you I could make you invincible?"

The soldier looks at him.

"I am a creature like you. We enjoy the same things. If you will accept me, I can help you fulfill your goals!"

The German sees the alien *thing* writhe in Joe's mouth. He looks closer, and nods his acceptance, and as the creature moves from Joe to the German, we see all the injuries Joe would have sustained suddenly appear on Joe's body! He convulses in terrified agony as bullet wounds burst open in his hands, arms, and chest, as pink foam fills his throat from the mustard gas he breathed years before! He collapses in a loathsome heap as the German smiles and looks down on the title of his book:

"Mein Kampf"

"Hobson's Choice"
August, 2002
(Story Pitch to the "New Twilight Zone")

Carl Hobson (late 30's) is a man with a mission: to become as wealthy as possible by being as unscrupulous as possible in every aspect of his life. His partner, Joe Dambreezy (early 30's), is little better. Though blessed with only a tiny modicum of wits, guile, and ingenuity, they none the less have successfully pulled off one of the largest bank heists in the short history of Nineteenth Century Louisiana. They plan on enjoying the fruits of their ill-gotten gains, but not until the storm of an investigation has blown over. Until then, their loot will be hidden from everyone, including themselves.

Stuffing the pouches of silver and gold coins into a box beside their revolvers, masks, rope and knives, Hobson proceeds to walk the blindfolded Dambreezy into the bayou. They march on in the haze for some time, their conversation revealing the bloodthirsty nature of Hobson, and the distrust both men feel towards one another. Then, checking his compass, Hobson pauses. It is his turn to don the blindfold as Dambreezy leads them the rest of the way into the swampy forest. In this manner, neither will have complete knowledge of the location of the treasure, and retrieval of the money will require the participation of *both* men. At the entrance to a large cave, Dambreezy stops. Hobson keeps his back turned as Dambreezy digs a hole inside, and buries the chest. Becoming agitated at how long his partner is taking, Hobson threatens to turn about, but Dambreezy reminds him of their promise, and tells him the whole plan will fall apart if they don't keep both ends of the deal.

Finally, Dambreezy is done, and they leave, returning through the woods in the same manner as they entered.

Five years go by, and Hobson returns to town, where Dambreezy has integrated himself into the community. In fact, Dambreezy has tried to become a law-abiding citizen, and the appearance of Hobson brings back memories of his criminal past. Hobson tells him it is time, time to get their fortune, and, despite his misgivings, Dambreezy's greed overwhelms him. Armed only with their compass and two shovels, they head off into the woods.

The forest has changed very little -- or so it appears to the outlaws, for as they move through the creepers and leaves, Dambreezy suddenly lurches forward! He tumbles into a wide, dank pit, a deep gray hole filled with quicksand! Desperate, he claws at the sludge around him, unable to get a hold. Hobson rushes to his side, telling him to calm down, but exposing his own nervousness as well. He tries to reach for his partner, but cannot. He searches about him for a branch, a vine, anything to help give Dambreezy something to hold.

"Please! Carl! I'm sinking!!! Carl!"

But Hobson can find nothing! There are only reeds and small twigs. He takes off his belt, but still cannot reach Dambreezy. The other man is falling fast!

Then, Hobson has an idea.

"The rope! We have rope in the chest! Tell me where it is!"

"If I tell you where it is, you'll leave me!"

"Don't be a fool! Tell me!"

Dambreezy is up to his shoulders.

"All right!" he says, and gives Hobson directions to the cave to find the loot.

Hobson stands up slowly, a wicked smile on his face.

"Thank you. That's what I wanted to know."

"What?!"

The older man just looks at him, grinning. He had no intention of helping his partner. As the deadly quicksand rises up to engulf Dambreezy's chin and lips, making him sputter and scream in abject terror, Hobson chuckles, watches the crazed Dambreezy sink beneath the surface, and walks away.

Soon, he moves into the dank recesses of the cave, ducking under vines and spider webs. He removes a flashlight from his pocket, and scans about. Ahead of him, the floor of the chamber stretches for yards, without a sign of disturbance. Then, Hobson notices something… A *wire*, running at an angle up from a small notch in the rock wall. The flashlight plays strangely on his features as he begins to realize:

"He laid out a trap! Dammit! He booby-trapped the thing!"

Hobson rushes back to the sand pit, but to no avail… His partner is long gone.

He stands there, frustrated, then gets an idea and stalks back in the direction of town.

There, hidden amongst the shanty shacks and brothels of a voodoo-infused, New Orleans-style Louisiana city, he steps down into the basement shop of an enigmatic woman named Mistress Viola (late 40's). He tells the voodoo queen he has a job for her -- to resurrect the dead body of his partner from the middle of the swamp, and *make* him tell them how to get to the gold without tripping the trap.

"What's in it for me," asks the strange woman.

"I'll give you his half of the money."

Viola agrees.

Soon, they are approaching the quicksand. The daylight is fading; Hobson tells her to make it quick. He watches in horrified amazement as she recites a strange, guttural spell, snapping her arms about with the words, and slowly pulling the grimy, soaked body of the dead Dambreezy up from the depths. The cadaver lurches, twists, and a hiss of air moves from its lips.

"What do you want?!"

"Tell us how to get to the gold!" she demands.

A bulging eyelid opens to stare balefully at Hobson.

"No! He let me drown! I will not let him have my gold!"

With a twist of her hand, the voodoo queen turns him about swiftly, commanding him to speak, to reveal the truth. And he does, telling them there is a pressure plate buried under the sand. The plate will set of poison darts from a device he secreted with him during their first journey to the cave. They can trip the darts by dropping a heavy rock before moving deeper into the cave. Then, Viola lets him go, telling him to rest, as his body sinks slowly back into the mire.

The two move to the cave, trip the plate, and unearth the treasure. All is as should be, nothing has been touched. But before Viola can stand up with her share of the money, Hobson hits her hard in the head. She falls, and he snatches up her bag of loot, racing off into the gloom of the forest.

The darkness surrounds him as Hobson runs, and he hears the rumble of thunder overhead. Lightning flashes above him, illuminating the woods in pools of purple and blue. His flashlight streaks about, making freakish arcs across trees, rocks, branches and vines. It's a blur to him as he races away with his money. After all this time. It's all his. He races forward, passing by the sandy pool...

And he FALLS! A HAND has caught him, a hand from the pool, around his ankle!

He screams. He's being dragged in! He gabs at anything to hold, but he slides, slides onward, into the quicksand! The body of his partner has him! His knees fall beneath the surface, then his waist...

The voodoo queen emerges from the gloom, barely lit by his shaking flashlight. Her features are implacable.

"Please! Help me!" cries Hobson.

Only his shoulders, arms and head remain.

"Give me the money," she demands.

Hobson shakes his head with disbelief and mistrust.

"NO! You'll just take it and walk away!"

"Give me the money, or I WILL walk away... You have very little choice, my dear."

The sand is up to his mouth. He strains to breathe. He yanks the bags up and out of the muck, tossing them to Viola.

Here eyes fix on the money. She picks it up, and smiles.

"Now get me out! GET ME OUT!!!"

She looks at him with a wry smile.

"You spent a lot of time away from town waiting for the heat to blow over, didn't you?" she says as a statement.

"Five years," she says, savoring every word, "and you know, a lot of things can change in five years. Your partner certainly changed a lot; he did many things..."

Viola leans towards him, extending her left hand.

"...Including getting married..."

As Hobson's eyes go wide with terror and amazement, and his screams become garbled under the pressure of the quicksand, Mistress Viola stands erect, and smirks.

"Have a nice time with my husband, Mr. Hobson."

Then, she turns and walks away as his dying body is dragged down to its doom.

LIVE FREE OR DIE

A Note on the Following Screenplay

The story you are about to read is a script originally designed for the television series "The Outer Limits". I never pitched the idea, but instead expanded it, and turned it into a full-length film screenplay.

Many of my friends are aware that in my stories I place references to the concepts and individuals that helped form the tenets of classical liberalism. In this tale, I did the same, though some might be surprised by the characteristics applied to some of the names. One cannot telegraph too much, valid?

This tale is dedicated to Mr. Rod Serling, and his wonderful wife, Carol, who was very nice to me as a teenager and beyond.

P. G. G.

"The Jewelbox of God"

A Screenplay
By
P. Gardner Goldsmith
1999

ACT ONE

FADE IN:

INT. FARSEER HELM/NAVIGATION

Seen in extreme close-up, a gold cross floats and twists on the end of a glittering chain, both suspended in mid-air. A HAND reaches forward to grab the necklace, and we PULL BACK to reveal OWEN LOCKE (35, tall, gray hair, wearing the blue uniform of the *Farseer* mission) as he floats into the pilot's seat near the large forward viewports. The viewports reveal strange trailers of color running out below the ship towards a point unseen. As we CONTINUE TO PULL BACK, we see Locke's co-pilot, CLAY ST. JAMES (25, wiry, uniformed as well), strap himself into his seat and don a headset. St. James watches Locke as he slides the necklace over his head, pulls on his headset, and straps himself in.

      LOCKE
     (into mic)
  All set, Commander.

We continue to PULL BACK, then REVERSE ANGLES to see five other men wearing similar uniforms and headsets who sit strapped into an angled bank of seats some thirty feet behind the pilots. The interior widens into a more spacious area here, one lined with computer consoles on the walls and video monitors on the ceiling. From left to right the other members of the team are: DR. GOTTLEIB NEIMEYER (45, balding, thin, nearly shaved head), KEVIN MAXWELL (20's, intense, close-cropped hair), COMMANDER FRANK LYDON (50, squat, tough, spiky hair), CHRIS GULLOTTI (early 30's, sharp profile, muscular) and HARRY BARNES (early 20's, thin, nervous). We CLOSE ON LYDON, who intensely watches the events on the screen.

      LYDON
  All right, Locke...

LIVE FREE OR DIE

ANGLE ON LOCKE

He listens, studying the controls.

> LYDON (O.S.) (CONT'D)
> (through headset)
> You know what to do.

Locke glances at St. James.

> LOCKE
> Okay, buddy. This is it...

St. James smiles, gives him the "thumbs up", and hunkers down over his controls. Locke leans forward, his fingers poised over a series of buttons.

> LOCKE (CONT'D)
> (into headset)
> Closing impact shields.

Suddenly, with a LOUD WHINE, two heavy metal plates slide down over the plex-glass portals to obscure the view.

> ST. JAMES
> Switching to monitors.

He taps a few buttons, and the pilot section suddenly comes to life with the light of video monitors showing the colorful streamers beneath the ship.

> LOCKE
> Changing to intercept vector...

He taps a command on the computer console.

ANGLE ON REST OF TEAM

The other members of the team prepare for something big. Locke's voice reaches all of them.

> LOCKE (O.S.) (CONT'D)
> (through headsets)
> We'll have secondary thruster burn for ten seconds on my mark...

Maxwell's expression is intense.

> MAXWELL
> (sotto, Sarcastically)
> Don't screw up, Fly Boy.

Neimeyer glances at him nervously.

RESUME

Locke holds the joystick, his thumb poised over a red button. As he brings his thumb down, he speaks with force.

> LOCKE
> Mark!

Suddenly, the ship swerves, pulling against the momentum of the astronauts. The strange colors in the viewports engulf their field of vision, blast the interior with light. At the same time, a RUMBLE EXPLODES like thunder, and the ship begins to violently shake. Locke seizes the control stick with both hands, pursing his brow. He is completely focused.

> LOCKE (CONT'D)
> (yelling, straining)
> We're in! We're in the coma!

> ST. JAMES
> Penumbra in thirty seconds!

ANGLE ON LYDON

His eyes are hard, steady. We move from him, past the tense face of Maxwell, to the dazzled gaze of Neimeyer as they experience the nerve-jarring decent into the coma.

LIVE FREE OR DIE

                    NEIMEYER
              God!

REVERSE ANGLES

Locke and St. James are about thirty feet away, two bizarre silhouettes hunched over the controls as the ship jostles and shakes.

                    LOCKE
              Fire retros in three...

We CLOSE ON St. James watching his controls, listening...

                    LOCKE (O.S.) (CONT'D)
              Two, one... Fire!

St. James hits a button, but there is no effect. Sudden alarm shoots across his face.

                    LOCKE (CONT'D)
                    (with immediacy)
              Hit it, Clay.

St. James' eyes dart across the control panel.

                    ST. JAMES
              It's cold!-- Re-routing!

His fingers punch at buttons.

                    LOCKE
                    (tensely)
              We're overshooting!

                    ST. JAMES
              Re-routing!

ANGLE ON MAXWELL

He shuts his eyes, speaks through clenched teeth.

                    MAXWELL
                    (intensely)
              C'mon...

RESUME

St. James punches more buttons, finally sees one flashing green.

                  ST. JAMES
            (as he hits the button)
    Go! Go! Go!

And the ship suddenly lurches. Locke and St. James hold on tight, hoping the burn has come in time. Slowly, the bright glare of the coma slides off to the periphery of the monitors like a halo, and the two men are looking out at the long tail from its clear and calm center.

                ST. JAMES (CONT'D)
            (relieved)
    We're through!
            (pointing at monitor)
    There it is!

The amazing image of a massive, brown and white celestial body appears through the ring of glowing, ionized dust that stretches out around the ship.

                ANGLE ON BARNES

His expression reflects amazement as he peers at the monitor above.

                BARNES
            (whisper)
    Would ya look at that...

RESUME

St. James reviews data on his computer.

                ST. JAMES
    Rate of decent, five meters per second. Retros are slowing us down...

LIVE FREE OR DIE

> (beat, reading data)
> Four mps... Altitude, three-point-two-five K.

Locke clenches his teeth.

> ST. JAMES (CONT'D)
> We've overshot our landing zone by about three kilometers.

> LOCKE
> Surface looks okay.

> ST. JAMES
> Two mps. Altitude, one thousand meters.

Locke adjusts the joystick, focussing on the video display.

> ST. JAMES (O.S.) (CONT'D)
> Seven hundred... One mps.

EXT. THE SURFACE OF TYCHO-B -- CONTINUOUS

The icy surface of the huge comet looms larger and larger. Suddenly, the shadow of the *Farseer* can be seen sliding along the alien landscape.

INT. FARSEER HELM/NAVIGATION -- CONTINUOUS

> ST. JAMES
> (tensely)
> Two hundred... This is it, Owen!

Lock stays focused. He reaches for a set of switches.

> LOCKE
> Engage tethers!

He flicks each switch and there is the EXPLOSIVE SOUND of something like cannons firing. From the video display we see four long cables shoot out and down.

EXT. THE SURFACE OF TYCHO-B -- CONTINUOUS

The cables, attached to long metal spikes, plunge down into the frozen surface We TILT UP to see the ship to which they are attached. From below, the *Farseer* looks like a huge, armored spider, with four main engines set around a circular central chamber. It moves down upon us as we watch, obscuring our field of view.

INT. FARSEER HELM/NAVIGATION -- CONTINUOUS

                LOCKE

        Engaging winches.

He hits a button, and the sound of powerful engines vibrates through the floor.

                ST. JAMES

        Ten meters. They look secure.

              ANGLE ON BARNES

who closes his eyes, waiting, hoping...

RESUME

              ST. JAMES (CONT'D)

        Five, four...

EXT. THE SURFACE OF TYCHO-B -- CONTINUOUS

The *Farseer* descends. The surface looms closer.

INT. FARSEER HELM/NAVIGATION -- CONTINUOUS

We move from Gullotti to Neimeyer as St. James counts the descent.

              ST. JAMES (O.S.)
           (through headsets)
        Three, two...

              ANGLE ON LOCKE

who watches the surface as the shadow of the ship begins to fill the screen. Suddenly... BANG! They're down, being thrust against their seats like dolls. There is a moment of sudden alarm, then, Locke looks at St. James.

LIVE FREE OR DIE

                    ST. JAMES (CONT'D)
                        (excited)
    That's it!

Over his headset, Lock hears Lydon

                    LYDON (V.O.)
                    (through headsets)
    Shut down landing systems. Good job!

                    ANGLE ON LYDON

As the sound of the engines dies down, Lydon looks at the rest of the crew beside him.

                    LYDON (CONT'D)
    Gentlemen... Welcome to Tycho-B.

We PULL BACK, THROUGH THE VIEWPORTS, away from the top of the ship, up, into space as the TITLE CREDITS ROLL. Soon, the ship and the cold surface of Tycho-B are obscured by the chaotic coma of the comet. Then, that too is dwindling into the distance, until it is nothing more than a tiny spec in the vast expanse of the solar system. As the CREDITS END, we turn away from the pinpoint of Tycho-B to the darkness of space and...

                                        DISSOLVE TO:

INT. FARSEER HELM/NAVIGATION -- MOMENTS LATER

Eager to get moving, Neimeyer, Maxwell, Lydon, Gullotti, and Barnes uncouple their seat harnesses.

                    BARNES
                        (excited)
    We made it!

Maxwell smirks.

                    MAXWELL
                        (sotto, stressed)
    Barely.

Lydon puts his hand to his headset.

> LYDON
>
> Alright, Locke. Let's open her up.

ANGLE ON LOCKE AND ST. JAMES

The two men exchange a smile, then Locke flicks a switch, and the massive metal shields begin to LOUDLY OPEN. Slowly, the icy, alien surface of the comet is revealed, crowned by the strange, wispy coma above.

St. James and Locke stare at the sight.

> ST. JAMES
>
> Damn. I never believed I'd see it.

RESUME

Lydon pushes himself off the seat. The weak gravity of the comet allows him to move forward in a small arc. When he lands, he checks a computer terminal on the ceiling.

> LYDON
> (reviewing data)
> Well, believe it, St. James. And get used to it. You'll be seeing more than you'll want in the days to come.

Behind him, the others rise in similar fashion, all moving toward the dazzling scene at the viewports. Lydon watches them go past, then he, too, is attracted by the sight. We FOLLOW as he leans into the helm section behind them.

> GULLOTTI
>
> It's the most beautiful thing I've ever seen.

Maxwell turns to him with a smirk, thumbs over his shoulder towards Locke.

> MAXWELL
>
> Except for the *Fly Boy's* pretty face.

An irritated Locke feigns a kiss to Maxwell, there appears to be some tension between them. Lydon looks at them with frustration, then pulls away.

> LYDON

Flirt on your own time, boys. Lets get it together.

The others turn to regard the commander.

> LYDON (CONT'D)

Everybody knows his place here.

> (nods at Maxwell and Gullotti)

Maxwell, Gullotti, you're old hands at construction in space. Your experience on the Lunar Installations will be invaluable.

> (nods at Locke)

By the same token, your *Fly Boy* may be new to the team, but he was one of the Space Corps' best, and he's our ticket home. So let's be nice to him, okay?

Maxwell sneaks an ugly, mock smile Locke's way.

> LYDON (CONT'D)
> (nods at Barnes)

Likewise with Barnes.

> (to Maxwell and Gullotti)

Might I remind you, he's a *geologist* not a Goddamn *dowser*? Without him, we won't be digging up anything except *ice*, so show him a little respect out there. Otherwise...

> (nods at Neimeyer)

Not even the Doctor will be able to help you after I whip your butts!

He moves over to a cargo bin, opens it.

LYDON (CONT'D)

Now let's get started...

He pulls out a clipboard and attached pen.

LYDON (CONT'D)

St. James, how far are we exactly from our target area?

St. James checks a readout.

ST. JAMES

Two point six kilometers, along a vector of...

(beat)

One degree longitude, minus two degrees latitude.

LYDON

Alright, that's manageable. Let's get the survey teams up and running.

The crew members move to other storage compartments, pulling out equipment, then walk over to an open porthole in the floor. Maxwell and Locke end up beside each other, both going for the opening at the same time. They pause in unison, and Maxwell extends his hand in an overly charitable sweeping gesture.

MAXWELL

(insincerely)

After *you*, fair pilot.

Locke looks at him harshly, then lowers himself down onto a thin ladder. One by one, they follow him down through the opening.

INT. FARSEER DECOM AREA -- MOMENTS LATER

Each of the members of the crew moves towards white space suits that hang against one wall. First, Gullotti, then Maxwell, then Neimeyer, then Barnes, then St. James, Locke, and, finally, Lydon. All climb into the suits, zip them up, then pull down the helmets hanging overhead to seal themselves in. Lydon steps forward to address them.

> LYDON
> (voice is slightly muffled)
> The Farseer Corporation is relying on us to find and retrieve two tons of the compound Ocsinnet. Spectroscopic analysis of the tail of Tycho-B indicates this rock is rich with it.

He walks over to the first decompression door, peering through the porthole and out the exterior hatch beyond.

> LYDON (CONT'D)
> We've got four days before our window to return to Earth will close.

He looks back at his men.

> LYDON (CONT'D)
> Four days.
> (beat)
> Let's make it worth their while.

He approaches the first decompression door, hits a control, and the door slides open.

EXT. THE SURFACE OF TYCHO-B -- MOMENTS LATER

Air bursts out of release valves on the *Farseer* to stir dust and ice from the surface, and a hatch opens at the base of the ship. The hatch is about twenty feet wide, ten feet high, and tilts down to form a ramp, along which the seven members of the crew descend. Each man carries a flashlight and surveying equipment. Behind them can be seen five wide radio dishes attached to retracted hydraulic towers on large, moveable bases. We CENTER ON LOCKE as he steps past the dishes and down onto the strange frozen surface.

EXT. THE SURFACE OF TYCHO-B -- LOCKE'S POV

We hear Locke's HEAVY BREATHING as he looks out at the amazing horizon of the comet, looks up at the streamers of ionized gas and dust. He watches Barnes move out in front of him

ANGLE ON BARNES

With the group behind him, he bends down to scoop a small amount of dust into a tiny glass phial. He plugs it with a stopper, then stands. (NOTE: All dialogue spoken outside the ship will require radio effects.)

LOCKE

What's that for?

BARNES

My wife's due in two months. I told her I'd bring back a memento for the baby.

He peers at the phial, then slips it into a pocket.

BARNES (CONT'D)

It's no teddy bear, but I think it'll do.

ST. JAMES

Damned right. Besides, I don't see a souvenir shop for miles!

Lydon steps out in front of the crew, scans the scene, then turns to them.

LYDON

Check your rangefinders.

RESUME LOCKE'S POV

Locke raises his left wrist to view a scanner attached to his suit. On it appears a radar-like display, indicating his proximity to the ship. There is also a life-sign meter indicating heart rate, temp., etc.

LIVE FREE OR DIE

ANGLE ON TEAM

Locke lowers his wrist.

                LYDON

    Pair up.

The men form into pairs. Locke is with St. James. Gullotti and Maxwell are together. Neimeyer and Barnes are paired. Lydon is alone.

              LYDON (CONT'D)

    You've been through the drills a hundred times. Now, it's for real. See you all back here in three hours.
    (beat)
    Good luck.

As he moves back to the ramp, the others spread out in their teams, moving away from the ship. WE TILT DOWN AND PULL UPWARDS, to see the men spread out in a "Y" with the *Farseer* at its center.

EXT. A RIDGE LINE ON TYCHO-B -- LATER

Two team members breath heavily as they approach the frozen ridge. As they move closer, we hear their voices.

              ST. JAMES

    Looks like you've made a real friend in Maxwell.

             LOCKE

    He's just a wise ass.

             ST. JAMES

    What's he got against you? He's been ribbin' you since the mission began.

             LOCKE

    Isn't is obvious? I used to be in the Space Corps.

> ST. JAMES
>
> So?
>
> LOCKE
>
> So, there are lots of people out there who really distrust and resent the government.
>
> (beat)
>
> And I can't say I blame them.

As if distracted, he pauses to check his rangefinder. St. James stops at his side, looks around.

> LOCKE (CONT'D)
>
> Four K. We're almost at our limit.
>
> ST. JAMES
>
> You wanna turn back?

Locke turns around, scans the area.

> LOCKE
>
> A little further.

The men resume their march, heading up the slope of the ridge. St. James struggles on the icy surface, Locke gives him a hand.

> ST. JAMES
>
> Why *did* you leave, Owen? You must have had a pretty good career...

They are almost at the top.

> LYDON
>
> It's different when you see it from the inside. Maybe I'll tell you about it when you've got a good month to spare.

With that, Locke and St. James step up to the top of the ridge. We follow OVER THEIR SHOULDERS as they rise and see a vast expanse of ice and rock... And something else.

LIVE FREE OR DIE

                    ST. JAMES

          Jesus Christ!

As we RISE OVER THE MEN to get a clear view, we
see it. A SHIP. It's an alien lander, sitting
in the middle of a wide, gray canyon. The ship
is octagonal in shape. Its base touches the
surface. Landing struts protrude from each
corner of the walls. There appears to be a
hatch, but we are currently too far away to make
out fine details.

                    ST. JAMES (CONT'D)

          This wasn't in the training, Locke.

                              TIME CUT TO:

EXT. A RIDGE LINE ON TYCHO-B -- LATER

Still holding their equipment, the rest of the
Farseer crew has gathered with Locke and St.
James. We MOVE IN on Neimeyer, Maxwell and
Lydon.

                    NEIMEYER

          Bloody Hell!

They all stare.

                    BARNES

          This changes things a little, doesn't
          it?

Lydon steps forward.

                    LYDON

          Let's check it out.

And the others follow down the ridge.

EXT. TYCHO-B -- ALIEN LANDER -- MOMENTS LATER

The crew members cautiously approach the large
metal ship. Barnes raises a flashlight, shines it
on the alien lander. His beam reveals strange
markings on the exterior, pock marks, and lots of
dust. The ship appears to be dead, derelict.

                    BARNES

          This is nuts! It's like finding the
          Titanic in the middle of the desert!

Lydon turns to Maxwell.

                    LYDON

          Max, you've worked on a lot of
          international crews. Anything you've
          seen before?

                    MAXWELL

          Zip, Commander. That's certainly no
          writing *I'm* familiar with.

Lydon's expression tightens. His eyes scan the
ship. Gullotti moves up behind him.

                    GULLOTTI

          Unbelievable! I don't know about
          the rest of you, but I'm beginning
          to think we're in a pretty unique
          position here.

                    BARNES (O.S.)

          Commander! Over here!

The others turn to see Barnes' beam playing on
another section of the ship. He stands about
twelve feet away. They walk towards him and
follow the beam.

Above them, they see a large square hatch, hinged
at the base and partially open. As Barnes'
light rises, the opening widens to an aperture
of nearly three inches. There is only darkness
beyond.

                    BARNES (CONT'D)
                    (to Lydon)
          Think we can get inside?

Lydon steps forward, determined.

                    LYDON

          Let's find out.

He drops his light and reaches around the door,
pulling back, to no avail.

                    LYDON (CONT'D)
               (over his shoulder)
          Barnes, Max, gimme some leverage.

Barnes extends a monopod over the Commander's
shoulder, and Lydon reaches back to grab it and
thrust it into the opening. Then, he begins
pushing against his end. Maxwell sees this, and
moves over to the corresponding opening on the
other side.

                    MAXWELL
               (to Neimeyer)
          Doc...

Neimeyer turns, sees Maxwell motioning for help,
and steps forward to place one leg of his tripod
into the opening just like Lydon's monopod.

Lydon strains against the pole, and suddenly, the
door budges! A small puff of dust pops off its
metal surface.

                    LYDON
          Ready, Max! On three!

Maxwell puts down his light, prepares.

                    LYDON (O.S.) (CONT'D)
          One, two...

Lydon bends into the bar.

                    LYDON (CONT'D)
          Three!

He pushes. And the hatch bursts open! Suddenly,
something flashes in the light, Lydon YELLS IN
SHOCK and jumps back as A surreal, horrific,
humanoid *thing* flies out at him, pulled by the

force of the door!

                    LYDON (CONT'D)
                  (shocked)

      God damn!

Strange eyes wide with terror, its skin gray and nearly mummified over tendons and bone, the creature slides out into space until half its body protrudes from the alien lander and bobs in the slight gravity.

                    MAXWELL
                  (stunned)

      Oh, man...

Barnes steps beside Lydon.

                    BARNES

      What the? What is it? I mean...
                (bends down beside it)

      What the Hell?

                    LYDON
                  (cautious)

      Doc...

As Maxwell climbs over his side of the hatch to get closer to the alien, Neimeyer comes up behind him. The others crowd behind Lydon and Barnes. The Doctor bends down to get a closer look, taking hold of one of the spindly arms that weaves up and down in the garish light.

                    NEIMEYER
                  (studying the alien)

      It's sure not from our neck of the woods.

                    LYDON

      How long do you think it's been here?

Neimeyer looks at the elongated face, the tight

lips and jaw. Behind him, Maxwell turns his light inside the craft.

NEIMEYER

I couldn't guess.

MAXWELL (O.S.)

Doc!

Neimeyer turns, sees Maxwell standing *inside* the lander, in front of a frightening pile of six dead alien bodies in one corner of the ship.

MAXWELL (CONT'D)

Look at this!

INT. ALIEN LANDER -- MOMENTS LATER

Neimeyer moves beside Maxwell as the others climb up the ramp.

GULLOTTI

(staring)

Oh, man...

ST. JAMES

This is unbelievable!

Locke sweeps his light over the open hatch and walls nearby, seeing another, interior, door open against the right wall.

LOCKE

There must have been something wrong with the seals.

ST. JAMES

Air leak.

Locke nods.

Barnes bends down to study another dead creature, sees the look of terror on its face.

BARNES

Man! This really *does* change everything!

Lydon peers at some of the controls along the walls.

> LYDON
>
> Not everything.
>
> BARNES
>
> What d'ya mean?

Lydon steps around the bodies to address him. The others watch.

> LYDON
>
> We can't let this dominate our time or distract us from our goal.
>
> LOCKE
>
> But Commander, this is the most monumental discovery in history!
>
> LYDON
>
> I know that, Locke. But we were sent here for a *reason*, we signed a contract, we gave our word.
>
> LOCKE
>
> But surely all *this* will be worth more than the company could have possibly dreamed!
>
> LYDON
>
> Yes, I agree. But we can't just change the goal of our mission. We can't just *assume* they'll be satisfied with us superseding their orders!

The men appear frustrated.

> LOCKE
>
> Commander! This is *alien life! Intelligent alien life!* Just *one* of those bodies, if brought back to Earth, would be priceless! Nothing could be more valuable!

Lydon raises his gloved hands in a calming gesture.

                    LYDON

     And I'm not saying we won't retrieve
     samples, make a record of our
     discovery.
          (beat)
     But we can't let this keep us from
     completing our original mission.

Locke appears crestfallen.

                    LYDON (CONT'D)

     We just can't.

Locke nods; the others see Lydon's point.

                    LOCKE

     I understand.

Lydon scans the interior of the ship once more.

                    LYDON

     Locke, Neimeyer, select a body to
     bring back to *Farseer* for analysis.
     We'll record everything we can, take
     samples of the metal, if we can.
     That'll be your job for the next
     twenty-four hours.
          (beat)
     The rest of you, let's pick a site and
     set up the array.

The men move towards the hatch, where Barnes pauses beside the rictus visage of the first dead alien, its eyes staring into oblivion.

EXT. ALIEN LANDER -- LATER

We PULL BACK from the lander towards and over the ridge, to see Locke and Neimeyer carrying an alien strapped to a makeshift gurney made from two tripods.

LOCKE

This seems so unreal...

NEIMEYER

What do you mean?

LOCKE

I mean it contradicts everything I've been taught!

NEIMEYER

Owen, you're a space jockey, for goodness sake. Don't tell me you've actually bought all that Creationism nonsense.

LOCKE

Why not? Why does there have to be a contradiction between faith and science? (beat)

There's never been any real evidence to support the theory of evolution.

NEIMEYER

That's rubbish! Not only is the theory *logical*, it's borne out by archeological facts.

LOCKE

Well... Not really. They've never found examples of cross-species evolution. There's never been any evidence to undercut the Creationist view.

Neimeyer hefts the body.

NEIMEYER
(pointedly)

Until now.

Locke stares at the creature, nods.

LOCKE

Until now.

NEIMEYER

You know, Locke, I wouldn't count on anything being resolved when we return.

LOCKE

Why not?

Neimeyer looks at the icy vista around them, remembering.

NEIMEYER

My father was a minister in the Anglican Church. We used to get into bloody screaming matches over the creationism/evolution debate.

(beat)

I don't think the religious will be too quick to accept this as disproof of their beliefs.

LOCKE

But it's right here. It's real. If *I* can't deny it, nobody can.

NEIMEYER

Didn't you just say it seemed *unreal*?

(beat)

When we land, the first thing the orthodoxy will claim is that our experience is a fraud, the creature is fake.

LOCKE

And if we prove it's not?

NEIMEYER

Then they'll find a convenient way to claim their doctrines have either already accommodated for this type of life, or predicted its discovery.

LOCKE
(interpreting)
It's all in God's plan.

NEIMEYER
Right.

The two walk on for a moment in silence.

LOCKE
I take it you don't believe in God, Gottleib.

NEIMEYER
No.
(beat)
But I'm sure this chap was never late for Sunday Service.

As they near *Farseer* they pause to glance at a large circle of lights that appears suddenly, near the horizon opposite the alien ship.

NEIMEYER (CONT'D)
Looks like they found a good location.

Locke prompts them up the ramp.

LOCKE
After six hours? They should have.
(beat)
Let's get started before the Commander decides he needs us.

EXT. TYCHO-B MINING SITE -- MOMENTS LATER

Our perspective is momentarily awash with blinding WHITE LIGHT as we PULL BACK from an intense Klieg rising on a large hydraulic scaffold. Also attached is a massive, circular microwave "radiator" -- which aims downward at the surface, twitching from commands being sent via radio control -- and a long metal beam that stretches forward beyond our perspective. As we continue to PULL BACK, a circle of nine similar lights some fifty meters in diameter becomes visible. All are connected by similar long metal beams, and at their center is a wide, circular dish pointing down at the surface. The entire complex network is known as "The Array", and this tower is the final of the ten to be erected. We TILT DOWN to see St. James working the radio control of the last scaffold, standing near its six-wheeled base. He turns to Lydon as he approaches.

            LYDON
        How's it coming?

St. James glances up at the tower as it locks into its full height, then checks his radio control.

            ST. JAMES
        Looks like they're all lined-up,
        Commander. We'll be ready to start a
        trial any time.

Lydon scans the rest of the the mining area. He sees Maxwell, Gullotti and Barnes standing under the central dish, working controls, checking digital readouts.

            LYDON
            (loudly)
        Barnes?

Barnes turns to him, raising a hand.

            LYDON (CONT'D)
        How's it look?

            ANGLE ON BARNES

as he studies an electronic device in his hand.

BARNES

This is the place, Commander! We've got concentrations of Ocsinnet going off the chart!

Maxwell moves up beside him to address Lydon. He points at the dish above their heads.

MAXWELL

Commander, I'm not so sure about this Collector. I've never worked with a magnetic polarizer before.

ANGLE ON LYDON

who shakes his head.

LYDON

Don't worry! Once the microwaves have vaporized the frozen CO_2 and loosened the ore, the polarizer will be able to concentrate it, pick it up, and deposit it in our collection bins on the treadmill.

(beat)

Just ask Barnes. He's seen it dozens of times.

ANGLE ON MAXWELL

Maxwell turns to Barnes, who shrugs.

BARNES

It works in the lab, anyway.

Maxwell's expression reflects skepticism.

RESUME

Lydon turns to St. James.

LYDON

Listen, Clay. You're new to this.

(beat)

I want you to be particularly careful out here. Once The Array is up and running, the perimeter of the dig can become extremely unstable. Any stray movement could send you over the edge.

St. James looks out at The Array.

                ST. JAMES
                      (nods)

    Got it, Commander.

Gullotti and Maxwell finish their readings under the central dish, and begin walking towards the other men, leaving Barnes to his work. As they walk, Maxwell scans the icy surface of the comet, somewhat in awe.

                MAXWELL

    Man. This place reminds me of my ex-wife.
               (beat, off Gullotti's
                reaction)
    Frigid, barren, and unfriendly.

                GULLOTTI
                (ironic laugh)

    Ya' know, Max? You've got such a pleasant demeanor. I can see why you have so much success with women!

Maxwell seems to take offense to this, in a jovial kind of way.

                MAXWELL
                (defensively)

    Hey. I'm doin' fine. I've met somebody.

                GULLOTTI
                (laughs)

    Really? What's she charge?

Maxwell smiles, pushes Gullotti playfully.

MAXWELL
(humorously)

Screw you, Gullotti.

GULLOTTI
(moc seriousness)

Sorry, man. I forgot what a miser you are.

(beat)

You'd probably go the plastic blow-up route.

Still smiling, Maxwell slaps Gullotti's helmet.

MAXWELL

Nice one, Cyreno.

(beat)

You know as well as I that the patch kits are too expensive.

They approach Lydon and St. James.

Suddenly, from the horizon behind them, something BURSTS UPWARD in a puff of white snow and dust. The four men turn, as does Barnes behind them, to see a shiny round object shoot off into space.

MAXWELL (CONT'D)

What the Hell was that?

Barnes turns back towards the others.

BARNES

Ice particle. Instability on the bright side causes shifts in the ice plates all over the surface.

Maxwell and Gullotti look at each other with trepidation.

BARNES (CONT'D)

We may see a lot more of that before our visit is through.

                    MAXWELL
                    (quietly)
          All the more reason to hurry the Hell
          up!

INT. FARSEER MEDICAL MODULE -- LATER

The module is part of the complex between the flight deck and the exterior ramp. In it are a series of high-tech computers and screens, vacuum wash basins, and a long silver operating table with metal poles at either end. Atop this table lies the mummified alien cadaver. Neimeyer and Locke, changed into surgery clothes and gloves as well as protective masks, approach from an adjoining chamber. Neimeyer carries a tray filled with gleaming surgical instruments, and Locke carries a digital camera, which he affixes to a pole atop the far end of the steel table.

                    LOCKE
                    (fiddling with the camera)
          Looks... Like it's set, Doc.
                    (beat)
          We're rolling.

Neimeyer hands him a paper mask, dons his own.

                    NEIMEYER
          Given the mummified condition of this
          creature, these are really just a
          formality, still...

                    LOCKE
                    (donning mask)
          Still...

Neimeyer lifts a tape measure.

                    NEIMEYER
          Alright! Let's get started...
                    (beat)

My name is Dr. Gottleib Neimeyer, medical specialist aboard the cometary mining ship *Farseer*. With me is former USSC captain Owen Locke, flight specialist aboard the ship.

(beat)

We're privileged to be part of an historic first, the first mission to mine a comet, and the first group to attempt such a monumental endeavor through solely private means. But our achievement is now dwarfed by what you see before you.

(beat)

Evidence of intelligent life beyond the confines of Earth.

(beat)

Owen?

Locke leans over the alien, peering at it.

LOCKE

When we landed on Tycho-B, we discovered someone had already been here before us... An alien race with space faring capabilities. There were seven, all vaguely humanoid, and all lifeless aboard a ship approximately two miles away. We've brought this sample back for examination.

Neimeyer measures the length of the body.

NEIMEYER

Length, two-hundred twenty centimeters. Weight, adjusted for gravitational differences, approximately five-hundred kilograms.

He wraps the tape around the forehead of the creature.

> NEIMEYER (CONT'D)
> Cranium circumference, seventy-two centimeters.

He puts down the tape, and begins pushing at the body with his fingers.

> NEIMEYER (CONT'D)
> The cadaver appears completely dehydrated. The skin is gray and leathery, drawn tight over what appears to be a skeletal structure similar to that of homo-sapiens.

He lifts the right arm, plays with the hand.

> NEIMEYER (CONT'D)
> The digits appear to be like our own, with the exception that they can bend in either direction.

He moves the alien's fingers, then lowers the hand.

> NEIMEYER (CONT'D)
> I will now make the "Y" incision across what seems to be the cardio-vascular system.

Locke moves behind the camera, zooming in on the site of the incision.

We watch as the Doctor leans onto the body with his left hand, and slowly pushes the sharp scalpel into the alien flesh. It cuts slowly, like rawhide. Neimeyer pulls hard, cutting down toward the abdomen.

> NEIMEYER (CONT'D)
> Owen, give me a hand here, could you?

Locke walks from behind the camera, pulling the tough skin apart as Neimeyer cuts. Slowly, it spreads open to reveal the dry organs beneath.

                    NEIMEYER (CONT'D)
            The dehydrated skin is thick and
            tough, I...

Suddenly, Locke's tugging pressure on the chest flap causes it to open unexpectedly fast. Neimeyer's scalpel races down and the blade slices into his left forefinger.

                    NEIMEYER (CONT'D)
            Blast! Locke!

Blood begins to pour out of the wound, running down his glove.

                    NEIMEYER (CONT'D)
                (distractedly)
            Where're the damned towels?

He reaches past the camera, knocking it as he pulls a towel from the shelf beyond, then turns back to the body.

                    NEIMEYER (CONT'D)
            Sorry, Owen, I...

            ANGLE ON CADAVER --
            NEIMEYER'S POV

As he turns to the table, he sees his blood seep into the dry alien cadaver, and the open chest of the horrific thing begins to *close back up*! In an instant, the gray flesh that was once dead begins growing, reforming!

                    NEIMEYER (CONT'D)
            Oh, my God...

Tendrils of flesh begin winding about chaotically.

RESUME

Horrified, Neimeyer drops the towel, backs away.

                    NEIMEYER
            Sweet mother of Jesus! Get back,
            Locke!

ANGLE ON CADAVER AND LOCKE
-- NEIMEYER'S POV

The gray skin is turning light blue, red veins are growing, tendrils lengthening... Neimeyer sees Locke's hands on the edge of the table...

NEIMEYER
(yelling)
For God's sake, Locke! Get back before it touches you!

The flailing tendrils whip down onto Locke's gloved hands, piercing the rubber, driving into his flesh. He dives back, screaming, the worm-like appendages disconnecting, but leaving long tendrils to weave about his arms and face.

NEIMEYER (CONT'D)
(screaming)
Locke!!

Locke rushes towards him, red veins now pulsing all over his body. His eyes are desperate, crazed.

NEIMEYER (CONT'D)
(fearfully)
No! Stay Back!

RESUME

Neimeyer races to the airlock, grabbing onto a steel support rod nearby.

NEIMEYER
(emphatically)
Stay back!

But as WE RUSH TOWARDS HIM, Neimeyer punches the hatch control. A VIOLENT CLAXON RINGS OUT, A RED LIGHT FLASHES, and, suddenly, the door slides open to the space beyond. Instantly, we WHIP LEFT, as pieces of equipment are swept up in the suction. The alien body is lifted off the table and hits the door frame above Neimeyer's head, shattering into dozens of dry pieces before flying out into the void. Locke is pulled towards Neimeyer in a blur, his back to us as he lands on top of the terrified Doctor. There is a moment's struggle, Neimeyer screams as his bloody fingers come loose. Then, he is tumbling into the vacuum of space. With the last of his strength, a normal-looking Locke hits the airlock control and stops the explosive purge.

ACT TWO

INT. FARSEER MEDICAL MODULE -- LATER

Our perspective is dominated by the image of a video monitor as it replays the beginning of the autopsy.

> NEIMEYER
> (in video replay)
> I will now make the "Y" incision across what appears to be the cardio-vascular system.
> (beat)
> Owen, give me a hand here, could you?

Locke appears. He moves to the other side of the table. We PULL BACK from the video screen to see St. James, Gullotti, Barnes, and Locke watching the video images. St. James holds the control keyboard for the replay. Maxwell stands a few feet farther back, watching Locke with a look of suspicion.

> LOCKE
> This is just about where it happened...

REVERSE ANGLES

As the airlock door WHINES open to admit an angry and worried Lydon, who rips off his helmet and turns to see the others already gathered around the display. They turn as he enters.

                    LYDON

              (angry, to Locke)

    What the Hell happened?!

                    LOCKE

    I don't know, Commander. He cut
    himself with the scalpel and went
    haywire. We're trying to piece it
    together.

Lydon moves beside the brooding Maxwell to watch as the video resumes.

                  NEIMEYER

              (in video replay)

    The dehydrated skin is thick and
    tough, I...

In the replay, the chest flap widens swiftly. Locke points at the monitor.

                    LOCKE

    There! There, that's it. You can see
    the blade cutting into his hand.

St. James freezes the action, zooms in. We can see the scalpel doing its damage.

                    LYDON

    Resume.

The replay continues.

                  NEIMEYER

              (in video replay)

    Blast! Locke!

The blood begins pouring out of the wound.

              NEIMEYER (CONT'D)

              (in video replay)

    Where are those damned towels?

He moves out of the frame, his elbow suddenly

jostling the camera. The image flutters for a moment, the sound is garbled... Then they come back, but the camera is pointing at the cabinet.

> NEIMEYER (O.S.) (CONT'D)
> (in video replay, with sounds of breaking glass)
> Locke!!
> (beat)
> No! Stay back!
> (beat)
> Stay back!

We HEAR THE AIRLOCK BURST OPEN, THE SCREAMS OF NEIMEYER, AND THE EXPLODING WIND. The camera whips up toward the ceiling, then goes black.

> MAXWELL
> (suspiciously, to Locke)
> What the Hell was that?

> LOCKE
> (nervously)
> Something's missing. He started acting strangely.

He rises, moves to the table.

> LOCKE (CONT'D)
> We were standing right here, doing the autopsy... But Neimeyer nicked himself with the blade. He reached for a towel... And... He just went berserk! Started screaming about the alien. Telling me to get away...

He walks over to the airlock.

> LOCKE (CONT'D)
> The next thing I knew, he'd hit the airlock! We ended up beside each other, holding on... And his hands

                    must have slipped!

Maxwell sneers.

                         MAXWELL
                      (sarcastically)
                    Must have.

Locke stares at him.

                         LOCKE
                         (angry)
                    What the Hell's that supposed to
                    mean?!

Maxwell's face is stern, accusatory. He rises to face Locke while the others watch with surprise.

                         MAXWELL
                    I didn't see anything like that in the
                    video. It sounded to me like he was
                    afraid of *you*.

A trace of nervousness flitters across Locke's face.

                         LOCKE
                    That's ridiculous.

                         MAXWELL
                    You know, I've been wondering about
                    you from the start.
                         (beat)
                    Why did you resign from the Space
                    Corps, Locke?

Locke is impassive.

                         MAXWELL (CONT'D)
                         (pressing)
                    It was after the Ganymede incident,
                    wasn't it?

St. James looks at Maxwell, the mention of the "incident" sparking recognition. Maxwell looks at St. James, and the rest, explaining.

                    MAXWELL (CONT'D)

I have a friend in the Corps. Before we launched, he told me that someone named Locke was *supposed* to have been part of the prep team for the first Ganymede mission. I never found out if it was the same guy.

                    (to Locke, harsher)

Something went *wrong* on the orbital platform, didn't it, Locke?

Locke is silent, red-faced.

                    MAXWELL (CONT'D)

A decom chamber malfunctioned. And one of your buddies ended up crippled.

                  (beat, gets in Locke's face)

But was it a *malfunction*, Locke?

Locke pushes him away violently. The others watch in stunned amazement, all save Lydon, who appears extremely wary, on edge.

                    LOCKE

                (angrily, defensively)

It was a malfunction, read the damned report.

But Maxwell rushes the other man, grabbing his shirt collar.

                    MAXWELL

                (fiercely)

It's kinda hard to get out here!

He shoves Locke, pushing him up against the wall. But Lydon jumps between them, pulling Maxwell back.

LIVE FREE OR DIE

> LYDON
> (yelling)
>
> All right, Max! That's enough!

Maxwell turns on him, breaking Lydon's hold.

> MAXWELL
> (to Lydon)
>
> Is it?! *You knew* about him, didn't you? You put him on the team without any notice because somebody pulled some strings!

Lydon stares at him intensely.

> LYDON
>
> Everybody deserves a second chance.

> MAXWELL
> (mock laughter)
>
> A second chance? Here? With our lives at stake?

> LYDON
>
> He was the best flight specialist in the Corps.

> MAXWELL
> (snide)
>
> *Was.*
>
> (beat)
>
> Thanks for making such a *wise* decision, Commander.
>
> (beat, fierce)
>
> I can see how well it's paid off.

He turns angrily and walks away. As he does, Lydon speaks.

>   LYDON
>   (to Maxwell)
>   You'd better watch yourself, Maxwell.
>
> Maxwell sits down, angry.
>
>   MAXWELL
>   (sotto)
>   You mean watch my *back*.
>
> Lydon moves to Locke's side. The others watch, looking for an explanation.
>
>   LYDON
>   (to all)
>   What happened aboard the Ganymede
>   platform was an unfortunate accident,
>   plain and simple.
>   (nods to Maxwell)
>   Yes, I knew about the incident. But
>   I can assure all of you, it was
>   mechanical failure, just like the
>   report said. Locke was not at fault.
>   If anything, Locke blamed himself too
>   much. While the authorities were
>   ready to dismiss the entire affair,
>   he wouldn't allow it. He voluntarily
>   resigned.
>
> Locke nods very slightly, his eyes downcast.
>
>   LYDON (CONT'D)
>   When I heard the circumstances behind
>   his resignation, I jumped at the
>   chance to have him as part of the
>   team. And I expect you to respect my
>   decision.
>   (beat, to Maxwell)
>   That's it. End of discussion. I
>   don't want to hear another word about
>   this during our entire mission.

He steps forward, points at Maxwell, St. James, and Gullotti.

> LYDON (CONT'D)
> I want you three to get back to the site and fire up the Array. We're wasting time.
> (to Locke, Barnes)
> Let's see if we can figure out what went wrong.

CUT TO:

EXT. THE SURFACE OF TYCHO-B -- LATER

Clad once more in their helmets and suits, Maxwell, St. James, and Gullotti walk down the ramp of Farseer. Above them there has been positioned an auto-winding winch, and a circuit of cable that leads off towards the mining site.

> GULLOTTI
> (to Maxwell)
> You really think Locke isn't to be trusted?

Maxwell approaches the winch, reaches up, and attaches a special hook that connects his suit to the cable via a short tether. The others line up behind him to begin doing the same.

> MAXWELL
> (over his shoulder)
> Let's just say this.
> (beat, checking fastener)
> The government has opposed this project from the start. I think it entirely conceivable that they'd try to sabotage it from the inside, by getting somebody they could control placed on the team.

                    ST. JAMES

          That's crazy. You heard the Commander
          yourself, he knew about the incident
          on Ganymede, and Locke wasn't at
          fault.

Maxwell turns on his tether to face the others.

                    MAXWELL

          That's what the *Commander* said. But
          what if he hasn't been told the truth?

                    ST. JAMES

          I trust Locke.

                    MAXWELL

          I trust my *instincts*. And they tell
          me I should believe the evidence on
          the tape before I believe the word of
          a guy who left the Space Corps under
          suspicious circumstances.
               (turns away)
          Let's go.

And Maxwell hits a control on his wrist. We
CENTER ON the large wheel of the winch as it
begins spinning, then RESUME on Maxwell, St.
James, and Gullotti as the cable yanks them off
towards the mining site.

INT. FARSEER MEDICAL MODULE -- MOMENTS LATER

Lydon stands beside the seated Barnes, who has
a computer keyboard on his lap. Both men face
the video monitor. Behind them, Locke watches
nervously.

                    LYDON
               (to Barnes)
          Okay. Let's see if we can make it any
          clearer. Work on that middle section.

Barnes taps on the keys.

LIVE FREE OR DIE

                    BARNES
          Right...
The video monitor sparks to life, picking up
as Neimeyer hits the camera. We see the same
jumble, hear garbled words.
                    BARNES (CONT'D)
          Hold on here...
He taps more commands on the keypad. The video
replay rewinds a bit, then begins again. The
jumbled image is now slightly improved.
                    NEIMEYER (O.S.)
                (jumbled, through replay)
          For God's sake, Locke!
Lydon glances at Locke, who looks back with
concern. Barnes stops the tape, rewinds, and
plays it again.
                    NEIMEYER (O.S.) (CONT'D)
                (jumbled, through replay)
          For God's sake, Locke! Get back
          before it touches you!
Now, it is Barnes' turn to peer at Locke with
surprise and concern. Locke recognizes the
expression, steps forward. The video continues.
                    NEIMEYER (O.S.) (CONT'D)
                (jumbled, through replay)
          Locke!
                (beat)
          No!
                (beat)
          Stay back!
We HEAR THE AIRLOCK BURST OPEN, THE SCREAMS OF
NEIMEYER, AND THE EXPLODING WIND. The camera
whips up toward the ceiling, then goes black.

                    LOCKE
               (relieved)
     See? He just went berserk! Kept
     screaming about the alien...
But Barnes continues to stare at him with
concern.
                    LOCKE (CONT'D)
               (to Barnes, off reaction)
     What?
He glances at Lydon, who is unreadable.
                    LOCKE (CONT'D)
               (nervous)
     It didn't *touch* me... *Nothing*
     happened! Look...
As he leans towards the keypad, Barnes quickly
leans away. The video rewinds, then re-starts.
                    NEIMEYER (O.S.)
               (through replay)
     For God's sake, Locke! Get back
     before it touches you!
Locke glances at Barnes beside him. The man is
becoming more nervous, staring at Locke.
                    LOCKE
               (nervous laughter)
     Wait, wait...
The tape freezes.
                    LOCKE (CONT'D)
               (relieved)
     There!...
He points at the screen, to a spot on the
reflective surface of the cabinet.

LIVE FREE OR DIE

>   LYDON
>   (inquisitively)
>   Enlarge.

Locke taps some controls, and the reflected image enlarges. It is a slightly blurry shot of the alien cadaver, motionless on the table, and of Locke behind it, peering at Neimeyer off screen.

>   LOCKE
>   You see? There's nothing. Nothing
>   there. He just cut himself... And all
>   Hell broke loose.

Barnes stares at the image, nods with satisfaction. Locke is right.

>   BARNES
>   (still staring)
>   But why?

EXT. TYCHO-B MINING SITE -- LATER

The microwave mining site is a spectacle of technology. All of the towers are now standing, each with its circular microwave "radiators" pointing down at the surface. The "Array" is almost complete. Working under a tower about ten meters away, near the drop-off point of the winch that shuttled the men over, Gullotti stands with a harpoon gun in his hands. He fires the gun, shooting a large steel spike, with a hoop in the close end, into the icy surface. Then he reaches up to grab a long steel cable that hangs down from one corner of the tower, and pulls it through the hoop. We PULL BACK to see Maxwell and St. James in the foreground, doing the same thing at two corners of another tower.

>   ST. JAMES
>   (as a statement)
>   So, you really think Locke could've
>   killed Neimeyer.

Maxwell concentrates on his work as he speaks.

MAXWELL

You saw the tape. You tell me.

He finishes locking the cable into the pike, and stands.

MAXWELL (CONT'D)

All I'm saying is, don't trust anybody from the government. They'll do anything they can to crush private business. I wouldn't be surprised if somebody found *us* all dead next time this rock came around.

ST. JAMES

Sounds paranoid to me.

Maxwell disregards him, and turns toward the distant Gullotti.

MAXWELL

What's taking him so long?

(to Gullotti)

Hey, Toucan Sam, you done yet?

Gullotti is busy tugging on an unruly cable, trying to get it tied down. The end just won't fit.

MAXWELL (CONT'D)

(to St. James)

What the Hell's the problem? Get the power cables ready, I'll be back.

He moves towards Gullotti. As St. James stands and turns to a large set of steel boxes, he hears Maxwell's voice.

MAXWELL (O.S.) (CONT'D)

(to Gullotti)

Hey, nosejob!

ANGLE ON GULLOTTI

Still, Gullotti struggles with the cable. His harpoon gun lies at his side. We CLOSE IN on him as Maxwell comes to a halt off screen.

MAXWELL (O.S.) (CONT'D)

What's the matter, you deaf?

Gullotti strains to pull the cable through the loop.

GULLOTTI

I could use a hand.

The sharp tip of the harpoon rises to point at his right ear.

MAXWELL (O.S.)

(devilishly)

C'mon, boy! Get those fingers working!

Gullotti irritably pushes the harpoon away with his right hand.

GULLOTTI

Give it a rest, will ya?

But the point returns to knock against his helmet. Gullotti twists angrily.

GULLOTTI (CONT'D)

Hey...

ANGLE ON MAXWELL --
GULLOTTI'S POV

Maxwell leers at him, the harpoon still raised.

MAXWELL

(threateningly)

C'mon, choirboy. Get a move on.

ANGLE ON GULLOTTI

Over Maxwell's shoulder, we see Gullotti staring at him with anger in his eyes.

> GULLOTTI
>
> (fiercely)
>
> What the Hell d'you think you're doing?!

We PULL AROUND Maxwell to see the man standing there, unarmed. The harpoon is still on the ground.

> GULLOTTI (O.S.) (CONT'D)
>
> Put it down, Max!
>
> MAXWELL
>
> (confused)
>
> What?

Gullotti quickly waves at the empty space beside his helmet once more.

> GULLOTTI
>
> I said, *put it down!*

And suddenly, he spins around on his feet, a long harpoon in his hands. He points it at Maxwell, breathing heavily.

> MAXWELL
>
> Hey!

But Gullotti is enraged.

> GULLOTTI
>
> Put it *down!*

And he rushes at the unarmed man. Shocked, Maxwell dives out of the way, pulling the harpoon, twisting. His arm is grazed, initiating the massive rotor of the winch. The weapon flies away, but so does Gullotti, who tumbles into the rotor.

> MAXWELL
>
> (desperate)
>
> Chris!

Gullotti's leg is yanked up towards a support arm for the cable. His SCREAMS ring out in the others' helmets as Max tries to reach him. But it's too late, his leg is pulled apart, sending bloody pieces into space. Then Gullotti's torso is tugged in. His SCREAMS GURGLE as his strong arms push against the support, then go limp as the lower half of his body is torn away, spinning into the fiery ion streamers of the comet.

          TIME CUT TO:

EXT. TYCHO-B MINING SITE -- LATER

The surviving members of the crew have gathered at the site. As Barnes and St. James pull the torn body of Gullotti from the motionless winch, Lydon turns from the grisly image to look at the agitated Maxwell.

    MAXWELL
     (defensively)
 He came at me with a harpoon. I had to defend myself.

    LOCKE
     (sarcastically, indicating
     body)
 Looks like you did a pretty thorough job.

    MAXWELL
     (angry)
 Go to Hell, Locke!

Lydon raises a hand to quiet the men down.

    LYDON
     (as a statement)
 You did nothing to provoke him?

    MAXWELL
 No way, Commander. I kidded him a little, sure, but...

LOCKE
(dismissively)
We all know how kind-hearted his jests can be.

Maxwell shoots him a hateful look. St. James, who is sealing Gullotti's remains inside a large silver bag, turns to the others.

ST. JAMES
I heard him, Commander. It wasn't anything.

Maxwell nods.

MAXWELL
All of a sudden he starts yelling at me to put something down. I don't know what he's talking about. And then he's got this harpoon...

He acts out the motions.

MAXWELL (CONT'D)
And he dives right at me! I twist, push his arm away, grab the harpoon. And he slams into the winch.
(beat)
There was nothing I could do.

St. James stands.

ST. JAMES
It's true. I saw them.

LOCKE
And where were you?

ST. JAMES
(pointing)
Over there, at the third tower.

LOCKE
That's over forty meters away.

Maxwell becomes angry, he takes a step towards Locke.

MAXWELL

What the Hell's your problem?

LOCKE

(to Maxwell)

Just following your example, Max. Kind of uncomfortable when the shoe's on the other foot, isn't it?

Lydon moves between them.

LYDON

All right. Cool it. You've made your point, Locke.

(to all)

It seems clear that neither of you is responsible for what's happening here.

(beat, surveys the site)

There must be another explanation.

(back to the crew)

We've got to ask ourselves, what could have set these two off?

BARNES

It's almost like they were seeing things, hallucinating.

LYDON

(nodding)

Right.

(to Locke)

Is it possible they could have contracted something from the alien body you brought aboard?

LOCKE

It's pretty unlikely. We took every

precaution.

LYDON

But Neimeyer cut himself just prior to losing control. He could have picked something up.

(beat)

And if there were airborne particulates that came from the cadaver...

(beat, forbiddingly)

We *all* could have been exposed upon returning without protective gear.

LOCKE

(shakes his head)

The chamber would have been vacuumed clean when he opened the hatch. It would be highly improbable for something to have survived.

LYDON

But would it be *impossible* for some microscopic amount of crystallized DNA to have remained, especially since you were able to *stop* the purge?

Locke considers it.

LOCKE

I can't say I can rule it out.

Maxwell throws his hands up in frustration.

MAXWELL

(angry)

Goddamn great! You just might have infected us all!

LYDON

Back off, Max. It was my call to bring that thing aboard.

LIVE FREE OR DIE

>   BARNES
>   (worried)
>   Oh, man...

Lydon looks at the men, thinking about how to proceed.

>   LYDON
>   Look. We're all justifiably upset, and
>   we're all tired. We've been going
>   almost thirty-two hours straight since
>   we began the decent. The first thing
>   we need to do is get some rest. Then
>   we've got to find out more about these
>   creatures.

>   ST. JAMES
>   I don't know if I could sleep at a
>   time like this.

>   LYDON
>   Well you'll have to try. Any more
>   time spent out here is just gonna wear
>   us down until we're completely unable
>   to function.
>   (beat)
>   Let's go back.

He turns, points at Barnes and Locke, who lift the bag containing Gullotti's remains and attach it to two hooks on the winch cable. The others follow them over to the cable, ready to return to the ship.

INT. FARSEER HELM/NAVIGATION -- LATER

Maxwell and Lydon climb up from the chamber below. Both men are exhausted, tugging at their uniforms to loosen them. As they move in, we see Barnes, St. James, and Locke in the FOREGROUND, all sitting on cots that have been unhinged from the walls.

LYDON

We placed Gullotti's remains in the cold locker.

Locke, Barnes, and St. James watch dejectedly as Maxwell moves over to the left wall, unlatches a cot and attached pillow that hang on a hinge, and plops down on the cot.

MAXWELL

What a nightmare.

Lydon finds a free cot on the right wall, unhinges it, and sits, staring at the others.

LYDON

We'll get out of this. Don't lose faith.

(beat, glancing at watch)

I'm gonna give us four hours to rest, we can't afford much more.

(to Locke)

Locke, set the ship's clock.

LOCKE

Aye, sir.

Locke turns to a digital panel beside his cot, begins punching buttons. The clock reads 04:30 AM.

LYDON

And I want all of you to set your watches. We can't slip up.

The other men set their alarms, then lie down. Lydon hits a control beside him, and the lights go out.

LYDON (CONT'D)

Try to get some rest. We'll attack the problem in a few hours.

He lies down, and closes his eyes.

LIVE FREE OR DIE

TIME CUT TO:

INT. FARSEER HELM/NAVIGATION -- LATER

Locke sleeps, his eyes moving in REM cycle.

DISSOLVE TO:

EXT. GANYMEDE PLATFORM

The huge, skeletal structure of the rotating circular orbiting Platform looms in the distance, floating high above the orange colored clouds of the huge moon. From those clouds appears a round, white, man-made object, a shuttle, traveling towards the Platform at a swift rate of speed. It passes our point of view, and we follow.

>   JENSEN (V.O.)
>   (through radio)
>   Ganymede Platform, this is Orion One,
>   requesting permission to dock.

INT. GANYMEDE PLATFORM -- CONTINUOUS

Wearing a bright green uniform with United States military markings, and a head set and mic, Owen Locke stands with confidence at the controls of Docking Bay One, the centrifugal force of the Platform's rotation acting as artificial gravity. He watches the shuttle approach through a large plexiglass window and presses a button on the control board.

>   LOCKE
>   Orion One, this is Ganymede Control.
>   You are cleared to dock at Bay One.

INT. ORION ONE -- CONTINUOUS

A tall, thin man, MIKE JENSEN (20's), also wearing the military uniform of the Space Corps, and a headset, speaks into his mic as he watches the Platform grow larger in his plexiglass viewscreen.

                    JENSEN

          Thanks, Control, nicest news I've
          heard all day.

INT. GANYMEDE PLATFORM -- CONTINUOUS

Locke smiles, nods.

                    LOCKE

          Long day, eh, Mike?

                    JENSEN (V.O.)

              (humorously, through radio)
          Day?! Hey, Locke, you call thirty six
          hours a day? I don't know which I've
          been deprived of more in the service,
          sex or sleep!

INT. ORION ONE -- CONTINUOUS

Jensen hits a series of buttons, watches readouts on a screen.

                    LOCKE (V.O.)

              (through radio)
          Well, you can get the latter here,
          but you'll have to live without the
          former.

                    JENSEN

          After ten months, I'm gettin' used to
          it, but I'll tell ya, Owen, I wouldn't
          call it livin'!

EXT. GANYMEDE PLATFORM -- CONTINUOUS

The Orion One approaches the outer curve of the Platform. Small jets of energy spray from navigation boosters on its hull, setting the shuttle on an intercept trajectory with a large, circular docking hatch some one hundred meters overhead.

INT. ORION ONE -- CONTINUOUS

Jensen wonders at the mighty station.

LIVE FREE OR DIE

                    JENSEN
          Man! What a sight!
                    LOCKE (V.O.)
                (through radio)
          Thanks, Mike!
                    JENSEN
                (smirking)
          Not you, you slob! The station!

INT. GANYMEDE PLATFORM -- CONTINUOUS

Locke looks at the controls before him, at the huge glass window.

                    LOCKE
          Well, I agree with you there, too.
          Almost as handsome as me!
                (beat)
          I wish I could take credit for
          designing her myself!
                (beat)
          You're at fifty meters. Everything
          looks good. Switch over to manual any
          time.
                    JENSEN (V.O.)
                (through radio)
          Thanks, Locke. Comin' in.

EXT. GANYMEDE PLATFORM -- CONTINUOUS

The Orion One slides through the ether towards the Platform Docking Bay. Closer, closer... Until it is only a few meters away.

INT. GANYMEDE PLATFORM -- CONTINUOUS

Locke watches the shuttle approach. This is business as usual for him.

                    LOCKE
          Ten meters...

> (beat)

Five.

> (beat)

Man, you're smooth, Jensen.

JENSEN (V.O.)
> (through radio)

Engaging magnetic couplings.

LOCKE

One...

JENSEN (V.O.)
> (through radio)

Pucker up, honey, here it comes!

There is a loud THUD as the shuttle makes contact with the Platform. Locke hits a pair of buttons, then walks over the curved floor to stop before a circular portal at his feet. Above the hatch is a sign reading "DECOM HATCH/BAY ONE", and in the portal's center is a glass window allowing us to view Jensen beyond the large decom chamber, behind his own hatch, inside the now attached Orion One. He grips a pair of handholds near his hatch. As he speaks, we hear the sound of AIR HISSING into the decompression chamber.

JENSEN (CONT'D)
> (through radio)

Whoa! That artificial gravity gets me every time!

> (beat)

All set?

The HISSING STOPS. Locke looks at a control panel nearby, seeing a light turn from red to green.

LOCKE

Okay, you're pressurized.

LIVE FREE OR DIE

INT. ORION ONE -- CONTINUOUS

Jensen hits a button on his hatch, and the round door SLIDES BACK, allowing him to climb up into the decompression chamber. He presses a button above his head in the chamber, and his hatch SLIDES CLOSED behind him. He presses another button, expecting something...

INT. GANYMEDE PLATFORM -- CONTINUOUS

Jensen smiles, a bit perplexed, looking up at Locke through the hatch at Locke's feet.

                  JENSEN
                (through headset)

    Hey, you lockin' me out or somethin'?

Locke looks at him, confused.

                  LOCKE

    What?

He checks a readout by his side.

                  JENSEN
                (through headset)

    I can't access the control. Must be a malfunction.

Locke turns a dial.

                  LOCKE

    Maybe...
                (beat)
    Here, let me do it.

He steps over to another set of buttons, and presses one. Suddenly a screaming CLAXON sounds, and red lights go off in a strobe-like display. Locke tenses with alarm, eyes darting over the controls.

                  JENSEN
              (frightened, through
              headset)

                    LOCKE!

Locke steps back to the hatch. Jensen is inside, scared. We can hear the HISS of escaping air.

                    JENSEN (CONT'D)
                    (through headset)
        Locke! That's my oxygen! You're
        decompressing!

Locke hits controls.

                    LOCKE
        I know! I know! Something's wrong!

INT. HATCH -- CONTINUOUS

Jensen is frantic. He presses buttons on the controls, but nothing happens. The HISS of expelling oxygen is very loud.

                    JENSEN
                    (nervous)
        I can't get back into Orion!

He looks up at Locke.

                    JENSEN (CONT'D)
                    (desperate)
        Locke!

INT. GANYMEDE PLATFORM -- CONTINUOUS

Locke races over to the manual override: a large metal lever and crank on the other side of the hatch.

                    LOCKE
        System malfunction! Manual override!

He bends down, strains against the lever, but it remains fixed. In front of him and below, Jensen is becoming terrified.

                    JENSEN
                    (yelling, through headset)
        Locke!

Locke can do nothing. He kneels down over the hatch, yelling at Jensen, whose face is up against the glass, his fists banging away in futility.

LOCKE

Hold on Mike!

He rises, runs over to the control panel, hits a button.

LOCKE (CONT'D)
(into headset)

Ganymede control, this is Bay One! We've got an emergency. Decompression system malfunction!

JENSEN (V.O.)
(desperate, through headset)

LOCKE! LOCKE!

LOCKE

Mike!

And we CENTER ON the struggling Jensen, as he fights like a crazed animal to break out of his tomb. Locke moves back over to him, watching in futility as the man slowly falls back against the opposite hatch of Orion One, losing his strength, still flailing away with his useless arms, mumbling...

JENSEN
(losing consciousness)

Locke... Locke...

DISSOLVE TO:

INT. FARSEER HELM/NAVIGATION -- LATER

Locke's sleeping face is awash in flashing red light as his body is tousled by unseen hands. A LOUD CLAXON sounds.

                    ST. JAMES (O.S.)
                (anxious, loudly)
            Locke! Locke!

Locke opens his eyes.

ANGLE ON ST. JAMES -- LOCKE'S POV

The room is bathed in red. St. James appears frightened.

                    ST. JAMES (CONT'D)
            Locke! Something's wrong!

RESUME

Locke sits up, grabs the anxious St. James.

                    LOCKE
            What's going on?

St. James looks over the room. Behind him, Barnes stands, barely awake.

                    ST. JAMES
            Somebody's opening the airlock!

Locke stands.

                    LOCKE
            Where're the Commander and Max?

St. James runs with him and Barnes to the ladder leading down to the lower level.

                    ST. JAMES
            Don't know! But somebody's trying to
            get out!

Locke drops down into the passage, sliding down the ladder with St. James and Barnes just behind.

INT. FARSEER DECOM AREA -- CONTINUOUS

Locke lands just ahead of St. James and Barnes to see a suited Maxwell pulling the limp form of Lydon towards the airlock. The near hatch of the airlock is open.

                    LOCKE
                (angry)
            Maxwell!

But Max seems not to hear. He continues dragging the commander, drops his body, and moves over to the hatch controls. Locke jumps forward with great speed.

                    LOCKE (CONT'D)
            No!

And as the inner hatch closes, he gets his arm around it, keeping it from sealing. Barnes and St. James join him, pulling on the door.

                    LOCKE (CONT'D)
                (to Barnes)
            Hit the control! Hit the control!

Barnes shifts to his left, hitting the control for the door. It slides open, and Locke dives on top of the lethargic Maxwell, knocking him to the floor. Max barely resists as Locke rips off his helmet, slapping him in the face.

                    LOCKE (CONT'D)
            What the Hell are you doing?

Max seems to snap to life, his eyes angry. With a bestial ROAR, he lunges at Locke, throwing him against the wall. But Locke takes the hit well, and throws back a powerful right fist. Max falls, and Locke is atop him, his fingers around Maxwell's neck. We MOVE IN on Max.

                    ST. JAMES (O.S.)
            Locke! Locke!

Locke continues to squeeze, anger coursing through him.

                    ST. JAMES (O.S.) (CONT'D)
            Locke!

DISSOLVE TO:

INT. FARSEER HELM/NAVIGATION -- CONTINUOUS

The light on Maxwell's terrified face becomes much dimmer, and his spacesuit is gone. But Locke's fingers still encircle the other man's neck.

ST. JAMES (O.S.)

Locke!

We PULL BACK to see that Maxwell is still in his bunk, defenseless, and Locke is strangling him, in some kind of trance. St. James and Lydon jump on him, pulling him away, and Maxwell rises to his feet, straining to breathe.

LYDON

(to Locke)

Wake up!

Lydon and St. James pull a yelling Locke away as Barnes steps into view and Maxwell gets his breath back.

BARNES

(concerned)

Maxwell, you okay?

Max feels his bruised throat.

MAXWELL

What the Hell?!

Then, anger in his eyes, he rushes towards the restrained Locke, smacking him in the stomach. Locke keels over, moaning.

MAXWELL (CONT'D)

Goddammit!

He steps forward, as if to kick the injured Locke, but Lydon restrains him.

LYDON

He flipped out, Max!

Maxwell tries again, but Lydon holds him back.

                    LYDON (CONT'D)

        He didn't know what he was doing!

St. James attends to Locke.

                    LOCKE

                    (moaning)

        What the Hell?..

                    ST. JAMES

                    (interrupting)

        Locke, can you hear me?

Locke's face reflects the pain he feels. He opens his eyes.

                    LOCKE

                    (angry)

        Yeah! What's goin' on?!

He looks around him, realizing he's on the floor. St. James helps him sit up.

Maxwell strains against Lydon, trying to get at Locke.

                    MAXWELL

                    (angry)

        What's goin' on my ass!

                    LYDON

                    (forcefully)

        Sit down, Max!

He pushes Maxwell back to his bunk.

                    MAXWELL

        That Goddamned bastard was tryin' to kill me!

Locke stands as Lydon pushes Max onto the cot.

                    LOCKE

                    (disoriented)

                    What?

Lydon turns to Locke.

                    LYDON

          You were hallucinating, Locke.

Maxwell tries to rise, but Lydon pushes him back.

                    MAXWELL

          Hallucinating?! He knew what he was
          doing!

Lydon holds Maxwell's shoulders firmly.

                    LYDON
                      (angry)
          He was *hallucinating*!

                    MAXWELL
          Commander, I don't trust that Fly Boy
          scumbag as far as I could spit!

                    ST. JAMES
          Go to Hell, Maxwell.

                    LYDON
                      (to St. James)
          Shut up, Clay.

                    LOCKE
                      (to Maxwell)
          I'm sorry. I though you were...

                    MAXWELL
                      (angry)
          Can it!

He feels his injured neck.

                    MAXWELL
                      (to Lydon)
          I want out of here! I wanna get off
          this Goddamned rock *now*!

Maxwell collapses in frustration, and Lydon pulls away from him, looking at each harried man in turn.

>   LYDON
>
> Alright Max! We *all* want out of here.
>   (beat)
> And we'd better work fast because we don't have much time.
>   (beat)
> Here's what we're gonna do. Locke, you okay?

Locke nods.

>   LOCKE
>
> Yeah, I'm alright, sir.
>
>   LYDON
>
> Alright. You and St. James will return with me to the lander. We'll try to get more information about the origin of these things, how they died, the possibility that they could be the cause of these hallucinations.
>   (beat)
> Max?

Maxwell, now under control, looks up.

>   MAXWELL
>
> Yeah?
>
>   LYDON
>
> You and Barnes will continue mining and retrieving the ore we came here to get. We may not be able to retrieve everything we wanted, but we *can't* go back empty-handed.
>   (beat)
> We've got just over fifteen hours. If

we do this right, we can get out of this mess with our lives. If we're lucky, we can still fulfill part of our mission. *If* we're lucky.

(beat)

Okay, let's go.

He nods. The worried men glance at each other, then walk towards the ladder.

ACT THREE

INT. ALIEN LANDER -- LATER

Flashlights ablaze, Lydon, Locke and St. James step through the half open hatch. They move around the octagonal chamber, momentarily peering at the strange controls, then kneel down to inspect the aliens in minute detail.

ST. JAMES

Look.

He points at two of the bodies. Locke and Lydon follow his finger.

ST. JAMES (CONT'D)

There are marks on some of them. Cuts.

We see what he's indicating, deep gouges in the flesh of the bodies, near their necks, and in their chests.

LYDON

And burns. Look at the discoloration around the wounds.

He points at the darker areas around the cuts.

LOCKE

I think I know where they came from.

He holds up a shiny, pen-sized metallic device, presses a button on its side. Suddenly, a bright red ray shoots out of the tip, projecting to a length of about eight inches.

LIVE FREE OR DIE

                    LOCKE (CONT'D)

   And there are more over here.

He moves to pick up two more.

                    LOCKE (CONT'D)
                      (intensely)
   That one in the hatch wasn't pulled
   against the wall by the air leak.
   He was trying to *escape*, from his
   crewmates!

We CLOSE ON LOCKE as he turns off the laser,
staring at the other men.

                    LOCKE (CONT'D)
   They all killed each other!

There is a depressing silence. They look at each
other. Then, the Commander's head set hisses.

                    BARNES (V.O.)
                      (through headset)
       Commander! Commander!

Lydon stirs from his worried thoughts.

                    LYDON
                      (into headset)
       Go ahead Barnes, what is it?

EXT. TYCHO-B MINING SITE -- CONTINUOUS

We HOLD CLOSE on Barnes' amazed face as he begins
to respond.

                    BARNES
                      (with disbelief)
       Commander...

We PULL BACK to reveal Barnes deep inside a wide
mine shaft. He is about twenty feet down in a
hole as wide as the Array; his body is dwarfed by
the scale as we see more of his surroundings.

                    BARNES (CONT'D)
            You'd... Better get down here.

And we REVERSE ANGLES to see that he is standing before an expanse of shiny, bronze-colored metal... The skin of a metallic orb hidden beneath the surface of the comet!

                                        TIME CUT TO:

EXT. TYCHO-B MINING SITE -- LATER

We move with Lydon as he, Locke, and St. James climb down into the shaft on a nylon rope ladder. After a few final steps, they join Barnes and Maxwell at the center of the dig. Before them is the metallic surface of the Orb, criss-crossed with thick grooves about one meter apart. All the men appear speechless, their eyes wide with disbelief.

                    ST. JAMES
            Oh, my God!

                    BARNES
            It's an orb! The entire comet! It's
            some kind of ship!

                  ANGLE ON LYDON

who steps close to the edge of the metal skin, kneels on one leg, and looks out over the strange object.

                    LOCKE (O.S.)
            But that would mean it's been orbiting
            our sun for millions of years.

Lydon tentatively lowers his right hand, runs his gloved fingers over the smooth surface.

                    ST. JAMES (O.S.)
            Could it have accrued all this ice and
            rock over that time?

Barnes squats beside the Commander, visually scans the surface, and the ring of the dig some twenty meters above.

                    BARNES
          I don't know. If it was a typical
          comet, with a regular orbit, any
          material accreted to its mass would
          eventually be burned off by solar
          radiation. Sooner or later, all
          comets break up into bits and pieces.
                    (beat)
          But it's possible that it hasn't been
          on this path for that long, that it
          got thrust into a different orbit from
          somewhere else, the asteroid belt, or
          beyond...

We FOLLOW as he stands.

                    BARNES (CONT'D)
          I just don't know.
                    (beat)
          Commander?

We TILT DOWN on a worried Lydon.

                    LYDON
          Everyone, back to the ship.

INT. FARSEER HELM/NAVIGATION -- LATER

The crew gathers inside the chamber, all are in
disbelief. Lydon, Barnes and St. James stand.
Maxwell sits in one of the pilot seats. Locke
leans over the open seat and looks out at the
surface of the comet through the front view
screens.

                    LOCKE
          This is the discovery of the
          Millennium!

                    BARNES
          And it does change things, now,
          doesn't it, Commander?

LYDON

Absolutely. I want to get off this rock immediately.

LOCKE

(turning, surprised)

What?! When we've only got a mystery and no answers?!

(beat)

We don't know anything about this, where it could have come from! It's been circling the solar system, returning every seven-hundred and ten years, for who knows how long? We've got to break through the shell and find out what's inside!

LYDON

(flatly)

Not under my command.

(to Maxwell)

Max, how much Ocsinnet have you been able to retrieve?

Max swivels the chair to face him.

MAXWELL

About half of what we want. There's still some yet to be placed on the conveyor and pulled up from the pit, but the total?.. I'd say maybe five hundred kilograms.

LYDON

We may have to be satisfied with that.

Locke shakes his head.

LOCKE

You can't be serious! Leave all this behind?

He turns to the others for support.

                    LOCKE (CONT'D)

We'll never have another chance!

Lydon begins to pace.

                    LYDON

Look.

                    (beat)

First of all, we don't even know if we *can* get in. And if we could, who's to say it's a wise idea? We've had two tragedies since we got here. And *we don't know why!*

He stops, places his hands on his hips, faces the men.

                    LYDON (CONT'D)

Those aliens are all dead. They killed each other. They could have had some kind of virus, and they just might have spread it to Gullotti and the Doc, and *possibly* to all of us! Or maybe, *just maybe*, there isn't a virus at all, and it's because of *where* we are!

                    (beat)

This thing isn't even a *comet*, God Dammit! It's some kind of giant, artificially constructed *Orb!* Don't you think it's possible that it might be having some sort of effect on us?

                    BARNES

You mean like some kind of defense mechanism?

Lydon points at him, nods.

                    LYDON

Right. It could be intentional...

> Or it could be a side-effect of its operations. What if this *thing* is emitting some sort of resonant electro-magnetic waves that can effect our subjective views of reality, mess up the ions in our heads?
>
> (beat, to Locke)
>
> What if it doesn't want us to get inside?

Locke will not be deterred.

> LOCKE
>
> We've got to try.
>
> LYDON
>
> *Something* caused those men to go insane, and we're running out of time. We've got to load up the ore and start the launch prep, before our window to return closes.
>
> MAXWELL
>
> (to Lydon)
>
> I'm with you, Commander.
>
> (to the others)
>
> None of us knows when the other may go haywire. The sooner we get out of here, the better.

Locke shakes his head.

> LOCKE
>
> (as a statement)
>
> You'd give up a chance to make a monumental discovery, just because of your fear.
>
> MAXWELL
>
> (angry)
>
> Fear?! It's self-preservation, God

> Dammit! You don't seem to get it, do you? I've got a girlfriend back on Earth. Barnes' wife's gonna have a baby! We take care of ourselves because we *owe it to them to return*!
>
> (beat)
>
> You'd better get your damned priorities straight, man. To me, this 'great discovery' is nothing next to seeing that Barnes gets to see his kid.

Lydon moves up beside him, peers out the viewport.

> LYDON
>
> Besides, opening the Orb presents so many dangerous possibilities. It's like opening a can of worms. I can't allow it.
>
> LOCKE
>
> This is crazy! We're standing here arguing about whether or not we should do something that all of humanity would want us to do?
>
> LYDON
>
> Look, I agree with you that we can't just disregard what we've seen here. But I'm not willing to risk the lives of these men to unlock this comet's secrets. That's all there is to it.
>
> (beat)
>
> I'll let you and St. James take some final shots of the alien lander, and retrieve one of the bodies for return to Earth, but that's it.

Maxwell becomes alarmed.

                    MAXWELL
                  (in warning)
            Commander, if those things *are*
            carrying some kind of contagion...

                    LYDON

            They'll be thoroughly examined, just
            like we will, before anything is
            allowed out of quarantine.

He glances at his watch, disregarding the worried
Maxwell and the disappointed Locke.

                    LYDON (CONT'D)

            Alright. No more discussion. We've
            got about twelve hours to get
            everything loaded and start the launch
            prep. Let's get moving.

EXT. A RIDGE LINE ON TYCHO-B -- LATER

Locke and St. James reach the crest of the ridge.
Each holds a pack in his hand, about the size of
a back-pack.

                    LOCKE

            He's making a mistake, Clay. I can't
            believe he'd let all this go.

                    ST. JAMES

            We won't be leaving empty-handed,
            Locke. Our return of the alien will
            still be the most incredible find in
            history.

                    LOCKE

            But it won't be everything! When the
            people back on Earth find out what
            we've left behind...

                    ST. JAMES

            I don't live for the people on Earth.
            I live for myself and my family.
            Screw what 'the people' want. I agree

with Maxwell.

LOCKE

Don't give me that...

ST. JAMES

(interrupting)

No. Really. I don't owe humanity anything.

LOCKE

That's a pretty damned cold attitude.

St. James offers Locke a hand up to the top of the ridge.

ST. JAMES

Is it? I think it's the only way societies can survive. I don't owe you anything, and you don't owe me. The minute you assume people are obligated to do things for one another, the system breaks down.

LOCKE

Clay, caring for one another is the glue that holds us together. We should have common goals and work towards them.

ST. JAMES

Just as long as you don't force your goals on me! You shouldn't have the right to *force* me to do anything, Owen. We should just leave each other alone. That doesn't take any effort at all.

They turn, seeing the alien lander off in the distance.

EXT. TYCHO-B MINING SITE -- LATER

Lydon stands on the edge of the mine, beside the end of a long treadmill device that runs up from the bottom of the dig. Large steel canisters, about a square meter apiece, slide up towards him at regular intervals, deposited at the lower end by Maxwell and Barnes, who toil at the base of the mine. Lydon removes each canister and stacks them near the wheel of the winch.

> LYDON
>
> How's it coming, Max?

Below, we see Maxwell tap his helmet. He steps away from the conveyor.

> MAXWELL
>
> Sorry, Commander. Gettin' some interference from the turbine!
>
> (beat)
>
> What did you say?

Lydon looks down at him.

> LYDON
>
> How much more?

Maxwell moves over to his own stack of canisters.

> MAXWELL
>
> (counting)
>
> Uh, twenty-one! Could take about another two hours!

He waves his hand at the ring of the mine, indicating the Array.

> MAXWELL (CONT'D)
>
> And we've still got to take all that down!

> LYDON
>
> I'll get started on the Array. You take my place. Let Barnes finish on that end.

LIVE FREE OR DIE

                    MAXWELL
                    (waving)
          Got it!

And he moves towards the rope ladder.

EXT. ALIEN LANDER -- LATER

Locke and St. James stand before the ramp of the alien ship. Locke is opening his pack.

                    ST. JAMES
          Where *did* this thing come from?

Locke removes the digital camera, turns it on, focusing on the strange writing on the side.

                    LOCKE
                    (sourly)
          I don't know. And thanks to Lydon, I
          don't think we'll ever know.

He finishes recording the symbols, and lowers the camera. Then they step up the short ramp and move inside.

INT. ALIEN LANDER -- CONTINUOUS

St. James puts down his pack on a nearby control panel, kneels beside one of the bodies.

                    ST. JAMES
          I still can't believe it.
                    (beat)
          Which specimen should we take?

Locke has the camera in his hand once more, recording the interior of the ship.

                    LOCKE
                    (waving his hand)
          It doesn't matter.

St. James stands, grabbing the arms of the nearest cadaver and pulling it out of the tangled pile. As he does, he backs into his pack, knocking it over. The pack falls onto a tiny button, which comes alive with light.

>   LOCKE (CONT'D)
>   (seeing the light)
>   What the...

St. James turns towards the panel. But before he can see what's happened, a LOUD RUMBLING sounds through the floor. Suddenly, the center of the floor WHINES OPEN like a camera shutter, and St. James tumbles down!

>   ST. JAMES
>   (unexpectedly)
>   Wha?!

He catches himself on the slick edge of the gaping hole, a hole that seems to have no end. Locke dives forward to grab his arm.

>   LOCKE
>   Hold on!

Slowly, Locke pulls the younger man up out of the pit. The light gravity makes it easier than a similar effort on Earth.

Together, the two men step back and stare into the deep, dark hole. Locke inquisitively leans forward, peering over the edge with his flashlight. He sees a ladder attached to one side of the well, a ladder that leads down farther than his light will illuminate.

>   LOCKE (CONT'D)
>   It's some kind of tunnel!

EXT. TYCHO-B MINING SITE -- LATER

We TRACK AWAY from Lydon lowering one of the hydraulic microwave stands, to CENTER ON Maxwell, who is now attaching the steel ore containers to the winch for transport to *Farseer*. As he finishes one more connection, he turns towards the conveyor. There, we see the belt carry an exhausted Barnes up over the edge of the dig.

BARNES

That's it.

He steps off the conveyor and comes to a soft landing on the surface.

BARNES (CONT'D)

Need a hand?

ANGLE ON MAXWELL

Maxwell turns his back to Barnes, loading another container on the winch.

MAXWELL

Yeah, just grab...

BARNES (O.S.)

(interrupting, angry)

What are you doing?

Without warning, Barnes SCREAMS.

BARNES (CONT'D)

Get away from her!

Max turns towards him.

BARNES (CONT'D)

That's my daughter!

And he rushes at Max, a steel pipe in his hands. Max is taken off guard, knocked back. He stumbles and falls, tripping over the pile of ore containers. On his back, he rolls out of the way of another vicious blow.

BARNES (CONT'D)

What the Hell're you doing to my daughter?

ANGLE ON LYDON

He catches sight of the attack.

                    LYDON
          Barnes!

He drops his equipment, begins running towards
them.

                ANGLE ON BARNES

The crazed man rips the pipe down for another
blow. This one hits Maxwell in the side of his
helmet, cracking the plexiglass. Sudden fear
erupts on Max's face as a powerful, white stream
of oxygen bursts through the crack. He rises
with great effort, wrestling the pipe out of
Barnes' hands. But Barnes will not give up; he
dives on Maxwell.

                    BARNES
          You've killed her! You've killed her!

The two roll. Max struggles, air leaking from
his helmet. They tumble towards the craggy edge
of the mine.

Holding Barnes' arm, Max tries to get atop him,
but he slips on the loose edge of the dig. It
begins to crumble around him. In a desperate
motion, he grabs at Barnes, who twists, and is
himself thrust onto the crumbling edge of the
mine. He slips and falls, losing his hold on
Maxwell, tumbling down into the dig with the
loose ice and rock.

Lydon rushes to Max's side.

                    LYDON
          You've got a leak!
                    MAXWELL
                (breathing hard)
          Gotta get back. I don't have much
          time!

Lydon helps Max over to the winch.

                    LYDON

          Go! I'll get down to Barnes.

Max hooks his suit on the winch and sets it in
motion, hurtling back towards *Farseer*.

Lydon scrambles down the motionless conveyor.

EXT. TYCHO-B MINE -- CONTINUOUS

We follow Lydon as he runs from the conveyor to
the still form of Barnes. He kneels, pulling
chunks of ice and rubble off the stricken man.

                    LYDON
               (desperately)
          Barnes!

He lifts the other man's left wrist, checking
the life-sign meter. There is activity. Lydon,
pushes his hands beneath the shoulders of Barnes
and lifts.

                    LYDON (CONT'D)
          C'mon, kid. We're gettin' you outta
          here!

                    ACT FOUR

INT. ALIEN LANDER -- MOMENTS LATER

Locke and St. James stand at the edge of the
mysterious well.

                    LOCKE
          It's a bore-well! A *mine*! They were
          doing the exact same thing we were!
               (beat, looks at St. James)
          Only... They broke through!

INT. ALIEN LANDER -- MOMENTS LATER

Locke and St. James stare at the well for a
moment as Locke moves the beam of his light onto
the ladder.

LOCKE

We've got to go down.

ST. JAMES
(surprised)

What?

LOCKE

We've got to find out what's down there!

ST. JAMES

Locke, we're *leaving*. The Commander gave us orders.

LOCKE

This easily takes precedence.

ST. JAMES
(with disbelief)

That's not for you to decide!

LOCKE

The decision's already been made.
(beat, points at well)
It's right here. Now. We've *got* to look.

ST. JAMES

Locke, we don't have time! We've got to get back and prepare for the launch! It's only out of the Commander's good graces that we were sent back to collect samples at all!

LOCKE

To Hell with the Commander.

He moves towards the other side of the well, where the ladder appears. St. James takes a tentative step in the same direction.

ST. JAMES

LIVE FREE OR DIE

> Locke! Was Maxwell right about you? About the Ganymede incident? Are you really that irresponsible?

Locke looks at him sharply.

> ST. JAMES (CONT'D)
>
> We've got orders, God Dammit!

> LOCKE
>
> Screw our orders, Clay.
>
> (beat, emphatically)
>
> *We can make it!*

St. James steps away, resolute.

> ST. JAMES
>
> Not me, Locke. I want off this comet, or ship, or whatever it is. You do this, you do it alone.

Locke stares at him.

> LOCKE
>
> So be it.

He straps his light to his suit, and begins climbing down onto the ladder. St. James steps forward in alarm.

> ST. JAMES
>
> Don't, Owen! You may not have enough time to get back!

Locke looks up at him, holds up the camera, and smiles.

> LOCKE
>
> Don't worry, Clay. I'll make it. Just save me a seat at the helm.

He reaches forward with his free hand, and St. James clasps it. The two exchange a hopeful look, then Locke begins the decent into the darkness.

INT. FARSEER HELM/NAVIGATION -- LATER

Lydon is strapping a bruised and tranquilized Barnes into his flight seat in the command module. He looks up as Maxwell rises from the floor below.

> MAXWELL
>> The ore's all set.

Lydon checks his bindings on Barnes, then looks at his watch.

> LYDON
>> He's pretty banged up. Might have a concussion. I've given him ten cc's of morphine. He should be okay for a while.
>> (beat)
>> Where the Hell are Locke and St. James?

He moves over to a control panel, lifts the mic of a headset to his mouth, and flips a switch.

> LYDON (CONT'D)
>> (into mic)
>> Locke, St. James, this is Lydon.

He listens to the earpiece and waits for a reply.

> LYDON (CONT'D)
>> (into mic)
>> Locke, come in.
>> (beat)
>> St. James...

Nothing. He puts the headset down and stares gravely at Max.

INT. ALIEN BORE-WELL -- LATER

Locke is about twenty feet below the opening of the bore-well, taking shots of the tunnel as he climbs down. Above him, a concerned St. James peers over the edge.

                    LOCKE
               (through headset, to St.
               James)
     It's weird! The whole tunnel looks
     seamless! Like it's all one long
     tube!

                    ST. JAMES
     Can you see the bottom?

Locke shines his light downward.

                    LOCKE
     Not yet, but...

And suddenly, the light from above fades. Locke
looks up quickly, to see the top of the well
swiftly sliding closed. For a moment, St. James'
face can be seen in the dwindling aperture.

                    ST. JAMES
               (alarmed)
     Locke!!

And then, the well is closed, and Locke is left
with only the beam of his flashlight to show him
the way.

                    LOCKE
               (through headset)
     St. James.
               (beat)
     St. James, can you hear me?

STATIC sounds through his headset. Locke's face
grows grave.

INT. FARSEER HELM/NAVIGATION -- MOMENTS LATER

Lydon and Max stand near the helm controls.
Lydon checks readouts, while Maxwell tries to
reach Locke and St. James on a headset.

MAXWELL

Locke, are you there?

(beat)

Still nothing, Commander.

Lydon turns from punching some commands into the computer.

LYDON

We've only got eight hours before the window closes, and it'll take three to check the launch systems.

He rises.

LYDON (CONT'D)

We'd better get after them.

He moves towards the passage to the lower level, and Maxwell follows.

INT. ALIEN BORE-WELL -- MOMENTS LATER

Locke continues to descend. He pauses, grabs his flashlight in his hand and points it above, where even the sealed opening is too distant to be distinguished. As he begins climbing down once more, his fingers lose their purchase on the light, and it slips from his hand.

LOCKE

Damn!

We watch as the light falls, spinning in tiny circles. But, without warning, it comes to a clattering stop some twenty feet below! He's reached the end of the well! Locke scrambles down to retrieve the light, and surveys his surroundings.

The area is dominated by the copper colored metal of the Orb. But a large hatch has been cut into the surface. Locke lifts his camera and runs a gloved hand over the closed portal.

> LOCKE (CONT'D)
> (whispering)
>
> I knew it!
>
> (beat, louder, for camera)
>
> I've reached the end of the well. The aliens were successful! Now the question is, do I go inside?

He pushes against the door, and it swings inward into darkness.

INT. THE ORB --LOCKE'S POV -- CONTINUOUS

Locke takes a tentative step in, flashing his light ahead of him. What he sees boggles the mind. It is a long, dark, obsidian colored hall that seems to stretch on for miles; a hall composed of such strange geometries that no human mind could have ever attempted to construct it.

> ANGLE ON LOCKE

He steps cautiously down the hall. There are separate alcoves on each side every thirty feet. He flashes his light inside the first few, seeing strange machines made of the same black metal.

> LOCKE
> (with awe)
>
> It appears to be some sort of highly advanced laboratory, or service area. I have no idea what these machines could be for.

He pauses, swinging his light back towards the entrance to the well, then resumes his exploration, walking deeper into the Orb.

> LOCKE (CONT'D)
>
> We know there are records of this comet as far back as the time of Ptolemy.
>
> (beat)

> To think I'm walking inside it, that it's been an alien ship all along...

We HEAR A DEEP RESONANT HUM. He stops in mid stride, pointing his light at the alcoves once again, swinging his camera around.

> LOCKE (CONT'D)
> Wait a minute...

He moves the light from one alcove to the next.

> LOCKE (CONT'D)
> *I hear something...*
> (beat)
> There are nine alcoves, and there seems to be some sort of sound emanating from one of them.

He turns to his right, then to his left.

> LOCKE (CONT'D)
> It's the fourth...

He moves towards the fourth, approaches its threshold, pauses.

> LOCKE (CONT'D)
> Yes. There's something...

And he steps inside.

Instantly, the chamber erupts in a profusion of color and sound. The color quickly coalesces into a HOLOGRAMATIC IMAGE of the solar system, with lines tracing the orbits of all the planets, the asteroid belt, and the Orb itself.

> LOCKE (CONT'D)
> (stunned)
> Oh, my God...

New lines appear, moving from Mars to the Orb, and a smaller, SUB-HOLOGRAM comes to life. It flashes brief images of bizarre forms of life, and their corresponding DNA structures; of forms of life and their evolutionary development, the changes in their DNA. Each new image prompts a small light to appear in a concavity atop the metal panel in front of the holograms.

                    LOCKE (CONT'D)
              (with awe)
    It's like one of those computer generated renderings of evolution.
             (beat)
    But it's not from *Earth*!

He steps closer, looking at the hologramatic diagram of the solar system, seeing one of the planets highlighted. It is the fourth from the sun.

                    LOCKE (CONT'D)
              (stunned)
    I... I think it's *Mars!*

EXT. A RIDGE LINE ON TYCHO-B -- MOMENTS LATER

Lydon and Maxwell reach the top of the ridge overlooking the alien lander. Pausing, Maxwell checks his watch.

                    MAXWELL
    Seven and a half hours.

                    LYDON
    I don't like the look of this.

The two proceed down the ridge towards the alien ship.

                                  TIME CUT TO:

EXT. ALIEN LANDER -- MOMENTS LATER

We FOLLOW as Lydon and Maxwell come to within ten meters of the ship.

                    MAXWELL
    There're no lights.

He follows Lydon up the ramp, into the lander.

INT. ALIEN LANDER -- CONTINUOUS

The two men wave their lights around the chamber, over the dead alien bodies. Two backpacks come into view.

LYDON

Their packs...

He bends down to check them out, then stands.

LYDON (CONT'D)
(to headset)
Locke, St. James, come in...

They hear only STATIC. Lydon and Maxwell exchange a worried glance.

MAXWELL

Where the Hell could they be?

Off the sound of the headset STATIC...

INT. THE ORB -- MOMENTS LATER

Locke holds his camera as the hologramatic images fly by with incredible speed.

LOCKE

There used to be life on *Mars*!
(beat)
And, somehow, the Orb was monitoring it!
(beat)
But why?

Suddenly, Locke sees a familiar sight, the image of creatures like the ones in the alien lander, working in verdant fields, traveling to towering cities. But, in an instant, the entire image is engulfed in an apocalyptic flash that leaves nothing but barren, lifeless rock. Locke looks down at the control panel. A crimson light blinks in the final concavity on the right, signifying the conclusion of the sequence.

                    LOCKE (CONT'D)

  They were the ones in the lander!
       (beat)
  But they must have destroyed themselves.

Suddenly, a powerful MECHANICAL HUM reaches him from the next chamber. He turns with the distraction, stepping back out into the black corridor.

INT. ALIEN LANDER -- MOMENTS LATER

Lydon and Maxwell stand beside each other in the derelict craft, moving their flashlights aimlessly.

                    MAXWELL

  This is goddamn crazy! Where the Hell are they?

                    LYDON

  We don't have much time. We can't cut the engine prep without risking an explosion.

He steps to the edge of the ramp.

                  LYDON (CONT'D)

  We'd better check around the ship.

Maxwell moves up beside him.

                  LYDON (CONT'D)

  It's possible one of them became deranged and ran off. But I don't understand why the other wouldn't have called for help.

                    MAXWELL

  What if they *both* went nuts?

Lydon looks at him, fearing the thought, then begins stepping down the ramp. Maxwell follows.

LYDON

Let's split up, make a circle with a radius of about two hundred meters. We'll meet on the other side of the ship.

Maxwell begins to turn to his left.

LYDON (CONT'D)
(catching him)
And keep in *constant* radio contact. I don't care if you're complaining about the weather, just *keep talking*.

INT. THE ORB -- MOMENTS LATER

Locke steps inquisitively towards the third chamber. The MECHANICAL HUM increases in volume as he approaches. Then, as his foot crosses the threshold, the room suddenly jumps to bright life. A hologram like the first appears, but this time a small metallic globe sits in the last of the strange concavities in the control panel.

LOCKE

It's just like the other display...

He stares at the images, seeing the position of the highlighted planet... The third from the sun.

LOCKE (CONT'D)

But... But this is *Earth!*

As if in answer, the holograms begin to show us depictions of early life on Earth, one celled animals, early fish.

LOCKE (CONT'D)

It's not possible! How could it gather all this information? How could it be *monitoring* life on Earth?!

The images continue to show the advancement of the evolutionary process: reptiles, early dinosaurs, birds. The DNA of each new species appears with it. And with each advancement, a light flashes in an empty concavity. Suddenly, Locke puts the camera down on the panel; he finally understands.

> LOCKE (CONT'D)
> (stunned)
> It's not just *monitoring*, it's *influencing* it!

He moves towards the concavities.

> LOCKE (CONT'D)
> Oh, Neimeyer, if only your dad could see *this*!
> (beat)
> The Creationists always claimed there were no *transitional* species to support the theory of evolution! That's because this Orb changed things!
> (beat)
> It's like the hand of God!

He traces his fingers around the concavities.

> LOCKE (CONT'D)
> It sends out these projectiles each time it passes by, with strands of DNA inside... Retro-viruses or something! And they influence our evolution! Kill off certain species, cause mass extinctions, or spontaneous mutations!

The images in the holograms fix on man, homosapiens. The last *open* concavity lights up, and we see images of the Middle Ages, the Bubonic Plague.

> LOCKE (CONT'D)
> The Black Death. That was in 1348, the last time the comet flew by! It

>   was seen as a harbinger of evil...

Modern man appears in the holograms.

>   LOCKE (CONT'D)
>
>   But if the last of these globes sent
>   to *Mars* somehow wiped them out...

He looks at the globe resting in the final socket.

>   LOCKE (CONT'D)
>   (fearfully)
>   What'll this do?

As if in answer, the light beneath the globe comes on.

EXT. TYCHO-B, SOUTH OF LANDER -- LATER

Maxwell is alone, searching on his side of the ship. He traces his flashlight beam over the blanched surface of the comet.

>   MAXWELL
>   (to himself)
>   Where the Hell are those stupid,
>   Goddamn, useless bastards?

He turns to his right, sees the distant image of Lydon conducting his search, then turns back to the ice before him.

>   MAXWELL (CONT'D)
>   (to himself)
>   This whole thing is insane! It's like
>   some kind of nightmare!

He turns back to Lydon.

>   MAXWELL (CONT'D)
>   You got anything, Commander?

In the distance, Lydon directs his beam towards Maxwell.

>   LYDON
>   Nothing.

Lydon turns back to his search.

                MAXWELL

    What the Hell?!

He resumes his search as well.

                MAXWELL (CONT'D)

    I'm startin' to get antsy, Commander.
    We're running out of time.

                LYDON

    I know, but nobody just disappears.

                MAXWELL
        (to himself)

    They could on *this* comet!

The two men move towards each other.

                LYDON

    I've got nothing, what about you?

                MAXWELL

    No sign of 'em.

Lydon looks around, frustrated.

                LYDON

    Let's double back, make one last try,
    on a little wider diameter.

INT. ALIEN LANDER -- LATER

Lydon moves up the ramp and inside. He turns to see Maxwell just a few feet behind.

                MAXWELL

    Nothing. Not even a footprint.
        (beat)
    It just doesn't make sense.

Lydon's face is grave.

                LYDON

    If we don't get back and start the
    final sequence in the next hour, that's

it. We'll all be stuck here.

He clicks on his radio once more.

                LYDON (CONT'D)

    Locke, St. James, can you hear me?

                (beat)

    Is anyone there?

He gives up, shakes his head, begins moving towards the ramp.

                MAXWELL

                (confused)

    Wait! Wait a minute...

                (beat)

    Say that again.

Lydon cocks a brow, turns on his transmitter once more.

                LYDON

    Locke, can you hear me?

He looks at Maxwell, who is bending down, placing the exterior of his helmet against the floor.

                LYDON (CONT'D)

    What are you doing?

                MAXWELL

                (distractedly)

    Turning down my receiver. I thought I
    heard something, a vibration...

                (beat)

    Transmit again.

                LYDON

    This is Lydon, come in Locke.

Maxwell's face reflects astonishment.

                MAXWELL

    There's something coming from under

>   the floor! The transmission is coming
>   out from under the floor!

A stunned Lydon moves beside him.

INT. THE ORB -- MOMENTS LATER

Locke stands before the glowing globe, hesitant to approach. Suddenly, the concave base supporting the globe opens up, and the device begins to sink into the panel. Locke jumps forward, trying to stop it.

>   LOCKE
>   (horrified)
>   No!

He grabs the globe, knocking his camera onto the floor, but he can get no purchase on the black metallic device. Beneath him, we can hear the broken camera's playback in a repeating loop.

>   LOCKE ON VIDEO (O.S.)
>   It's like the hand of God!... It's
>   like the hand of God!... It's like
>   the...

Locke struggles in vain as the thing slips from his fingers and disappears into the panel. Desperate, he turns around in the chamber, searching for a way to stop the device.

>   LOCKE
>   There's got to be a way!

Then, realization. He pats a pocket on his suit, unzips it, and removes one of the small, pen-sized lasers from the alien lander. He holds the device before him, and turns it on. A bright red beam shoots up in front of his eyes. Instantly, he drops to his knees, and begins cutting a hole into the shell of the console.

INT. ALIEN LANDER -- MOMENTS LATER

Lydon and Maxwell strain against a long piece of metal that they've thrust into a crack in the floor panel.

                    LYDON

     Just one more time...

                    (beat)

     Push!

And with great effort, the panel rises. The two men quickly drop to their knees and thrust their fingers under it. They pull together, raising it up to discover...

Not a tunnel, as Locke saw, but a storage alcove, in which the bloody, burned corpse of St. James has been stuffed. A shocked Lydon looks at Max, then jumps to his feet, turning on his transmitter.

                    LYDON (CONT'D)
                  (frantically)

     Barnes!

                    (beat)

     Barnes! Wake up!

INT. THE ORB -- MOMENTS LATER

Locke tears away the panel, seeing the globe glide into a round socket and sink down into the floor. But he jumps forward with the laser, cutting into the globe, bringing forth clouds of smoke, sparks and flames. He tosses the laser aside and rips at the globe with his hands, screaming with pain as a powerful electric current charges through his body. All the while the camera repeats:

                    LOCKE ON VIDEO (O.S.)

     It's like the hand of God!...

INT. FARSEER HELM/NAVIGATION -- CONTINUOUS

We CLOSE ON BARNES as his drugged mind is roused from its haze by Lydon's call.

LYDON (V.O.)
(through headset)
Barnes! Barnes!

Barnes blinks, realizes he's strapped into his seat, tied down.

BARNES
(into mic)
What is it, Comman?..
(beat, looking toward helm)
What the?..
(horrified)
No!!

INT. THE ORB -- CONTINUOUS

Locke kneels before the smoldering remains of the Orb's controls, smiling with satisfaction. He's done it. He's stopped the delivery of the globe. Slowly he hears the sound of his camera replaying.

LOCKE ON VIDEO (O.S.)
...The hand of God!... It's like the hand of God!...

Then he cocks his head, hearing something else: Barnes, becoming more detectable over the sound of the camera.

BARNES (O.S.)
(horrified)
Locke!
(beat)
Locke! What have you done?!

ANGLE ON THE PANEL

From LOCKE's POV we see the burning, smoldering Orb controls, and slowly, THE IMAGE BEGINS TO MELT AWAY...

DISSOLVE TO:

INT. FARSEER HELM/NAVIGATION -- CONTINUOUS

... And the sight is replaced by the real control panel of *Farseer*, the control panel that Owen Locke has just destroyed.

ANGLE ON LOCKE

He stares in horror, looks at the aghast Barnes, then turns to his video camera, where the small eyepiece display shows a loop of the interior of Farseer, and repeats his words:

LOCKE (O.S.)
(through video replay)

> It's like the hand of God!... It's like the hand of God!... It's like the hand of God!...

Locke realizes he has just hallucinated everything, just determined the fates of everyone left alive on comet Tycho-B.

We PULL BACK, THROUGH the plexiglass viewports of *Farseer*, UP, and INTO the CHAOTIC COMA, until the comet and its prisoners are left far behind, little more than specs in the limitless void.

FADE OUT

END ACT FOUR

END

"Beautiful Chaos"

An Intellectual Construct in Favor of Laissez Faire Capitalism over Government

In the pages of this book, and throughout history, we have seen numerous examples of the inefficiency and moral bankruptcy of the statist mindset. Government regulates our lives and businesses, takes our money, and competes with many of us in our own professions. It is, as John Locke defined it in his ground-breaking *Second Treatise of Government*, imposing on us a "State of War" by infringing on our Natural Rights and retarding our economic development. Where it is only supposed to garner funds in order to protect us, it now acts as a thief and takes our property (both physical and non-physical assets) to give favors to others.

As tools to facilitate critical analysis of this modus operandi, we thus far have utilized economic analysis, and the historically valid underpinnings of American civics, most of which are based on the ideas set forth in the aforementioned *Second Treatise*. Of course, in doing so, the strength of the Lockean philosophy has not been challenged. It appears to be a very workable system, and has been deemed acceptable by many proponents of individual liberty throughout history[48].

But logically, and ethically, Locke's theory deserves more scrutiny, and such study leads one to not only question many of the assumptions

---

[48] Locke's *Two Treatises of Government* is often best remembered for its *Second Treatise*. The *First Treatise* is notable as a refutation of the so-called "divine right of kings" as expressed by Robert Filmer, in his work *Patriarcha*, published in 1628. In *Patriarcha*, Filmer not only used what he viewed to be Biblical scholarship to defend the power of the Sovereign to rule, he also stated that to deny the God-granted authority of a King would be to deny Adam his dominion over Eve, and over the beasts of the Earth. Locke brilliantly tore Filmer's argument apart, revealing that the Old Testament says that God gave *them* – i.e. man, in general – dominion over the Earth, all human beings had this power, not just Adam and his male descendents. Filmer claimed that to deny the royal authority would be to make each man his *own* king, and, in fact, Locke came close to acknowledging and extolling that idea of pure autonomy. The *First Treatise* is a fascinating window into the practical religious and political thinking of that time. The *Second Treatise* moves much further, towards radical individualism. It does, however, stop short of promoting the elimination of the state entirely.

underlying our contemporary political institutions, but also to postulate effective, moral alternatives.

The basis of Locke's thesis is that you are created with, as Thomas Jefferson said in the *Declaration of Independence*, certain unalienable rights. These are the right to life, liberty and property (the "pursuit of happiness"); the latter two rights are essential for the fostering of the first, and all three are inextricably connected.

According to Locke and the intellectuals of the 18th Century who turned his philosophical construct into a practical rule book for government, we form "the state" to *protect* these rights, and vest in government certain "police powers" based on the consent of the governed. These powers are to be used solely to protect our lives, liberty and property from encroachments by others. Once a government begins to do that which a malicious person would do – namely threaten our lives, liberty or property – it works against its very raison d'etre, and is therefore invalidated.

But if, as we assume, legitimate government is created to stop us from plundering one another and threatening one another's lives, property and freedom, how is it justifiable to *take* a person's property in order to fund the very government that is established to *protect* that property?

The inconsistency is obvious, and reminiscent of the Platonic conundrum of "who watches the watchers?"

How can we justify government confiscating some of our property in order to protect our property? How much is enough? How is that decided? What if one does not want to comply?

Locke's answers in support of his argument for individual liberty do not address these questions. He first states that, "the supreme power cannot take from any man (singular) any part of his property without his *own* consent (italics added)." Later, however, while providing his rationale for granting government the police power, Locke explains that if a man enjoys the protection that the state provides, he is duty bound to give up some portion of his property in the support of it, concluding with this internally contradictory statement, "But still, it must be with his own consent, that is, the *consent of the majority*, giving it either by themselves, or their representatives, chosen by them (italics added)."

The problem here is clear. If one is to give his *own* consent, how does that correlate in any way to policy making by the *consent of the majority*?

It does not. It does not support the rule of the majority, even for the establishment of the police power of the state. Individual consent is not reflected through majority rule. Individual consent would connote volition, thus voluntarism, and thus, the elimination of the state apparatus altogether. The "state", in its generic form, is only needed to institute force upon one unwilling to join or comply, and yet it is the prevention of force which is the rationale for establishing the state. If the state must use force on us in order to arrest force, what purpose does it really serve?

The Lockean dilemma is much larger than this logical inconsistency reflects, and its ethical and economic implications are closely linked. But before one analyzes the problems of Locke's rationale in favor of limited, "negative" government, it is important to study the larger panoply of government services, and praise Locke's powerful argument against "positivist" state action. This will allow us to see in a different light what we typically assume are justified, "negative" roles for the state.

The Conceit That Drives Positivism

As Locke might say, it is only with the greatest conceit that one attempts to *force* individuals to pay for a product or service after they have opted *not* to pay. Yet we see this happening in government all the time. A ski hill is failing in the private market because not enough people find it attractive to recreate there, and as a result, to "save" it from development, politicians propose using tax money to purchase the land and turn the area into a state park[49]. Inevitably, this park will not turn a profit, and more tax money will be used to keep it operational.

Or perhaps it is a particular industry, one which stands to lose to more efficient, foreign competition. American consumers might like to choose the *foreign* product, thus saving themselves money and letting them have

---

[49] This is the case in New Hampshire, circa 2007, where state Representative Ann Marie Irwin, of Peterborough, has proposed taking $400,000 from NH taxpayers in order to "save" Temple Mountain from "development." Temple Mountain has failed more than once to turn a profit as a ski hill and recreation spot, but Ms. Irwin does not seem to realize that this form of "development" has been rejected by the consumers and the mountain is most likely better suited (it is a small mountain, in the southern region of the state, and often lacks snow) for some other use. She does not want to form her own company to try to operate it for the sake off recreation. Instead, through taxation, she wants to force people to pay who already decided *not* to frequent it for that purpose.

more capital left over to purchase something else or invest. But politicians disagree. We "need this essential American industry", they might say, or "the 'trade imbalance' is enormous"[50], and therefore the government must place tariffs on foreign products (this also applies to restrictions on immigration, based on the fallacious idea that foreign-born workers depress native wages).

In so many cases, the government is utilized to force us or our neighbors to pay for something we would not have paid for, or paid for in a different amount, had we been given our own druthers, whatever those are. This is coercive, malicious, and unsupportable in a free society. The ethics of forcing someone to pay against his will are clearly malignant and run contrary to the Golden Rule. Would you like it if you had an inescapable "buying buddy", who tagged along with you everywhere you went, and imposed his will each time you attempted to buy or sell a product? If you agreed to a certain price with a businessman, would you not find it the height of arrogance for your "buddy" to step in and tell you that you need to pay more, or to tell you as the seller you need to sell for less? What if you completed the purchase, and then the "buddy" told you to give that product, or the profit from its sales, to someone else? If such a person existed, he would be quickly shunned,

---

[50] In his book *The Fair Trade Fraud* (New York, NY. St. Martin's Press, 1991), James Bovard conducts a thorough and systematic analysis of the economic effects of protectionism. In study after study, he notes that protectionist policies designed to lend favors to domestic businesses harm consumers up to eight times what they might bring in to the favored domestic businesses helped by this government intervention. This is money that could be used to buy other products, both domestic and foreign, and would expand our economy through the growth of vibrant, efficient and productive businesses. Our well-being is retarded by trade barriers imposed by our own government, but many people don't look at the issue as closely as they ought. Likewise, many people are not aware that when media pundits warn of a "trade deficit" with other countries, it merely means that our dollar is strong enough to buy a lot of foreign goods for a good price. The deficit is nothing of the sort. It is American consumers buying foreign products with their own money, and this is only *half* of the equation, because the money the foreign businesses receive is in Dollars, and must come back to the United States. It does so in capital investment, liquidity, which spurs even more growth of domestic US business, higher employment, and a stronger Dollar. The trade "deficit" is a fallacy, promulgated by politicians and members of the media in order to gin up fears of foreign workers, and to promote domestic special interests. In fact, there is always a balance between the products we buy, and the investment that returns to the US. That is why it's called the "balance of trade", but you will rarely hear this unless you are watching Lawrence Kudlow on television.

and become nobody's buddy in very short notice, because the ethics of his actions are unacceptable. Yet this is what politicians try to be all the time, and they set up bureaus to act as our invisible "buying buddies" for every private transaction.

The Economic Drag of Positivism

As stated earlier, the ethics and economics of "positivism" are linked. On the economic side, government provision of goods and services has grave consequences as well, but these consequences often go overlooked. They fall victim to the dynamic of "opportunity costs", or what Frederic Bastiat called "what is seen and not seen". While the public *sees* the gymnasium or wildlife refuge that is created through the taking of tax money and the application of that money to the purposes the majority chose, the same taxpaying public *does not see* the innumerable products left unproduced, the jobs not created, the productivity lost, due to this redirection of usable capital. As it turns out, the losses far outweigh the gains, for, as has been noted earlier, if the government *forces* people to pay for things they had already chosen not to buy -- or would never choose to buy if given the freedom to decide -- these expenditures are, *by their nature*, losses to the taxpayers, not gains. The aggregate economy is harmed, not helped.

Bastiat's argument was reinforced by the members of the Austrian School of economics. In the 19th and 20th Centuries, men such as Ludwig von Mises, Karl Menger, and FA Hayek showed that the valuation of one's property is purely subjective. As a result, each of us creates our own definitions of what are efficient expenditures of our capital. We subsequently take those definitions and interact with others to get what we want in the market, and through those freely chosen transactions we create price information that helps other providers of products and services to attenuate their own actions most efficiently. This market process allows people to produce the most for the least amount of work, or buy the most for the least amount of money.

Without a fully functioning price mechanism created by free individuals, there cannot be a proper management of resources. Producers will not know how much to produce, prices will not reflect the real value of the product to consumers, and time and capital which could be spent in more efficient ways will be squandered on creating or buying products and services that people do not want. Life is not bettered in this manner. Living standards are not improved by taking away the prerogative of the individual to decide for himself whether to engage in a transaction with another person. By definition, waste is created, for would one not call something a waste of money if he had it taken from him and spent on things he did not want?

Bastiat, the Austrians, Adam Smith and other economists understood that living standards rise most rapidly when the individuals *living their own lives* get to define what betters their lives. If we trust our neighbors to use the fruits of their labor as we would like to be trusted with our own, not only the ethics of the Golden Rule are upheld, but the practical advantage of increased productivity is facilitated, and the lives of men are improved.

How Government Competition with Private Industry is More Widespread Than One Might Think

It is easy to overlook these kinds of long-held economic axioms when faced with a constant barrage of pro-government propaganda in the media. Likewise it is easy to forget that the acceptance of "positivist" government for certain goods or services leads to its use in regulating, cartelizing or monopolizing other areas of our lives which we don't immediately see as being tied to economics and market exchange. People begin to think it is appropriate for government to address other societal needs, needs we could fill ourselves through the use of private exchange and capitalism. As a result, the line between "protection" and "provision" becomes blurred.

Today, the government engages in activities which we initially assume to be "protective" in nature – things such as restaurant health inspection, and building code inspection – but are, in reality, positivist provisions of services that crowd-out or openly exclude market participants from competing with government in these fields of endeavor.

Let's look at "safety" inspection as the first example. In the winter of 2003, a Rhode Island nightclub called "The Station" caught fire due to pyrotechnics being lit by a band on stage. Ninety-six people were killed. Shortly thereafter, politicians were calling for more stringent fire codes, this despite the fact that the fire began due to actions that were illegal in the first place. The laws did not stop the tragedy. In addition, many New England papers and broadcast media soon reported that their own state inspectors were finding all sorts of "safety" violations in their own visits to local clubs.

Keen observers might have wondered why there was a sudden barrage of violations. Were the nightclubs working in concert to violate the codes at that specific time, or is it more likely that the increase in violations was due to a higher number of inspections? Perhaps the government bureaucrats who were suddenly finding all sorts of snow-blocked back doors and flammable materials at the nightclubs simply hadn't visited the clubs as they were supposed to have done, or their scheduled visits would have proven insufficient to police the standards. Seeing a sudden spike in violations just after a high-profile nightclub tragedy certainly seems driven by politics, not collusion on the part of nightclub owners to break fire codes.

Of course, none of this offers observers much confidence in the consistency or thoroughness of the inspection regime as operated by the government.

Add to that the historical fact that many nightclub owners bribe politicians, and many safety inspectors extort owners, and you have a recipe for an opaque, corrupt, inefficient, untrustworthy regime of so-called inspection that many people blithely trust to tell them they are "safe" in crowded bars, rather than a transparent, honest, efficient, trustworthy system of inspectors whose livelihoods depend on satisfying the customers who frequent the clubs and also depend on satisfying insurance agencies that offer protections against hazards.

This problem is repeated over and over, in field after field, from food inspection[51] to elevator inspection, from the licensing of nail stylists, to the licensing of gas pipe fitters. Government does not do the job properly, efficiently, or with addressability. Corrupt government employees and politicians use the safety codes and licensing laws to shake down competing businesses and help favorites exclude competition, and the populace is not only directly financially harmed by the interference in the competitive marketplace, it is also indirectly harmed by believing in the fantasy of government protection. The government inspectors certainly weren't

---

[51] On March 27, 2007, Jessica Fargen, of the *Boston Herald*, reported that auditors in Massachusetts found fewer than one food inspector working on any given day in the entire state. The auditors also revealed that local inspectors were often corrupt, and made special deals with those they were supposed to be monitoring. For more, go on line to this address:
http://news.bostonherald.com/localRegional/view.bg?articleid=191065

around the night "The Station" became a deathtrap. Realistically speaking, it would be cost-prohibitive for them to be in every club. But the threats of lost business, liability suits and possible bankruptcy help inspire businesses to avoid such calamities before they occur.

Consumers have choices, and they will be the final deciders. Every consumer can approach a club employee, or talk to a nail "technician", or ask a friend about a doctor, and find out about how that person handles his safety issues. Each person's commercial exchange with anyone offering a product or service in the market is uniquely his to decide. The consumers themselves have the power to put people out of business simply by not doing business with them. Likewise, they have the power to make businessmen dazzlingly successful. The more comfortable one feels with the quality of a seller's product or service, the more likely he will be to engage in commerce. Businessmen recognize this, and, as a result, respond best to market incentives brought about by the consumer, not abstract regulations imposed by politicians.

Besides, ethically, who are politicians to decide for others how they live their lives when engaging in peaceful commercial interaction with others? Even if one posed a radical hypothetical wherein customers knew their safety was in jeopardy, but visited a club or rode on rides, or ate meals, or drank drinks that could kill them, what business would it be of government to stop them? Rock clubs are also dangerously loud, does that mean government "sound inspectors" should be enlisted to check the levels of every amplifier about to be played by every guitarist in every club in a particular jurisdiction? Would the hearing problems people might encounter after concerts justify the government ordering all concert-goers to wear earplugs?

Whether the people are aware or unaware of the dangers, their lives are their own, and it is not the place of government to protect them from their own actions. Such activity by government is not protection at all. It impedes the natural growth of market participants and private watchdogs who would naturally cater to those who want to look out for themselves, and it encourages people to look to government to handle other areas of their lives that could better be handled by private industry.

Roads are an excellent example. For many Americans, indeed for many people all over the world, the assumption that only government can create and run roads is unquestioned. Government has always run roads, and it always will, they believe. The forced seizure of land through use of eminent domain, the widespread taxation of people who might not even use specific roads upon which the tax money will be showered, the inefficiency of upkeep, improper speeding laws and ticketing, and the mixing of bad drivers and good on the same pavement are all viewed as mere nuisances one must accept if one wants to be mobile. It is seen as virtually impossible for private interests to be able to surmount the huge costs and property hurdles any attempt to build a private road might present. How is it possible, then, that in the first half of the 19th Century, private turnpikes not only existed, they flourished and turned sizable profits?

As economist Daniel Klein wrote:

> "Between 1794 and 1840, 238 private New England turnpike companies built and operated about 3,750 miles of road. New York led all other states in turnpike mileage with over 4,000 as of 1821. Pennsylvania was second, reaching a peak of about 2,400 miles in 1832. New Jersey companies operated 500 miles by 1821.... Between 1810 and 1845 over 400 turnpikes were chartered and built."[52]

Despite popular misconceptions, private companies succeeded in building roads without having to coerce anyone to pay for them or give up land to build them. The argument offered by critics, even conservative ones, that only *government* can "generate" enough money to undertake such large and expensive projects is belied by the facts. Likewise, the red herring often tossed out by leftists, who argue that there is a "free rider" problem (wherein potential beneficiaries of a project will not participate in the investment if they know they can still reap benefits by being in close proximity to the project when it is complete) is shown by history to be inapplicable, because exclusivity and competition against other projects drives people to invest out of their own self-interest.

Unfortunately, the more government has insinuated itself into our lives in a "positivist" manner, the more people expect it to do. Sometimes, this

---

[52] Daniel B. Klein, "The Voluntary Provision of Public Goods? The Turnpike Companies of Early America," *Economic Inquiry*, October 1990, 788-812. As quoted by Tomas J. DiLorenzo, in *How Capitalism Saved America* (New York, NY, Three Rivers Press, 2004) p. 84.

comes about due to certain special interests, and the public eventually comes to believe that the world has always operated in this fashion.

Marriage is a perfect example of this entrance of government in our private lives. In this, the beginning of the 21st century, there is a clamor for state and national laws or constitutional amendments that would codify a legal "marriage" as a licensed union between one man and one woman. This has set off a firestorm of debate. Homosexuals are upset because marriage brings heterosexuals certain legal advantages they cannot acquire with the same ease. Heterosexuals counter that it is unjust to redefine a word that has meant one thing for centuries. Marriage between one man and one woman is the bedrock of society, they say; it protects the children from abuse. In fact, many "pro-marriage" activists have actually said that they want to legalize only heterosexual marriage because it is "the optimal environment for raising a child." In response, critics ask if all other, "sub-optimal" child-rearing situations would be *outlawed*. Would a single parent be unable to legally adopt, even though the living situation for the child might be better than a foster home or an orphanage? What about grandparents, or homosexual couples? What about heterosexual couples on the low end of the earning scale? Homosexuals also point out that there have been cultures in the past that allowed for many kinds of "official" marriage situations. They want the state, in its generic sense, to recognize their "right" to be married under the same laws that heterosexuals employ. They want the state to recognize their "Fourteenth Amendment rights" to equal protection under the law.

Unfortunately, neither side is willing to acknowledge that state licensing of marriages is a relatively new phenomenon. They have had their minds blurred in two ways. First, they assume that because the state plays a certain role now, it always has done so. This is caused by simple ignorance of history. Why one reflexively turns to the state to get a *license* to wed another is a complete mystery, unless one acknowledges that most Americans don't know that marriage licenses and government involvement are relatively recent phenomena in the United States. As has been noted in this book, George and Martha Washington did not ask permission from the government to get married. Marriage used to be the purview of one's church. The state has now been put before God in order of importance for the sanctioning of one's bond with another. But since Americans don't study the history of marriage, they don't question the implication of having the government get involved.

The problem is not that homosexuals want to encroach on a traditional area of heterosexual life, it is that heterosexuals have ceded to the state the power to grant permission for marriage and many other activities. Even if they are successful in passing laws or constitutional amendments that will define marriage the way they want it defined *today*, heterosexuals have to understand that by putting the power to define words and societal traditions in the hands of the state, they leave the definitions and traditions up to majority rule, and one cannot say with any sense of surety that majorities even a few years down the line will believe as they believe at this time. The attempt to "preserve marriage" will last only as long as the vocal minority or the majority agrees, and then, so-called "traditionalists" will be sorry to see a dramatic change in what the word "marriage" means.

Since many special interest lobbyists do not look back at history to see the origins of what they assume to be a legitimate government purview (in this case, it was religious and racial animosity that fueled certain established churches in the US to begin pushing for government licensing and for the exclusive power to marry people) the combatants in today's marriage debate are unable to see that there is a different way, a system that forgoes government in favor of private, voluntary association.

But there is a second factor revealed in the marriage debate, something more significant than simple laziness or ignorance of history, something that tells us about not only human nature, but also the flaw at the heart of Locke's *Second Treatise*. What is most revealing is that many Americans believe that the Fourteenth Amendment is applicable in the case of marriage, and in many other instances of "positivist" provision of government "services", or licensing thereof.

Read with "strict scrutiny", the Fourteenth Amendment's "equal protection" clause is simply that. It requires that all citizens of all states be *protected* equally by the laws of their state and federal government. It does not mean, as is the common fantasy, that all citizens must be *treated* equally under the law. As much as one would like to think that all citizens should be treated equally, the clause does not use those terms, and no amount of legal wrangling can change this fact. This distinction between *protection* and *treatment* lies at the heart of the Lockean code. Government is only supposed to *protect* us, not offer goods and services such as legal arrangements like marriage that equate to *treatment* under the law. In any instance where such over-stepping of the Lockean system occurs, government has become illegitimate.

Unfortunately, the Lockean system's false assumption that the positive provision of the service of police protection is truly a "negative", and thus justified, role of government leaves open the possibility that other services will be viewed as justified, and, of course, if government can take a portion of our property in order to "protect" our property, why not expand the "protective" role of government beyond the police service?

Very few people in the field of political-philosophical disputation engage in this debate, but it is important, for the assumptions manifest themselves more and more, in many ways, and always undercut the efforts of those who try to hold the line in favor of limited, "negative" government established solely to protect our lives, property and peaceful interactions.

Such problems lead one to question the wisdom of basing a governmental system on Locke's theory. But it is not enough to criticize or pick apart his paradigm. It is incumbent on those who would say that Locke's ideas do not go far enough -- or rest upon contradictory statements, or open the Pandora's Box of larger government -- to present a better alternative, a moral, ethical, and workable alternative that avoids the practical Lockean pitfalls.

In a word, that alternative is the market.

The free-market, the organically created, spontaneous outgrowth of human individuality and peaceful human interaction, solves the ethical problems of Locke's theory. It allows every man to give his consent, avoids the pitfalls of government preying on the slothful side of human nature, and promotes man's positive attributes: creativity, work and thrift. It allows us to get services, even police services, provided to us voluntarily, without forcing others to pay for something they do not want, or do not want to the same degree, and it fosters bonds between those in need of charity and those who provide it. It is truly the noblest achievement of society, and, at the same time, that which allows society to exist.

The Market Paradigm, and How It Can Replace Government

Recall Locke's excellent criticism of "positivist" government activity. It is simply not ethical to take someone's money to pay for something he could have voluntarily purchased in the market. Likewise, any product or service that people want can be provided, and provided most efficiently, through the market. If there is not enough demand for it in the market, there certainly is not a rationale for *forcing* those who would have chosen to spend their capital on other goods and services to pay for what politicians compel them to buy. By getting involved in these subjective decisions and trying to manage a constantly fluctuating, self-correcting market, the government retards productivity.

But how would those needs we have assumed only government can fulfill be better provided by markets? Surely people must be compelled to pay for the things that "only government can do."

People don't need to be compelled to pay for anything, ranging from building, food, and service safety, to road construction and maintenance, to marriage licensing, to trash collection, fire protection, and even the so-called rationale for government under the Lockean system, police protection.

There is a market for safe buildings, food, and services. People don't want to be poisoned, burned, or defrauded. Not only do food suppliers and restaurateurs, club owners and service providers know this, and know that the better they cater to the consumer desires the more prosperous they will be, other entrepreneurs know this as well, and will explore the market to see if there is a role for them to act as watchdogs for the consumer interest.

As opposed to government bureaucrats and politicians, who are insulated from the harm their bad decisions and lack of attention can do to their bottom lines, market watchdogs have great incentives to be thorough, sharp, open to analysis, and open to new ideas. They need to be honest, for any report of favoritism will deter future customers from giving them business, and the threat of competition will keep even the dominant watchdogs from abusing their positions.

Consumer Reports is an excellent example of a dominant watchdog service that has remained vigilant about its quality for decades. It is the "gold standard" of consumer magazines, and leads a pack of sector-specific publications that also give consumers excellent, unbiased advice one would never trust the government to give[53].

---

[53] Never trust a government ad campaign or a study funded by the government. Anytime one hears "brought to you by the Ad Council" in a broadcast commercial, he ought to be skeptical. Millions have been spent to tell people about nutrition, drugs, "fair housing" and race relations. Even NASA has spent thousands paying "performance artist" Laurie Anderson to do "works" promoting its agenda. In the past, people actually had the choice of whether to buy her CDs or pay for her concerts. Perhaps she wasn't making enough money when people could decide for themselves.

"Underwriters Laboratories" is a private entity funded by people who work in the electric and construction businesses. As the watchdog on electric cable and component safety, it is unrivaled, and one would be hard-pressed to see any piece of electric equipment put into a house by a contractor if that piece did not have the "UL" seal of approval.

Walt Disney World is a private enterprise that sees thousands of people pass through its gates each day. It has highly complex pieces of machinery that entertain people repeatedly, day after day. Breakdowns mean dissatisfied customers; injuries and death lead to lawsuits, bad publicity and lost business. Pleasurable experiences lead to good publicity and higher profits. As a result, Disney World has very high standards for its rides and employees, and as a result of those standards, Disney has had very few injuries or fatalities in its thirty years of operation. Compare the highly complex operation of Disney with the unmonitored, poorly maintained public playgrounds in your state or city. Not only are there more injuries per capita, the public parks cannot sustain themselves without taking tax money from people who don't even use them[54].

Disney also has its own roads, as do most shopping malls and private condominium complexes around the United States. Compare the maintenance of the private roads with the government roads, and take particular notice of the northern states in the winter. It is a very good bet that you will see the privately owned pavement cleared first, and better, than the government roads. After all, no one is forced to drive the roads and parking lots at the mall or in the condo associations. The safety paradigms are arranged by those who own them, based on how they want to cater to their clientele.

In California, certain stretches of highway are being returned to the private paradigm mentioned by Daniel Klein. They operate in the black, safely, and efficiently. Certainly many people who are excellent drivers stuck on a government highway that has to admit people with many levels of

---

[54] For many years, the New Hampshire Department of Parks and Recreation operated on "license fees" and fees for entrance into parks. The "license fees" for fishing, use of snowmobiles, and hunting have increased and widened over the years, yet, as of 2007, the head of the department has asked for tax money to keep the system in the black. Despite this impending bankruptcy, more land is going to be added to the parks system for hiking trails and snowmobile use. If the parks system were a private entity, it would be selling off assets, not acquiring more to be a heavier burden. Silly? Indeed. It's government, baby.

driving skills would prefer to have private highways that would allow them to get to their destinations without having to put up with those who are a drag on their own abilities. This seems a perfect allegory for many roles government takes on. By doing so, it impedes our abilities to excel at what we do best, be it driving, cooking, entertaining, or reporting on the services of others. Get this arrogant, political force out of our way, many of us say, and just let us do what we do best.

Many people are skeptical of this approach. They believe that only the "elite" would receive safe goods and services if it weren't for government. The poor, they claim, are helped by having government rules for entrance in the market.

The trouble is that these government rules are the very things that often make it impossible for the poor to afford certain products and services. Regulations are expensive, and often arbitrary, having little to do with real safety. These expenses are passed on to the consumer, making it impossible for some to afford certain products, or restricting their ability to use leftover capital to buy other things they need. Licensure excludes competitors of lower skill, competitors who could, if allowed to, provide services to people of lesser means. By creating expensive licensing laws, government restricts the pool of people who can enter the market, and allows them to charge more because they have fewer potential competitors. Surely poor people would prefer having the choice of getting an inexpensive, though possibly inferior, product or service rather than not having the choice of buying anything because the price is artificially high due to conceited, egalitarian government intervention.

That's all well and good, some might say, but there are certain things that just cannot be left to the market. Sure, one can make an argument that even protection against bad food and dangerous buildings is not really protection in the "negative", Lockean tradition, and one can show how these services can be provided more fully by private entrepreneurs, but what about things like fire protection, police protection, and adjudication? Surely they fall into Locke's view of the acceptable "negative" role of government?

One wonders whether Locke would have supported government fire services. Within the Lockean construct, people do not form governments to protect them from naturally occurring phenomena. Fires, storms, earthquakes, and other dangers posed by life are just that. According to Locke, we form governments to prevent *human beings* from harming other human beings. Provision of fire fighting services is a "positivist" action by government. It is a provision of a service that is not legitimate under the Lockean paradigm.

Contemporary leftists claim that it would be impossible to secure market services for things like firefighting, because the "free rider" problem would inspire those who live nearby, and thus pose a threat if their property should catch fire, to simply not pay. These "riders" would know that neighbors who really want to protect their property would also try to stop a fire nearby, because that fire could spread and damage their own home.

But this overlooks many factors. First among them is liability. In a market society, neighbors will arrange liability paradigms, most of which will cover the possibility of fire. One neighbor in a market community will be inspired to work with another to make private arrangements for potential threats. Much like insurance companies work with clients to hedge against future liabilities, private firefighting forces would work with private communities to arrange broad coverage, and those living within would have an incentive to work together to make such a system work.

Additionally, history shows us that the "free rider" dilemma was not encountered when communities fought fires in the early United States. Instead, they formed volunteer firefighting teams, much like the volunteer philanthropic organizations that were created in town after town. In such cases, neighbors helped neighbors, volunteering their time or donating their money to a pool, upon which members in distress could call. When the need had passed, the neighbors who had been helped tried to return the favor, and thus the voluntary organization was sustained and fostered.

Firefighting is not something one need look to government to do. It can be done more efficiently, and cover only those who want it, by *charging only those who want it*, or by people working together voluntarily.

Police protection, that fundamental role of Locke's "legitimate state", operates under the same rules. Though many people might at first be skeptical, police protection is also a "positive" provision of a service[55], and one that could be more efficiently supplied through private means.

First, one must acknowledge that a government-provided police force is rarely going to stop a crime. Even today, more crimes are stopped by private

---

[55] Hence the popular motto: "To Protect and Serve."

citizens brandishing private weapons than police, simply due to the fact that police cannot be everywhere. Likewise, police protection is often uneven, and favoritism between politically connected parties and members of police forces is not uncommon.

But the provision of protection by an armed, or at least potentially physically injurious, force of men is still seen as a preventative, a deterrent against crime.

That being the case, and acknowledging the erroneous nature of Locke's view that granting the state police power is a "negative", rather than "positive" act, one must provide an alternative that would work.

This alternative comes in the form of private police forces working for private communities, forces subject to the demands of the market, forces that must answer to customers with honesty and efficiency.

Just like any other service provider, those offering protection to potential customers would have reputations to uphold. They would have to do their jobs well and cheaply, answering to their clients.

But, one might ask, what if their clients are interested in preying upon their poorer neighbors, and hire the police force to invade and plunder. Meanwhile the poorer neighbor does not have the financial where with all to hire a strong enough police force to fight back? Couldn't "ganglandism" ensue, wherein the richest hire the strongest force to steal from those who cannot compete?

This is highly unlikely for numerous reasons.

History has shown that warfare is extremely expensive. "Warfare states" cannot sustain themselves against the forces of the market. In a market-governing society, comprised of many private communities, the very existence of the market communities would imply the understanding of this fact about war versus peaceful market exchange. The freer and more peaceful the community, the more prosperous it is, and the more it has to spend on its own defense. Take a look back at the United States and the USSR. The US, with its relatively free market structure, was able to fund a military that surpassed that of the USSR in almost every regard. The USSR imploded after trying to invade nation after nation, all in an effort to keep its war machine funded. Admittedly, when one is painting a picture of a stateless society that provides for its own defense, the United States is not a perfectly analogous system because tax money was forcibly taken from the freer market system in order to pay for the defense force. However, in a general sense, the higher prosperity of market-driven societies can not only outpace warlike societies in provision of food, clothing and leisure opportunities, it can also surpass the warlike societies in the provision of defense forces to insure the peace.

In addition, market structures that successfully provide goods and services, even services such as police protection and adjudication, require extraordinary degrees of sophisticated coordination that arise in response to consumer demand. In order to offer protection services to any community, of any size, a private police force would be required by the consumers to show that it could and would coordinate with, and be accepted by, the police and justice systems of other communities. Not only would these other community forces promise to remain peaceful, they would all work together to create emergency defense unions to repel any market participant who turns "rogue" and engages in aggressive activities.

The ability to unite and shun -- the ability to exclude through mutually beneficial arrangements -- is key to market operations in all fields. Often, it is not the stigma of breaking a *statute* that stops someone from committing a crime, it is the possibility that he or she will be caught, stigmatized for being a predator, and punished through financial means, imprisonment, or outright exclusion.

When novelist Janet Dailey admitted to copying in her book "Notorious" the work of fellow writer Nora Roberts, it was not the stigma of breaking any law that prompted her to publicly apologize, it was the humiliation of exposure to readers, and the possible loss of her livelihood. Support structures fall apart, goodwill of publishers, publicists and bookstores disappears. The same is true for companies. Those that do not operate honestly in the market do not last long. Their reputations get around, not only to the consumers, but also to the suppliers of products upon which the offending company relies to stay in operation. Support structures erode due to the supporting companies turning to more reliable, honest and stable buyers.

Integrated police and justice systems are essential for different communities to get along and prosper. It would run counter to human nature, and counter to the forces of the market, for a police force operating in "Toughville" to arbitrarily arrest and shakedown anyone entering the city. Obviously, no one would visit "Toughville", "Toughvillians" interested in visiting other cities would not be welcome, and they would not receive reciprocal justice arrangements to protect them away from home.

This is not to say that rogue market societies would not arise. No system is perfect. The market is, however, blessed with certain advantages over the state. First, its police forces would have to be more addressable to consumer demands than are the forces of the state. The very process of majority rule, upon which Locke relies to fund the police power of the state, rarely, if ever, showers 100% approval on every government act. Different percentages of the populace want different things at different times. As a result, police forces cannot satisfy all of their consumer demands, cannot address new demands in an efficient manner, and have no way to match the feedback mechanism that provides information so quickly to market entrepreneurs.

The court systems tied to the police protection of each market-based community would also have to be more addressable to the public. Arbitration companies will not last long if they do not satisfy the consumers who demand some kind of assurance that disputes will be handled justly.

There are those who say that this is all fine for the "rich", who can afford to pay for the bests services, but they still distrust the market to provide justice to the poor. This is intriguing, for in all other aspects of our lives, we see market efficiency providing the essentials of life more and more cheaply. What used to take days of work to buy now takes hours. Televisions, once the playthings of only the richest Americans, can be purchased by teenagers working part-time for about a week. Computer capacity that used to cost millions and take up entire rooms in order to function properly now costs about fifteen Dollars and fits in the palm of one's hand. How is it that all of these non-essentials can be provided with increasing efficiency, and with greater efficiency than the state can provide, yet we believe that the poor would be excluded from a useful and just police and court system?

A look back at history might be worthwhile, for, in fact, there was once a society that operated without even the Lockean paradigm that many in the United States assume is necessary for our protection.

It was located in Iceland, and was created and run by the Vikings beginning in the late 9th century. For nearly four-hundred years (during a time when Al Gore was not around to save the planet from man-made global warming), the Vikings survived and prospered in Iceland without a government, employing only voluntary defense and justice systems for protection and adjudication.

At the heart of the Viking order was the bundle of private property rights called the Godard. Cheiftans who built temples or areas of congregation held the primary Godard, and could sell their rights to others. This allowed people to join in a justice system whereby one could swear allegiance to a Chieftan and become a "Thingman". Your allegiance was voluntary, and permitted entrance into the network of voluntary justice houses the Chieftans set up from village to village. All Cheiftans had votes in the creation of the court system, and competed for the allegiance of the Thingmen.

Within the courts, every Thingman had an equal chance to get a fair hearing for a claim against another, and favoritism was avoided through the use of the market. As David Friedman explains:

> "A claim for damages was a piece of transferable property. If you had injured me and I was too weak to enforce my claim, I could sell or give it to someone stronger. It was in his interest to enforce the claim in order to collect the damages and establish his own reputation for use in future conflicts."[56]

Of course, nowadays, it might surprise some Americans to know that the Vikings were more than a football team or the bases for comic book characters, but taking the time to look at how smoothly their society functioned without government is a rewarding task, and could go far to convince many that both "positive" and "negative" states are wasteful and unnecessary.

Some will remain unconvinced. They worry about particular issues that they believe only the state can address. The heterosexual marriage proponents are an example of this kind of group. Many of them remain steadfast in their belief that the state must legalize only heterosexual marriages because they believe that the state has a justified role in protecting people from aggression, and they fear that children could be hurt if homosexual child rearing and adoption were allowed.

The trouble with this kind of thinking specifically -- and in a general sense about other issues where people believe the government must be involved to afford us protection -- is that it never addresses the Platonic conundrum of "who watches the watchers?"

---

[56] Friedman, David. *The Machinery of Freedom* (La Salle, Ill, Open Court, 1995) p. 203.

If one cannot be trusted to handle his own life, and to raise his children peacefully and with care, then how is one to be trusted to vote for a distant politician with no ties to his life, or the life of his child, and to believe that the politician can not only better handle raising one's own child, but raising other peoples' children? As we have seen, such thinking leads to profound economic and ethical troubles, yet people continue to assume they need to get government involved.

As a perfect example, there is the other side of the marriage coin: divorce. In Indiana, a surprising court case recently arose involving two divorcing Wiccan parents. In the proceedings between Thomas E. Jones Jr. and Tammie U. Bristol, Marion County Superior Court Chief Judge Cale J. Bradford ordered that the parents "take such steps as are needed to shelter [their child] from involvement and observation of these non-mainstream religious beliefs and rituals." The judge decided that the nine year old child could not be taught Wicca, for "while the two of you are free to engage in any kind of behaviors you want to that are lawful, or that you don't get caught at," he said. "I suppose, where you've got a child involved, that freedom can be somewhat limited."[57] Since the parents had gone to the state to get *permission* to marry, they also had to go to the state to get permission to divorce, and to have the state be the arbiter for their claims at the end of their legal relationship. They had not counted on a judge who did not like Wicca, and had not counted on the judge deciding how their son would be taught. The parents were forced to file an appeal to a higher court, where the new case was eventually decided in their favor. But the systematic problem is clear, regardless of the outcome in that instance. Systematically, the mechanism of state licensing of marriage presents the state with innumerable opportunities to regulate our lives, and we must recognize that the impact the state has is both emotional, and economic.

If these Wiccan parents had not lived in a world where the state took it upon itself to grant licenses for marriage, where marriage was a private affair, with private contracts recognized by private arbiters and churches, all of their associations would have been voluntary, and thus the results of their

---

[57] The Judge also thought that Wiccans worshipped Satan, which had to be corrected by Jones, who said, "I can't worship something I don't believe in." The Wiccan religion is based on the worship if nature. For more, check this report: http://blog.au.org/2005/08/18/discriminatory_/

actions would have been sanctioned by them from the start. Any arbitration organization, i.e. a private court system, adjudicating the case would have had to answer in the market for future clients, and thus the likelihood of its judges making rulings based on capriciousness or prejudice against the Wiccan religion, the Mormon religion, Catholicism, or any other, would be minimized. Reputations are established quickly in the private market, and businesses prosper or fail based on them. Satisfied customers return and recommend the businesses to their friends. Unsatisfied customers do not.

But this market feedback and information dissemination system does not exist under the government paradigm. In fact, the political mechanism increases the likelihood that decisions will be made contrary to the sense of justice for all parties involved. As has been shown time and time again, the insulating effect of political appointments and occasional elections based on the investments of mercantile special interests produces a perverse incentive for politicians and bureaucrats to rule not in the public interest, but in the interest of themselves and those who will help them retain power. Bad decisions rarely cause a politician or bureaucrat to lose business. Just the opposite, when bureaus fail, politicians clamor for higher funding, for more staff members, and the cycle ratchets upwards. Amtrak has never turned a profit, NASA wastes billions, the Import-Export Bank hands out money for foreign advertising of US products, the Massachusetts food inspection team is a useless and wasteful bureaucracy, Social Security is a Ponzi scheme, yet the mantra is that they need *more* money to be successful. Is the public interest truly served in this manner?

As a matter of economic and ethical fact, the answer is no. The term "public interest" itself would best be defined by the individual members of society acting in the private market, for only when each of us decides for ourselves, can one claim that anyone's "interest" has been reflected. 51% majority rule does not reflect the interest of the other 49%. But each of those people could show his own interest if he were not prohibited by law to do so in the private market.

Many people take this example of the Wiccan divorce (as opposed to Steely Dan's great song, "Haitian Divorce") and initially agree with the logic against state control of marriage. But then they think about the child, and they wonder, "Sure, perhaps these parents are responsible, and caring, and it was wrong for the judge to impose his prejudices in this area of the divorce. But we need the state to protect against other parents, ones who won't be so kind and loving towards their children. It is the presence of the state, with its police force and child protective services, that spreads a blanket of security, and curtails the likelihood of miscreants causing harm to their kids. Shouldn't we have the state establish certain parameters for child rearing and against abuse, so that the punishments dolled out for crimes against kids will act as deterrents for potentially abusive parents?"

First, one must ask about the definitions of "abuse" and "parameters for child rearing". When do parental actions constitute neglect or abuse? How do we write laws that define these under a state paradigm?

Second, one must reiterate this question: If we cannot trust our neighbors to raise their children in a loving and careful way; if we cannot rely on the people who, in most cases, gave birth to the child and are closest to him or her to take the best care of that child, then how can we rely on these untrustworthy people to not only vote for politicians and a system of bureaucrats to care for *their* child, but for their *neighbor's* child as well? Or, to put it another way: If we can trust people to elect politicians who will decide not only for them but for others how to raise their children, then why would we not have faith that the parents themselves, working in voluntary association with other parents, could form their own societies and their own market legal structures to address their needs and leave other people alone to address theirs?

If one were to live in a private community, established voluntarily, through market exchange and free association and succeeding or failing based on consumer satisfaction, would one not see the same kinds of checks against parental abuse? Would one not also see a more responsive, less expensive, judicial system based on what we already assume are the interests of good people?

One would think this is a convincing argument, but critics of laissez faire societies might then bring up one more point: what does one do about abortion?

This is a fascinating question, for if, as John Locke and most proponents of individual liberty believe, we are created (be it by natural means or by supernatural means such as the work of God) with certain inalienable rights, and one of those is the right to life, then how does one protect the life of a created, yet unborn, human being still in the womb? Wouldn't *that* at least, be a rationale for the existence of a limited government? After all, the child in the womb is completely incapable of defending himself or herself.

Certainly the child's existence justifies the provision of a police force to provide protection.

Unfortunately, like the example of education, one must realize that simply because people *need* something, and may be incapable of providing it for themselves, it does not mean that these people have a legal *right* to the fruits of another's labor in order to provide what is needed. We must remember that, like teaching services, police protection is a *service*, and must be provided by someone. If we can take money from person "A" to pay for the police protection for the unborn child of person "B", then we are, in fact, enslaving person "A" for a certain period of time to provide that payment. If that is the case, we can use the same rationale to simply enslave the protection force – the police, prosecutors, judges, etc. – and make *them* perform services at the behest of the government.

Ethically, this cannot be justified.

Practically, it does not work well, because once one admits that the state can have a role in monitoring and enforcing how a woman or couple care for their child upon conception, the door is left open to arbitrary standards for what constitutes proper care. In a recent New Hampshire court case, a woman who was taking cocaine while pregnant was going to be charged with child endangerment, yet if she had decided to abort that child, she would have been acting within the law and had no legal troubles. Clearly, the standards do not jibe. The state does not have a consistent position regarding what is a human life deserving of legal protection against injury or death caused by another.

If the state *were* to move in the direction many Lockeans would have it move, i.e. to protect the child against abortion, then the practical question arises: how far can the state insinuate itself in the pregnancy in order to insure the protection of the child? Certainly, stopping the mother from taking cocaine would be justified under this paradigm. But what about checking on the mother for other drugs, or alcohol, or cigarette smoking, which all have negative effects on the child? What about nutrition? Can the state make sure that a woman is eating properly, and if she is not, what will the state do? Will it provide food? The federal government and many states already do this for expectant mothers (the program is "WIC", which stands for "Women and Infant Children"). But what if the mother eats too much, or doesn't follow the state commands? What if she engages in risky behavior such as sports?

In all of these instances, we see the potential for the state to begin micromanaging a woman's life in ways that are completely contrary to what she might want, and what she and her partner might have agreed. Many conservatives think that pressure from the state to manipulate the minute activities of a pregnant woman would be attenuated by the "balancing forces of the majority", whom, the conservatives claim, we can trust to come up with reasonable restrictions and rules of conduct for expectant mothers, within the context of the justified state role in protecting the individual right to life.

The trouble is that these are the same people who often rail against government intervention in so many other aspects of our lives, and trust us to make decisions in them. Their stance is inconsistent. Mistakes by the state regarding parenting arise often, and conservatives are the first to promote the right of parents to care for and educate their children as they see fit. Why, then, do they not trust parents to make decisions for their children even when they are in the womb? For many, it is a matter of degree. But, while people believe the forces of politics can produce a workable paradigm under which rules for protecting the life of the unborn can be written and enforced without impinging on the expectant mother's prerogatives, the argument could just as easily be taken in the opposite direction.

Based on this supposition, it is possible that the state could make expectant mothers their wards, and, in the extreme, arrest and imprison them until their children are born. After all, the state has a role in protecting the child, and extensive police power insures such protection.

Obviously, this is not likely. However, it is worthwhile to consider the possibility that it could happen.

If one believes that the majority of people can be trusted to raise their children properly, because they care most for the children and know the most about their needs, then it is logical to assume that, left to their own devices, they could create voluntary associations that protect their children just as well, or better, than government can.

Through the creation of such market societies, people could insure that each participant agrees to certain checks on his behavior. All such voluntary restrictions would be policed by forces hired by the voluntary association, and would carry with them the right of the association to work with a private arbitration group to carry out judicial proceedings against wrongdoers. Be they expectant mothers who tried to have abortions, parents who mistreated their children, or criminals who had aggressed against other members of the association, the market society would have rules for entrance, and would retain the prerogative to act on those rules to insure the protection of the other members. Any legal framework inside which we live today could be replicated with greater efficiency, savings, and freedom through private societies competing with one another for participants. With the forces of exclusion and competition at work, there is no reason to think that we who treat our neighbors as we would like to be treated would not be able to live in peaceful, state-less societies that protect our natural rights to the fullest extent possible.

Conclusion

One understands that not all of these arguments will convince every individual to embrace the advantages of the market paradigm over the state. There are many circumstances that have not been addressed in this article. However, it is worthwhile to push any analysis of contemporary political issues as far as one can towards the market approach, and to see if one thinks such problems could best be solved by free individuals working within the capitalist system. Human morality and development depend on this kind of effort.

By conducting such analysis, I have come to the conclusion that the ethical and practical operations of the market are superior to those of the state, but I understand that such a world is a long way off. Until then, I will be satisfied working within the constitutional parameters laid out by the founders of both the US and my home state of New Hampshire. With such frameworks, the thinkers of the 18th century created an approximation of market competition based on small spheres of government authority. If one did not like the operations of a town or state, he could move to another. He had the ability to leave, and he had constitutional rules laid out to protect his rights against infringement by the government.

While one might not be able to convince every reader that the market approach is optimal in every instance, at least he can point to the people who created our governments, and note that they did so in order to give us competing spheres of control, the right to exit, and a large measure of independence under the Lockean government paradigm.

It is possible that Jefferson and Madison, Paine and Mason did not go far enough in dismantling the apparatus of the state in its generic sense, but their efforts were truly remarkable, and one can be satisfied that they made their arguments very clear, set them down in plain text, and tried to insure for us that government would not interfere to a large extent in our lives.

I believe that it is important to honor their efforts, and expand the defense of individual liberty for future generations.

Gardner Goldsmith
Biographical Details

P. Gardner Goldsmith has an extensive background in television scriptwriting, broadcast and print journalism, political philosophy and economics.

His television experience includes work in the script departments of **"The Outer Limits"** and **"Star Trek: Voyager"**, commercial copywriting and editing. He was the recipient of a **Writers' Guild West** fellowship in 1998, and the recipient of the **Institute for Humane Studies Young Communicators' Fellowship** in 1996. His journalism background traces back to 1989, when he attended the **National Journalism Center**, in Washington, DC. Following in the footsteps of earlier graduates such as John Fund, now of the Wall Street Journal, and controversial columnist/author Ann Coulter, Goldsmith covered Capital Hill, learning the ins and outs of the political world on the federal level.

His radio experience includes the state-based program **"Against the Grain"** and fill-ins for nationally syndicated programs.

Mr. Goldsmith's articles and opinion pieces have appeared in numerous print and electronic publications, including *Investor's Business Daily, TechcentralStation.com, Human Events, The Freeman, FEE.org, Mises.org, LewRockwell.com, The Manchester Union Leader, The Nashua Telegraph, SFX* **(UK),** and *Naked* **(UK).**

A life-long resident of New Hampshire, Mr. Goldsmith has utilized its motto for *"Live Free or Die"*, and he will soon be featured in the non-fiction anthology **"Serenity Found"**, a collection of essays about the popular science-fiction series **"Firefly"**, and its concluding motion picture, **"Serenity"**. The book will be published by Smart Pop, a division of Ben Bella Books.

He was recently named **Libertarian of the Year** for 2006 by the New Hampshire Libertarian Party, and thinks very highly of all the dedicated people making such a difference in the Granite State.

Drop Gard a line with your thoughts any time. He would enjoy hearing from you. Visit www.libertyconspiracy.com for more information.

Made in the USA